Chosen Capital

Chosen Capital

*The Jewish Encounter
with American Capitalism*

EDITED BY REBECCA KOBRIN

RUTGERS UNIVERSITY PRESS
NEW BRUNSWICK, NEW JERSEY, AND LONDON

Library of Congress Cataloging-in-Publication Data

Chosen capital : the Jewish encounter with American capitalism / edited by
Rebecca Kobrin.

   p. cm.

   Includes bibliographical references and index.

   ISBN 978–0–8135–5307–8 (hardcover : alk. paper) — ISBN 978–0–8135–5308–5
(pbk. : alk. paper) — ISBN 978–0–8135–5329–0 (e-book)

   1. Jews—United States—Economic conditions—Congresses.   2. Capitalism—United
States—History—Congresses.   3. Capitalism—Religious aspects—Congresses.
4. Free enterprise—Religious aspects—Judaism—Congresses.   5. Economics—
Religious aspects—Judaism—Congresses.   I. Kobrin, Rebecca.

   E184.36.E25C49 2012

   330.12'2—dc23   2011038426

A British Cataloging-in-Publication record for this book is available from the British
Library.

Visit our website: http://rutgerspress.rutgers.edu

Manufactured in the United States of America

Contents

Acknowledgments

The idea of a conference to explore the ways in which Jews shaped and were shaped by American capitalism was born on a long subway ride I shared with Tony Michels. The subway—whose rumblings shape New York City in countless ways—served as an apt midwife to such an important and, at times, explosive topic. While it may be rarely discussed in the annals of American Jewish life, few would deny that Jews have long served as both American capitalism's greatest innovators as well as its harshest critics. Jews' encounter with this country and its economy has fundamentally altered both the United States and the practice of Judaism over the course of the twentieth century.

Tony Michels and I both enjoyed a wonderful year at New York University—he as a Goren-Goldstein fellow and I as an American Association for Jewish Research fellow. There, we encountered many thoughtful colleagues, many of whom participated in the conference. I want to thank particularly Hasia Diner, who was a staunch supporter of the conference from the outset. Without the financial support of New York University's Goren-Goldstein Center for American Jewish History and Columbia University's Institute for Israel and Jewish Studies, the international conference Tony and I organized could have never taken place. The logistics of travel and food for the conference were aptly taken care of by Shayne Figueroa, Malka Gold, Kiley Lambert, and Tamara Mann. The conversations that took place at the conference were provocative and engrossing. All who participated agreed that our debates marked the beginning of a larger conversation and that our insights and reflections could spark further critical research and must be made available to the larger world. That task of rethinking Jews' relationship to America's economic development became more pressing, and more difficult, following the fall of Lehman Brothers and the financial crisis of 2008. I thank Marlie Wasserman and Allyson Fields for their appreciation of the importance of this volume and for patiently seeing it through the process, particularly after the unexpected early arrival of my son.

For me, the completion of this volume represents the culmination of a long journey, during which I have been fortunate to have the support of a number of individuals and institutions. Columbia University provided me with both a stimulating environment and the time to transform these proceedings into a book. Conversations with Ira Katznelson, Ken Jackson, and Betsy Blackmar on American capitalism as well as the encouragement of Michael Stanislawski and Jeremy Dauber, directors of the Institute for Israel and Jewish Studies, provided the support to make the proceedings available to a wider public. A book subvention grant from the Harriman Institute helped move this book through the final stages of production. I thank each author for working with me to hone his or her individual piece so that the larger message of the volume would be a cohesive one. Jerry Muller's thoughtful comments and incisive questions transformed each of the essays in this volume. Eric Wakin, Columbia's curator for American history, provided speedy and instrumental help in procuring an image for the cover of this volume.

Finally, I would like to thank my family. My parents, Ruth and Lawrence Kobrin, continue to inspire me with their dedication to both their family and the life of the mind. The countless hours of babysitting they provided for my editing made this volume possible. I am profoundly indebted to my husband, Kevin Feinblum, whose unflagging support and patience helped me through the ups and downs of such an editorial project. Indeed, his expertise in finance helped me sort through many of the more technical descriptions and charts in the volume. My daughters, Ariela and Simone, and my son, Eitan, whose early arrival forced all the contributors to follow my strict deadlines, were always understanding of my need to work on weekends. It is to them that I dedicate this book, as their giggles and smiles enrich my life every day.

Note on Orthography
and Transliteration

In transliterating Russian and Hebrew words, the authors in this volume have generally followed the systems used by the Library of Congress, with the exception of certain well-known names for which other transliterations are commonly used. In general, Yiddish words, phrases, titles, and names of organizations, places, and persons have been rendered according to the transliteration scheme of the YIVO Institute for Jewish Research, except that no attempt has been made to standardize nonstandard orthography. All translations have been made by the authors unless otherwise indicated.

PART I

Reframing the Jewish Encounter with American Capitalism

∾

The Chosen People in the Chosen Land

THE JEWISH ENCOUNTER WITH AMERICAN CAPITALISM

Rebecca Kobrin

More than a century ago, German sociologist and economist Werner Sombart (1863–1941) marveled at two remarkable economic "exceptionalisms" in the world.[1] First, he focused on the exceptionality of the United States, a nation that in just a few short decades had emerged as an industrial juggernaut, replete with huge mills, transcontinental railroads, and large cities. Writing in 1906 Sombart pondered why, despite this new nation's rapid growth and expanding economic inequality, the United States and its capitalist system did not nurture a mass socialist movement among its working class like its counterparts in Europe.[2] What exceptional forces made workers in the United States, imagined by some as a "chosen nation," seem more content and less inclined to protest their condition? Equally as exceptional, argued Sombart, was the unique role played by the Jews, or the self-proclaimed "chosen people," in the development and expansion of capitalism in Europe.[3] Revising Max Weber's vision of capitalism as linked to Protestant ethics, Sombart contended that Jews' intrinsic proclivities made them central provocateurs in the creation of modern capitalism. Indeed, as historian Jonathan Karp points out, Sombart's portrayal of Jews as "capitalist pioneers"—rooted in his vision of Judaism as a rational, law-oriented and acquisitive religion—molded the ways in which interwar intellectuals, anti-Semitic writers, and politicians discussed the Jews.[4]

Sombart's summoning of the idea of exceptionalism to describe both America's and the Jews' engagement with the developing economic system known as capitalism hints at the complex set of charged ideas, questions, and reflections that undergird this volume. During the long century in which industrialization and mass migration reshaped the United States, Jews, like many immigrant groups, were transformed by their encounter with America's ever-expanding and ever-evolving system of capitalism.[5] The essays in this collection, most of which were adapted from presentations first delivered at a conference at Columbia University and New York University in March 2008, try to assess these encounters, but they all remain cognizant of the looming ghost of Sombart, who was the first to argue for the alleged economic exceptionalism of the Jews and the United States. As discussions of American capitalism have become commonplace in the past two decades since the fall of the Soviet Union, we often forget, as historian Howard Brick aptly points out, that American "capitalism has a history."[6] And Jews, some posit, were central to this history, just as they are alleged to have been in Europe.[7] But we cannot assess this claim because the study of Jews and their relationship to American capitalism has remained anecdotal. In fact, we know very little about the real or imagined role of Jews in the creation, expansion, and maintenance of American capitalism, a lacuna that must be filled if we ever hope to fully understand the economic forces shaping the fateful encounter of Jews and the United States.

This lacuna is nothing particular to American Jewish history. In general, the larger field of economic history does not see the subject of Jewish history as particularly urgent, and the overwhelming bias of modern Jewish history has been toward the life of the mind rather than the toil of the hand. The forebearers of modern Jewish history may have pondered how economic thought intersected with intellectual discussions of emancipation, but they rarely assessed the actual day-to-day business practices of Jews throughout the modern world.[8] As Polish Jewish historian Ignacy Schipper pointed out in 1911:

> Thanks to them [the nineteenth-century leaders of Jewish historiography], we possess an impressive picture of the spiritual directors of Diaspora Jewry. But what is completely lacking is the history of hundreds of thousands of Jews who have left few traces for the future, not of the spiritual riches [of their world] but of their toil and drudgery as well as of their speculative abilities. In short, we know about the Sabbath Jew and his extra [Sabbath] soul. But it is time we got to know the history of the weekday Jews . . . [and] the history of Jewish working life.[9]

This volume follows Schipper's programmatic call to map out the daily business activities, economic strategies, and fiscal mechanisms deployed by Jews as they strove to succeed economically and to adapt their religious practices to the American marketplace.[10] American economic historians and sociologists have long focused on the ways in which specific individuals engineered innovations in American business, and this volume will allow those interested in the world of business to see how Jews, as one exemplary ethnic and religious group, adapted, took advantage of, and expanded particular niches of the American economy.[11]

So how does this volume tackle its examination of Jews' and Judaism's encounter with American capitalism? Perhaps it was the anti-Semitic overtones of Sombart's writings that initially discouraged economists, business historians, and scholars of Jewish history from analyzing the patterns and strategies utilized by Jews in their economic encounter with the United States.[12] Indeed, it has been decades since scholars seriously considered these topics, as the economists Arcadius Kahan and Simon Kuznets did in their pioneering studies of American Jewish immigrant economic mobility.[13] So little scholarship exists on American Jewish economic life that the beautifully realized portraits of Jews in specific industries, unions, and political parties presented in this volume enter a virtually uncharted scholarly terrain. Approaching the Jewish encounter with American capitalism from "the bottom up," the essays in this volume demonstrate the power of well-crafted case studies, as they bring the fields of American economic and business history (fields that rarely consider questions of ethnicity or religion) and American Jewish history (a field more interested in culture than economics) into direct dialogue with on another.

While the essays in this volume fill many lacunae, they do not constitute a history of the encounter of Jews with American capitalism. Rather, they highlight the "selective involvement" of Jews in the ambit of American capitalism through niches they created in specific cities, regions, industries, and occupations.[14] A wealth of literature exists around the study of contemporary immigrant groups' involvement in America's capitalist society, but we know far too little on the spatial and occupational niches that served as safe launching pads for immigrant Jews into the American economy at the turn of the twentieth century, even though these niches were abundantly clear to most contemporary observers.[15]

A prime example of such contemporary observations is a 1936 *Fortune* magazine issue focused on the "Jews in America." Penned to assess and to refute the "charge that Jews have monopolized or are monopolizing economic opportunity," this expansive and problematic survey of Jewish economic activity in the United States was geared toward proving that "there is no basis whatever for the suggestion that Jews monopolize U.S. business and industry"; in fact, Jews' participation in peak capitalist roles was limited to the margins—to industries such as clothing manufacturing and scrap-metal collection. To be sure, *Fortune* acknowledged that in their marginal niches Jews "were highly visible" if not dominating presences: for example, Jews constituted just under 4 percent of the population of the United States in 1936, but they remarkably composed 90 percent of participants in the scrap-iron industry; 95 percent of the entrepreneurs in waste management of nonferrous scrap metal, paper, cotton rag, and rubber; 85 percent of the owners of factories specializing in the manufacture of men's clothing; and 95 percent of women's clothing manufacture.[16]

Since *Fortune* conducted this survey more than seventy years ago, few others have ventured to survey or analyze Jews' business endeavors, how these businesses may have altered the course of American capitalist development, or how life in this capitalist system may have molded the contours of Jewish life.[17] This volume begins to fill these lacunae by asking three simple questions. First, through which specific niches, and at which specific moments, did Jews play a role in the evolution of America's brand of capitalism? To be sure, economists have considered some aspects of this question, but far more writers have commented on the astonishing speed and fascinating paths through which Jews ascended into America's middle and upper classes without considering the larger economic context.[18] Second, how and through what methods did Jewish workers, entrepreneurs, and businesspeople achieve this mobility? As historian David Hollinger points out, the failure to conduct a "straight-forward historical and social-scientific study" of what enabled immigrant Jews to succeed economically so quickly in the United States "perpetuates the mystification of Jewish history and subtly reinforces invidious distinctions between descent groups in American society."[19] Third, how and in what ways did capitalism alter the practice and experience of Judaism itself? The growing scholarly appreciation of American Jews' distinct material culture is integrally linked to Judaism's encounter with American capitalism.[20] This volume, through straightforward historical analysis, answers some questions while raising many more for those interested in American Jewish history, immigration history, and economic history.

Immigration and entrepreneurship are two central themes in the history of the Jews in the United States. To be sure, there is a wealth of literature on late twentieth-century Asian and Latin American immigrant entrepreneurs, but we know far less about their Jewish predecessors. The curio dealers, liquor distributors, and scrap-metal dealers discussed in the following pages were the "forgotten siblings"—to use the term coined for the discussion of German immigrant entrepreneurship—of the much-chronicled Jewish banker and garment worker.[21] Was immigrant Jews' outsider status, to use the words of sociologist Charles Hirschman, "an asset that spark[ed] creativity," creating "new possibilities for entrepreneurship"?[22] Or was, as Andrew Godley found in his comparative analysis of Jewish immigrants in London and New York, American society's value system the reason why so many Jews pursued entrepreneurial endeavors?[23]

While focused on North America in its examination of such diverse topics as Jewish developers in the world of New York real estate or Jewish executives in the rhythm and blues recording industry, since many of the historical actors discussed were immigrants, this volume situates the American Jewish past in a transnational framework. Was there a specific predisposition for entrepreneurship among Jews as a result of selective immigration? What political ideologies and knowledge did Jewish immigrants bring with them that led some to pursue entrepreneurial endeavors and others to pursue radical politics? Or did Jews simply seize on opportunities presented to them in the United States, obtaining the skills and forming the political parties they needed here? The case studies on the following pages concerning Jews' engagement with American capitalism deepens our knowledge of the American Jewish past, providing a new prism through which to understand the intersection of immigration and ethnic history and the development of the larger American economy.

This volume also brings to the forefront how Jewishness as a category of analysis is useful in the study of American business. As Ron Chernow observes, "Political, ethnic, and religious differences among bankers permeated Wall Street in the early 1900s. The Yankee-Jewish banking split was the most important fault line in American high finance." If Jewishness was an engine driving "the saga of American finance" in the United States, as Chernow argues, it was also a key factor in defining the boundaries in a host of other industries as well.[24] The attention devoted to the careers and family connections of German Jewish bankers by scholars of American Jewish history needs to be expanded to other areas of economic activity.[25] While Jews have moved from the margins of the United States to its mainstream in the arenas of social, political, and cultural life, we know relatively little about the economic underpinnings that enabled Jews to make this shift and conversely how their monumental progress may have affected the course of American capitalist development.

The volume opens with Ira Katznelson's sweeping overview of the empirical, theoretical, and methodological questions facing those interested in assessing the Jewish encounter with American capitalism. Reflecting on the "exceptionalist" strands that have shaped the field thus far, Katznelson calls for more descriptive information "about the position of Jews in the United States at different moments, regions, cities, and sites of trade and industry." Such empirical studies, he believes, will help scholars address whether Jews were absent from certain niches in the American economy because of formal and informal exclusions or from self-denial. Indeed, Katznelson charges all interested in the fateful encounter of Jews and American capitalism to consider the following key questions: "in explaining outcomes, how much causal weight should be credited to preferences—that is, to the habits, ideas, practices, beliefs, values, interests, and cultural assets of persons as agents—and how much to the structure of the situations in which they are found? Irrespective of the relative emphasis given to each, how should agents [specifically the Jews] and structures [such as capitalism and industry] be conceptualized and analyzed?"

Identifying, exploring, and analyzing the specific niches created and occupied by Jews in the American economy is the goal of the second section of the volume. Jews, like other arriving immigrants a century ago, participated in new areas of economic distribution and production that opened up to them as a result of America's industrial revolution and the virtual end of various forms of social and legal discrimination. Focusing on garment production, probably one of the most well-known Jewish niche industries, Phyllis Dillon and Andrew Godley chronicle the development of garment production beginning in the early nineteenth century and argue that we need to look at this industry over the *longue durée* and in places beyond New York if we hope to understand Jews' role in transforming the production of clothing in the United States. Indeed, the emergence of New York as the center of garment manufacturing and as a Jewish niche industry was far from inevitable. The development of the garment industry, as Andrew Dolkart discusses, led some Jewish factory owners to experiment in the field of urban real estate development. Through his discussion of Abraham Lefcourt's instrumental role in the development of the Garment District, Dolkart explores how entrepreneurial Jewish garment shop owners made the field of commercial real estate development in New York a niche Jewish enterprise and, at the same time, transformed this city's architectural landscape. While perhaps the most well known, New York was far from the only American city transformed by niche-occupying Jewish entrepreneurs, as Jonathan Z. S. Pollack highlights in his discussion of the scrap-metal industry. Jews' dominant role in the development of this industry—created as a result of Jews' appreciation of the need for refuse removal—transformed Jewish life in Chicago and other smaller cities throughout the Midwest.

Jewish entrepreneurs in regions spanning from the American South to the western frontier capitalized on specific racial dynamics and divides to insert themselves in America's expanding system of capitalism.[26] Marni Davis's chapter on Jewish liquor distributors in the South highlights how Jewish economic success, achieved by serving a growing African American working class, often placed Jews at the center of heated discussions of race, religion, and morality in America. Jonathan Karp examines Jewish entrepreneurs in the rhythm and blues industry in the Midwest. These entrepreneurs offered African American musicians the unprecedented opportunity to record their music and acquire fans but also exploited these artists who had little independent capital on which they could draw. Indeed, as Karp sums up, "the story of these business pioneers is a morally ambiguous one . . . [but their] Jewishness cannot be ignored; if these men and women tended to be infrequent attendees at synagogue, they nevertheless evolved a kind of Jewish subculture" that requires recognition and analysis. A similar Jewish subculture can be found among the figures analyzed by David S. Koffman on the western frontier. Koffman explores the experiences of Jewish pioneer businessmen who traded with American Indians, introducing this group to American capitalist markets while simultaneously creating a curio market among European and American collectors for American Indian ritual objects.

Beyond dominating specific niches of America's economy, Jews' formative engagement with American capitalism also took place in the arena of American politics. As the volume's third section explores, from the beginning of the twentieth century, Jewish socialists served as key figures in rethinking the relationship of capitalism to the American body politic. Through a close study of the International Ladies' Garment Workers' Union and other labor unions, Daniel Katz explores how Russian Jewish socialists in New York introduced the idea and ideal of multiculturalism to New York City politics in the 1930s. Katz argues that multiculturalism was a "natural extension" of Jewish radical resistance to the ethos of capitalism, as Jewish union leaders used their experiences in Russian revolutionary movements to integrate new racial-ethnic groups into the garment industry workforce. Beyond forming multiracial unions in New York, socialist-minded Jews were instrumental in the reshaping of the state's larger political landscape. As Daniel Soyer discusses, between 1933 and 1944 the American Labor Party and the Liberal Party served as crucial political entities that helped elect progressive political figures such as Mayor Fiorello La Guardia. Founded as a result of some peculiar New York State election procedure laws, these parties relied on Jews for their leadership, support, and electoral base. Through these parties, Soyer argues, Jewish socialists redefined themselves as progressive in America's body politic and thus entered the mainstream of postwar American liberalism.

Eli Lederhendler shifts our attention away from the realm of electoral politics to the heated world of Jewish politics, highlighting how debates over capitalism reshaped American Jewish communal debates in the mid-twentieth century. Lederhendler's discussion of the Yiddish writings of Isaac Rivkind explores the dour appraisal of capitalism harbored by many Yiddish intellectuals. Rivkind, as Lederhendler points out, saw capitalist individualism as undermining Jewish communal life. Grappling with the larger question of whether the open features of capitalism could accommodate group particularity, Rivkind ruefully mused that American capitalism might even be worse for the Jews than the former oppressive societies in which they lived.

In the fourth section of this volume, the discussion shifts from looking at the ways in which Jews participated in, thought about, or altered American capitalism to a close examination of the innovations and changes introduced to Jewish rituals and their observance as a result of the demands of America's mass market. Jeffrey Shandler explores the career of the cantor Yossele Rosenblatt, who conjoined piety and entrepreneurship. Deploying "new media and new cultural practices . . . to promote his artistry," Shandler argues, Rosenblatt's life suggests that even pious Jews, who might argue in public that the United States and its capitalist ethos were inimical to traditional religiosity, could not resist the opportunities offered to them by mass marketing and consumption. Rosenblatt was not alone in linking religious rituals and entrepreneurial innovation, as evidenced by Jonathan D. Sarna's analysis of the business of Behr Manischewitz. "Yok[ing] modern technology to the service of religion," Sarna points out, Behr Manischewitz and his company transformed the process of matzah making and the character of matzah, as well as the Jews' experience of eating this ritual food. Passover would never be the same as a result of Manischewitz's ingenuity and desire to spread his matzah throughout the nation.

By focusing on the late nineteenth and twentieth centuries—when American capitalism was redefined by industrialization, war, mass migration, and the emergence of the United States as a superpower—this volume engages how the experiences of Jews in the United States molded and were molded by the development of America's particular economic system. To be sure, through its analysis of the relationship between one specific ethno-religious group and the development of American capitalism, this volume raises as many questions as it answers. The fine case studies presented in the following pages illustrate not only how much concrete, resonant, and archive-based information there is concerning the kaleidoscope of variables shaping Jews' encounter with the United States and its economic system but also new ways to theorize, conceptualize and narrate the Jewish encounter with American capitalism. In the end, this volume does not seek to offer the final word but rather invites other scholars to further conversation, investigation, and analysis of the fateful encounter of Sombart's exceptionalisms: the Jews and the United States.

NOTES

1. Werner Sombart was most famous in his time for his multivolume treatise *Der moderne Kapitalismus* (Leipzig, Germany: Dunker and Humblot, 1902).

2. Werner Sombart, *Warum gibt es in den Vereinigten Staaten keinen Sozialismus?* (Tübingen: Mohr, 1906)

3. Werner Sombart, *Die Juden und das Wirtshaftsleben* (Leipzig, Germany: Dunker and Humblot, 1911); Werner Sombart, *The Jews and Modern Capitalism*, trans. Mordechai Epstein (1913; repr. New Brunswick, NJ: Transaction, 1982).

4. Jonathan Karp, *The Politics of Commerce: Economic Thought and Emancipation in Europe* (Cambridge: Cambridge University Press, 2008), 265.

5. Calvin Goldscheider and Alan Zuckerman, *The Transformation of the Jews* (Chicago: University of Chicago Press, 1984)

6. Howard Brick, "The Postcapitalist Vision in Twentieth-Century American Social Thought," in *American Capitalism: Social Thought and Political Economy in the Twentieth Century*, ed. Nelson Lichtenstein (Philadelphia: University of Pennsylvania Press, 2006), 21.

7. Karp, *Politics of Jewish Commerce*; Jerry Muller, *Capitalism and the Jews* (Princeton, NJ: Princeton University Press, 2010).

8. Karp, *Politics of Jewish Commerce*; Derek Penslar, *Shylock's Children: Economics and Jewish Identity in Modern Europe* (Berkeley: University of California Press, 2001).

9. Ignacy Schipper, quoted in Raphael Mahler, "Yitzhak Schipper (1884–1943)," in *Historiker un vegveizer* (Tel Aviv: Farlag Israel Bukh, 1967), 260.

10. Indeed, this call was part of a larger movement among Polish Jewish historians in the interwar years who devoted themselves to building Jewish scholarship in Poland under the guidance of Majer Bałaban (Meir Balaban) and specifically concentrated on the economic and social history of Polish Jewry. See Natalia Aleksiun, "Ammunition in the Struggle for National Rights: Jewish Historians in Poland between the Two World Wars" (PhD diss., New York University, 2010), 76–77.

11. Several notable studies on individuals who changed American capitalism are Alfred Chandler, *Henry Varnum Poor: Business Editor, Analyst, and Reformer* (Cambridge, MA: Harvard University Press 1956); Alfred Chandler, *Pierre S. du Pont and the Making of the Modern Corporation*, with Stephen Salsbury (New York: Harper and Row, 1971); W. Bernard Carlson, *Innovation as a Social Process: Elihu Thomson and the Rise of General Electric, 1870–1900* (New York: Cambridge University Press, 1991); David A. Hounshell and John Kenly Smith Jr., *Science and Corporate Strategy: Du Pont R&D, 1902–1980* (Cambridge: Cambridge University Press, 1988). Ivan Light and Steven Gold, *Ethnic Economies* (San Diego: Academic Press, 2000), offers a stimulating discussion of the impact ethnic business had on the United States. Also see Roger Waldinger, Howard Aldrich, and Robin Ward, *Ethnic Entrepreneurs: Immigrant Business in Industrial Societies* (Newbury Park, CA: Sage, 1990).

12. American Jewish historians have expressed interest only in the economic success of German Jewish bankers, paying slight attention to their actual business practices. See, for example, Stephen Birmingham, *Our Crowd: The Great Jewish Families of New York* (Syracuse: Syracuse University Press, 1996); Barry Supple, "A Business Elite: German-Jewish Financiers in Nineteenth-Century New York," *Business History Review* 3 (Summer 1957): 143–178. American historians have similarly delved into examinations of America's economic expansion without ever mentioning Jews. See Alfred D. Chandler Jr., *The Visible Hand: The Managerial Revolution in American Business* (Cambridge, MA: Harvard University Press, 1977), the classic study of the growth of capitalist enterprise in America. Also see Alfred D. Chandler Jr., *Scale and Scope: The Dynamics of Industrial Capitalism* (Cambridge, MA: Harvard University Press 1990), as well as his "Organizational Capabilities and the Economic History of the Industrial Enterprise," *Journal of Economic Perspectives* 6 (Summer 1992): 79–100; Paul Uselding, "Business History and the History of Technology," *Business History Review* 54 (Winter 1980): 440–459; Alfred D. Chandler Jr., Thomas K. McCraw, and Richard S. Tedlow, *Management Past and Present* (Cincinnati, OH: South Western College Publishers, 1996); Mansel G. Blackford and K. Austin Kerr, *Business Enterprise in American History* (Boston: Houghton Mifflin, 1990); C. Joseph Pusateri, *A History of American Business* (Arlington Heights, IL: Davidson, 1984); Richard S. Tedlow and Richard R. John, eds., *Managing Big Business: Essays from the Business History Review* (Boston: Harvard Business School Press, 1986); Maury Klein, *The Flowering of the Third America: The Making of an Organizational Society, 1850–1920* (Chicago: Dee, 1993); Stuart Bruchey, *Enterprise: The Dynamic Economy of a Free People* (Cambridge, MA: Harvard University Press 1990); Robert Sobel and David B. Sicilia, *The Entrepreneurs: An American Adventure* (Boston: Houghton Mifflin, 1986); James Oliver Robertson, *America's Business* (New York: Hill and Wang, 1985); Walter Licht, *Industrializing America: The Nineteenth Century* (Baltimore: Johns Hopkins University Press, 1995); David A. Hounshell, *From the American System to Mass Production, 1800–1932: The Development of Manufacturing Technology in the United States* (Baltimore: Johns Hopkins University Press, 1984); and William G. Roy, *Socializing Capital: The Rise of the Large Industrial Corporation in America* (Princeton, NJ: Princeton University Press, 1997).

13. Simon Kuznets, "Immigration of Russian Jews to the United States: Background and Structure," *Perspectives in American History* 9 (1975): 35–124. Arcadius Kahan, "Economic Opportunities and Some Pilgrim's Progress: Jewish Immigrants from Eastern Europe in the United States, 1890–1914," *Essays in Jewish Social and Economic History* (1986): 101–117

14. Ira Katznelson, "Jews on the Margins of American Liberalism," in *Paths of Emancipation: Jews, States, Citizenship* (Princeton, NJ: Princeton University Press, 1995), 160, 190–196.

15. The vast body of sociological literature concerning contemporary immigrant, ethnic, and racial minorities' relationship to American capitalism cannot be summarized here, but a few noteworthy exemplars can be found in Ivan Light's and Roger Waldinger's work.

Soo Light's *Ethnic Enterprise In America: Business and Welfare among Chinese, Japanese, and Blacks* (Berkeley: University of California Press, 1972); Light and Edna Bonacich, *Immigrant Entrepreneurs: Koreans in Los Angeles, 1965–1982* (Berkeley: University of California Press, 1988); Light, *Immigration and Entrepreneurship: Culture, Capital, and Ethnic Networks* (New Brunswick, NJ: Transaction, 1993); Light and Carolyn Rosenstein, *Race, Ethnicity, and Entrepreneurship in Urban America* (New York: Aldine de Gruyter, 1995); Light and Gold's *Ethnic Economies*; Waldinger, Aldrich, and Ward, *Ethnic Entrepreneurs*; Waldinger, *Through the Eye of the Needle: Immigrants and Enterprise in New York's Garment Trades* (New York: NYU Press, 1986); Waldinger, "Immigrant Enterprise: A Critique and Reformulation," *Theory and Society* 15 (1986), 249–285.

16. "Jews in America," *Fortune* 13, no. 2 (February 1936): 79–133. Quotations appear on 79–80 and 131–132.

17. The general avoidance of these questions is evident on many levels. For example, in the series Studies in Contemporary Jewry, which has overall set the topic of Jews and capitalism aside, volume 8, dedicated to the subject of Jews in the United States, contains only one brief article on "the postwar economy by American Jews." Barry Chiswick, "The Postwar Economy of American Jews," in *Studies in Contemporary Jewry* (Jerusalem: Avraham Harman Institute of Contemporary Jewry, 1992), 85–101. To be sure, economic historians such as Simon Kuznets and Arcadius Kahan have produced insightful studies with impressive empirical analyses of the occupational structure of Jews in America, but their work contains virtually nothing about large-scale historical issues or how Jews have shaped the larger trajectory of American capitalism.

18. Arcadius Kahan, *Essays in Jewish Economic and Social History* (Chicago: University of Chicago Press, 1986); Simon Kuznets, "Immigration of Russian Jews to the United States: Background and Structure," *Perspectives in American History* 9 (1975): 35–124. Among those who comment on immigrant Jews' rapid ascent into the middle and upper classes are such classic studies as Deborah Dash Moore's *At Home in America* (New York: Columbia University Press, 1983) and Jenna Weisman Joselit's *The Wonders of America: Reinventing Jewish Culture, 1880–1950* (New York: Hill and Wang, 1994). The notable exception is Eli Lederhendler, *Jewish Immigrants and American Capitalism: From Caste to Class* (Cambridge: Cambridge University Press, 2009).

19. David Hollinger, "Rich, Powerful, and Smart: Jewish Overrepresentation Should Be Explained Rather Than Mystified or Avoided," *Jewish Quarterly Review* (Fall 2004): 596.

20. Some of the most influential work on American Jewish material culture includes Weissman Joselit, *Wonders of America*; Susan L. Braunstein and Jenna Weissman Joselit, eds., *Getting Comfortable in New York: The American Jewish Home, 1880–1950* (New York: Jewish Museum, 1990); Ken Koltun-Fromm, *Material Culture and Jewish Thought in America* (Bloomington: Indiana University Press, 2010); and Vanessa L. Ochs, "What Makes a Jewish Home Jewish? Stuff in a Jewish Home Is More Than Just Stuff; It's Jewish Stuff," *Cross Currents* 49, no. 4 (1999–2000): 491–510.

21. The term "forgotten siblings" was coined by Hartmut Berghoff and Uwe Spiekermann, "Immigrant Entrepreneurship: The German-American Business Biography, 1720–Present Research Project," *Bulletin of the German Historical Institute* 47 (Fall 2010): 75. Examples of literature on German Jewish bankers are Barry E. Supple, "A Business Elite: German-Jewish Financiers in Nineteenth-Century New York," *Business History Review* 31 (Summer 1957): 99–113; and Naomi Cohen, *Jacob H. Schiff: A Study in American Jewish Leadership* (Hanover, NH: University Press of New England, 1999). Several noteworthy works on Jewish garment workers include Moses Rischin's classic *The Promised City: New York's Jews, 1870–1914* (Cambridge, MA: Harvard University Press, 1962); Susan Glenn, *Daughters of the Shtetl: Life and Labor in the Immigrant Generation* (Ithaca, NY: Cornell University Press, 1990); and Hadassa Kosak, *Cultures of Opposition: Jewish Immigrant Workers, New York City, 1881–1905* (Albany: SUNY Press, 2000).

22. Waldinger, "Immigrant Enterprise," 249–250; Charles Hirschman, "Immigration and the American Century," *Demography* 42 (2005): 595–620.

23. Andrew Godley, *Jewish Immigrant Entrepreneurship in New York and London, 1880–1914: Enterprise and Culture* (New York: Palgrave Macmillan, 2001).

24. Ron Chernow, *House of Morgan: An American Banking Dynasty and the Rise of Modern Finance* (New York: Grove, 2001), 89, 90. See Susie Pak's *Gentlemen Bankers: The World of J. P. Morgan and Investment Banking, 1895–1940* (Cambridge, MA: Harvard University Press, forthcoming) for a discussion of how Jewishness and anti-Semitism shaped business and investment banking practices in the United States.

25. Birmingham, *Our Crowd*; Vincent P. Carosso, "A Financial Elite: New York's German-Jewish Investment Bankers," *American Jewish Historical Quarterly* 66, no. 1–4 (September 1976–1977): 67–88.

26. In the realm of American culture, several scholars have penned fine studies that explore the ways in which Jews identified with and engaged America's racial outsiders. See Michael Alexander, *Jazz Age Jews* (Princeton, NJ: Princeton University Press, 2001); Eric Goldstein, *The Price of Whiteness: Jews, Race and Identity in America* (Princeton, NJ: Princeton University Press, 2006); and Michael Rogin, *Blackface, White Noise: Jewish Immigrants in the Hollywood Melting Pot* (Berkeley: University of California Press, 1996).

CHAPTER 1

Two Exceptionalisms

POINTS OF DEPARTURE FOR STUDIES OF CAPITALISM AND JEWS IN THE UNITED STATES

Ira Katznelson

Even as academic Jewish studies have moved ahead by leaps and bounds in the past half century, "the relationship of the Jews to capitalism," as Jerry Muller limpidly puts the point, "has received less attention than its significance merits."[1] Within American studies, the main exceptions to this rule, Arcadius Kahan's and Simon Kuznets's rich scholarship, date from more than three decades ago.[2] One might speculate about the reasons for this neglect. Certainly, a high degree of caution, even skittishness, is warranted, for the charged subject of Jews and capitalism has been marked not only by scholarly challenges but also by public perils. Yet the cost of neglect to historical understanding has been high.

From the early Republic, Jews brought networks of trust and experience with commerce to a country with a prominent and growing role in the development of global capitalism. In the nineteenth century the United States became an increasingly important economic center for the Jewish world. In the twentieth a combination of calamity and opportunity made the United States its cultural and demographic focal point.[3] Yet we know, and understand, far too little about how and when Jews have helped form the ethos, institutions, and trajectory of U.S. capitalism or, in turn, how the group's members have been affected by the economy's character and course. With capitalism, as Muller writes, having "been the most important force in shaping the fate of the Jews in the modern world," I wish to ask how this relationship might be moved from peripheral inattention to a more central scholarly location in American studies.[4]

With the recent renewal of interest in these subjects, not least by the contributors to this volume, it is timely to consider how scholarly considerations

concerning Jews and American capitalism might proceed.[5] Offering both sub-
stantive and methodological points of departure, this essay makes two principal proposals. First is an insistence on the inherent complexity and changing
qualities of segmentation. The history that has marked the group's experience
in the United States has been characterized by an extraordinary but only partial and skewed economic integration. It has also been marked by a distinctive,
if changing, Jewish economic sphere, by visible but not constant niches. Second
is a consideration of how we might combine assessments of distinctive historic
situations with accounts that highlight the preferences and decisions of key
actors. In so doing, I invoke Salo Baron as a practical and ethical guide.

––––––

The United States has been the globe's most hospitable and least insecure location for mass Jewish settlement in modern, perhaps all, human history. No
other Jewish population ever was as swiftly and surely inserted into a world of
physical security, cultural permissiveness, and civic membership. American
Jews were emancipated from the start. The Constitution specified no religious
tests for office. Anti-Jewish feeling, which certainly existed in civil society,
never took national political form, even if some states persisted in restricting
the full civic membership of Jews well into the nineteenth century. Jewish office
holding came early, even, perhaps especially, in areas where few had settled.
Until the early 1920s the right to enter the country was nearly untrammeled. A
pluralism of faiths prevailed; there was no state religion nor a dominant Christian profession. Patriotism trumped nationality as the basis for loyalty to a
regime dedicated to individual rights. Racial divisions between black and white
directed civil society's racism, deflecting it from the Jews, especially after they
moved from the category of a race to that of an ethnic group. As *Fortune* argued
in 1936, "there is no . . . clinical record" of anti-Semitism, which the magazine
defined as "the deliberately incited, affirmative racial phobia which has produced the social and economic and sometimes physical pogroms of modern
Germany just as it produced the murderous pogroms of Czarist Russia."[6]

The contrast between these felicitous circumstances in the country of entry
and the harsher conditions from which Jews had come long has been a staple
of American Jewish historiography and wider cultural understanding. Jews,
after all, escaped more than the economic destiny of European Jewry. On that
continent some Jews had become less segregated and more visible when they
had moved from embeddedness within the ancien régime's political economy
based on land, hierarchy, and status to the new commercial economy based
on urban capital and social class. They demonstrated that they could seize
beckoning economic opportunities, however partial. In less enclosed and more
economically emancipated cities such as Budapest, Berlin, and Warsaw, even
in Moscow and St. Petersburg, Jews pioneered in capitalist finance and gained

highly visible roles in the various liberal professions.[7] In other settings, most notably the Pale of Settlement, they lost traditional functions without gaining access to new ones. The result was Jewish poverty and superfluity.[8] Jews came to compose a segmented and dependent population. At a time of nationalist assertion, these patterns generated resentment and contempt. Ultimately, such obloquy convoked tragedy.[9]

Born commercial and capitalist, the United States was different. The long-settled and mostly legitimate market economy offered places to Jews when they arrived. As newcomers, they did not stand out or stand apart from other Americans, and their economic participation largely was welcomed. Notwithstanding the existence of social anti-Semitism and discriminatory practices, Jews were able to join the country's economy from the start without attracting or inciting disproportionate attention or hostile regard. Set in comparative terms, existing strictures and limits were relatively mild.[10] By the time the mass migration of Russian Jewry began, America's mostly German Jewish community had achieved much economic accomplishment and cultural integration.[11] Arriving later and moving "from caste to class" between the 1880s and the 1920s, that era's mostly Russian newcomers joined the long-standing capitalist structure of the United States at a moment of immense industrial growth and development and thus secured places on the first rungs of what proved to be an attainably high ladder.[12]

An emphasis on the uncommonly integrated standing of Jewry within American capitalism is correct but insufficient, for it understates the complexity and contradictions that characterized this relationship. Of course, any specification of the distinctive features of this encounter cannot but begin with an assessment of the uncommon circumstances that were hospitable to the commercial role of Jews and that facilitated the incorporation of the Jewish masses into a modern class structure. But significant distortions can result when portraits of economic inclusion and integration do not take in concurrent patterns of economic segmentation and exclusion. Well into the twentieth century, American Jews were subjected to sharp exclusions from key areas of the economy and professional training, often based on fierce resistance to Jewish entry.

Three complicating features characterized the tenor of Jewish links to the mainstream economy. First is the patchy nineteenth-century economic integration of even the most successful German Jews. Second is the remarkable clustering of Russian Jews when they entered America's modern class structure. Third is the set of barriers that separated both German and Russian Jews from much of the country's core economy, at least until the end of World War II.[13]

Initially, members of the Jewish immigrant stream from Germany, who first arrived in number in the 1830s, formed a distinct section of the larger movement of Christian Germans to the United States and tended to live within the country's dispersed German areas of settlement. It was this pattern that contributed to the reduction in Jewish visibility that Muller emphasizes. At this point, Jews belonged to secondary associations that were as likely to be German in an inclusive way, spanning religious lines, than distinctly Jewish. For sure, the Jews were distinguished from fellow Germans on the basis of creed, but much like the way German Protestants were distinguished from German Catholics. By contrast, after the post-1848 upsurge in migration from Germany to the United States, the Jews became increasingly visible and segmented, with a separation marked by a growing institutional independence. They now were less a subgroup of a larger ethnic population than a distinctive population from which other Germans distanced themselves, especially as the number of Jews grew significantly. In these circumstances, economic and occupational impediments grew more rigid. Bounded exclusion impelled Jews to create separate institutions, including banking houses led, among others, by the Kuhn, Seligman, Loeb, Guggenheim, Strauss, and Lehman families.

In short, great and unprecedented economic achievement was accompanied by the development of a distinctively Jewish economic sphere, similar to, integrated with, but clearly separate from the larger capitalist political economy. Even the most assimilated in religious and cultural terms could not escape, and many did not wish to escape, their social and economic identities as Jews.

The massive post-1880 migrant stream reproduced and exaggerated this segmented pattern, combining imposition with choice. Jewish economic enclaves in the main were more concentrated than those of other migrants who came from eastern and central Europe at the same time. Most extraordinary was their density in New York City, especially the Lower East Side, the home of one in ten of the world's Jews at the turn of the century, and half of those in America, where the leading source of employment was the garment industry, led primarily by Jewish employers in neighborhood worksites. To be sure, in contrast with their Russian experiences, the newcomers experienced what Eli Lederhendler calls class-based integration, but it was of a particular, discrete, and insulated type.[14] It offered a form of economic integration on relatively equal terms, but with uncertain margins. Experiencing inclusion alongside segmentation and shut doors at the edges of American life before World War II, Jews were induced to engage the wider society from the vantage of "city niches," a set of spatial and institutional locations "from which they could relate to an uncertain and unpredictable wider society." Being both strangers and at home, they "sought to preserve their distinctiveness not only as an end in itself but as a strategic resource capable of forwarding their engagement with America on terms as favorable and secure as possible."[15]

Uneven incorporation and occupational concentration were central themes marking how an empirically rich assessment of "Jews in America" described the economic position of Jews in the mid-1930s. In what remains an unrivaled account of their position within American capitalism, this essay (attributed to "the editors of *Fortune*" but written by Archibald MacLeish) recorded their absence from banking ("there are practically no Jewish employees of any kind in the largest commercial banks—and this in spite of the fact that many of their customers are Jews") and especially from the most important investment banks (noting that the Jewish houses "do not compare in power").[16] Concluding "that there is no basis whatever for the suggestion that Jews monopolize U.S. business and industry," it took note of the limited place for Jews in the country's stock exchanges and of the non-Jewish character of the automobile and steel industries—the country's most important—as well as aviation, chemicals, coal, oil, rubber, shipbuilding, railroads, telephones, heavy machinery, lumber, and engineering. The article observed how, by contrast, Jews specialized in furniture, clothing, scrap metal, liquor, furniture, cigars but not cigarettes, the distribution but not the production of tobacco, and parts of publishing and entertainment, especially the movies.[17]

Those positions were highly visible. They centered in big cities and perceptible locations like the mass media and department stores. A 1949 reanalysis of the data in *Fortune*'s study by the University of Pennsylvania sociologist William Kephart, himself a student of anti-Semitism, sought to place the information the article had contained within the frame both of population numbers and practices of exclusion. He reminded his readers that in 1936 Jews had composed just under 4 percent of the population of the United States (a quarter of world Jewry at the time), yet 90 percent of participants in scrap iron and steel; 95 percent in waste products of nonferrous scrap metal, paper, cotton rag, and rubber; 85 percent in men's clothing and 95 percent in women's; 50 percent of radio and theater; and 80 to 90 percent in the film industry. Not bigotry alone, but the Jewish presence in such proportions, far more than their absence, say, in coal production, lumber, or agriculture, underpinned the period's widespread apprehension that Jews commanded too much economic power.[18] Shortly after World War II, and following postwar revelations about the Shoah, fully 36 percent of respondents to a 1947 poll conducted for *Fortune* named Jews as a group that is "getting more economic power in the United States than is good for the country." Catholics were named, in contrast, by 12 percent, and Protestants, who undoubtedly possessed the most economic capacity, were identified by only 2 percent.[19]

Seeking to comprehend the rabble-rousing potential of Jewish economic success during the 1930s, the time of Father Coughlin and Gerald L. K. Smith, the German-American Bund and the Silver Shirts, the Crusader White Shirts and the Defenders of the Christian Faith, and situating its detailed empirical portrait within the grip of fear, *Fortune*'s 1936 overview observed,

> The apprehensiveness of intelligent Jews springs from this fact. Realizing
> that Jews have been the scapegoats of all Western history, that they have

been made to bear responsibility for everything from the Black Death to the economic ills of the Germans, these observers fear that the enormous increase in Jewish numbers and America will lead to charges that the Jews have monopolized the opportunities for economic advance and that these charges will pave the way for fascism here as they paved the way for Hitler in Germany. Non-Jews who prefer democratic institutions to dictatorship share the fear. To determine whether it is a fear of deserving of serious attention it is necessary to inquire . . . whether there is any factual basis for charges of Jewish monopolization of American economic opportunity.[20]

The point of the article was to answer negatively. Because it worried that "a disproportionate Jewish participation in the economic life of a country has been found capable of arousing anti-Semitic feeling," its economic survey sought to counter a view of such disproportion by refuting the "charge that Jews have monopolized or are monopolizing economic opportunity in the United States."[21] Read closely, however, the *Fortune* article, though written explicitly to protect America's Jews, actually exposed powerful countercurrents and revealed the precarious qualities that characterized the relationship of Jews to capitalism in the United States.

Three aspects stand out.

First, the study exposed the depth of mass ambivalence, at just the moment when the extrusion of Jews from German society was visibly under way. The article reported on a January 1936 survey the magazine had carried out. To the question, "Do you believe that in the long run Germany will be better or worse off if it drives out the Jews?" fully 45 percent replied either that it would be better off or answered that they did not know. The magazine put a positive spin on this finding. It concluded that American anti-Semitism was relatively feeble, arguing that the "don't know" response was "equivalent to indifference. And indifference, though Jews may think it callous, is the most effective prophylactic against the pestilence of hate; those who don't care either way will smash no windows."[22] This does not seem persuasive.

Second, the article revealed just how difficult it is even for enlightened observers to write about the American economy and discrimination without implying or saying that those who face its effects are being oversensitive. *Fortune* argued that "any man who loathes fascism will fear anti-Semitism. Fearing anti-Semitism he will also fear the various conditions which encourage it, of which the apprehensiveness of the Jews themselves is one." The article further wondered "specifically whether the growing apprehensiveness of American Jews has any justification in fact." It answered, "There is no reason for anxiety so far as concerns the record to date of the organized forces of anti-Semitism." But it worried how, despite this fortunate reality, "the apprehensiveness of American Jews" had become "one of the most important influences on the social life of our time." And it went on to warn that "fearful minorities become suspicious minorities and suspicious minorities, their defensive reactions set on a hair trigger of anxiety, create the animosities they dread."[23]

Third is the way *Fortune* sought to account for Jewish economic patterns, including their concentration in particular locations and their absence from the peaks of American capitalism. The analysis presented by the article did not differ much from the line of reasoning the German sociologist and economist Werner Sombart had offered a quarter century earlier in a contentious study of Jews and modern capitalism.[24] Jews, the magazine claimed, have a taste for particular economic roles as an aspect of their non-Christian cultural heritage. They have acquired "a universal strangeness," "an exotic character," and "a strong sense of difference and hence of clannishness." Other groups assimilate; "all other immigrant peoples accept the culture of the country into which they come." But Jews "have refused to accept it. . . . The habit of pride . . . is too strong in them. Even many of those who have deserted the traditions of their people and accepted in every detail the dress and speech and life of the non-Jewish majority are still subtly but recognizably different." And it is this cultural, if not racial, difference that impels Jews to seek economic niches marked by a "crowding together in particular businesses and particular localities." This wish to be apart, it further argued, explains "the very existence of discriminatory . . . barriers . . . in education and industry" for these were not instances of "Gentile injustice" but, rather, understandable response to the "Jewish tendency to inundate a field where other Jews have made an entrance."[25]

————

From the perspective of historical economics and economic sociology, the *Fortune* study of 1936 was lacking in many ways. Its data sources were very uneven, with a tilt toward economic activity in New York and a few other large cities, so it was not fully representative geographically, leaving out the kinds of patterns chronicled by Elliot Ashkenazi for New Orleans and Ewa Morawska for Johnstown, Pennsylvania.[26] It failed to specify when Jews were absent because of formal and informal exclusions and when by self-denial. It lacked measures of discrimination. It did not link economic integration to trends in global migration or population movements within the country. It did not distinguish fully those economic niches that were integral to and largely enclosed within the Jewish community and those that were connected and central to the larger American economy. It was silent about Jews and organized labor; indeed, about Jewish workers and their prospects. It only briefly took up the relationship between Jews and the liberal professions and the development of their place within American capitalism. It had no measures of income or wealth or mobility. Its methodology was obscure. It did not reveal its sources nor is there reason to believe that it cross-checked them.

With all that, this single article persists as a reminder of what we do not have. Thus, as an example, Beth Wenger's excellent treatment of the Jewish ethnic economy during the Great Depression had little choice but to draw on this source, despite these flaws and omissions that have not been mitigated by subsequent studies or by accounts of later periods.[27] There is an enormous amount that we simply do not know empirically about the position of Jews in the United States at different moments, regions, cities, and sites of trade and industry. Thanks to Jonathan Israel, Jonathan Karp, and other scholars of early modern Europe, we almost certainly are more informed about the vertical and horizontal economic standing, linkages, and networks of the Jews then and there than in the United States.[28] To my knowledge, there currently is no body of work with a comparable ambition that offers sweeping and accurate overviews of the kind *Fortune* produced at the end of President Franklin Roosevelt's first term.[29]

As an example of this elision, notice how one of the most important publications in Jewish studies, the impressive annual, *Studies in Contemporary Jewry*, has largely set these issues aside, all the while probing other important topics that include relations between Jews and the state, Jews and the city, and Jews and gender. Even volume 8, dedicated to Jewish patterns in the United States since World War II, devoted only one brief article to economic questions, a learned essay by the economist Barry Chiswick that charts the postwar occupational structure of American Jews. But that discussion is virtually silent about larger historical issues. In this respect, it resembles other significant sources of empirical information, including treatments of American patterns in *The Transformation of the Jews* by Calvin Goldscheider and Alan Zuckerman and of economic affairs in Marshall Sklare's landmark volume on *The Jews: Social Patterns of an American Group*. Nor has the literature on Jews and capitalism adequately considered reciprocal questions of how the contours of modern Jewish life have been shaped by living within the ambit of capitalism.[30]

Such silences reflect concerns about the fraught qualities of the subject, but they also are the product, at least in part, of the way knowledge is organized and produced. Within the discipline of economics, economic history ranks low in prestige, and the field is not populated by scholars concerned with Jewish history. Ethnic studies, in sociology and other disciplines, rarely makes the Jewish past or present a central concern. As the group has become more integrated and less threatened, it also has become less interesting. Furthermore, historians of the Jews, whose numbers are flourishing, largely lack the requisite economic and statistical competence.

All the more reason to celebrate the growing accumulation of fine qualitative case studies, including those written for this book. We have begun to possess resonant archive-based knowledge about a kaleidoscope of subjects, including the place of Jews in peddling, scrap dealing, and industries from feathers to music; about the ways religion, including cantorial skill, have been marketed;

about activities on the edges of economic criminality; and about how the Jewish role in the economy has been represented within Jewish life and literature. Such studies have enlarged what we see and how we understand a wide range of economic experiences, but the intellectual harvest presented even by beautifully realized portraits of this kind cannot stand alone. Microhistories are not enough. Such work demands a larger frame, or more than one large frame, to guide inquiries that wish to probe how Jews have penetrated, shaped, and lived within American capitalism, and, in turn, how economic arrangements have influenced and affected American Jews individually and collectively.

Such a research program cannot be successful unless it is based on a much stronger empirical basis than we currently possess; unless it moves beyond pointillist description to develop accounts about Jews and capitalism in which the causal arrows face not just in one, but in both, directions; unless we identify not just correlations between capitalism and Jews but specify as precisely as possible the mechanisms that underpin these relationships; and unless we carefully designate eras and distinguish epochs. Such a multidimensional research program also invites strategies of comparison. An analytically directed and rounded portrait would not only evaluate the experiences of Jews before and after coming to the United States but would assess Jewish history in tandem with that of contemporaneous immigrant groups, especially Catholic and Protestant Germans, and Catholics from southern and eastern Europe. Further comparisons beckon, both with American racial minorities, recalling that Jews frequently were coded as a race and not just by anti-Semites, and with other Jewish communities of consequence in the Americas, including those in Argentina, Brazil, Canada, Chile, and Mexico.

————

No robust research endeavor about Jews and American capitalism will thrive unless it confronts the ghost of Werner Sombart. Best known for his six-volume study, published in 1902, that offered a broad historical portrait of *Der moderne Kapitalismus*, he identified what he thought to be two economic "exceptionalisms"—for the United States and for modern Jews—that continue to challenge our comprehension of American Jewish history, notwithstanding the unsettling and famously unpleasant features of his work about the role of Jews in the making of modern capitalism.[31]

Published in 1906, his *Warum gibt es in den Vereinigten Staaten keinen Sozialismus?* famously explained key features of American working-class history, including the absence of effective socialist appeals, by underscoring how prosperity had blocked the pathway to proletarian consciousness.[32] A half decade later, Sombart's *Die Juden und das Wirtschaftsleben*, translated in sometimes expurgated English editions as *Jews and Modern Capitalism*, analyzed the contribution Jews and Judaism had made to the development of modern capitalism. Identifying this group and its religious orientation as prime movers, this book revised the hypothesis Max Weber had offered just five years earlier about capitalism and the Protestant ethic.[33] Rather than focus on Calvinists and their theology, Sombart argued that the rootless mentality, urban-oriented culture, acquisitive nature, and rationalistically inclined religion of the Jews had placed them at the head of western capitalist development by advancing their egoism, promoting their love of money, and enlarging their capacity for abstract calculation. Less tendentiously, he identified how the dispersal of the Jews often produced nimble adaptations to local situations.[34]

Within Central Europe's increasingly hostile, anti-Jewish atmosphere, Sombart's identification of Jews with capitalism was not simply a social scientific or historical claim but an incendiary ideological provocation. In 1902 *Der moderne Kapitalismus* had lamented the decline of an integrated and natural precapitalist world. *Die Juden* placed responsibility for this deterioration on Europe's foreign element of ultrarational Jews, drawn to commerce by their religion and acquisitive nature. As progenitors of such basic instruments of financial capitalism as banknotes and securities, the Jews, in this history, were reported to have played a decisive role in developing the institutions of modern banking and stock exchanges that made money abstract and speculation rampant. Unlike Max Weber's *The Protestant Ethic*, Sombart's *Jews and Modern Capitalism* treated its historical protagonists as a hardwired race, "ethnically pure . . . for some twenty generations," a stance that heralded his *Deutscher Sozialismus*, his 1934 text that explicitly contrasted the triumphant spirit of the young Third Reich with the doleful spirit of the ancient Jewish people.[35]

Notwithstanding the ugly aspects of Sombart's scholarship, the questions he raised that concern relationships among faith, religious attitudes, and economic orientations persist as important challenges in understanding Jewish economic history. However statistically advanced or descriptively robust, even the most full empirical portraits cannot elide the problems Sombart probed. Serious inquiry must reckon with *Die Juden und das Wirtshaftsleben*, or at least with the research questions it raises about whether and how a causal affinity links Jews to capitalism.

When *Die Juden* was translated in 1913, the English edition omitted much of the racist biological analysis that undergirded its claims about the "natural" affinities of Jews. Indeed, Sombart himself understood that this orientation might prove difficult for many readers. He thus adopted a voice more like that found in his scientific and sociological writings than the emotional tone he had used in writing an overtly anti-Semitic pamphlet concerned with the future of the Jews just a year earlier. As Natalie Davis has observed, Sombart "kept his text uncannily free of normative statements that would disclose his strong aversion to the capitalistic calculation allegedly invented by the Jews."[36] As a result, some learned historians, including George Mosse, Fritz Ringer, and Hugh

Trevor-Roper, wrongly believed, in Mosse's words, that "Sombart was not con-
demning the Jews, but merely, as he thought, providing a historical analysis of
the evolution of capitalism."[37] Indeed, Sombart's portrayal of Jews as insistent
modernizers sometimes has been a source of approbation from outside the Jewish world, looking in, and inside, looking out.

However motivated, the decision to favor a language of scientific moderation by Sombart and by his translator, Mordechai Epstein, does us a favor. The
repression of anti-Jewish prose and feeling helps facilitate our engagement
with the claim that Jews, across a range of historical circumstances, have been
inclined to cultivate the skills to thrive in a commercializing modern world.
This theme, of course, is not unique to Sombart; it appears, for example, as a
central feature in Werner Mosse's detailed treatment of the positive influence of
Jewish economic elites on the development of capitalism in nineteenth-century
Germany.[38] Stripped of its racial content, *Jews and Modern Capitalism* identi-
fies hypotheses about mechanisms that have characterized this relationship.
An example is the ironic claim that as outsiders (strangers, in Georg Simmel's
terms) who were enclosed in a separate culture, distinct networks, and partially
isolated and institutionally segregated environments, Jews could become con-
summate insiders, formative influences, and leaders of trends.[39]

For Sombart, propensities counted for more than situations. The aptitude
of Jews to successfully engage capitalism was fashioned over the centuries not
simply by their circumstances as dispersed outsiders but by deeply embedded
orientations situated within the most fundamental qualities of Jewish religious
doctrines, regulations, and practices. On this reading, there was a deep affinity
between the requirements of modern capitalism and how traditional Judaism
sanctioned the pursuit of gain. Rational and law-oriented Judaism, he argued,
is a religion with a capitalist ethos, a capitalist spirit. It opposes mysticism and
unreservedly accepts wealth. It promotes entrepreneurship and facilitates economic dealings based on mutual reliance among Jews and on maximizing profit
in dealings with non-Jews, because its code permits such differential relations.[40]

This mode of argumentation raises fundamental questions that are familiar
to historians and social scientists. In explaining outcomes, how much causal
weight should be credited to preferences—that is, to the habits, ideas, practices,
beliefs, values, interests, and cultural assets of persons as agents—and how
much to the structure of the situations in which they are found? Irrespective
of the relative emphasis given to each, how should agents and structures be
conceptualized and analyzed?

There are, of course, no simple or singularly correct answers. Inquiries
profit when they refuse choices that are too stark. They gain when they experiment with different valences, when they offer a wide array of accounts about
the sources and character of the economic preferences of Jews as shaped by, and
located within, particular historical conditions. The analysis of Jewish agency

gains force, in short, when it is embedded within structural accounts about where and how they were permitted to be economic actors.[41]

While the religious, and the ideational, aspects of culture and circumstances clearly have a role to play, the kind of exaggerated and often crude representation of Judaism that Sombart offered hardly can suffice. When any group, including Jews, is shown to have an affinity for particular economic behavior, argument by provocative correlation, such as that between a putatively rational religion and rational economic action, is always insufficient. Nor, though, can his focus on propensities simply be dismissed, for cultural assets do change the probabilities of action. Thus, I am drawn to the work of historians who have grappled with his writing critically, who have taken his account of Jewish preferences seriously, and who persuasively think that only an elaborated conceptual and more specific historical understanding of the situations Jews experienced can help us craft better answers than Sombart provided.[42]

Critiques of Sombart by Werner Mosse and Natalie Davis are two such examples. Both underscore how the idea of an inherent proclivity or predisposition has to vie analytically with the particularities of historical situations and thus with the full range of group circumstances. Speaking at a 1978 conference of economic and social historians at the University of Bielefeld, Mosse strongly argued that understanding specifically Jewish institutions and attitudes, including those that promote cohesion and solidarity, is inherently insufficient. Rather than paint with a broad brush, as Sombart had, scholars should depict with quantitative and qualitative exactness how Jews were embedded within particular capitalisms. Based on his own learned investigation of the German-Jewish capitalist enterprise, he further argued that when an uneven distribution of Jews in different sectors of a given economy is identified, a systematic and comparative analysis of institutions, networks, opportunity patterns, and other structural arrangements must be mounted to discover persuasive causal explanations. Mechanisms particular to individual historical situations should be compared with those in other times and places as a means to develop more general and portable hypotheses.[43] This, in short, was an elegant plea on behalf of a focus on "situation" rather than "propensity."

An essay by Natalie Davis on merchant culture in seventeenth-century German-speaking Europe similarly confronted Sombart.[44] Treating economics as a cultural activity in the tradition of Clifford Geertz, Davis stressed how a wide-ranging constellation of factors shaped the orientation that Jews then and there developed to deal with an emerging commercial society. The evidence she considered includes a communal roll of honor compiled in tandem with measures of wealth within the Jewish community. This practice, she argued, reveals money's multiple meanings.[45] It also discloses how commercial and family matters were tightly integrated. So, too, were struggles about religious prestige and the meaning of law.

Davis further emphasized the particular character of Jewish networks and the advantages of secrecy, including linguistic secrecy, all the while taking care to demonstrate similarities as well as differences between Jewish and non-Jewish behavior. Strongly cautioning against historical reification, the article reminds readers to consider the role of Jews in the development of modern capitalism by taking into consideration important scholarship that is not primarily concerned with this group.[46] A leading example is Alexander Gerschenkron's evaluation of models of economic modernization in England, France, Germany, and Russia in a work that undermines simple ideas about singular pathways. Particularity matters, even within broadly general theory.[47]

Sombart's story, Mosse and Davis showed, is both too crude and too general.[48] Stressing careful and focused accounts shaped by theory and comparison, they implicitly identified grounds on which significant work might proceed at four distinct levels of analysis. First is the objective structure of the particular capitalist economy to which Jews were connected, including its organizational and industrial structure, the character of its class structure and economic opportunities, and its social geography. Second is how these circumstances were experienced by Jews as businesspeople, workers, professionals, and consumers. Third is an account of the range of dispositions about capitalism that Jews came to have within the penumbra of these experiences. Fourth are patterns of individual and collective action as they unfolded across a practical and ideological range within the ambit of these dispositions. Inquiry along these layered lines must be sensitive to temporality and sequence and should seek to distinguish critical junctures and moments of inflection, including those characterized by economic crises, mass migration, industrial transformation, and war.

——————

Focusing on how the particulars of the American experience conditioned the insertion of Jews into the political economy of the United States and how Jews acted within these often complex and uneven circumstances, such analyses could enrich our empirical knowledge and provide means with which to engage the two "exceptionalisms" Sombart identified. But the deep flaws both in his analysis and in the character of his person rule him out as an orienting guide for this endeavor. Instead, we might gain perspective and intellectual sustenance, and lose our reluctance to deal with the subject of Jews and capitalism lest we free the demons, by turning from the spirit of Sombart to the far more attractive spirit of Salo Baron.

As historians of the Jewish experience, we live in the house of Baron. Writing in the *Menorah Journal* in the summer of 1942, he offered reflections on "modern capitalism and the Jewish fate."[49] With liberal capitalism under enormous stress from the Bolshevik Left and from the fascist Right, he urgently inquired about the operation of market economies and assessed the price for Jews should capitalism collapse in the face of these ideological assaults. Baron's appraisal was dour. Capitalist development over the course of four centuries had offered Jews big advantages and unprecedented opportunities to break out of enclosed, mostly poor, traditional environments. New outlets for migration had opened up. Capitalist imperatives had helped Jews return to places from which they once had been excluded, and it had facilitated a radical growth in the group's population, while allowing Jews to deploy their economic skills on an ever-larger stage in big cities devoted to trade and industry. Long experienced with money and credit as a result of having been excluded from the land, Jews, both at court and more broadly, learned to deploy capital and utilize cross-national networks as inherent aspects of power and economic advancement. Overall, private enterprise widened their once-cribbed prospects. Where capitalism and industrialization prevailed, Jewish living standards improved, often dramatically, despite persisting poverty. Nowhere were these trends and possibilities, he observed, more vital and welcoming than in the United States.

But these dramatic gains exacted a high price. "In fact," Baron wrote, "it was capitalism, operating from its inception in the direction of political emancipation and cultural assimilation, that began to threaten the very survival of the Jewish people even more menacingly than had the antagonism and large-scale exclusion of the previous feudal system." Capitalist individualism undermined Jewish communal life, thus raising the larger question of whether, and under which conditions, the broadly open features of capitalism, especially in liberal polities, would accommodate group particularity.[50] In countries, notably the United States, where church and state were distinct realms, communal disorganization threatened because Jews lost their status in public law, instead becoming a voluntary association. Jews as individuals, he summarized, "benefited by early and advanced capitalism" but "undoubtedly lost a great deal *qua* Jew, that is, as a member of his group and faith." Not surprisingly, Orthodox rabbis often sought to stem the tide of modern commercial society. But the end of capitalism, Baron ruefully mused, might even be worse.[51]

What is compelling about Baron's reflections is less his specific cost-benefit analysis than his willingness to make situations determinative of preferences, and preferences the shapers of situations. He also insisted that we should reckon with this dynamism within a framework that contains an explicit scheme of periodization—in this case, in an ironic borrowing from Sombart, "early," "advanced," and "late" capitalism. I have many reservations about this terminology, but it suggestively reminds us that the snapshot offered by *Fortune* in 1936, or for that matter any other quantitative or qualitative portrait of Jewish economic participation and roles, has meaning only within a given temporal framework. Usually, American Jewish history is compartmentalized by migration streams—the early Sephardic, the nineteenth-century German, and the late nineteenth- and early twentieth-century movement from the Pale of Settlement; indeed, I have done just that earlier in this essay. But this familiar division in time implies a much wider range of questions. How were the assets—religious, intellectual, economic, social, political, and educational—that each immigrant stream brought distinctive? How, and within which situations, had such resources been produced? In which ways did they combine to shape the economic propensities of newcomers? In what form and with what degree of change were they transmitted forward, or reshaped, in new individual and communal circumstances? What dynamics were internal to the experiences of each stream in America, and how did each relate to and affect the patterns of later groups? We should be prepared for answers that might surprise us.

Another essay by Baron, dating to 1938 and dealing with nineteenth-century transformations, exemplifies the kind of scholarship I hope will guide the revival of scholarship on Jews and American capitalism.[52] That article documents remarkable economic changes within European Jewry that opened up as a result of the Industrial Revolution, including their participation in new areas of economic distribution and production and their penetration into occupations that previously had been closed by various forms of social and legal discrimination. Baron emplaced these shifts inside demographic and spatial changes, including a doubling of the proportionate share of Jews in the population, their widened geographic area, their movement into parts of the West from which they had appeared only in a limited way in prior centuries, their accelerating urbanization, and the process of political emancipation that altered what once had been a closed Jewish corporate status. What is so striking about this text is less its details than its analytical sensibilities. For in advancing empirical information, probing Jewish propensities and situations, and asking causal questions about the effects of Jews on economic development and of economic development on the Jews, all with a keen sense of temporality, it presents us with a model for what we currently lack.

But there is yet another feature of Baron's writing that we might also bear in mind. Ever mindful that information can have a relationship to danger, he nonetheless never repressed or distorted knowledge in the name of Jewish security. For this and much more, he deserves the last word. Professor Baron closed his 1942 essay on "Capitalism and the Jewish Fate" by reflecting about choices and dilemmas under determinate historical conditions:

> The identification of modern capitalism with "the spirit of Judaism," false and profoundly misleading even in the heyday of early or advanced capitalism, has become a tragic irony during the recent critical decades. We should also constantly bear in mind that the great crisis of Jewish life did not begin

in 1933, and it will not automatically resolve itself by the defeat of Hitler, crucial as that will be for the immediate future of Jewry. Even if out of the ruins of contemporary Europe and Asia there emerges a new type of social democracy—in some respects adumbrated by the American New Deal and the social transformation of England, but in many other ways as yet wholly unpredictable—there will remain the insistent need of constant creative readjustment of the Jewish economic, social, and cultural structure.[53]

As we probe the story of Jews and capitalism, it is good to know that the house Salo Baron built not only stands but is being reinforced.

NOTES

1. Jerry Z. Muller, *Capitalism and the Jews* (Princeton, NJ: Princeton University Press, 2010), 1. Muller's work is a provocation directed at redressing this elision.

2. See the posthumous collection of essays by Arcadius Kahan in *Essays in Jewish Economic and Social History* (Chicago: University of Chicago Press, 1986); see also Simon Kuznets, "Economic Structure and Life of the Jews," in *The Jews, Their History, Culture and Religion*, ed. Louis Finkelstein (New York: Harper and Brothers, 1960), 2:1597–1566; and Simon Kuznets, *Economic Structure of U.S. Jewry: Recent Trends* (Jerusalem: Hebrew University Institute of Contemporary Jewry, 1972).

3. See David Berger, ed., *The Legacy of Jewish Immigration: 1881 and Its Impact* (New York: Columbia University Press, 1983); and Arthur A. Goren, *The Politics and Public Culture of American Jews* (Bloomington: Indiana University Press, 1999).

4. Muller, *Capitalism and the Jews*, 1.

5. A noteworthy recent effort dealing with these matters in the modern European experience is Gideon Reuveni and Sarah Wobick-Segev, eds., *The Economy in Jewish History: New Perspectives on the Interrelationship between Ethnicity and Economic Life* (New York: Berghahn Books, 2011).

6. Archibald MacLeish, "Jews in America," *Fortune* 13 (February 1936): 79.

7. These reflections draw on Muller's stimulating chapter, "The Jewish Response to Capitalism," in *Capitalism and the Jews*, 72–132.

8. Louis Bloch, "Occupations of Immigrants Before and After Coming to the United States," *Quarterly Publications of the American Statistical Association* 17, no. 134 (1921): 750–763; Simon Kuznets, "Immigration of Russian Jews to the United States: Background and Structure," *Perspectives in American History* 9 (1975): 35–124.

9. Underneath these deleterious trajectories lay a long-standing Christian suspicion of commerce, especially of interest-generating finance, the location historically associated with Jews and their exemption from bans on usury. Critiques of commerce, which accelerated in the nineteenth and early twentieth centuries with the dramatic conquest of older forms of economic life by capitalism, often made Jews their targets. Concurrently and ironically, attacks were also directed at Jews as leading forces in left-wing, anticapitalist movements. Jews thus were seen as guilty parties, identified with uprooting traditional life, capitalist insecurity, and radical opposition thought and movements. See Muller, "The Long Shadow of Usury," in *Capitalism and the Jews*, 15–71.

10. Muller, *Capitalism and the Jews*, 95.

11. Naomi W. Cohen, *Encounter with Emancipation: The German Jews in the United States, 1830–1914* (Philadelphia: Jewish Publication Society, 1984); Hasia R. Diner, *A Time for Gathering: The Second Migration, 1820–1880*, vol. 2 of *The Jewish People in America* (Baltimore: Johns Hopkins University Press, 1992).

12. Stanley Lieberson, A Piece of the Pie: Blacks and White Immigrants since 1880 (Berkeley: University of California Press, 1980). For class tensions and conflict, see Hadassa Kosak, *Cultures of Opposition: Jewish Immigrant Workers, New York City, 1881–1905* (Albany: SUNY Press, 2000). Lederhendler underscores key distinctions between "there" and "here." Russia and its Polish extensions, he shows, were marked by economic backwardness and underdevelopment, especially in areas to which Jews were confined. There, Jews were restricted to economic niches that lay outside an emergent class structure. Their economic standing was characterized by more than impoverishment. More important was "the lack of any real standing—that is, class—and thus virtual caste status." Russian Jewry thus composed "a population subject to economic and national policies . . . that resulted in a deficiency of stable class formation and class structure." A sharply different pattern prevailed in rapidly industrializing America, where "Jewish immigrant workers and small trades people lived mainly in the nation's largest industrial and commercial cities and worked in trades that were on the rise . . . at the heart of the economic and social system." This situation conferred valuable "integrative advantages." Eli Lederhendler, *Jewish Immigrants and American Capitalism, 1880–1920: From Caste to Class* (Cambridge: Cambridge University Press, 2009), xxii.

13. For a more extended version of the discussion in the following paragraphs, see Ira Katznelson, "Between Separation and Disappearance: Jews on the Margins of American Liberalism," in *Paths of Emancipation: Jews, States, and Capitalism,* ed. Pierre Birnbaum and Ira Katznelson (Princeton, NJ: Princeton University Press, 1995), esp. 171–204. This argument is consistent with the economic niche theory presented by Simon Kuznets in his classic article, "Life of the Jews."

14. See also Arcadius Kahan, "Jewish Life in the United States: Perspectives from Economics," in *Jewish Life in the United States: Perspectives from the Social Sciences,* ed. Joseph B. Gittler (New York: New York University Press, 1981), 237–269.

15. Katznelson, "Between Separation and Disappearance," 205.

16. After appearing in the February 1936 issue of *Fortune,* the essay "Jews in America" was published as *Editors of Fortune, Jews in America* (New York: Random House, 1936); for a discussion of this article and its composition, see Alan Brinkley, *The Publisher: Henry Luce and His American Century* (New York: Knopf, 2010), 162.

17. MacLeish, "Jews in America," 128, 130, 133.

18. William M. Kephart, "What Is the Position of Jewish Economy in the United States," *Social Forces* 28 (December 1949): 153–164.

19. Quoted in William M. Kephart, "The Sociology of a Minority: Group Economy," *Phylon,* 11, no. 1 (1950): 43. For a contemporaneous overview of barriers to full Jewish entry into American mainstream institutions, notably including economic ones, see Carey McWilliams, *A Mask For Privilege: Anti-Semitism in America* (New York: Little, Brown, 1948).

20. MacLeish, "Jews in America," 128.

21. Ibid.

22. Ibid., 85.

23. Ibid., 79.

24. Werner Sombart, *Die Juden und das Wirtshaftsleben* (Leipzig, Germany: Dunker and Humblot, 1911); Werner Sombart, *The Jews and Modern Capitalism,* trans. Mordechai Epstein (1913; repr., New Brunswick, NJ: Transaction, 1982).

25. MacLeish, "Jews in America," 130.

26. Elliot Ashkenazi, *The Business of Jews in Louisiana, 1840–1875* (Tuscaloosa: University of Alabama Press, 2003); Ewa Morawska, *For Bread with Butter: The Life-Worlds of East Central Europeans in Johnstown, Pennsylvania, 1890–1940* (Cambridge: Cambridge University Press, 1986).

27. Beth S. Wenger, *New York Jews and the Great Depression* (New Haven, CT: Yale University Press, 1996), ch. 1, pp. 10–32.

28. Jonathan I. Israel, *European Jewry in the Age of Mercantilism, 1550–1750* (Oxford: Oxford University Press, 1985); Jonathan I. Israel, *Diasporas within a Diaspora: Jews, Crypto-Jews, and the World of Maritime Empires* (Boston: Brill, 2002); Jonathan Karp, "Economic History and Jewish Modernity: Ideological versus Structural Change," *Simon Dubnow Institute Yearbook* 6 (2007): 249–268; Jonathan Karp, *The Politics of Jewish Commerce: Economic Ideology and Emancipation in Europe, 1638–1848* (Cambridge: Cambridge University Press, 2008).

29. Although there are no such treatments written in English, there is a Yiddish scholarly literature that does address some of these issues. Examples include Isaac Rivkind, *Yidishe gelṭ in lebensshṭeyger, ḳulṭur-geshikhṭe un folḳor: Leksikologishe shtudye* (New York: Ha-Aḳademyah ha-Ameriḳanit le-mada'e ha-Yahadut, 1959); and Herman Frank, "Di yiddishe treyd-yunion bevegung in amerike," *Yivo yorbukh fun amopteyl* 2 (1939): 104–107.

30. Barry R. Chiswick, "The Post-War Economy of American Jews," in *A New Jewry? America since the Second World War, 1948–1968*, ed. Peter Y. Medding, Studies in Contemporary Jewry 8 (1992); Calvin Goldscheider and Alan S. Zuckerman, *The Transformation of the Jews* (Chicago: University of Chicago Press, 1984); Marshall Sklare, ed., *The Jews: Social Patterns of an American Group* (Glencoe, IL: Free Press, 1958); see also Sklare, ed., *America's Jews* (New York: Random House, 1971). In contrast to these various silences, there is a robust literature on the places Jews have occupied in the stratification hierarchy. For examples, see these essays by Barry R. Chiswick: "The Occupational Attainment and Earnings of American Jewry, 1890 to 1990," *Contemporary Jewry* 20 (1999): 69–98; "The Skills and Economic Status of American Jewry," in *Terms of Survival: The Jewish World since 1945*, ed. Robert S. Wistrich (London: Routledge, 1995), 111–126; and "The Occupational Attainment of American Jewry, 1900–2000," *Contemporary Jewry* 27 (2007): 80–111.

31. Werner Sombart, *Der moderne Kapitalismus* (Leipzig, Germany: Dunker and Humblot, 1902).

32. Werner Sombart, *Warum gibt es in den Vereinigten Staaten keinen Sozialismus?* (Tubingen, Germany: Mohr, 1906).

33. Max Weber, *Die protestantische Ethik und der Geist des Kapitalismus* (1905; repr. Tubingen, Germany: Mohr, 1934). For a discussion of Sombart's complicated but largely sympathetic relationship to Nazism, see Friedrich Lenger, *Werner Sombart, 1863–1941: Eine Biographie* (Munich: Beck, 1994).

34. Sombart, *Jews*, ch. 10.

35. Ibid., 288; Max Weber, *The Protestant Ethic and Spirit of Capitalism* (New York: Scribner's Sons, 1958); Werner Sombart, *Deutscher Sozialismus* (Charlottenburg, Germany: Buchholz and Weisswange, 1934). Weber thought Sombart to be wrong. For a discussion of Weber on such racial explanations, see Harry Liebersohn, "Weber's Historical Concept of National Identity," in *Weber's "Protestant Ethic": Origins, Evidence, and Context*, ed. Hartmut Lehmann and Gunther Roth (Cambridge: Cambridge University Press, for the German Historical Center, 1993), 123–131. An important overview of the place of Jews in European scholarship about the development of capitalism is Derek Penslar, *Shylock's Children: Economics and Jewish Identity in Modern Europe* (Berkeley: University of California Press, 2001); for his discussion of Sombart, see 163–173. See also the treatment of Sombart in Jeffrey Herf, *Reactionary Modernism: Technology, Culture, and Politics in Weimar and the Third Reich* (Cambridge: Cambridge University Press, 1984), 130–151. Another useful discussion can be found in Mitchell B. Hart, "Jews, Race, and Capitalism in the German-Jewish Context," *Jewish History* 19 (2005): 49–63. Hart notes that critics from the Right, especially Catholic conservatives,

~~thought Sombart to be insufficiently critical of what they viewed as the degenerate role~~ of Jews in fostering modernity.

36. Natalie Zemon Davis, "Religion and Capitalism Once Again? Jewish Merchant Culture in the Seventeenth Century," *Representations* 59 (Summer 1997): 58.

37. George Mosse, *The Crisis of German Ideology: Intellectual Origins of the Third Reich, 1914–1933* (1964; repr. New York: Schocken Books, 1981), 141.

38. Werner Eugen Mosse, *Jews in the German Economy: The German-Jewish Economic Elite, 1820–1935* (Oxford: Oxford University Press, 1987).

39. Georg Simmel, "The Stranger," in *The Sociology of Georg Simmel*, ed. Kurt H. Wolff (Glencoe, IL: Free Press, 1950), 402–408. For an assessment of this theme in the American context, see Peter Temin, "An Elite Minority: Jews among the Richest 400 Americans," in *Human Capital and Institutions: A Long-Run View*, ed. David Eltis, Frank D. Lewis, and Kenneth L. Sokoloff (New York: Cambridge University Press, 2009), 248–264. Temin asks two questions: "First, are Jews among the very rich because they were discriminated against in other activities? Second, are Jews among the very rich because of some aspect of minority behavior? I suggest that the answer is no to the first question and yes to the second." His identification of the richest Jews is based on the annual publication since 1982 in *Fortune* of the most wealthy four hundred Americans in the United States.

40. Muller pursues these themes, showing how we should prefer the formulations in Georg Simmel's *Die Philosophie des Geldes* that consider Jews not as "central to the genesis of capitalism" but as "disproportionately successful at a phenomenon that is central to the modern world," a role Simmel broadly welcomed. *Capitalism and the Jews*, 53.

41. For discussions that situate human preferences in determinate contexts, see the introduction and essays in Ira Katznelson and Barry Weingast, eds., *Preferences and Situations: Points of Intersection between Historical and Rational Choice Institutionalism* (New York: Russell Sage Foundation, 2005).

42. See Paul R. Mendes-Flohr, "Werner Sombart's *The Jews and Modern Capitalism*: An Analysis of Its Ideological Premises," *Year Book of the Leo Baeck Institute* 21 (1976): 87–107.

43. Werner Mosse, "Judaism, Jews and Capitalism: Weber, Sombart and Beyond," *Leo Baeck Institute Yearbook* 24 (1979): 3–15.

44. Davis, "Religion and Capitalism."

45. See Viviana A. Rotman Zelizer, *The Social Meaning of Money* (Princeton, NJ: Princeton University Press, 1997).

46. Consider, as examples, literature both on ethnicity and American capitalism that would be informed by more focused attention on the Jewish experience: Richard Alba, *Ethnic Identity: The Transformation of White America* (New Haven: Yale University Press, 1990); Gary Gerstle, *Working Class Americanism* (New York: Cambridge University Press, 1989); Mary Waters, *Ethnic Options: Choosing Identities in America* (Berkeley: University of California Press, 1990); John Steele Gordon, *Empire of Wealth: The Epic History of American Economic Power* (New York: Harper and Row, 2005); and Alfred D. Chandler Jr., *The Visible Hand: The Managerial Revolution in American Business* (Cambridge, MA: Harvard University Press, 1993).

47. Alexander Gerschenkron, *Bread and Democracy in Germany* (Berkeley: University of California Press, 1943). For studies of the garment industry that underscore just such particularity, see Andrew Godley, *Jewish Immigrant Entrepreneurship in New York and London, 1880–1914* (New York: Palgrave Macmillan, 2001); and Nancy L. Green, *Ready-to-Wear and Ready-to-Work: A Century of Industry and Immigrants in Paris and New York* (Durham, NC: Duke University Press, 1997).

48. Davis, "Religion and Capitalism."

49. Salo W. Baron, "Modern Capitalism and Jewish Fate," *Menorah Journal* 30 (Summer 1942): 116–138.

50. For a discussion of the cultural costs of Jewish entry, see Ira Katznelson, "Broken Chains of Memory: Reflections on Negotiated Membership for Jews in the United States," in *Anxieties of Democracy: Tocquevillean Reflections in India and the United States*, ed. Partha Chatterjee and Ira Katznelson (New Delhi: Oxford University Press, 2012).

51. Baron, "Modern Capitalism," 126, 127.

52. Salo W. Baron, "The Jewish Question in the Nineteenth Century," *Journal of Modern History* 10 (March 1938): 51–65.

53. Baron, "Jewish Fate," 129.

PART II

Jewish Niches in the American Economy

CHAPTER 2

The Evolution of the Jewish Garment Industry, 1840–1940

Phyllis Dillon and Andrew Godley

The apparel industry in the United States has provided a home for Jewish businesspeople and workers for more than one hundred and fifty years. Indeed, one cannot fully understand this industry or its place in the U.S. economy over the course of the nineteenth and early twentieth centuries without addressing the central role played by Jews as American entrepreneurs and apparel capitalists.[1] German Jewish immigrants played a major role in the expansion and growth of the men's suit industry in the United States between 1840 and 1880. They moved into it in large numbers once it was already established as big business by non-Jewish clothiers and merchant tailors, who were the first to industrialize the clothing industry. But by 1870 the industry was primarily Jewish owned. The ethnic characteristic of the industry was transformed during the 1890s and 1900s, as a far greater share of the much larger east European Jewish immigrant population moved into the clothing industry.

The purpose of the chapter is therefore to provide an overview of the Jewish involvement in the U.S. clothing industry from the very earliest years, rather than, as the existing literature is guilty of, focusing on one particular period or group of Jewish immigrants. The explanatory framework is broadly economic, although the study is explicitly internationally comparative to provide a superior contextualization of Jewish immigrant entrepreneurial strategies. Our hope is that the chapter provides a clearer explanation for why the clothing industry provided such a significant occupational home for so many of the German and east European Jewish immigrants to the United States over such a long period. The persistent themes are that Jewish entrepreneurs were well

suited to enter the clothing industry on arrival and that domestic demand for
U.S. manufactured clothing was for most of the period expanding sufficiently
quickly as to allow for Jewish entrepreneurs and workers to accumulate capital and savings. But the industry itself changed dramatically over the period,
meaning that the ethnic entrepreneurial strategies had to adapt.

The First Period of Industrialized Clothing Production: 1820–1860

Pioneering non-Jewish manufacturers were the first clothing capitalists, and
they established the basic parameters of the business in the East Coast cities
of New York, Philadelphia, and Boston by the 1850s.[2] Increased urbanization
and industrialization in the antebellum period stimulated the manufacturing
of ready-made apparel. As the new country expanded geographically through
the western frontier and demographically through immigration, the garment
industry grew in response to the increased demand for men's business dress
for new managers and clerks. The black business suit became the mark of
American gentility and was adopted by all classes as standard business wear.
New York City's small, midsize, and large manufactories became the leading
producers of high-quality ready-mades between 1820 and 1860; moreover, New
York emerged as the main center for shipping clothing and other products to
the South and West, areas with little local manufacturing capacity of their own.
Half of the garments and ready-to-wear clothing produced in New York City
was shipped south.[3]

The first major transformation in the production of clothing in the United
States began in the 1820s, as Michael Zakim describes, when the industrialization of tailoring took place and the rise of clothiers was set in motion.[4] Initially, tailors in East Coast cities industrialized their production to make extra
ready-made clothes called "slops" for travelers, sailors, and new businessmen.
Tailors and enterprising clothiers increased production and moved into making better ready-mades in response to two factors. When the city population
soared, business grew and trade with the South and West created wholesaling
opportunities. Zakim describes how innovations in measuring and fitting
suits prepared the groundwork for the expansion of the business well before
the introduction of the sewing machine and mechanization. Many custom
tailors went into the ready-made business or worked for the large ready-made
firms. By the 1840s cheaper, well-made ready-made suits were beginning to be
accepted by all classes.

The leading clothing capitalists in the initial period of the 1840s and 1850s
were non-Jewish clothiers who sold ready-made suits, shirts, and furnishing
items retail and wholesale in large elegant emporiums.[5] One such gentile establishment, Lewis and Hanford, by 1849 had 72 working on their premises and

3,600 on the outside.[6] Cloth was cut by master tailor cutters in-house and distributed to females working at home. Profits were high because of the huge immigrant pool of seamstresses, who kept the labor costs low. The textile industry in the United States had matured sufficiently in this period to supply the growing suit industry. New York City was the style and trading center of the nation, headquarters for the booming New England textile industry, the dry goods suppliers, the importers of foreign textiles, and the clothing manufacturers.[7]

The clothing business by its very nature suffered from many cash-flow problems. Manufacturers had to buy fabric, pay tailors to cut it, and pay seamstresses before they sold the clothes. While local shoppers paid cash, country merchants made purchases on credit. The leading clothing manufacturers or clothiers described by Edwin T. Freedley, an 1856 commentator on U.S. manufacturing and the economy, solved their financing problem by receiving credit from the fabric intermediaries, who were jobbers or commission agents. The successful large clothiers pioneered liberal credit policies. Freedley also noted how merchant tailors first entered retailing of self-produced ready-made clothing. Soon a new niche opened up for "clothing jobber wholesalers," who got the fabric, cut it on their premises, and then subcontracted the garment assembly to tailors. At first, mill owners did not want to extend credit to clothing jobbers. They preferred dealing with just the commission dealers and dry goods houses. Commission dealers and wool importers did not want to extend credit to clothing jobber wholesalers either. They preferred selling retail or to dry goods stores and small stores in the South.[8]

However, according to nineteenth-century observers like Freedley and many contemporary scholars, the large clothiers succeeded because they could smooth their profits by selling fabric of different qualities both retail and wholesale as well as undercut tailors by manufacturing on a large scale.[9] They also were more apt to extend credit to country merchants than a small manufactory or a tailor. The successful large producers also offered an array of innovations. Some had set prices, others bargained, and most published advertisements in city directories. Clothiers also jumped into the manufacturing of boys' clothing very early. As children outgrew their garments, so the demand for replacement clothing created a market. (Girls' clothing was mostly home manufactured.) Older boys also needed suitable clothing for work.

The difficulties suffered by small producers and seamstresses in the New York apparel system have been described by historians Christine Stansell and Sean Wilentz in their work on the growth of the labor movement in nineteenth-century New York.[10] The system relied on outwork. Tailors often took contracting work from the bigger firms. The female seamstresses who worked for smaller producers often risked not getting paid. The small craft workshops could not compete with the large manufactories, who supplied an ever-expanding local population as well as large wholesale trade. New York

City, for example, grew from 166,000 in 1825 to 515,000 by 1850. Wilentz also reaffirms what Freedley observed, that the clothiers were revolutionaries at extending "credit" to country merchants.[11] The large emporiums therefore made their profits by having a rich combination of operations under one roof. They sold to locals ready-mades and fabric of different qualities and also made custom-made clothing. They also sold wholesale to country merchants and engaged in coastal trading.

The large clothiers were also innovators in bringing the sewing machine into their operations. The first ready-made suits were completely made by hand. The 1840s sewing machine sewed poorly, was too clumsy and costly. But a series of patented innovations in the 1850s led to the machine's rapid diffusion through the clothing industry.[12] The shirt manufacturing industry was the first to incorporate it. It greatly speeded up the volume produced and also allowed for a breakdown of the production processes.

By 1850 New York City served not only as the fashion capital of the nation but as the commercial and manufacturing capital, consisting mostly of small and midsize shops and manufactories.[13] Among the non-Anglo immigrants, the German and Irish arrivals were heavily concentrated in the building trades, apparel production, and shoe making. By 1855, as Robert Ernst notes, "some 20,000 foreign-born tailors, dressmakers, hatters, furriers and clothiers included nearly 13% of the immigrant working population of the city."[14] By the 1850s they evolved into small manufacturers also supplying the southern and western merchants. Output grew steadily through the 1850s and the "NYC Chamber of Commerce reported that NYC sold $40,000,000 of men's clothing wholesale in 1858." A small number of German Jewish firms can be found listed as clothiers as early as the 1830s in the city directories, but by the 1850s it is clear that Jewish workshops and factories produced a larger share of the ready-to-wear market.[15]

New York City remained the largest producer before the Civil War and later, but new satellite manufacturing centers appeared as German Jews migrated to new cities on the evolving frontier.[16] Cincinnati and Rochester, early examples of satellite cities, began manufacturing in the 1840s. Chicago followed in the 1870s.[17]

Cincinnati was the home to an early German Jewish manufacturing phenomenon. The city, called the Queen of the West, became a magnet for Jewish migration as it developed in the 1830s and 1840s. The earliest Jews there were English immigrants, but German Jews joined them as early as 1820, when there were about 10,000 inhabitants. The first Jewish migrants formed a congregation and built their first synagogue in 1829. Between 1840 and 1860 the Jewish population grew from 1,000 to approximately 10,000 out of a total of 161,000. By 1840 Cincinnati produced $1.2 million worth of clothing in eighty-six small shops of fewer than ten employees each. It was up to $1.9 million by 1850 and was the leading western center for manufacturing clothes. Women at home supplied the labor. Of seventy wholesale firms listed in the 1860 city directory, fully sixty-five were Jewish owned.[18]

The Civil War changed the clothing industry by demanding more professional and standardized modes of production and by presenting new challenges to many firms that were entwined with southern markets. First, new firms came together to get government contracts to supply the troops. Large orders helped firms to professionalize their operations.[19] In Cincinnati, where the Jewish clothing manufacturers had supplied the surrounding states of Kentucky and Indiana, they turned to making uniforms. The other important impact of the war was to hurt the business of many of the large northern clothing firms that were dependent on business with the South. Many of those firms left the industry.

German Jewish Antebellum Strategy: Step-by-Step Migration and Credit Networks

A recent study of the Dun and Bradstreet records for 471 Cincinnati German Jewish merchants describes an economic strategy to enter the American clothing sector before and just after the Civil War, based around "step-by-step migration" and internal community-based credit.[20] The competitive climate in Cincinnati required lots of experience and savvy. Most of the established merchants in Cincinnati did not migrate directly to Cincinnati from Germany. Instead, after coming through eastern port cities, they first peddled for a few years and then moved to owning small general stores to accumulate the capital and gain necessary experience and contacts to set up wholesale manufacturing.

Long-distance peddling was a clear entry strategy for German Jewish entrepreneurs to accumulate funds and know-how to start a business. They knew how to peddle from past experience in Germany. And there was considerable demand for peddling in the mid-nineteenth-century United States. Far-flung farmsteads and isolated village homemakers relied on visits by peddlers for housewares, sewing supplies, and fabrics. Jews could also easily maintain their dietary observances on the road. The shift to the western frontier saw the creation of a new type of relationship between peddlers, retailers, and wholesalers. In the East, peddlers could return to the eastern cities to get more supplies. Farther west on the frontier, peddlers had to get supplies from local retail merchants or country stores, who themselves were provisioned by the Jewish wholesalers in Cincinnati.

The tale of dry goods merchant Lewis Eichberg's history offers a fine example. Eichberg arrived in the 1840s. A few years later he was in Newcastle, Illinois, and by 1851 he was in Atlanta, Illinois. He had peddled and then bought out a small store and paid it off. His worth was two thousand dollars in 1854. His brother Samuel joined him that year. In 1858 the Dun and Bradstreet records noted that his dry goods firm was considered the best in Atlanta, Illinois. In that year Eichberg moved to Cincinnati, where his new firm, Eichberg and Friedman, supplied the branch store in Atlanta with goods. Friedman had been a merchant in Bloomington, Illinois, before he and Eichberg pooled their capital and moved to Cincinnati to begin manufacturing.[21] Jews also regularly relied on Jewish brethren for credit. That trend is described in the Dun and Bradstreet reports where the correspondents mention that a particular firm has good credit from brethren but was not trusted by non-Jewish acquaintances.

The history of many German Jewish clothing firms repeats this pattern of step-by-step migration and reliance on relatives and Jewish networking for credit. The famous Levi Strauss Company is another obvious example of German Jewish immigrants entering the business of men's wear. The older Strauss brothers, Jonas and Louis, came first to the United States and founded a wholesale dry goods business, J. Strauss & Company, in New York City. Born in 1829, Levi came in 1847 from Buttenheim, Bavaria, with his recently widowed mother and two sisters. His father had been a long-distance dry goods and notions peddler. He learned the business in New York City working for his brothers and then peddled. In 1853 he headed west to San Francisco, where he set up a business first in his own name but that also served as a West Coast branch of his brothers' firm. His brother-in-law David Stern had been the first family member to go to San Francisco in 1851. Strauss was an "importer and jobber" of dry goods, which he sold to country stores to supply the miners. He sold clothing, fabrics, underwear, umbrellas, handkerchiefs, imported Irish linens, Belgian lace, and Italian shawls, as well as items from his brothers' firm in New York City.

The first store called Levi Strauss was at 90 Sacramento Street close to the docks, where the dry goods auctions were held. David Stern joined the firm, and by 1863 the firm was called Levi Strauss & Company. The firm had five partners: Levi; his brothers, Jonas and Louis; and two brothers-in-law, William Sahleins and David Stern. He moved to his final headquarters in 1866 at 14–16 Battery Street when he had ten salesmen on the road with his samples.

Strauss did not invent blue jeans. Jacob Youphes, a Jewish tailor born in Riga, Lithuania, in 1831, invented the riveted jeans. Youphes came to New York City in 1853 and changed his name to Jacob Davis. He moved to San Francisco in 1856 and then went to western Canada for eight years, where he worked as a tailor. In 1867 he moved to Virginia City, Nevada, where he opened a cigar store. After that failed he resumed tailoring and then lost his money investing in a brewery. By 1869 he was a tailor again in Reno, Nevada, making tents and wagon covers with fabric that he purchased from Levi Strauss & Company. In 1870 a woman asked him to make a strong pair of pants. He made them out of fabric supplied by Strauss, a white cotton duck, made at the Amoskeag mill in New Hampshire. He had rivets that he used to attach straps to horse blankets and he decided to attach the rivets to strengthen the pockets. Within months he had many orders for the pants, and he was beginning to be imitated. He then wrote to Levi Strauss for help in applying for the patent and offered him a partnership. Strauss agreed and asked Davis to come to San Francisco to oversee the production. The patent was approved in 1873. Initially the pants were made by women working at home, but the Levi Strauss firm eventually built a factory, which Davis supervised. Around 1907 Davis sold his interest in the patent to Levi Strauss.[22]

While Eichberg and Strauss were German Jewish pioneers in men's wear, after the Civil War the numbers of German Jewish businesses in the sector grew and the industry overall began to concentrate in New York City. By 1873 Hammerslough Brothers were at 50 White Street in Manhattan as wholesale clothiers, after a journey from Baltimore to Springfield, Illinois. Julius Hammerslough, born in Hanover, Lower Saxony, came to the United States in 1846, at the age of fourteen. By 1850 he joined his brothers in Baltimore as a dry goods clerk. In 1856 he went to Springfield, Illinois, to run a clothing business with two of his brothers. He left the business in Springfield to go to New York City in 1865 to form what became a substantial business there. From his days in Springfield he retained the friendship of Abraham Lincoln his entire life and frequently called at the White House. He became the first president of the New York Clothiers Association in 1874. Hammerslough Brothers went on to become one of the most reputable clothing firms in the country.[23]

Hammerslough Brothers is also noted for its training of Julius Rosenwald, the future president of Sears and Roebuck. Julius Hammerslough's sister Augusta married Samuel Rosenwald from Westphalia, who came to the United States in 1854 and ended up in Talladega, Alabama. He married Augusta in 1857 in Baltimore. Samuel Rosenwald bought Julius Hammerslough's business in Springfield, Illinois, and sent his son Julius (born in Springfield in 1862) to New York City to learn the clothing business from his Hammerslough uncles in 1876 when he was fourteen years old. Soon after 1885 Julius Rosenwald started his own suit-manufacturing business in Chicago with two brothers and a cousin and supplied suits to Sears and Roebuck. After the panic of 1893, Roebuck left Sears, and Richard Sears invited Rosenwald's brother-in-law, Aaron Nusbaum, to buy half the business. Nusbaum asked Rosenwald for financial help, and in 1895 they bought half the company for seventy-five thousand dollars. As vice president of Sears, Rosenwald expanded the offerings and grew the company to sales of $50 million in 1907. Rosenwald became president in 1908.[24]

After New York City, Chicago developed into the second largest men's garment center after the completion of the transcontinental railroad in 1879. The earliest Jews in Chicago were small retail merchants who sold ready-made clothing made in New York City. The history of Hart, Schaffner & Marx is a good example. Harry Hart, born in Eppelsheim, Germany, in 1850, came with his parents in 1858 to Chicago, Hart and his brother Max opened their own retail store in 1872 with $2,700 saved from working for other retailers. In 1875 they opened a second store and began manufacturing suits in Chicago to supply their own stores. With two brothers-in-law, Abt and Marx, they formed a company in 1879. Abt dropped out but a cousin, Joseph Schaffner, from a retail store in Ohio, joined them in 1887. Against advice, Schaffner used $5,000 to launch a national advertising campaign in 1897, which became the industry standard.[25]

The number of examples could easily be multiplied. But some overall explanation of why so many German Jews moved into the American men's wear business in the years surrounding the Civil War needs to be offered. Robert Liberles and Steven M. Lowenstein suggest that occupational affinity for the dry goods and clothing business is a factor in this Jewish propensity.[26] In Germany the Jews since the late eighteenth century had lived by petty trade and commerce. Because of restrictive legislation and control by the government and guilds, they primarily dealt in textiles, clothing, and agricultural products such as cattle, hides, and raw wool. They often peddled old clothes, fabrics, and trimming supplies and when possible moved into shopkeeping of those same items. They therefore had expertise about textiles, which are the raw materials of the clothing business. Dry goods firms provided places to learn business by keeping accounts and dealing with customers. They sold on credit and took interest on unpaid balances. They also were nimble. They moved from business to business, when profits dwindled and from sector to sector in the dry goods business. After 1800 and the beginning of emancipation in Germany, formal business apprenticeships in the stores were more common, as well as craft apprenticeships.[27] They lived in villages and towns of fewer than ten thousand inhabitants. But they had a level of sophistication from livelihoods spent in commerce. The textile business and retail dry goods trade meant that they also dealt in imports and knew about sophisticated luxury goods such as trimmings and ribbons as well as fabrics. Their personal experience included dealing with non-Jews, and many lived in proximity to non-Jews. They also often had non-Jews as business partners.

Jews often emigrated in family groups of brothers and sisters. This was more prevalent among Jewish immigrants from Germany than non-Jewish German immigrants. They then planned their expansion into shopkeeping with their brothers in mind.[28] This pattern of initial entry into peddling and then incremental diversification into clothes dealing and then retailing is also seen among the German Jews emigrating to the United Kingdom in the first half of the nineteenth century, where Alsatian Jewish immigrants transformed clothes retailing.[29] Emigrants often came along with friends from the same village or followed fellow neighbors. They always could go to a synagogue for help and advice. The first organizations founded by German Jewish settlers were their own synagogues and religious day schools. The American Jewish newspapers

Figure 2.1. Advertisement for Hart, Schaffner & Marx sack suits in *Munsey's Magazine*, circa 1900. The advertisement notes that "dressy men" will appreciate the style, durability, and low cost of these suits. A large strike by the firm's clothing workers was settled in 1911 with recognition of the Amalgamated Clothing Worker's Union. The agreement became a model for other industries. The firm is still in business as Hartmarx. Courtesy of Phyllis Dillon. Author's collection.

served as a form of national mass media, because they had reports on the different Jewish settlements. Jews were also active in the Masonic movement, so lodges of businessmen were formed quickly for mutual aid and networking. In New York City the King Solomon Lodge 279 was founded in 1852 by Jews from Bavaria who were primarily merchants.[30] Cincinnati founded the second group of B'nai B'rith in 1849 after it was founded in New York City in 1843.[31]

Their Western European occupational background, assimilation of modern cultural values, and ease of acquiring commercially relevant information and credit after arrival through communal networks enabled German Jews to move into apparel easily and quickly. The industry rapidly developed many trade organizations and trade publications for rapid communication. Local organizations of clothiers were founded in the 1880s in every city of manufacturing, and the first national organization, the National Clothiers Association, was founded in 1884. The *Clothiers and Haberdashers Weekly*, published in New York City, carried news about business efforts to solve problems and also reported on bankruptcies nationwide. Clothiers also created city-wide associations to discuss government trade policy and help in their relations with mill owners.

In this period the leading tailors at the ready-made firms also professionalized their expertise and went from being called "foreman cutters" to "designers" who managed production. They learned to make patterns graded for many sizes for wholesale production. They formed their own professional associations and founded publications such as the *American Tailor* and the *American Tailor and Cutter*, published by the John J. Mitchell Company. In 1884 the leading American ready-made tailor, Daniel Edward Ryan, the son of an English immigrant tailor, arranged for an exhibition of American-made ready-made suits to be displayed in London to an audience of English tailors and tailoring societies, which was said to have created serious respect for American ready-mades.[32] By 1889 there were 4,867 firms in the United States making men's clothing for a value of $251,020,000, a fivefold increase from the 1840s, and the German Jewish immigrant entrepreneurs had acquired a central role in the emergence and maturing of the U.S. men's wear industry by the 1880s.[33]

FASHION AND STYLE IN WOMEN'S WEAR AND MEN'S WEAR

While the men's wear business was stimulated by population expansion and industrialization, the women's wear business first grew in relation to the fashion imperative posed by European imports. Ambitious dry goods dealers of women's fabrics began manufacturing copies and adaptations of Parisian mantles, while also selling the imported models in the 1850s. These dealers, such as George Brodie and Molyneux Bell, were also innovators in using sewing machines to increase production.[34] These dry goods dealers also specialized in the latest French fabrics and European trimmings. American women as a matter of course esteemed imported fabrics and trimmings in the nineteenth century, because Paris had worldwide fashion cachet. The French introduced the notions of new styles for a "season" and the "colors" of the season as well as engraved fashion plates as early as the seventeenth century. The idea that styles change rapidly and that consumers have to be kept informed were intrinsic to the traditions of artisan dressmaking and logically became part of the ready-made industry as it developed. Paris fashion would remain the fashion ideal and source of inspiration for the women's industry to a greater and lesser degree until the last quarter of the twentieth century.[35]

Men's clothing was far less seasonal. It was influenced mostly by traditions of hand tailoring and style from London and by the innovations popularized by Beau Brummel. Therefore, English hand tailoring was the initial inspiration for American tailors and ready-made manufacturers. "Good taste" incorporated esteem for the most beautifully made and designed English prototypes tempered by practical considerations of functionality and cost for appropriately styled American versions. Along with style, fit was a significant part of the essence of good quality. Ready-made manufacturers had to compete with custom merchant tailors to achieve the best fit that they could, but men's designs were less likely to succumb to a diminishing of popularity from fashion. Thus, demand for individual items of men's clothing tended to be far less volatile than for women's items. Conversely, frequent changes in fashion meant that women's wear was a much easier sector for an immigrant entrepreneur to enter.

Frequent trips and contact with Europe ensured the ability of American manufacturers of ladies' fashions to move quickly with the latest styles. In the nineteenth century fashion trends were communicated through trade publications within the artisan community, but fashion ideas for the general public were covered routinely in newspapers and ladies magazines. *Harper's Weekly* had articles about the ready-wear industry, columns about the latest in New York fashion, and coverage of Paris fashion with small amounts of fashion advertising on its back pages. By the 1880s illustrated mail order catalogues with drawings brought instant fashion trends to an ever-wider audience throughout the United States. Ready-made offerings for women in mail order catalogs and department stores consisted of mantles or cloaks, a small selection of suits, children's cloaks, millinery, underwear or chemises, night dresses, corset covers, and corsets. But only a small amount of ready-made suits were offered and sold compared to the pages of ladies' costumes that could be ordered by supplying extensive measurements.

An 1881 Lord and Taylor catalog sums up the fundamental problem for entrepreneurs wanting to increase their sales of women's ready-mades. It demonstrates why the ready-made industry for women could grow only once female clothes became simpler. Lord and Taylor offered ten styles of ready-made suits ranging in cost from fourteen to forty-five dollars, which were described prefaced by the following important paragraph.

> The following are kept in stock in diminishing quantities as the season advances. The bust measure and skirt length only are guaranteed, the other measures are in proportion; if other measures are necessary to insure a fit, the garment will need to be made to order.[36]

Women's ready-mades were, in other words, sized proportionately only from one measurement, the bust measurement. They were different from "made to measure," where the customer supplied extensive measurements in addition to the bust, including waist, hip, neck circumference, length from neck to waist in front, inside sleeve length, neck to waist in back, bottom of waist band in front to shoe, side length from waist and back length. Given the variability in the shape of the female body, and the relative complexity of women's fashion and its need for a close fit, the potential market for ready-mades was restricted at the time. "Custom-made" clothes by a dressmaker or tailor, with individual fitting, continued to be preferred by most American women. But where styling demands were different, American women were evidently happy to buy ready-made goods.

Hoopskirts became a necessary fashion undergarment during the 1860s. Cage crinolines or hoopskirts to hold up the fashionable large skirts popularized by Empress Eugenie of France were mass-produced. The cage crinoline made with circles of light steel suspended by cloth tapes was invented in France and quickly replaced heavy cloth crinolines. Jewish immigrants moved quickly into this business in New York City after it was established to make hoopskirts for the huge western and southern trade.[37]

German Jewish entrepreneurs combined dry goods sales and importing with cloak and suit manufacturing. By 1880 a firm such as Blumenthal Brothers & Company at 452 Broadway called itself "Importers and Manufacturers of Ladies Cloaks and Mantles." They sold a number of styles to retail cloak departments. "Sherman, Samuels and Company at 132 Bowery, four doors from Grand St.," advertised "Clothing, cloaks and Dry goods, on credit without security." They sold ladies' jackets from $2.20 up, ladies' plain and combination suits $6.50 up, stylish capes $4.00 up, as well as dry goods, silks, satins, plushes, and velvets.[38]

In *Wilson's Business City Directory* of 1879–1880 there are eighty-three cloak and suit manufacturers. About half have obviously Jewish names such as Freitag and Vogel, at 196 Church Street; Goldman Brothers at 25 Greene; Jonasson, Meyer & Company at 356 Broadway; Oppenheim Brothers at 2 White; Oppenheimer & Company at 154 Church; S. Rothschild & Brother at 54 Walker; Seligman & Company at 191 Church; Simonson & Weiss, at 10 White; and Wechsler, Abraham & Collins at 45 Worth.[39] Some of them stayed in business through the 1890s and become the premier suppliers of cloaks and suits to the department stores. Wechsler, Abraham & Collins evolved into the Abraham & Straus department store in downtown Brooklyn. Jordan Marsh, a Boston department store in 1891, featured advertisements of twenty-four wholesale suppliers they used in their mail order catalog.[40]

THE GREAT TRANSITION: FROM MEN'S TO WOMEN'S WEAR AND FROM GERMAN JEWISH TO EAST EUROPEAN JEWISH

After 1900 simpler women's clothing in the form of shirtwaist blouses and skirts, which could be manufactured easily and cheaply, became popular. Washable wrappers, tub dresses, and other garments quickly followed. The emergence of this simpler styling enabled a revolution in the American apparel sector to take place, which also coincided with a transition in the ethnic composition of the workforce from German Jewish to east European Jewish from around 1900 to the 1930s.[41] While apparel was an important economic niche for German Jewish immigrants seeking economic advancement, for the east European Jews it was essentially their only route into the American mainstream. This distinction can be reflected in the degree of specialization that took place in the first decades of the twentieth century. By the mid-1930s the Jewish population represented 27 percent of the New York City workforce overall, yet as many as three-quarters in clothes manufacturing and 80 percent of all the workers in clothes stores.[42] A 1936 survey by *Fortune* magazine found that Jews owned 95 percent of all women's wear firms and 85 percent of all men's wear businesses in the United States.[43] But the true difference was even more profound, with German Jews concentrating in men's wear, and east European Jews in women's wear. Accounting for this difference is less straightforward than might at first appear, especially the reasons why east European immigrants continued to cluster in women's wear manufacturing several years and even decades after their arrival.

As already noted, German Jews arrived with appropriate past experience and skills to move into the rapidly growing clothing sector of the middle decades of the nineteenth century, which was dominated by the production of men's wear. But east European Jewish immigrants in the 1890s and 1900s had no prior experience in manufacturing women's wear, for there was no production of ready-made women's wear in Russia and Poland then. The patterns for the Jewish immigrant economies in Britain and Canada displayed similar levels of occupational specialization in the early decades of the twentieth century among east European Jewish immigrants.[44]

The Jewish economies of the United States, Britain, and Canada were essentially variants of a one-sector, export-led economy, producing and distributing vast quantities of clothing to export to the non-Jewish populations of those countries.[45] If those providing communal services are deducted from the employment totals, then the broad clothing group provided employment for more than three-quarters of all Jewish immigrants in New York City and London as they arrived and settled in increasing numbers during the 1880s, 1890s, and 1900s. But women's wear began to dominate.[46]

To some extent this specialization was the straightforward result of the sheer unattractiveness of the clothing industry. As survey after survey revealed, the clothing industries in these countries suffered from appalling conditions, with very poor wages, unsanitary conditions, and very long hours. The east European Jewish immigrants flooded into the clothing industry because no one else would; conditions were too poor. In other sectors in these urban economies, from construction to transport, heavy industry to services, wages and conditions were better, and so east European Jews were confronted with strong competition from other more advantaged immigrants and natives. Whether through discrimination or not, the Jews typically lost out.

But it was not simply that the clothing industry was a refuge from competitive labor markets for the east European Jews. As Roger Waldinger and Michael Lichter have recently emphasized, when unskilled or low-skilled immigrants enter a labor market, they typically follow ethnic chains of recruitment.[47] Where a surplus of ethnic labor exists, immigrant preference for working within an "ethnic" environment can have the effect of allowing employers to further reduce wages and conditions, even if the labor market overall may be tight.

As the numbers of entrants increased, so the innovative master tailors reorganized the flow of work. They specialized tasks, deskilled, speeded throughput, and, effectively, cut wages. As the supply of laborers increased with Jewish immigration from 1883 to the early 1890s, so wages and conditions were bid down. In London the retail price of men's coats and suits fell from around six to seven pounds in the 1870s to forty-five shillings by the early 1890s, as Jewish workshops increased their market share through undercutting competitors. In human terms it was not a pretty sight.[48]

So poor did conditions become in the clothing industry that east European Jewish immigrants typically left the industry to move into other sectors as soon as they could. In the United States, economist Joel Perlmann has shown that the longer a Jewish immigrant stayed in the country, the less likely he was to remain in clothing manufacturing.[49] Studies of Jews in Ireland confirm from 1911 Irish census data that Jews aged forty and older were much more likely to have moved out of clothing manufacturing and into its distribution and retailing.[50] Similar evidence comes from the occupations of Jewish bridegrooms in London, with 71 percent of immigrant grooms up to twenty-five years old in the clothing industry, compared with only 56 percent twenty-five years and older. Older Jewish immigrants in London, like elsewhere, were much more likely to move into a host of ancillary trades, especially distribution.[51] East European Jews may have been forced everywhere to take jobs in the clothing industry, but wherever they were they quickly aspired to leave. London and Ireland were far from exceptional, as Arthur Goren points out: the clothing industry was "the backbone of the Jewish neighbourhood economy in New York, Boston, Philadelphia, Baltimore and Chicago."[52] But it was the emergence of women's wear in New York City that had truly enormous ramifications for the entire Jewish community and this, rather than clothing overall, needs to be properly outlined.

While the clothing industries in Anglophone countries grew in the second half of the nineteenth century, the presence of the Jews within them was overall modest. Jews probably have accounted for 15 percent at most of clothing industry employees in the United States, far less elsewhere by the 1880s. Yet despite their small numbers, Jewish entrepreneurs and workers were employed in almost all sectors of the trade, in men's, women's, and children's garments, from the heavier stitching in coats and jackets to the lighter work in shirts. The only areas where Jews were typically absent were in those sectors that had been able to organize into larger factories (like rubber overcoats or footwear) or were dependent on social connections with the elite, like the bespoke trade.[53] Nevertheless, as immigration increased during the final years of the nineteenth century, the impact was seen in the disproportionate growth of Jews in the clothing industry. But within a few short years, however, the Jewish clothing industry itself had decisively shifted in most immigrant centers to focus on women's wear.

This was not the case everywhere. In Montreal, Canada, most Jewish tailors remained in men's wear even by 1920. In Leeds, England, the men's wear industry remained utterly dominant.[54] But in the other principal areas of settlement, in New York, London, and Toronto, the move into women's wear was dramatic. It was not that Jewish entrepreneurs left men's wear, but rather that the less frequent changes in styling from the less seasonal men's wear enabled these manufacturers to scale up production, invest in mechanization, and relocate out of the urban center and away from the Jewish immigrant populations. The clothing manufacturing that was left behind in the urban heartlands of Manhattan, Toronto, or London's East End was increasingly women's wear.

In New York, for example, the Jewish immigrants dominated the clothing industry, with three-quarters of all workers in 1897.[55] By 1913 almost all the factories and workshops were owned by Russian Jews, and three-quarters of the workforce remained Jewish.[56] But during this period of growing Jewish influence in the New York industry, the growth sector was women's wear. From a very small base in 1880 the ready-made production of women's garments accelerated rapidly. Between 1899 and 1909 the output of ready-made women's wear in the United States increased by 159 percent, the number of workers by 111 percent, and the number of establishments by 86 percent.[57] New York had come to dominate the entire American women's wear industry by the 1920s.[58]

The specialization in the Jewish clothing sector was also very marked in London. Unfortunately British census data are less detailed than the American. What is clear from the censuses is that very significant regional specialization occurred in the United Kingdom clothing industry from 1851 to 1935, a slower and more drawn-out version of what was happening contemporaneously in the United States. London's East End and Leeds emerged as the dominant regional centers; by 1935 the two centers accounted for almost half of the industry's total output in the United Kingdom, compared with only one sixth in 1911.[59] Underlying this regional concentration was a specialization between the two centers, as Leeds-based firms grew to dominate men's wear, and firms in London's East End focused on women's wear.[60] It was this regional concentration of the women's wear in London's East End that gave the sector its very specific ethnic association in Britain as well as in the United States. As early as 1909 it was alleged in London that "most of the ladies' tailors are foreigners" (meaning east European Jewish immigrants), a trend that merely accelerated over the coming years.[61]

Peter Hall's series of maps published in 1962 displays how the women's wear industry increased rapidly in London's East End from 1901 to 1951. A local government survey of the East End economy shows how there were nearly twice as many women's wear as men's wear firms there by 1939. Moreover, the women's wear firms were more recent entrants. More than one in five men's wear firms surveyed had started before 1900, compared with only 1 percent of women's wear firms, indicating the different periods when each sector was expanding.[62] An official British government survey in 1950 discovered that half of the UK women's wear industry was then based in London. The sector was overwhelmingly Jewish-owned and had by then begun to migrate across London, leaving the East End and moving closer to the headquarters of the big retail chains and department stores in the West End.[63] In London, like in New York, the Jewish immigrant economy became ever more focused on women's wear.

Elsewhere this specialization was less acute. Jewish clothing entrepreneurs in Chicago, Boston, Philadelphia, and Baltimore in the United States were less dominated by women's wear. Indeed, in Montreal and Leeds, men's wear continued its dominance through to the 1920s and beyond. In these secondary population centers, Jews either remained in men's wear or began to leave the clothing industry and enter new, nonclothing sectors.

Even though concentrated in just three cities, with New York City, London, and Toronto the largest Jewish population centers in their respective countries, the overall degree of specialization in women's wear was nevertheless forceful. By 1920 the most likely occupation of an east European Jewish immigrant anywhere in the Anglophone Diaspora was no longer a peddler, nor even a tailor, but rather a tailor in the women's wear sector.

This conclusion is of great importance. First, it is clear that there cannot have been any American-specific determinant of such occupational specialization when similar patterns can be seen elsewhere. This suggests that the explanation for east European Jewish concentration in women's wear was more a result of near-simultaneous secular changes in the demand for women's clothing in all these countries. Thus, the underlying economics of the women's wear industry are different from the other branches of the clothing industry.

The best way of explaining the novel economics of the emerging women's wear sector is first to turn to census statistics to describe its pattern of growth. Once again the best census data come from the United States census of manufacturers. Table 2.1 compares the development of the U.S. clothing industry from 1914 to 1935. The table indicates that women's wear had become a bigger industry than men's wear immediately after World War I, reflected in a larger aggregate value added from 1923 onward, and a larger workforce from 1927 onward. This reflects the relative position in other countries too at this time. In the United Kingdom the retail value of women's wear was roughly twice that of men's wear, for instance.[64]

While employment levels were, broadly speaking, declining overall in both sectors from World War I onward, this was mostly because of the exiting of

TABLE 2.1

THE UNITED STATES CLOTHING INDUSTRY, 1914–1935,
EMPLOYMENT AND VALUE ADDED

Year	Women's wear wage earners	Women's wear value added	Men's wear wage earners	Men's wear value added
1914	168,907	221543	173,747	228179
1919	165,649	528136	175,270	557234
1921	144,865	454933	165,206	487231
1923	133,195	597123	158,173	532795
1925	126,466	569406	141,511	474773
1927	154,459	684881	146,099	484937
1929	187,500	775167	149,868	460599
1931	173,890	587994	121,964	287741
1933	196,423	371797	120,175	185395
1935	259,042	522939	154,583	257746

Source: United States, Census of Manufactures (Washington, DC: Bureau of the Census, 1899–1935).

smaller regional firms from the market. As we have seen, employment in New York and among the Jewish immigrants was growing.

The table also indicates why women's wear was outstripping men's wear. From World War I onward the women's wear industry enjoyed a higher productivity, or value added per wage earner, than men's wear, and this arose from a change in the characteristics of demand rather than any change in production methods, namely the emergence of a demand for fashionable clothing among the broad mass of women in these nations in the years around 1900. New publications, such as the *Ladies' Home Journal* in North America, circulated patterns emphasizing a relative simplicity of design and construction.[65] This spilled over into demand for ready-mades, where the cheapness of the new style clothing and the increasing purchasing power of young women led to rapidly growing sales.[66] Shirtwaist workers, for instance, young girls of fifteen and up either working as trimmers or finishers, earned anywhere from five to twelve dollars a week. After paying room and board, sending money home to relatives in Europe, club dues, and an occasional night at the theater, they increasingly spent the rest of their income on new shoes at two dollars a pair and a ready-made skirt for five dollars.[67]

The merchandising of these new fashionable garments was also transformed as the retail landscape in the United States saw new women's specialty shops such as Filene's, as well as low-cost chains like Sears and Roebuck that established retail stores in the 1920s. Department stores in the 1920s responded to new competition from lower-priced chains by developing new strategies like buying offices, building fancy additions, and attempting mergers. The Retail Research Association, founded in 1918 by a group of department stores to study how to improve merchandising, led to the formation of the Associated Merchandizing Corporation, or AMC, for mass buying of goods. Buyers in the department stores soon became the arbiters of style and they had power over the garment manufacturers.[68]

In the same period after World War I, advertising became more sophisticated as fashion became more important for sales. The stores became taste-makers. Cheapness was increasingly less important than style. Condé Nast, the editor who bought *Vogue* in 1909, changed it from a social gossip sheet to a magazine reporting on fashion for both New Yorkers and women across the nation, whom he believed had the right to inside fashion advice. He professionalized the magazine and revolutionized its advertising. The apparel industry became crucial to his advertising success and financing. Local newspapers also benefited from department store advertising, which became a crucial source of their income. Fashion journalists in newspapers and magazines developed as crucial insiders along with manufacturers, buyers, and department stores to make up the world of the American fashion industry. *Women's Wear Daily*, founded in 1910, became the daily pulse of the apparel industry, with news about style and business and extensive coverage of the textile industry, manufacturers, and department stores as well as style changes. Nearly everyone subscribed and even had it delivered to their hotels while on vacation in Miami.[69]

The immediate pre- and postwar years saw new fashion designs appealing to women in ordinary households, as opposed to those in the elite sectors, the focus of the nineteenth-century fashion industry. In consequence, women's wear firms began to compete less and less on price, and more and more on design. Compared with men's wear output, which was less constrained by fashion, women's wear prices increased.[70]

Chart 2.1 compares the value added per worker in the two sectors in the period of women's wear expansion and shows that the total income received per wage earner began to outstrip men's wear from 1919 onward. This was not because of any novel feature of production that enabled women's wear workers to be more efficient than those in men's wear. There were no significant technological changes that enabled output per worker to be so increased in either branch of clothing production. The sewing machine, the most significant innovation, had entirely diffused through the clothing industries well before the east European Jewish immigrants began to take these sectors over. Other innovations, such as pressing machines, automated cutting machines, and electric lighting, were introduced somewhat later (the Hoffman Press diffused with any significance only in the 1930s) but had in any case a far less significant impact on productivity.[71] In fact, the divergence in the value added per worker in the two sectors reflects a difference in pricing behavior. Women's wear prices rose by much more than in men's wear.

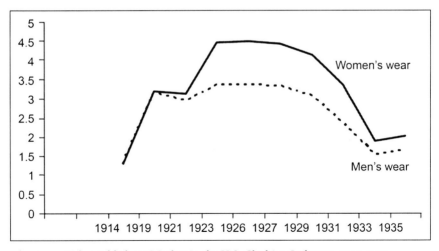

Chart 2.1. Value Added per Worker in the U.S. Clothing Industry, 1899–1935.
Source: Calculated from table 2.1.

This increase in prices is surprising because it followed a period of price falls in the clothing industry, falls resulting from an oversupply of labor bidding down the cost of production. While men's wear continued to experience only a very slight increase in real prices after 1900, the real gains in women's wear prices approached 50 percent. The easiest way to understand the divergence in pricing behavior in what were essentially two very similar branches of one industry is to concentrate first on why price rises were so much more muted in men's wear.

Men's wear benefited from growing ability of producers to exploit very substantial economies of scale in production. The key to efficiency gains was less in technology and more in organization. A detailed survey of production methods in the Anglo-American Productivity Council's Report of 1950 highlights the significance of large batch sizes and predictability in production runs in the American men's wear industry, emphasizing that the source of higher productivity was more in economies of throughput gained by task specialization and minimizing employee downtime. These organizational gains were common throughout men's wear and so plant size had increased, these economies of scale had diffused, and all firms produced and sold at similar prices. It had become a textbook industry.

While the technology used by the typical firm was little different to that in men's wear, women's wear firms were instead characterized by less specialization, minimal planning, great uncertainty in production runs, low batch sizes, and high levels of downtime. Women's wear firms inevitably enjoyed less productive efficiency than their equivalents in men's wear. But nevertheless they enjoyed a higher value added per worker because they were able to sell their output at significantly higher prices.

From the textbook perspective, this divergence in pricing behavior was rather surprising. Ordinarily the more efficient firms succeed over the less. But it was women's wear firms that were generating higher profitability. This was purely a consequence of different characteristics of demand between women's wear and men's wear sectors. As described earlier, demand for women's wear became increasingly dominated by fashion during the early twentieth century, and this had several important implications for the Jewish clothing industries. First, the price consumers were willing to pay for a fashion product was relatively high because it carried more utility than a nonfashion equivalent product, the value of display.

But while prices earned by women's wear firms were relatively high compared with men's wear firms, the corollary was that they were unable to predict which particular model of a fashion garment would sell for high prices in any particular season. With retailers' end-of-season sales clearing stocks of unsold garments at below-cost prices, producers had no incentive to second-guess the consumer and stockpile particular models in expectation of their success. The potential gain at being better able to plan workflow was more than outweighed by the risk of not being able to sell stock. Rather, producers had to wait until retailers restocked with successful designs. With such high risks associated with any kind of investment in capacity, firms remained small, poorly equipped, labor intensive, and highly seasonal. Most Jewish women's wear firms were simple contracting workshops, with no brand designs and producing nothing for stock. Instead, they worked together with several other companies in a network of producers able to meet demand for whichever products were successful and being restocked within a short period of time.

The net result was an industry where firm organization was often inefficient from a technical perspective. Firms were small, labor-intensive, and clustered close together to respond quickly to subcontracted orders from other small producers unable to meet retailers' and wholesalers' demands. They were chronically insecure, unable by definition to predict the future and plan work, and dependent on others for additional orders. Perhaps it was precisely this nature of the women's wear sector that led to the widespread sense of insecurity among Jewish immigrants. As Thomas Kessner observes about the New York Jewish community, "despite their obvious economic achievements, they felt the least secure of the immigrant groups."[72] For so many small contractors, the key to their survival was continuing close contact with the principal buyers in the main wholesalers and retail chains, and so to benefit from the early signals of which designs were successful in any given season and to be able to gain orders for restocking. It was not especially pretty, but it was profitable, especially in contrast to the 1880s and 1890s.[73]

The east European Jewish immigrants in New York and London were therefore experiencing some very considerable good fortune. The Jewish immigrants had crowded into tailoring in the 1880s, 1890s, and 1900s, principally because it was the least attractive sector available to entrants and the Jews were the least advantaged entrants. Jewish immigrants at the bottom of the labor market queue were therefore concentrating in something of a refuge from an otherwise hostile labor market. But from the 1900s onward the characteristics of demand began to change, with women in Britain and the United States becoming increasingly willing to spend more money on clothing with a higher fashion content.

The Jewish immigrants in the clothing industry centers were faced with a choice. Either they responded to the competitive forces in men's wear for increasing the scale of production, reducing labor costs, and competing on price, or they responded to the demand for fashion goods in the women's wear sector, where prices and profit margins were higher, where there was very little impetus for increasing the scale of operations, but where insecurity was endemic. In those cities where it was possible, the leading centers of women's wear production close to the principal wholesale and retail buyers, Jewish firms grew to dominate this higher margin sector.

Given the evident insecurity in such an immigrant economy, dependent on volatile, unpredictable fashion demand, mediated through short-term contracts, it may not have felt to the individual actors that they were prospering much in their new country. But the facts are clear. Of all immigrants arriving in the years immediately before World War I, the east European Jews were the most successful. And this success arose almost entirely from the rapid growth in demand for relatively high margin products—fashionable women's wear garments.

This fortune was compounded by one other event that underpinned the tendency for financial returns to increase to Jewish business: World War I. While this was one of the greatest tragedies of modern times, for those immigrants who had already left Europe, almost paradoxically it provided some tangible economic gains, through the war's effect of cutting off all subsequent migration flows after August 1914. For those tentatively prosperous entrepreneurs in the women's wear industries in New York and London, the net effect was for competitive entry from other potential east European Jewish entrepreneurial entrants to be halted. There were, of course, some new entrants from among the existing stock of immigrants. In New York, for instance, there was an increase in non-Jewish entrepreneurs in the years before 1914, which no doubt also continued after.[74] But the inflow of new entrants was far less than it would otherwise have been had war not occurred and the borders remained open.

CONCLUSION

This chapter has provided the first overview of the role of the Jewish immigrant entrepreneurs in the American clothing industry from its very genesis as an industry to the 1940s. The chapter has suggested that while German Jewish immigrants were favored with a relevant set of skills from their European background to move into peddling, which then enabled many of them to move ultimately into wholesale men's clothes manufacturing, the path followed by the east European Jews was different and not so easily explained by their past experiences. East European Jewish immigrants to the United States moved overwhelmingly into women's wear by the 1900s, as indeed was the case among similar immigrants settling in the main immigrant centers in Britain and Canada. There was no intermediate stage, as had been the case with the German Jewish immigrants earlier. Moreover, their occupational experience in Russia and Poland could not be a strong argument for explaining why they moved into clothing. Rather, a more likely explanation is that so poor were conditions in the clothing industry at that time, that east European Jew experienced the least competitive pressure from other immigrant arrivals in that sector. Quite extraordinarily, however, the characteristics of demand for women's wear changed in the years after 1900, and a mass market for fashionable garments emerged. East European Jewish entrepreneurs were well placed here to capitalize on this opportunity. And in all those immigrant centers in the leading destinations, which also happened to be the centers for women's fashion, the east European Jewish entrepreneurs found themselves able to improve profits and workers' wages.

NOTES

1. The apparel sector is central to the broader story of immigrant entrepreneurship in U.S. history. See, for example, Thomas McCraw's "Immigrant Entrepreneurs in U.S. Financial History, 1775–1914," *Capitalism and Society* 5, no. 1 (2010): 1–47.

2. Michael Zakim, *Ready-Made Democracy: A History of Men's Dress in the American Republic, 1760–1860* (Chicago: University of Chicago Press, 2003), 37–155; Edwin Troxell Freedley, *Leading Pursuits and Leading Men: A Treatise on the Principal Trades and Manufactures of the United States* (Philadelphia: Young, 1856), 121–148; Claudia Kidwell and Margaret C. Christman, *Suiting Everyone: The Democratization of Clothing in America* (Washington, DC: Smithsonian Institution Press, 1974), 1–133. See also Egal Feldman, *Fit for Men: A Study of New York's Clothing Trade* (Washington, DC: Public Affairs Press, 1960); and Harry Cobrin, *The Men's Clothing Industry: Colonial through Modern Times* (New York: Fairchild, 1970).

3. Feldman, *Fit for Men*, 35.

4. Zakim, *Ready-Made Democracy*, 37–95.

5. Shirts, like hosiery, were often mass-produced in specialist manufactories. They were generally called "furnishing goods," as were cravats, handkerchiefs, and gloves. A clothing warehouse primarily sold suits and dress jackets and pants. See Freedley, *Leading Pursuits*, for the style and size of buildings; and Kidwell and Christman, *Suiting Everyone*, for illustrations.

6. Kidwell and Christman, *Suiting Everyone*, 48.

7. Carolyn Milbank, "Ahead of the World: New York City Fashion," in *Art and the Empire City, New York 1825–1861*, ed. Catherine H. Voorsanger and John K. Howat (New York: Metropolitan Museum of Art, 2000), 243–257.

8. Freedley, *Leading Pursuits*, 132, 130.

9. Ibid., 133. See also Zakim, *Ready-Made Democracy*, 48.

10. See Christine Stansell, *City of Women: Sex and Class in New York, 1789–1860* (Urbana: University of Illinois Press, 1987), 120–129. See also Stansell, "The Origins of the Sweatshop: Women and Early Industrialization in New York City," in *Working Class America*, ed. Michael H. Frisch and Daniel J. Walkowith (Urbana: University of Illinois Press, 1983), 78–103; and Sean Wilentz, *Chants Democratic: New York City and the Rise of the American Working Class 1788–1850* (New York: Oxford University Press, 1984), 104–142.

11. Wilentz, *Chants Democratic*, 110, 120.

12. See Andrew Godley, "Singer in Britain: The Diffusion of Sewing Machine Technology and Its Impact on the Clothing Industry in the United Kingdom, 1860–1905," *Textile History* 27 (March 1996): 59–76; Godley, "Pioneering Foreign Direct Investment in British Manufacturing," *Business History Review* 73 (Autumn 1999): 394–429; Godley, "The Global Diffusion of the Sewing Machine, 1850–1914," *Research in Economic History* 20 (November 2001): 1–45; and Godley, "Selling the Sewing Machine around the World: Singer's International Marketing Strategies, 1850–1920," *Enterprise and Society* 7 (June 2006): 266–314.

13. Wilentz, *Chants Democratic*, 107.

14. Robert Ernst, *Immigrant Life in New York City: 1825–1863* (Syracuse, NY: Syracuse University Press, 1994), 73, 75.

15. Cobrin, *Men's Clothing Industry*, 26.

16. Yeshiva University Museum, *A Perfect Fit: The Garment Industry and American Jewry* (New York: Yeshiva University Museum, 2005), 12–13.

17. The National Association of Clothiers had branches in thirteen cities dating from the last quarter of the nineteenth century. In 1911 New York City had eighty-three member firms, followed by Chicago's eighteen firms. Philadelphia had seventeen, Rochester had sixteen, Baltimore had fourteen, Boston had thirteen, Cincinnati had twelve, St. Louis had four, Syracuse had two, Buffalo had two, Milwaukee had two, Louisville had one, and Detroit had one. Letter from National Association of Clothiers, September 9, 1911, D220, box 1, L. Adler Bros. collection, University of Rochester Library, Rochester, New York.

18. Stephen G. Mostov, "A Jerusalem on the Ohio" (1981), 109–111, quoted in Jonathan Sarna and Nancy H. Klein, eds., *The Jews of Cincinnati* (Cincinnati: Center for the Study of the American Jewish Experience, 1989), 38.

19. For uniform suppliers, see Mark R. Wilson, *The Business c̓ Civil War* (Baltimore: Johns Hopkins University Press, 2006).

20. Stephen G. Mostov, "Dun and Bradstreet Reports as a Source of Jewish Economic History: Cincinnati 1840–1875," in *Central European Jews in America, 1840–1880: Migration and Advancement*, ed. Jeffrey S. Gurock (New York: Routledge, 1997), 333–353. The Dun and Bradstreet agency provided reports on businesspeople in American cities to establish their credit worthiness. Local correspondents collected information about firms, which was kept locally in a branch office and also sent to the headquarters in New York City.

21. Ibid., 342–343.

22. Lynn Downey, *This Is a Pair of Levi's Jeans: The Official History of the Levi's Brand*, with Jill Novack Lynch and Kathleen McDonough (San Francisco: Strauss, 1995). See also archivist Lynn Downey's essays on her website, as well as the Levi-Strauss Museum in Buttenheim, Germany, website. "Levi Strauss: A Short Biography," Lynn Downey, Levi Strauss & Company, Historian, 2008, http://www.levistrauss.com/sites/default/files/library.

23. Mentioned in an article about Mr. Thomas W. Walsh as foremost tailor in the United States in "Mr. Thomas W. Walsh," *American Clothier and Furnisher* 19, no. 2 (September 1889): 44–45.

24. Cobrin, *Men's Clothing Industry*, 49–50.

25. See Rob Schorman, *Selling Style: Clothing and Social Change at the Turn of the Century* (Philadelphia: University of Pennsylvania Press, 2003), on advertising at HSM. On Hart, Schaffner, and Marx; Hammerslough Bros.; and Rosenfeld, see Cobrin, *Men's Clothing Industry*, 49–51.

26. Robert Liberles, "On the Threshold of Modernity: 1618–1780," in *Jewish Daily Life in Germany 1618–1945*, ed. Marion A. Kaplan (New York: Oxford University Press, 2005), 9–92; Steven M. Lowenstein, "The Beginning of Integration, 1780–1870," in Kaplan, *Jewish Daily Life*, 93–158. For occupational affinity in general, see Roger Waldinger, *Through the Eye of the Needle: Immigrants and Enterprise in New York's Garment Trades* (New York: New York University Press, 1986); Yeshiva University Museum, *Perfect Fit*; and Phyllis Dillon, "German Jews in the Early Manufacture of Ready-Made Clothing," in *A Perfect Fit: The Garment Industry and American Jewry, 1860–1960*, ed. Gabriel Goldstein and Elizabeth Greenberg (Lubbock, TX: Texas Tech University Press, 2012).

27. Lowenstein, "Beginning of Integration," 109.

28. Rudolph Glanz, "The German Jewish Mass Emigration, 1820–1880," in Gurock, *Central European Jews*, 22–28.

29. Andrew Godley, "Moses, Elias (1783–1868)" and "Marsden, Isaac Moses (1809–1884)," in *New Dictionary of National Biography* (Oxford: University Press, 2004), accessed December 4, 2011, http://www.oxforddnb.com/view/article/57650 and http://www.oxforddnb.com/view/article/57651; Godley, "The Development of the Clothing Industry: Technology and Fashion," *Textile History* 28 (Spring 1997): 3–10; Godley,

"Comparative Labour Productivity in the British and American Clothing Industries, 1850–1950," *Textile History* 28 (Spring 1997): 67–80.

30. Original document about King Solomon Masonic Lodge in Jewish Collection, box 1, Warshaw Collection of Business Americana, National Museum of American History, Smithsonian Institution, Washington, DC.

31. Sarna and Klein, *Jews of Cincinnati*, 44.

32. As reported in the obituary for Daniel Edward Ryan, "Dean of Clothing Designers," *Clothing Trade Journal*, April 1925, 35, 49.

33. See census total in the chart in Cobrin's *Men's Clothing Industry*, 47.

34. Freedley, *Leading Pursuits*, 214.

35. For the decline of influence of the francophile fashion press and the rise of "branding," see Teri Agins, *The End of Fashion: How Marketing Changed the Clothing Business Forever* (New York: HarperCollins, 2000).

36. Original catalog, Lord and Taylor, 1881, box M3–1880, Special Collections, Fashion Institute of Technology Library, New York.

37. For hoopskirts and corsets, see Yeshiva University Museum, *Perfect Fit*, 27–29. See also Milton Gottesman, *Hoopskirts and Huppas: A Chronicle of the Early Years of the Garfunkle-Trager Family in America, 1856–1920* (New York: American Jewish Historical Society, 1999).

38. Catalogs, Ladies Clothing Collection, boxes 14–16, Print Room ephemera collection, New York Historical Society.

39. *Wilson's Business City Directory* (1878–1879), microfilm, ZAN G404, reel 3, 8, Local History Room, New York Public Library.

40. See the reprint of the *Jordan Marsh Illustrated Catalogue of 1891* (New York: Atheneum of Philadelphia/Dover Publications, 1999), 93–116.

41. There was also an important gender difference, as German Jewish immigrant women rarely worked in the apparel trade, but almost all East European Jewish immigrant women spent some time in paid employment in the needle trades. For brevity's sake, we are omitting this important distinction from our discussion.

42. See Nathan Reich, "The Economic Structure of Modern Jewry," in *The Jews: Their History, Culture, and Religion*, ed. Louis Finkelstein (New York: Harper Brothers, 1949), although he builds on Nathan Goldberg, "Occupational Patterns of American Jews," *Jewish Review* 3 (1945–1946): 3–24, 262–290. See also Noah Barou, *The Jews at Work and Trade* (London: Jewish Trades Council, 1946), for the first assessment of the UK situation, and Louis Rosenberg, *Canada's Jews: A Social and Economic Study of Jews in Canada* (1939; repr., McGill University Press, 1993). See also Ernest Krausz, "The Economic and Social Structure of Anglo-Jewry," in *Jewish Life in Modern Britain*, ed. Julius Gould and Shaul Esh (London: Routledge; Kegan Paul, 1964), as well as summaries in Vivien Lipman, *Social History of the Jews in England, 1850–1950* (London: Watts, 1954), and Harold Pollins, *Economic History of the Jews in England* (London: Watts, 1982).

43. Reich, "Economic Structure," 1253. Note how at least automobiles represent a counterexample to the oft-cited view that Jews were much more likely to move into "emerging areas" to avoid competition. See, for example, Nachum Gross, "Entrepreneurship of Religious and Ethnic Minorities," *Zeitschrift fur unternehmengeschichte* 64 (1997): 19–34.

44. Reich, "Economic Structure," 1254, on Canada and the United Kingdom.

45. See Thomas Kessner, *The Golden Door: Italian and Jewish Immigrant Mobility in New York City, 1880–1915* (New York: Oxford University Press, 1977), which builds on Moses Rischin, *The Promised City: New York's Jews, 1870–1914* (Cambridge, MA: 1962); Gerald Tulchinsky, *Taking Root: The Origins of the Canadian Jewish Community* (Toronto: Lester, 1992).

46. Andrew Godley, "Jewish Soft Loan Societies in New York and London and Immigrant Entrepreneurship, 1880–1914," *Business History* 38 (July 1996): 101–116. See also

Dan Hiebert, "Discontinuities and the Emergence of Flexible Production: Garment Production in Toronto, 1901–1931," *Economic Geography* 66 (1990): 229–253; Herbert A. F. Barker, *The Economics of the Wholesale Clothing Industry in South Africa, 1907–1957* (Johannesburg: University of South Africa Press, 1962); Isaac M. Rubinov, *Economic Conditions of the Jews in Russia*, Bulletin 15 (Washington, DC: United States Bureau of Labor, 1907), quoted in Tulchinsky, *Taking Root*, 131; and Cormac O'Grada, *A History of the Jews in Ireland* (Princeton, NJ: Princeton University Press, 2006), ch. 4, p. 74, table 4.1. See also Hilary Rubinstein, *The Jews in Victoria, 1835–1985* (London: Allen and Unwin, 1986), especially the appendix by Bill Rubinstein, 260–270; Gustav Saron and Loius Hotz, eds., *Jews in South Africa: A History* (Cape Town, South Africa: Oxford University Press, 1955); Louis Herrman, *History of the Jews in South Africa* (London: Gollancz, 1930); and Hilary Rubinstein, Dan Cohn-Sherbok, Abraham Edelheit, and William Rubinstein, *The Jews in the Modern World: A History since 1750* (London: Arnold, 2002). Aubrey Newman, "Directed Migration: The Poor Jews' Temporary Shelter, 1885–1914," in *Patterns of Migration, 1850–1914*, ed. Newman and Stephen Massil (London: Jewish Historical Society of England, 1996) indicates that there was a strong transmigratory link between Kovno, Lithuania, and Cape Town, leading to perhaps half the South African Jewish population of 1914 coming from Eastern Europe, especially Lithuania. See also Newman, "The Poor Jews' Temporary Shelter: An Episode in Migration Studies," *Jewish Historical Studies* 40 (2005): 141–156.

47. For queue theory, see Roger Waldinger and Michael Lichter, *How the Other Half Works: Immigration and the Social Organisation of Labor* (Berkeley: University of California Press, 2003), 8–9.

48. Stephen Aris, *The Jews in Business* (London: Cape, 1970), 96. For examples, see Andrew Godley, *Jewish Immigrant Entrepreneurship in New York and London, 1880–1914* (London: Palgrave Macmillan, 2001).

49. Joel Perlmann, "Selective Migration as a Basis for Upward Mobility? The Occupations of the Jewish Immigrants to the United States, ca 1900" (working paper 172, Joel Levy Economics Institute, Bard College, 1996), 17, table 5, accessed November 8, 2011, http://www.levyinstitute.org/publications/?docid=294. Note also that Kessner, *Golden Door*, chapter 5, tells a similar story for New York.

50. O'Grada, *Jews in Ireland*, ch. 4; and Baron et al., *Economic History of the Jews* (New York: Schoken Books, 1975), 264.

51. See Godley, *Jewish Immigrant Entrepreneurship*, table 3.4.

52. Arthur Goren, quoted in Shelly Tenenbaum, "Shops, Stands, and Stores: Jewish Immigrant Businesses in the United States, (paper presented to the conference on Jews in American Business, Temple University, October 2004), 3–4.

53. Ibid., 4–5, on Boston footwear.

54. Tulchinsky, *Taking Root*, ch. 11; Anne Kershen, *Uniting the Tailors: Trade Unionism among the Tailors of London and Leeds, 1870–1939* (London: Cass, 1995); and especially Katrina Honeyman, *Well Suited: A History of the Leeds Clothing Industry* (Oxford: Oxford University Press, 2000).

55. Hadassa Kosak, *Cultures of Opposition: Jewish Immigrant Workers, New York City, 1880–1905* (Albany: SUNY Press, 2000), 67.

56. Tenenbaum, "Shops, Stands, and Stores," 3; Rischin, *Promised City*.

57. Quoted in Kosak, *Cultures of Opposition*, 64. For the decline of Philadelphia, see Godley, "Comparative Labour Productivity." and Phil Scranton, "The Transition from Custom to Ready-to-Wear Clothing in Philadelphia, 1890–1930," *Textile History* 25 (1994): 246–258.

58. For New York's share of U.S. output, see Steven Fraser, "Combined and Uneven Development in the Men's Clothing Industry," *Business History Review* 57 (1983): 541–542.

59. Andrew Godley, "The Development of the UK Clothing Industry, 1850–1950: Output and Productivity Growth" (discussion paper, University of Reading, 1994), and

"Immigrant Entrepreneurs and the Emergence of London's East End as an Industrial District," *London Journal* 21 (March 1996): 38–45, tables 1 and 2A.

60. Godley, "London's East End."

61. Quoted in Kershen, *Uniting the Tailors*, 138. See also Kershen, *Off the Peg* (London: London Museum of Jewish Life, 1988).

62. Peter G. Hall, *The Industries in London since 1861* (London: Hutchinson University Library, 1962), ch. 4; Dennys Munby, *The Economy of East London* (Oxford: Oxford University Press, 1954), 177, table 24; see also 32–33 and 62–63.

63. Wray, *The Women's Outerwear Industry* (London: Duckworth, 1957), 23–67; Chris Breward, *The History of the London Clothing Industry* (Oxford: Berg, 2004).

64. Jeffreys, *Retail Trading* (Cambridge: Cambridge University Press), 453, table 85.

65. Taylor, *The Study of Dress History* (Manchester: University of Manchester Press, 2002); Breward, *London Clothing Industry*; For the *Ladies' Home Journal*, see Laird, *Advertising Progress* (Baltimore: Johns Hopkins University Press, 1988).

66. Taylor, *Study of Dress History*; Winifred Aldrich, "The Impact of Fashion on the Cutting Practices for the Woman's Tailored Jacket: 1800–1927," *Textile History* 34 (2003): 134–170.

67. See Sue Ainsle Clark and Edith Wyatt, "Working–Girls' Budgets: The Shirtwaist-makers and Their Strike," *McClure's*, 1910, 70–86.

68. Jan Whitaker, *Service and Style: How the American Department Store Fashioned the Middle Class* (New York: St. Martin's Press, 2006), 9

69. For example, accompanying hotel ads in *Women's Wear Daily* 60 (January 2, 1940) offer hotel delivery.

70. On price data for the United Kingdom, see Godley, *Jewish Immigrant Entrepreneurship*.

71. *Anglo American Productivity Council Report on the Clothing Industry* (London: British Productivity Council, 1948), esp. 18, para. 195, on "no difference" between capital intense U.S. and UK industries' productivity.

72. Quoted in Beth Wenger, *New York Jews and the Great Depression: Uncertain Promise* (New Haven: Yale University Press, 1999), 15.

73. Margaret Wray, "Uncertainty, Prices, and Entrepreneurial Expectations: An Applied Study," *Journal of Industrial Economics* 4 (1956): 49–66. For the lack of accounting techniques in London fashion houses and the closeness to buyers, see Breward, *London Clothing Industry*.

74. For the role of Italians, see Kessner, *Golden Door*.

∽

CHAPTER 3

From the Rag Trade to Riches

ABRAHAM E. LEFCOURT AND THE DEVELOPMENT OF NEW YORK'S GARMENT DISTRICT

Andrew S. Dolkart

An article in the *New York Tribune* in 1925, extolling the meteoric growth of New York City's Garment District, noted, "Men who have risen from obscurity are in the foreground as the owners of property in the new garment center. Some came to these shores without a cent, and from the humblest surroundings on the East Side, have risen to the front through hard work and sincere effort. To-day they are the owners of businesses supplying retail merchants all over the country with the clothing necessary to make the American woman 'the best dressed in the world.'"[1] This "new garment center," the focus of the design, manufacture, sale, and distribution of a large percentage of the clothing worn by American women and children in the middle decades of the twentieth century, occupies a small area of New York City, a mere fifteen blocks bounded by West 35th Street and West 40th Street, and Broadway and Ninth Avenue, centering on Seventh Avenue, the street that has lent its name to the entire district.

This new Garment District developed with extraordinary rapidity, mostly in the ten years between 1920 and 1930, and became famous as a manufacturing center, its streets clogged with trucks unloading bolts of fabric and loading finished garments; handcarts carrying dresses, skirts, and coats guided by "push boys" careening through the congested streets; and thousands of workers crowding the sidewalks during their lunch breaks. "Noon," according to a writer for the International Ladies' Garment Workers Union, "is the signal for concentration twice multiplied. Thousands of workers niagara out to the streets, jam the sidewalks and flow over the curbs nonchalantly blocking traffic while husting truck drivers shout purple indignation. They crowd into the

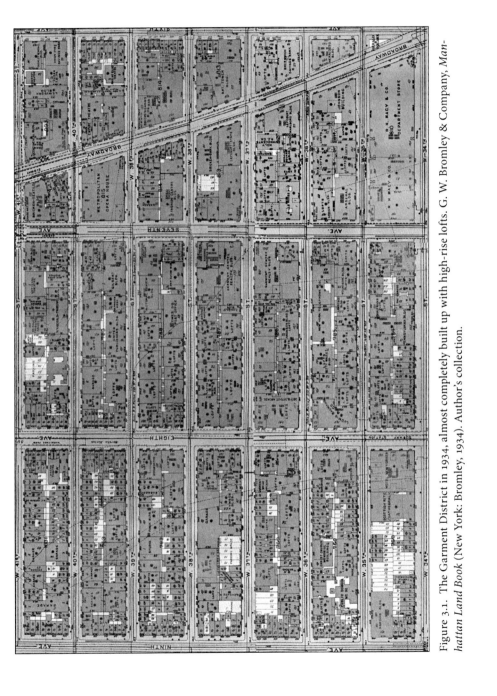

Figure 3.1. The Garment District in 1934, almost completely built up with high-rise lofts. G. W. Bromley & Company, *Manhattan Land Book* (New York: Bromley, 1934). Author's collection.

numberless cafeterias dotting the district, congregate over food and talk, then flood back across the pavements, perhaps for a cigarette and more talk in the warm sun."[2] Even today, as manufacturing has declined (but certainly not disappeared), "Seventh Avenue" remains a synonym for American fashion and the district retains its place as a center for the design and distribution of clothing.

While much is known about the history of fashion in the United States and about the garment-worker unions that played such a key role in the American labor movement, almost nothing is known about the physical fabric of the district and those who created it, a district developed almost entirely by and for Jewish garment manufacturers. Indeed, no place in the United States more fully reflects the interrelationship of Jews and American capitalism than New York City's Garment District, for it is a neighborhood largely created by Jewish developers who employed many Jewish architects to design the factory and showroom buildings leased to Jewish-owned businesses that employed primarily Jewish workers.

The author of the *New York Tribune* article extolling the men who created the new Garment District was Abraham E. Lefcourt, the "Miracle Man of Realty," the district's largest builder and a major force behind the creation of this new industrial center.[3] Lefcourt is largely forgotten today, even among those familiar with New York City's architecture and development. He was, however, a key player in the building boom of the 1920s, which created or transformed many of the commercial districts of the city. In 1928 the *Wall Street Journal* declared, "probably no individual has contributed more to New York City's office building requirements than A. E. Lefcourt"; the authors of *The Jews Come to America* listed Lefcourt as one of the "outstanding" men in the building profession; while the *Jewish Forum* placed Lefcourt among the "Jewish pioneers in the construction of New York City."[4] Lefcourt erected eighteen loft and office buildings in the city between 1910 and his death in 1932, most between 1921 and 1930. Some were built on a huge scale, with an aggregate of 5 million square feet of floor space, or 115 acres, spread over 477 floors, occupied each day by two hundred thousand people.[5] Lefcourt, born Abraham E. Lefkowitz, was a product of the Lower East Side Jewish immigrant community, and the trajectory of his career exemplifies the careers of the Jewish men who created this dynamic new district in the city. Lefcourt's loft buildings typify both the architectural character of garment lofts and the speculative nature of much of New York City's early twentieth-century construction, a building pattern largely dominated by Jewish developers.

THE GARMENT INDUSTRY AND THE
GARMENT DISTRICT IN NEW YORK CITY

Lefcourt and the other men who developed the Garment District in the years after World War I would not have succeeded if New York City had not already come to dominate the American ready-to-wear clothing industry.[6] Advantageous geography, historical circumstances, and the ambitions of entrepreneurial New Yorkers resulted in the centralization of the women's and children's clothing industry in New York, a development previously analyzed by historians.[7] New York's merchants exploited the city's exceptional harbor, easily accessible from European ports, transforming the city into a major shipping center by the early nineteenth century. The natural advantages of the port were augmented by the construction of canals, railroads, and highways, all leading directly to and from the port. This transportation network resulted in easy access to the raw materials needed for clothing manufacture—cotton and woolen cloth from New England mills, fine European fabrics, and the buttons, buckles, and other accessories mass-produced in American and international factories—and also permitted the efficient shipment of finished goods to department stores, dry goods establishments, and specialty shops across the continent. Ships sailing into New York Harbor brought not only fabrics and other materials that would be turned into clothing but also tens of thousands of immigrants, many of whom would become garment workers, garment factory owners, and, in a few cases, the developers of garment lofts. In addition, these ships brought fashionable Europeans to New York and transported New Yorkers to Europe. Thus, the city also became a gateway for new fashion trends, which were incorporated into the design of the latest clothing lines, popularized by New York–based magazines distributed to consumers across America. Finally, the banks and mortgage houses that made New York America's financial capital were easily accessible to the city's garment manufacturers and loft builders who needed capital to expand their businesses or erect new manufacturing lofts.

In the mid-nineteenth century, a ready-to-wear clothing industry developed for the production of men's wear. Unlike women's clothing, men's wear lent itself to mass production since it was generally not subject to rapid changes in fashion. New York was a major center for men's wear, but it shared this industry with other cities, including Baltimore, Chicago, Philadelphia, Rochester, and San Francisco.[8] New York, however, dominated the manufacture of women's clothing. By the end of the nineteenth century, the manufacture of women's wear was increasingly industrialized, as sewing machines became more efficient and as new machines were invented that could complete the intricate tasks of creating women's garments. In addition, department stores and other retail establishments catering to the growing middle- and working-class markets were expanding. These stores required large stocks of ready-to-wear, sized clothing. By the early twentieth century, only clothing for the wealthiest segment of American society was still custom made. Even with this industrialization, New York remained the nexus of design and manufacture for women's cloaks and suits, blouses and shirtwaists, dresses and skirts, furs and hats. From the start, the clothing industry in New York City was dominated by Jewish owners and workers; in the mid-1890s 75 percent of the workers were Jews.[9]

The development of loft buildings erected primarily for the garment industry began circa 1900. In the decades prior to this, most manufacturing was done by Jewish immigrants working as individuals or families in their own apartments or in small factories, often referred to as "sweatshops," also located in tenement apartments.[10] These tenement factories became extremely controversial, not necessarily because of the poor working conditions, but because of fears among more affluent people that germs might breed in clothing while it sat in tenement apartments and factories, and infectious diseases might then be spread to wealthy consumers. In his 1892 report, James Connolly, the factory inspector for New York State, expressed concern that Asiatic cholera and other epidemics might result from the manufacture of clothing in tenement apartments.[11] Beginning in 1892 the state legislature passed a series of laws that regulated tenement factories and made legal manufacturing in these venues increasingly difficult. As a result, garment factories opened in old and new loft buildings, most located on or near Broadway south of 14th Street, an area within easy walking distance of the tenements on the Lower East Side, where most of the workers lived. The factories were hardly ideal, as many lacked adequate toilets and other necessities and had poor fire proofing, a fact that became evident to the American public when a fire at the Triangle Shirtwaist Company's factory, located in a loft building erected in 1900–1901, claimed 146 lives.[12]

As the women's garment business expanded, hundreds of new eight- to twelve-story lofts were erected in the first two decades of the twentieth century, largely just north and south of 23rd Street between Fifth and Seventh Avenues, close to the city's leading department stores, which lined Broadway and Sixth Avenue. Among these new lofts was the Lefcourt Building at 48–54 West 25th Street, erected in 1910 by cloak and suit manufacturer A. E. Lefcourt, who moved his business into some of the space in the completed building (figure 3.2).[13] This twelve-story building, designed by George & Edward Blum, with large windows, fireproof construction, and open floors serviced by both passenger and freight elevators, typified the industrial buildings erected in the early years of the twentieth century that were rented primarily to women's clothing manufacturers.

New loft development continued to move northward. In 1914, for example, Lefcourt had the Blums design a loft at 134 West 37th Street, between Broadway and Seventh Avenue (figure 3.3), farther north and west than most garment-industry construction at the time. He soon moved his business into this building. More significant to contemporary concerns about the garment industry were the lofts appearing on or just off of Fifth Avenue, north of 34th Street, including one built by Lefcourt in 1915 at 42–46 West 38th Street. Construction

Figure 3.2. 48–52 West 25th Street, Abraham E. Lefcourt's first loft building. *The Work of George and Edward Blum Architects: New York City* (privately printed, 1935). Author's collection.

of these lofts in the early years of the twentieth century coincided with the appearance of luxury department and specialty stores on Fifth Avenue in the same area. Affluent women shopping at B. Altman's or Tiffany & Company found themselves sharing the sidewalks with the working-class, immigrant men from the cloak and suit factories out on the street during their noontime lunch breaks, which was also a fashionable shopping hour.[14] The store owners feared that this unwelcome interaction would affect their business.

Figure 3.3. 134 West 37th Street, Abraham E. Lefcourt's earliest building in the future Garment District. *The Work of George and Edward Blum Architects: New York City* (privately printed, 1935). Author's collection.

THE "SHALL WE SAVE NEW YORK" CAMPAIGN
AND THE CREATION OF A NEW GARMENT DISTRICT

By 1916 the concern among business owners that the new Fifth Avenue luxury shopping district would be diminished by the presence of garment workers had become public, with newspaper articles appearing with headlines such as "Menace to Trade on Fifth Avenue."[15] The conflict between the Fifth Avenue merchants and the garment industry would ultimately result in the development of a totally new Garment District on the West Side north of 34th Street, far removed from the Fifth Avenue shopping district. Under the auspices of the Fifth Avenue Association, store owners, hoteliers, bankers, and others with financial interests in the Fifth Avenue area began a campaign to force the garment factories from a "restricted zone" that they proposed between 33rd and 59th Streets between Third and Seventh Avenues. The proponents of this zone threatened to boycott any garment business still in this zone on February 1, 1917. The public campaign began in March 1916 with full-page advertisements in almost every local newspaper beginning with a bold challenge: "SHALL WE SAVE NEW YORK? A Vital Question for Everyone Who Has Pride in This Great City."[16] This was a strong statement with widespread support from local businesses and from the media—almost every New York City newspaper editorialized in favor of the Shall We Save New York campaign. The garment manufacturers soon acquiesced to the demand that new factories avoid the restricted zone and that businesses already within the zone move out. The proposed boycott was a threat that manufacturers had to take seriously. In truth, they had little to lose from agreeing to the restrictions, because rents in the new lofts north of 33rd Street were high and the expense of relocating would be minimal since the sewing machines and other equipment used in garment factories were easily transportable.

The main issue for the garment industry was to determine where to relocate their factories. Owners were not happy about the idea of moving back into older lofts that did not meet standards for light, electrical output, fireproofing, and sanitation. The Save New York Committee proposed the construction of modern factories in an area south of 31st Street between Sixth and Eighth Avenues. Just as debate about an appropriate new location for garment lofts got under way, World War I intervened, delaying new construction. Immediately after the war, the garment manufacturers and not the Save New York Committee decided that the blocks north of Pennsylvania Station (at Seventh Avenue between 31st and 33rd Streets) were the most appropriate place for their businesses, since new subway lines there connected to the residential neighborhoods where both workers and factory owners lived; buyers arriving from across the country at Penn Station would be close to new showrooms; and real estate was cheap in this section of the Tenderloin, a neighborhood of old and rundown tenements and row houses.

In late 1919 it was announced that a pair of enormous garment lofts, to be known as the Garment Center Capitol, would be erected on the west side of Seventh Avenue, flanking 37th Street (figure 3.4). This center was a cooperative venture by a syndicate of high-end manufacturers, including some of the largest employers in the industry. Both the twenty-two-story north building and the seventeen-story south building are L-shaped structures planned with all of the amenities required of a modern industrial loft building. Designed by the

Figure 3.4. The Garment Center Capitol, Seventh Avenue between 36th and 38th Streets. *Architecture and Building*, September 1920, plate 101. Author's collection.

obscure architect Walter M. Mason, the Garment Center Capitol is an inconspicuous complex, despite one fanciful description of the building's "Italian Renaissance" facades.[17] These little-known structures are, however, of major historical importance in the development of New York. Their construction was the joint idea of dress manufacturer Mack Kanner, born on Ludlow Street, the youngest of eighteen children of Jewish immigrant parents, and Russian Jewish cloak and suit manufacturer Saul Singer. Speaking about Singer, the hyperbolic 1932 publication *New York: The Wonder City* exclaimed that "this enormous project was conceived and carried through to achievement by a man who thirty years or so ago, was a poor little Jewish boy who lived in Russia and came to America practically penniless."[18] Kanner and Singer also represent another important characteristic of many of the builders who created the Garment District; that is, they were Jewish immigrants, or the children of immigrants, who worked in sweatshops, then became successful garment manufacturers, only to later close their factories as they became real estate developers and investors. Kanner became an active loft builder in the district and later a residential developer in Freeport, Long Island, while Singer became an officer of the Bank of United States, with its active interests in the Garment District, until its failure in 1931 resulted in his imprisonment.[19]

The Garment Center Capitol opened in July 1921 with stores on the first story, showrooms on the next three stories, up-to-date factories on the upper floors, and a manufacturers' club, with a gymnasium and large dining room, on the top floor of the south building. The complex was enormously successful. Indeed, one startled commentator reported that "more people are employed in the Garment Center Capitol buildings than in any women's garment manufacturing city in the United States outside of New York."[20]

Singer and Kanner predicted that the Garment Center Capitol would become the "gateway to the garment trade," establishing a new district for manufacturing.[21] They could not have imagined, however, how extensive and how rapid the development of new garment lofts would proceed, creating an entirely new industrial district of skyscraper lofts in only a decade. Almost all of the development was undertaken by Jewish builders and developers who had long been associated with the garment industry. Even before the Garment Center Capitol was completed, Jewish developers began constructing other loft buildings on speculation, hoping to fill their buildings with rental tenants. Russian-born Max Aronson, for example, closed his cloak and suit factory and invested in loft development, erecting two garment buildings between 1920 and 1922, both designed by Schwartz & Gross. Demand was suddenly so great in the area that one of Aronson's buildings was 60 percent leased from plans (i.e., leases were signed before construction was completed).[22] Joseph E. Gilbert, whom the *Jewish Forum* listed as one of the city's "great builders," teamed up with three manufacturers, William Fischman, Joseph Heit, and Hyman D. Rubin, in 1921 to erect the enormous, sixteen-story Gilbert Building at 205–219 West 39th Street, designed by George & Edward Blum. The three manufacturer/builders moved into the completed structure, each occupying two floors. The Gilbert Building's builders were especially cognizant of the need for uninterrupted natural light and air in the lofts, purchasing the lot to the north on 40th Street and erecting a two-story building on this valuable property, thus assuring that no building would ever rise on this plot and block the north-facing windows at the rear of the new loft building. The new lofts attracted tenants from the older loft district of the city, draining the tenant rolls of these earlier structures.[23]

A. E. LEFCOURT AND THE DEVELOPMENT OF THE GARMENT DISTRICT

Abraham E. Lefcourt, who had already built several garment lofts, also planned new buildings in the area and soon began taking credit for the establishment of the entire West Side Garment District. Lefcourt had erected a loft on West 37th Street between Broadway and Seventh Avenue in 1914 (see figure 3.3), but this building was an anomaly at the time. However, after the success of the nearby Garment Center Capitol, Lefcourt began actively building additional lofts in the area and exploited the presence of his earlier loft building, marketing himself as the "pioneer" in the new Garment District.[24] As he described it, his

Figure 3.5. Abraham E. Lefcourt. From *Building Investment and Maintenance* 2 (June 1927): 28. Library of Congress, Washington, DC.

friends had advised him against building a loft in an out-of-the-way area like 37th Street west of Broadway, but he had rejected this advice because he had come "to believe that sooner or later the entire garment industry of New York would finally be located from 36th to 39th Streets and from Broadway to Eighth Avenue."[25] The truth of this claim is belied by the fact that two years after he built the 37th Street loft, he erected a loft on West 38th Street between Fifth and Sixth Avenues, in exactly the area the Save New York Committee was trying to rid of garment factories. In addition, Lefcourt was active in the protection of his financial interests in the older Madison Square Garment District, serving as treasurer of the short-lived Madison Square Garment Association, established in 1921 by real estate and business interests in that area. This group was "emphatic in its statements that the Madison Square section is still the center of the garment-manufacturing industry in New York."[26] Thus, Lefcourt, the self-made man, carefully crafted his public persona as a great New York builder. *Women's Wear Daily*, the newspaper that closely watched the garment industry, lauded Lefcourt following his sudden death in 1932:

> A. E. Lefcourt, the builder who rose from obscurity in the garment trades to a position of affluence in these great industries, and subsequently to a veritable monarchy in real estate circles, was one of the most compelling personalities ever developed in the ready-to-wear trades. He was the industry's shining example of the story-book heroes of Horatio Alger and Oliver Optic.[27]

Lefcourt's origins remain somewhat unclear. Generally known throughout his life as "A. E.," he was born Abraham E. Lefkowitz in 1877, probably the child of Russian Jewish immigrants. The family officially changed its name to Lefcourt in 1909, although they had been using the less ethnic surname for several years before that. In fact, Lefcourt is the name that appears in the 1900 United States Census. He may have been born on the Lower East Side, as some records and biographies claim. In 1914, when returning from a trip to Europe, the ship's manifest lists Lefcourt as having been born on "Christy St. N.Y.," undoubtedly referring to Christie Street on the Lower East Side. A *New York Times* biography on the occasion of the opening of one of Lefcourt's garment buildings states that "another New Yorker born on the lower east side fulfilled America's favorite legend of success last week," although it places his birth on Delancey Street. Lefcourt's own 1932 death certificate lists him as American born. But the 1900 United States Census lists him and his parents as all being from Russia; the 1910 and 1930 census enumerations give Lefcourt's birthplace as England; and the 1920 census gives his place of birth as New York. His obituary in *Women's Wear Daily* states that he was born in Birmingham, England, and a lengthy article in the *New York Times* summarizing his career following his death asserts that "it has been generally understood that Mr. Lefcourt was a native of the lower east side of Manhattan. As a matter of fact, he was born in Birmingham, England, and came to this country with his parents when he was 5 years old." If this is correct, it would explain why the family does not appear in the 1880 United States Census. Weighing this confusing documentary evidence, it seems probable that Lefcourt was born in England to Russian Jews (his father's death certificate states that both he and his wife were from Russia), who journeyed to New York in about 1882, settling on the Lower East Side.[28]

Although the specifics of his birth may never be definitively known, it is clear that Lefcourt rose from poverty to great success. As he loved to relate, he began his industrious life as a newsboy and then opened a bootblack stand on Grand Street, hiring two Italian boys to run the stand during the day while he sold newspapers, before returning to the business at night. Of course, as luck would have it, so the tale goes, Lefcourt later purchased the site on the southeast corner of Broadway and West 38th Street, where he had once stood selling newspapers, and transformed it into the monumental Lefcourt Normandie Building. Lefcourt soon began working in a dry goods store as a shipping clerk, but decided that his future was not in retail. He then found employment in a women's clothing factory, serving as clerk, bookkeeper, buyer, and traveling salesman. When his employer retired he asked to take over the business on credit, but he needed customers. His success resulted from a seven-thousand-dollar sale to a leading Pittsburgh department store. However, without the money to pay for the materials and labor, he took a train to Pittsburgh and persuaded the president of the store to advance him five thousand dollars.[29]

From this beginning, Lefcourt's cloak and suit business developed into one of the most successful in the city. Records from 1913 indicate that he employed a monthly average of 185 workers—128 men and 34 women involved in manufacture and 23 as office workers.[30] He became a founder and first president of the industry's Cloak, Suit, and Skirt Manufacturers' Protective Association, formed in 1910 in response to a major strike and the related rise of union activism. Lefcourt was closely involved with the arbitration under the auspices of lawyer (and later Supreme Court justice) Louis Brandeis, resulting in the "Protocol of Peace" between his organization and the International Ladies' Garment Workers Union, which governed labor-management relations for some years.[31] Also in 1910 Lefcourt became a builder, investing more than one million dollars in the construction of the loft at 48 West 25th Street in the Madison Square Garment District. This was followed in 1913 by his venture into the west side, at 134 West 37th Street, and in 1915 by his loft on 38th Street near the 34th Street luxury shopping district.

All three of Lefcourt's early buildings were twelve-story lofts built out to the lot line, the typical form of industrial buildings in Manhattan erected in the early years of the twentieth century. While the 25th Street loft has a refined Beaux-Arts style facade not unlike that of contemporaneous lofts, the 37th and 38th Street buildings have innovative facades, with unusual Arts and Crafts–inspired terra-cotta and limestone ornament designed by George & Edward Blum, the firm eventually responsible for Lefcourt's first seven industrial buildings.[32] Like other Jewish developers active in the construction of garment lofts in the first three decades of the twentieth century, Lefcourt turned to Jewish architects, such as the Blums, for most of his buildings. The Blums were of French Jewish ancestry; George was born in the United States and Edward in France. Since Jews (and other immigrants as well) were generally not commissioned to design the most prestigious skyscrapers or the luxurious mansions and apartment houses of the city's wealthy Protestant elite, their careers focused largely on the design of speculative buildings, including lofts and apartment houses. Thus, these were building fields dominated by Jewish immigrants and their children. As a result, Jewish developers frequently turned to other Jews for designs. In the Seventh Avenue Garment District, the most prolific architects were all Jews: Schwartz & Gross designed twenty-five Garment District buildings (Simon Schwartz and Arthur Gross met while studying at the Hebrew Technical Institute), George & Edward Blum designed nineteen, Buchman & Kahn fourteen, Gronenberg & Leuchtag ten, and others were by Emery Roth, Shampan & Shampan, and Sugarman & Berger; with the exception of Buchman & Kahn, all were also well known for their speculative apartment house designs.

With the announcement in early December 1919 of the impending construction of the Garment Center Capitol, Lefcourt, whose cloak and suit business was not part of this cooperative venture, realized that the future of garment loft development was in the Seventh Avenue area. A week after Kanner and Singer made their plans public, Lefcourt announced his plan to construct a large twelve-story loft on West 38th Street between Seventh and Eighth Avenues. His announcement, echoed the rhetoric of the Save New York Committee, while minimizing the significance of the Garment Center Capitol:

> The "Save New York" movement can only be made successful by the build-
> ing of sufficient quarters for the entire manufacturing trade which is now
> encroaching on the retail district. For sixty manufacturers [in the Garment
> Center Capitol] to be located on Seventh Avenue and hundreds to remain in
> the Fifth Avenue district does not solve the problem confronting those who
> have the pride of the city at heart. We must all move out from our present
> quarters and by doing so we not only play an important role in ridding the
> most beautiful avenue in the world of its crowds at the noon hour, but also
> save thousands of dollars a year by paying lower rent and thus help reduce
> the cost of clothing to a considerable extent.

Ultimately, plans for the 38th Street loft building were abandoned when Lefcourt arranged a lucrative deal with the United States Post Office to erect the two-story Times Square Station at a cost of 1 million dollars, with the government agreeing to pay 3.5 million dollars for a twenty-year lease.[33]

It is notable that in 1919, Lefcourt made no claim to have been the pioneer in the Seventh Avenue Garment District. It was only in 1921, when he announced the impending construction of a new loft at 237–239 West 37th Street between Seventh and Eighth Avenues (figure 3.6), that he saw the commercial value of inventing this formative legend.[34] The new 37th Street loft would be erected, according to Lefcourt, in response to "the interest being manifested in the new permanent Seventh Avenue district, and there is no doubt in my mind that all manufacturers will eventually realize the desirability of making their business home in a neighborhood so convenient and attractive for visiting buyers."[35] This relatively small midblock loft and similar buildings at 246–250 West 38th Street (1922; figure 3.6), immediately behind the new 37th Street loft, and at 148–156 West 37th Street (1924), were all designed by the Blums.

These fourteen-story buildings are representative of the design and massing of the lofts in the new Garment District that were erected in the 1920s. All are relatively simple buildings with little money expended on extraneous architectural detail—gone is the unusual and costly terra-cotta found on Lefcourt's and the Blums' earlier lofts. Each has a two- or three-story stone base, with central storefronts that could be leased to fabric stores; shops selling buttons, zippers, or garment accessories; or to other businesses willing to pay high rents for prominent street frontage. Entrances flanked the stores, one leading to a modest lobby with passenger elevators, and the other leading to the freight elevators.

Figure 3.6. 237–239 West 37th Street and 246–250 West 38th Street, built by Lefcourt in 1921 to 1922. *The Work of George and Edward Blum Architects New York City* (privately printed, 1935). Author's collection.

These lofts were the first erected by Lefcourt that manifest the new requirements of the city's comprehensive zoning law of 1916. The zoning code required
setbacks on the facade so that light and air would reach the sidewalks. The
Blums, who had mastered the massing requirements of the law, creating a series
of dynamic setbacks on each building, with subtle Renaissance-inspired ornament emphasizing each step.[36] These were the last modestly scaled, midblock
industrial lofts that Lefcourt built, as he turned to the construction of monumental loft and showroom buildings on Broadway and then to the completion
of skyscrapers in other parts of the city.

Lefcourt developed four large Broadway lofts—one on each corner from 36th
to 39th Streets, erected between 1923 and 1929. Shortly after he purchased his
first property on Broadway, the Hotel Marlborough on the northwest corner of
West 36th Street, Lefcourt closed his cloak and suit factory and focused exclusively on real estate development. As Lefcourt told C. A. Rieser, the author of the
earliest of several articles that publicized his success, "During my last years in the
business I did not seem to get my usual amount of fun out of the manufacturing
of cloaks and suits. So I just carried out the promise I had always made to myself
that whenever a certain form of activity ceased to give me stimulus that I craved
I would quit it and go in for something more exciting."[37]

Lefcourt's announcement that he would build a garment loft on Broadway,
just north of Herald Square and the large department stores of Macy's, Gim-
bel's, and Saks 34th Street, caused the same concern among retailers that had
led to the 1916 Save New York campaign. According to an article published in
Broadway, the journal of the Broadway Association, merchants "feared that the
probable presence of great numbers of needleworkers, which the nature of the
businesses to be housed in the building seemed to make necessary, would create
one of the nuisances which the zoning law seeks to prevent."[38] The 1916 zoning
law would not, however, have permitted a building entirely used for manufacturing, for this section of Broadway was located within a commercial zone that
limited such use to only 25 percent of the floor area. This limitation would still
have allowed a substantial amount of manufacturing after stores, showrooms,
lobbies, halls, elevators, toilets, and other public spaces were subtracted from
the total square footage. But Lefcourt was able to placate the retailers' concerns,
writing to the Broadway Association that "I, personally, am as much interested
as any other individual in regard to keeping up the standard of Broadway,"
so the new building at Broadway and 36th Street "will be the highest type
of commercial building in the City of New York and I have no intentions to
permit manufacturing to be done in a building of this type."[39] The building
would house the showrooms and offices of garment firms and, emphasizing
the nonmanufacturing purpose of the building, Lefcourt announced that his
company's executive offices would be located on the top floor.

Lefcourt replaced the Hotel Marlborough with the Lefcourt-Marlboro Building, with the name prominently carved into the facade above the third story on each street facade. Lefcourt continued to name each of his successive buildings after himself, leading one chronicler of New York's real estate world to quip that Lefcourt was "touched by a Napoleonic complex, he named eight or nine of his buildings after himself . . . until the midtown areas were spotted with Lefcourt this and Lefcourt that."[40] Over the next few years New York saw the construction of buildings dubbed Lefcourt-Central, Lefcourt-Manhattan, Lefcourt-Madison, Lefcourt-Empire, Lefcourt-State, Lefcourt-National, Lefcourt-ITT, Lefcourt Clothing Center, Lefcourt-Normandie, Lefcourt-Colonial, and Lefcourt-Alan (figure 3.7).

No other builder in New York history had so many buildings named for himself. Together, Lefcourt referred to these buildings as "Lefcourt City"; his 1930 marketing book of that name claimed that the structures that he built, "when considered all together, do indeed comprise a city in themselves."[41] Artists drew composite images of all the buildings, creating dramatic, yet imaginary urban agglomerations of buildings rising from his two-story post office and modest early lofts to his later skyscraper towers (figure 3.8).[42]

Lefcourt considered himself to be a builder, that is, one who purchased land, improved it with a suitable high-quality building, rented space, and then managed the property. He strongly objected to being called a real estate operator or a speculator, since to him these terms implied the construction of cheap buildings sold for instant profit immediately after construction was completed.[43] "Sometimes," he said, "I wonder why men who spend so much money for property spoil it by erecting cheap looking buildings. They are bound to feel the effects in the long run. Pride in appearance works the same way in a building as it does in a dress."[44]

While it is true that Lefcourt was a builder who hoped to profit from long-term rental income on his many properties, he was also part of a larger movement of

Figure 3.7. Lefcourt's name inscribed on three of his loft buildings on Broadway. Photograph by author.

speculative construction in New York City that was dominated by immigrants and their children, largely Jewish immigrants, in the early decades of the twentieth century. Most of these speculative builders were small-scale investors who were responsible for only a few buildings, sometimes even a single building, but others, such as Lefcourt, Irwin Chanin, and Abraham Bricken, erected many monumental structures. These builders, whether they intended to retain ownership of their buildings or to sell as soon as the building was completed and take what they hoped would be a short-tem profit, were all speculative builders, in that they almost never had a client who was going to occupy the building upon its completion.

They erected the city's industrial lofts but were also responsible for many of its office towers and were largely responsible for the creation of its residential neighborhoods. Jewish speculative builders erected the vast majority of the city's early twentieth-century apartment buildings, ranging from expensive buildings on West End Avenue and Central Park West to the hundreds of more modest five- and six-story working- and middle-class buildings of the Bronx

Figure 3.8. "Lefcourt City": composite drawing of all of Abraham E. Lefcourt's New York City buildings. Almost all of the mid-rise buildings are garment lofts and showrooms. *New York Times*, November 20, 1922, General Research Division, New York Public Library, Astor, Lenox and Tilden Foundations.

and Brooklyn, where many garment workers lived. Like Lefcourt, these builders generally did not work with the premier architects of the day, rather they
commissioned designs from lesser-known architects who came from a similar
background. Indeed, Jewish loft architects such as George & Edward Blum and
Schwartz & Gross also had active practices in upper-middle-class apartment
house design, and Jewish architects such as Jacob Felson, Israel Crausman,
Springsteen & Goldhammer, and Horace Ginsbern in the Bronx and northern
Manhattan; and Cohn Brothers, Shampan & Shampan, Kavy & Kavovitt, and
Benjamin Finkensieper in Brooklyn created the streetscapes that have come to
define New York.

The four Broadway loft buildings, the Lefcourt-Marlboro, Manhattan,
State, and Normandie, each on a major, highly visible corner site, are massive
buildings with limestone bases, simple brick superstructures, and distinctive
crowns, often capped by a tower. The two earliest, the Marlboro and Manhattan, were designed by George & Edward Blum, but after the completion of the
Lefcourt-Manhattan Building, Lefcourt's relationship with the Blums inexpli-
cably ended. The Lefcourt-Normandie Building and a few of his buildings outside of the Garment District were designed by Bark & Djorup, a rare instance
of a Garment District building designed by architects who were apparently not
Jewish.[47] Other late buildings by Lefcourt, including the Lefcourt-State Building on Broadway and 37th Street (figure 3.10), were the work of Buchman &
Kahn, the Jewish firm responsible for many of the most prominent garment
buildings on Broadway and Seventh Avenue.[48]

Although none of Lefcourt's buildings are architectur... masterpieces, each
was carefully planned and built for its market and each has well-proportioned,
simply ornamented facades and an impressive lobby. Lobby design was especially important to Lefcourt: "Twenty-five per cent of your sale of a building
is made the first time a man enters the lobby. If he likes its appearance, the
decorations, lighting, and other features, this psychological first impression of
the entire structure will influence him strongly as a prospective tenant or as
a customer of someone in the building."[45] The lobby of the Lefcourt-Marlboro
Building, for example, had an L-shaped arcade with marble walls, terrazzo
floor in ornamental design, bronze storefronts, and an arched plaster ceiling
decorated with coffers highlighted in color (figure 3.9).[46]

The four Broadway loft buildings, the Lefcourt-Marlboro, Manhattan,
State, and Normandie, each on a major, highly visible corner site, are massive
buildings with limestone bases, simple brick superstructures, and distinctive
crowns, often capped by a tower. The two earliest, the Marlboro and Manhattan, were designed by George & Edward Blum, but after the completion of the
Lefcourt-Manhattan Building, Lefcourt's relationship with the Blums inexpli-
cably ended. The Lefcourt-Normandie Building and a few of his buildings outside of the Garment District were designed by Bark & Djorup, a rare instance
of a Garment District building designed by architects who were apparently not
Jewish.[47] Other late buildings by Lefcourt, including the Lefcourt-State Building on Broadway and 37th Street (figure 3.10), were the work of Buchman &
Kahn, the Jewish firm responsible for many of the most prominent garment
buildings on Broadway and Seventh Avenue.[48]

Lefcourt carefully planned a marketing campaign to attract appropriate
tenants to each of his newly developed properties. Appropriate marketing was
crucial since he was not the only builder erecting large loft buildings on prominent corner sites along Broadway and Seventh Avenue in the Garment District.
Others, including Louis Adler, Abe N. Adelsohn, and Abraham Bricken, all
Jewish garment manufacturers who became developers, were competing with
Lefcourt for tenants. Speaking of Lefcourt and these three competitors, real
estate broker Charles Noyes noted that "in all of the upbuilding of New York

Figure 3.9. Lobby of the Lefcourt-Marlboro Building. *Architecture and Building* 62 (May 1925), plate 101. Avery Architecture and Fine Arts Library, Columbia University in the City of New York

City during the past 10 years probably no four men have contributed more to the growth of the city and the production of better space for the city's manufacturers and merchants than four men previously identified with the garment industry."[49] Lefcourt maintained that he managed his buildings personally and maintained a high level of service. Conjuring garment imagery, Lefcourt said, "A building, like a suit of clothes, has to be respected. Neglect a suit, throw it around carelessly and it becomes unfit for use, shabby in its appearance and reflects discredit of its owner. The same idea can be applied to a building. If it is neglected and nobody cares about its appearance, nobody wants to be in it and it depreciates in value."[50] For the convenience of tenants at each of his buildings, Lefcourt kept the elevators running twenty-four hours a day, employed only carefully selected uniformed elevator operators, and banned cigar stands in his lobbies and luncheonettes near the freight elevators:

> We do not permit cigar stands in the lobbies or luncheonettes near the freight entrances. They are liable to attract crowds who block the passages to and from the elevators and otherwise make a lobby the opposite of what it should be—a wide, clear, pleasant place. . . . We constantly strive to give

Figure 3.10. Lefcourt-State Building. *Lefcourt City* (New York: Lefcourt Realty, 1930), 16. Wolfsonian-FIU.

the best of service through the building. If you don't please the tenant he is going to move out, and no price that you may offer will keep him if he is unhappy in the location.[51]

Lefcourt added that the ban on cigar stands continued even after he was offered a lucrative twenty-one-year lease on lobby concessions.[52]

Each of the Broadway buildings was immediately successful, generally opening with all of the space leased. The primary tenants were dress, and coat and suit companies.[53] It is not clear how many of the firms manufactured garments in the buildings and how many were jobbers who contracted out their manufacturing and used their space on Broadway for showrooms and warehousing. Legally, the zoning placed a limit on how much manufacturing could take place in each building, but it is also not know how vigorously the city policed this zoning rule.

All four of Lefcourt's Broadway buildings, and his side street lofts as well, were built for the women's garment trade. Although New York City did not dominate the men's wear trade in the same way that it dominated in women's wear, the design, manufacture, and sale of men's and boys' garments was still a substantial employer in the city. Unlike in Chicago and Rochester where enormous factories, employing thousands of workers, completed all aspects of the manufacture of a suit or a coat, New York's men's wear factories were largely small operations where a substantial amount of work in the 1920s was still completed by home workers. The men's wear industry largely remained in the old lofts south of 14th Street, concentrated on the blocks between Bleecker Street, 14th Street, Broadway, and Lafayette Street, where rents were extremely low, but where conditions were poor.

By the 1920s the industry was beginning to disperse from Manhattan, with factories opening in Brooklyn and the Bronx, as well as in New Jersey.[54] Lefcourt saw an opportunity to provide modern space for men's wear manufacturers. He purchased large Seventh Avenue plots, and in 1925 announced plans for the first of what he hoped would be three buildings creating a men's clothing mart between 22nd and 26th Streets. Lefcourt's public relations touted the planning of the building, declaring that "the Lefcourt organization, once more taking its place as the leader of a great movement, planned the clothing center with the needs of this big industry in mind."[55] Buchman & Kahn was the architect firm hired for the large, twenty-six-story building, known as the Lefcourt Clothing Center, which rose on the west side of the avenue between 25th and 26th Streets beginning in 1927 (figure 3.11). Although Lefcourt was able to rent the space in this men's clothing center, he never made any effort to build the other men's clothing mart buildings planned for land he had purchased for that express purpose.[56]

All of the attention that Lefcourt gave to positioning himself as a builder and not a speculator, and the care involved in the design, construction, and maintenance of his buildings was not enough to overcome the very personal criticism of elite architect and critic Kenneth Murchison, who named Lefcourt

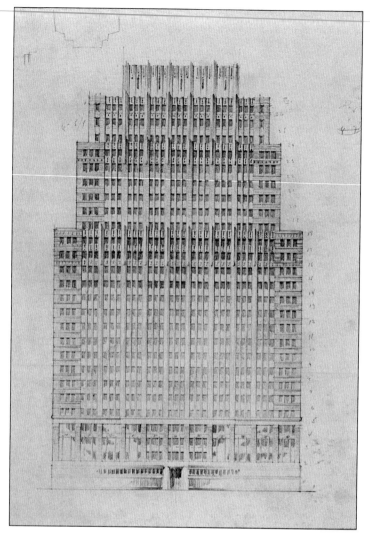

Figure 3.11. Drawing of the front elevation of the Lefcourt Clothing Center by Ely Jacques Kahn. Avery Architecture and Fine Arts Library, Ely Jacques Kahn Collection, Columbia University in the City of New York.

as an example of what he saw as the worst excesses of Jewish builders. In a short piece titled "Hebrew Architecture," written in 1929 in his monthly column in the journal the *Architect*, Murchison declared,

> The speculative builders of New York are . . . building merchants and building brokers. They are mostly of the Hebraic persuasion and they can out-trade us Christian martyrs eleven times out of ten. They build as they buy

any other goods, where they can get them cheapest. Occasionally, but rarely, they swallow hard and hire a good architect. But not often. They care nothing for tradition, nothing for architectural beauty, nothing for any of those ideas and purposes for which the Ecole des Beaux-Arts and our American schools of architecture were founded.

After describing one of Lefcourt's buildings, Murchison concludes, "Mr. Lefcourt's architects are of course unnamed. But Mr. Haas [Louis Haas, Lefcourt's assistant, who supervised construction] is. And there you are, fellow architects, there you are."[57] With his name prominently displayed on many building, Lefcourt was an easy target. This disparaging piece published in a prestigious journal counteracted everything Lefcourt claimed to stand for, including quality construction and good design, and it was couched in overtly anti-Semitic terms. Lefcourt complained to the journal's editor, George S. Chappell, who responded with an editorial published a few months after Murchison's initial statement:

> In our July issue our animated correspondent, Mr. Murchison, made certain comments on speculative builders and their often anonymous architects, specifying with perhaps unnecessary directness those of the Jewish race in general and Mr. A. E. Lefcourt in particular. Mr. Lefcourt has taken these remarks very much to heart and charges *The Architect* as a publication and Mr. Murchison as an individual with bitter race prejudices and religious animosity. . . . We consider this interpretation exaggerated and unwarranted by the text itself. . . . We realize that an affront has been given where none was intended and we are heartily sorry for it. We tender to Mr. Lefcourt and his associates our sincere apologies for any unintended hurt and we trust that he and they will accept them in the friendly spirit in which they are offered.[58]

Lefcourt was a great success within his world of Jewish developers, with assets valued at over $100 million.[59] During his life he was lauded in real estate publications and honored at banquets. But he could never transcend the world of Jewish speculative development, at least not in the eyes of the elite architecture world. This, however, did not stop Lefcourt from planning ever more ambitious projects. In 1929 construction was completed on the Lefcourt-National Building, on the southeast corner of Fifth Avenue and East 43rd Street, the tallest office building on Fifth Avenue, rising higher even than the namesake building of another major builder of the era, Fred F. French, located only two blocks to the north. Ironically, the Lefcourt-National Building replaced one of New York's most famous synagogues, Temple Emanu-El's grand Moorish style building that had been sold in 1926; Lefcourt, who was a member of the congregation, purchased the property from a land speculator in 1927.[60] Also in 1929 he announced plans, ultimately unsuccessful, for the world's tallest building on the northwest corner of Broadway and 49th Street.[61] As his building portfolio expanded, Lefcourt

moved into finance and banking. He established the Lefcourt Realty Corporation in 1928, a stock company that took control of five of Lefcourt's buildings,
with the option to purchase others at cost. The intent of this corporation was
to sell stock to large numbers of individuals, including building tenants, to help
finance construction. A year later, he founded the Lefcourt National Bank &
Trust Company, with its banking hall in the corner of the Lefcourt-Normandie
Building. Lefcourt's timing could not have been worse. With the onset of the
Great Depression and the resulting collapse of the real estate and finance markets, neither venture succeeded. In August 1930 Lefcourt resigned as president of
the bank, ostensibly because he could not devote the necessary time to this job
and manage his real estate and construction business, but, in reality, because of
the precipitous decline in the stock of the bank and of its affiliate, the Normandie
National Securities Corp., held largely by tenants in Lefcourt's buildings.[62] Law-
suits ensued over management of the securities company, but the suits were
settled out of court and Lefcourt's culpability cannot be determined.[63] In 1932
Lefcourt resigned from the realty company and, as tenants sought to cut back on
their space, rent rolls declined, and foreclosures loomed.

In January 1929 Lefcourt told a *New York Times* reporter that "if something
should happen tomorrow to sweep away every dollar I have in the world, I don't
believe I would be frightened. With the experience of the past thirty years to
guide me I could rebuild my fortune in half the time it has taken me to make
it."[64] Lefcourt was never able to validate this claim, for he died of a heart attack
only a few months after losing his business. A man who had once run a "veri-
table monarchy in real estate circles," a man whose marketing prowess resulted
in his being dubbed "the man who never fails," a man who built a business worth
well over $100 million, died with an estate valued at only $2,500.[65] Although
his empire had collapsed, in death he was eulogized as one of the great builders
of New York. More than one thousand people attended his funeral at Temple
Emanu-El, including many of the leading manufacturers and real estate owners
in the Garment District.[66]

Lefcourt's life was an iconic Jewish American rags-to-riches story—immigrant
youth brought up in a Lower East Side tenement apartment; pluck, luck, and hard
work resulting in success in the quintessentially Jewish garment business; and
then further success as a major real estate tycoon. Lefcourt was the largest developer in the new Garment District and his buildings remain a major presence in
that district. He also expanded his building empire to other sections of the city,
notably in his construction of office buildings on prestigious Midtown and Lower
Manhattan sites. While the sheer scale of his accomplishments dwarfs that of
most other builders of the period, he was not the only Jewish developer who rose
from immigrant poverty to success in New York's speculative real estate world.
Abraham Bricken, working largely in the Garment District; Irwin Chanin, building in the nearby fur district before erecting the magnificent Chanin Building on

Lexington Avenue and East 42nd Street; Abe N. Adelsohn, a garment loft builder, who went on to build the prominent Squibb Building on Fifth Avenue and 58th Street; and Henry Mandel, builder of skyscrapers and the monumental London Terrace apartment complex on West 23rd and 24th Streets, are but four of the most successful of Lefcourt's peers. These four men, like Lefcourt himself, rose to the peak of their profession in the 1920s and early 1930s, before the real estate slump caused by the Depression thwarted, at least temporarily, their ambitions and their fortunes. They were such successful developers that they were lauded by their contemporaries as creators of the city's skyline. But they were unusual only in the scope of their real estate enterprises. Other Jewish developers, working on a smaller scale and at times only as a professional sideline, erected thousands of buildings in New York during the boom years of the 1920s, ranging from modest apartment houses to great commercial skyscrapers.

Jewish immigrants and their children seized on speculative building as a way to make a living or augment an income in an era when discrimination and quotas restricted their access to many career paths.[67] Indeed, speculative development had long been a field open to immigrants since the developer, working independently, was not limited by discriminatory hiring practices and could generally rely on his compatriots for financial investment. Thus, Irish builders erected many of the nineteenth-century row houses that line the streets of Manhattan and Brooklyn, and German immigrants built many of the tenements that appeared on the Lower East Side and in other immigrant districts of the city in the 1860s and 1870s. As the character of immigration to New York changed, so too did the ethnicity of speculative builders. By the early twentieth century, Jews had come to dominate the speculative building world.[68] Abraham Schepper, writing in the *American Hebrew* in 1913, explained that Jews were especially attracted to property ownership and building because they "lived for many years under political conditions which practically prohibit land owing, [thus] the foreign Jew becomes intoxicated with the idea of being able at last to buy land and build in safety, and he considers the privilege of owning land without molestation as one of the great outward symbols of American freedom."[69]

Jewish immigrants prospered as real estate developers, but as architect Kenneth Murchison's anti-Semitic comments in his column in the journal the *Architect* made clear, the elites of New York abhorred speculative design and construction, especially because many successful buildings were erected by Jews. While Murchison's criticism clearly stung Lefcourt and insulted scores of other Jewish builders, it certainly did not stop them from building. Lefcourt and his compatriots, working in the Garment District or in the new apartment house neighborhoods of Brooklyn and the Bronx, building upper middle-class apartment buildings on West End Avenue and Central Park West and skyscraper office buildings in Lower Manhattan and Midtown came to dominate the world of speculative building in New York and established the foundation

~~on which later generations of Jews~~ continued to build up the New York. Indeed, among the earliest developers in the Garment District was Alexander Tishman, who established a family building empire that continues to this day.

Abraham Lefcourt never had the chance to rebuild his lost fortune after his real estate holdings collapsed with the onset of the Depression, but he left an impressive legacy of buildings in the Garment District that remain vital to New York City's economy, some of which are still used by firms in the garment business. Today the name Lefcourt means little to most New Yorkers, but his name is still emblazoned on at least half a dozen prominent buildings, testament not only to his importance to New York, but also to the importance of other Jewish builders—well-known and anonymous, large and small, and their mostly little-known architects who were responsible for creating the fabric of many of New York City's twentieth-century neighborhoods.

APPENDIX: BUILDINGS ERECTED BY A. E. LEFCOURT

Date given is year building permit was issued. All buildings are extant.

48–54 West 25th Street, between Broadway and Sixth Avenues. Loft. George & Edward Blum, 1910.

132–142 West 37th Street, between Sixth Avenue and Broadway. Loft. George & Edward Blum, 1913.

42–46 West 38th Street, between Fifth and Sixth Avenues. Loft. George & Edward Blum, 1915.

Times Square Station Post Office. 223–241 West 38th Street, between Seventh and Eighth Avenues. John T. Dunn, 1921.

237–239 West 37th Street, between Seventh and Eighth Avenues. Loft. George & Edward Blum, 1922.

246–250 West 38th Street, between Seventh and Eighth Avenues. Loft. George & Edward Blum, 1923.

Lefcourt-Marlboro Building. 1359 Broadway, northwest corner of West 36th Street. Loft. George & Edward Blum, 1923

Lefcourt-Central Building. 148–156 West 37th Street, between Broadway and Seventh Avenue. Loft. George & Edward Blum, 1924.

Lefcourt-Empire Building. 989 Sixth Avenue, between West 36th and 37th Streets. Loft. Buchman & Kahn, 1925.

Lefcourt-Madison Building. 20 East 34th Street, between Fifth and Madison Avenues. Loft. Buchman & Kahn, 1925.

Lefcourt-Manhattan Building. 1412 Broadway, northeast corner of West 39th Street. Twenty-three-story loft. George & Edward Blum, 1925.

Lefcourt-State Building. 1375 Broadway, northwest corner of West 37th Street. Loft. Buchman & Kahn, 1926.

Lefcourt Clothing Center. 275 Seventh Avenue, between 25th and 26th Streets. Loft. Buchman & Kahn, 1927.

Lefcourt-National Building. 521 Fifth Avenue, northeast corner of East 43rd Street. Office building. Shreve & Lamb, 1927.

Lefcourt-Colonial Building. 295 Madison Avenue, southeast corner of East 41st Street. Office building. Bark & Djorup, 1928.

Lefcourt-Normandie Building. 1384 Broadway, southwest corner of West 38th Street. Loft. Bark & Djorup, 1928.

Lefcourt-Manhattan Building Addition. 1418 Broadway, between West 39th and 40th Streets. Loft. Victor A. Bark Jr., 1929.

Lefcourt-Newark Building. Centre Market Plaza, Newark, New Jersey. Office building. Frank Grad, 1929.

Lefcourt-Alan Building (Brill Building). 1619 Broadway, northwest corner of West 49th Street. Office building erected in place of proposed world's tallest building. Victor A. Bark Jr., 1930.

Lefcourt-ITT Building. 67 Broad Street, southeast corner of Beaver Street. Office building. Buchman & Kahn, 1927; addition, Louis S. Weeks, 1930.

Seville Towers (now Essex House). 160 Central Park West, between Sixth and Seventh Avenues. Apartment building. Frank Grad, 1930.

NOTES

The author would like to thank graduate students Cristiana Peña, Angela Curmi, Mary Nastasi, and Jørgen Cleeman for their research assistance, and the University Seminars, which supported the acquisition of images. Research at Cornell University's Catherwood Library Kheel Center was supported by a grant from the Leon Levy Foundation. The acquisition of images was supported by a grant from the Warner Fund at the University Seminars at Columbia University; material in this article was presented in a lecture "Hiding in Plain Sight: The Vernacular Buildings of New York City," at the University Seminars Annual Tannenbaum Lecture.

1. Abraham E. Lefcourt, "Needle Trade District Not Yet Completed," *New York Tribune*, January 25, 1925.

2. *Our City—Our Union* (New York: International Ladies' Garment Workers Union, 1940), n.p.

3. Clarence I. Freed, "Romance of Realty: Men Who Have Become Masters of the Metropolis through Real Estate Enterprise," *American Hebrew* 120 (April 1927): 742.

4. "Lefcourt Buildings Investment Large," *Wall Street Journal*, July 28, 1928; Paul Masserman and Max Baker, *The Jews Come to America* (New York: Bloch, 1932), 447; Helen Hirsch, "Jewish Pioneers in the Construction of New York City," *Jewish Forum* 31 (September 1948): 183–184.

5. *Lefcourt City* (privately printed, 1930), 4; "A Builder Who Changed Mid-Manhattan's Skyline," *New York Times*, November 20, 1932, sec. 10, p. 1.

6. For the ready-to-wear industry, see, for example, Nancy L. Green, *Ready-to-Wear and Ready-to-Work: A Century of Industry and Immigrants in Paris and New York* (Durham, NC: Duke University Press, 1997), 20–24; Florence S. Richards, *The Ready-to-Wear Industry 1900–1950* (New York: Fairchild, 1951); Claudia B. Kidwell and Margaret C. Christman, *Suiting Everyone: The Democratization of Clothing in America* (Washington, DC: Smithsonian Institution Press, 1974); and Gabriel Goldstein, ed., *A Perfect Fit: The Garment Industry and American Jewry 1860–1960* (New York: Yeshiva University Museum, 2005).

7. Nancy L. Green, "Sweatshop Migrations: The Garment Industry between Home and Shop," in *The Landscape of Modernity: Essays on New York City, 1900–1940*, ed. David Ward and Olivier Zunz (New York: Russell Sage Foundation, 1992), 214–215; and Daniel Soyer, "The Rise and Fall of the Garment Industry in New York City," in *A Coat of Many Colors: Immigration, Globalism, and Reform in the New York City Garment Industry*, ed. Daniel Soyer (New York: Fordham University Press, 2005), 5–11.

8. *Perfect Fit*, 34–41.

9. United States Factory Inspector, *Report* (1897), 45, cited in Judith Greenfeld, "The Role of the Jews in the Development of the Clothing Industry in the United States," *YIVO Annual of Jewish Social Science* 2–3 (1947/1948): 203.

10. For tenement factories, see Daniel Soyer, "Cockroach Capitalists: Jewish Contractors at the Turn of the Twentieth Century," in Soyer, *Coat of Many Colors*, 99–102.

11. James Connolly, *Seventh Annual Report of the Factory Inspectors for the State of New York* (Albany, NY: Lyon, 1894), 14; Andrew S. Dolkart, *Biography of a Tenement House in New York City: An Architectural History of 97 Orchard Street* (Santa Fe: Center for American Places, 2007), 55–56.

12. David Von Drehle, *Triangle* (New York: Atlantic Monthly Press, 2003); Leon Stein, *The Triangle Fire* (Philadelphia: Lippincott, 1962); and Gale Harris, *Brown Building (originally Asch Building) Designation Report* (New York: Landmarks Preservation Commission, 2003).

13. "In the Real Estate Field: Sixteen-Story Loft for 25th Street," *New York Times*, March 18, 1910, 16.

14. Will Irwin, *Highlights of Manhattan* (New York: Century, 1926), 318.

15. "Menace to Trade on Fifth Avenue," *New York Times*, January 16, 1916, sec. 7, p. 5.

16. See, for example, *New York Sun*, *New York Times*, *New York Tribune*, and *New York World*, March 5, 1916; and *New York Evening Post* and *Women's Wear*, March 6, 1916.

17. "New Garment Centre," *New York Times*, June 19, 1921. For the Garment Center Capitol and the Shall We Save New York campaign, see Andrew S. Dolkart, "The Fabric of New York's Garment District: Architecture and Development in an Urban Cultural Landscape," *Buildings and Landscapes* 18, no. 1 (Spring 2011): 14–42.

18. W. Parker Chase, *New York: The Wonder City* (New York: Wonder City, 1932), 214.

19. For Kanner, see "Mack Kanner, 93, Major Builder Who Developed Garment District," *New York Times*, April 8, 1979. For Singer, see "Immigrant Lad in 1900 Is Bank Executive Now: Business Chiefs to Pay Honor to Saul Singer," *New York Times*, February 25, 1925; "Saul Singer, Ex-Aide of Bank of U.S., 66," *New York Times*, March 2, 1948; "Rites Today for Saul Singer: Dynamic Figure in Many Fields," *Women's Wear Daily*, March 3, 1948.

20. "350 Honor Officers of Garment Centre," *New York Times*, March 5, 1922.

21. "Garment Centre Expands Westward," *New York Times*, July 31, 1921.

22. "Many New Buildings for Garment Trades Reveal Seventh Avenue's Business Growth," *New York Times*, August 27, 1922; "Max Aronson Dies: Realty Investor, 83," *New York Times*, January 9, 1959. Aronson's two early loft buildings were located at 229 and 242 West 36th Street.

23. Hirsch, "Jewish Pioneers," 184; "Many New Buildings."

24. "Active Trading in the Midtown Loft Zone: Many Deals Closed Last Week," *New York Times*, December 18, 1921; see also "Many New Buildings" and Martin Cleary, *Mid-Manhattan* (New York: 42nd Street Property Owners and Merchants Association, 1929), 178.

25. Abraham E. Lefcourt, quoted in "$20,000,000 Involved in Three Midtown Deals: New Structures for Plots Bought by Lefcourt," *New York Times*, June 17 1923; see also C. A. Rieser, "Achieving Success in Two Conspicuous Fields of Industry," *Real Estate Magazine of New York* 11 (September 1923): 501; Harry A. Stewart, "Don't Keep Half Your Brain Busy Trying to Hide Something," *American Magazine* 97 (January 1924): 213; Abraham E. Lefcourt, "Housing the Garment Trade," in *Broadway: The Grand Canyon of American Business* (New York: Broadway Association, 1926), 136; *Mid-Manhattan*, 215; and "Lefcourt Calls Adler Courageous," *Women's Wear Daily*, December 17, 1929.

26. "Push Madison Square as Center of Women's Garment Trade," *New York Tribune*, July 8, 1921.

27. "Trade Shocked by Sudden Death of A. E. Lefcourt, Long Realty, Garment Leader," *Women's Wear Daily*, November 14, 1932.

28. For the name changes of Samuel Lefkowitz, Charles S. Lefkowitz (Abraham's brother), and Abraham E. Lefkowitz, see "Name Changes," October 16, 1909, *Laws of the State of New York State*, 2:2095, Albany; United States Department of Commerce and Labor, Immigration Service, New York Passenger Lists, List of United States Citizens, S. S.

Imperator, May 3, 1914; Standard Certificate of Death, Abraham E. Lefcourt, registered no. 24300, November 13, 1932, Bureau of Records, Department of Health of the City of New York; United States Census, 1900, ED 889; 1910, ED 706; 1920, ED 694; 1930, ED 31–566; all previous information is provided in http://www.ancestry-library.com. See also "Trade Shocked"; "Mid-Manhattan's Skyline"; C. G. Poore, "A Skyscraper Builder Began as a Newsboy," *New York Times*, January 20, 1929; Standard Certificate of Death, Samuel Lefcourt, registered no. 14937, May 23, 1923.

29. Several versions of this story were published, including "Mid-Manhattan's Skyline"; "Owns Corner Where He Once Sold Papers, *New York Times*, January 5, 1926, 1; Stewart, "Half Your Brain," 66; Lefcourt to Build on Hotel Normandie Site," *New York Times*, January 5, 1926; "His Real Estate Creed is 100 Per Cent Location," *Building Investment and Maintenance* 2 (June 1927): 29; and Poore, "Skyscraper Builder."

30. New York State Department of Labor, *Second Annual Industrial Directory of New York State* (Albany: State Department of Labor, 1915).

31. Gus Tyler, *Look for the Union Label: A History of the International Ladies' Garment Workers Union* (Armonk, NY: Sharpe, 1995), 67–74; Tyler incorrectly gives Lefcourt's initials as "E. J." See also "Cloakmakers Unite to Fight Strikers," *New York Times*, July 12, 1910.

32. For the Blums, see Andrew S. Dolkart and Susan Tunick, *George and Edward Blum: Texture and Design in New York Apartment House Architecture* (New York: Friends of Terra Cotta Press, 1993).

33. "Another Building in Seventh Avenue Zone for Needle Trade," *New York Tribune*, December 14, 1919, sec. 3, p. 7;"Plan New $1,000,000 Post Office Building for Times Square Section to Relieve Congestion," *New York Times*, August 8, 1920; and "Gov't Gets $1,000,000 Postal Station in Times Sq.," *New York Tribune*, June 20, 1921.

34. "Active Trading."

35. "Garment Centre Buildings," *New York Times*, August 20, 1922.

36. "Two New Lefcourt Buildings to Be Ready Early Next Year," *Women's Wear*, March 25, 1922; "New Lefcourt Building," *New York Times*, March 26, 1922; "Garment Trade Building," *New York Times*, March 26, 1922; "New Millinery Centre Building to Be Erected on Seventh Ave.," *New York Times*, January 7, 1923; *Lefcourt City*, 26–27.

37. Rieser, "Achieving Success."

38. "Ultra Modern 'Garment Palace' to Replace Old Marlborough Hotel," *Broadway* 3 (December 1923): n.p.

39. "Garment Palace."

40. Arthur Pound, *The Golden Earth: The Story of Manhattan's Landed Wealth* (New York: Macmillan, 1935), 229.

41. *Lefcourt City*, 4.

42. Artist E. H. Suydam created one such image in black and white in 1928, published in C. Y. Taylor, "A Master Builder," *Edison Monthly* 20 (November 1928): 244, and reprinted in Clary, *Mid-Manhattan* (New York: 42nd Street Property Owners Association, 1929), 16. Later colorized, this image appears as the cover of *Lefcourt City*. In 1932 a more expansive drawing, including all of Lefcourt's buildings, was published in "Mid-Manhattan's Skyline."

43. "Lefcourt Building Investment Large," *Wall Street Journal*, July 28, 1928.

44. Lefcourt, "Needle Trade District."

45. Taylor, "Master Builder," 247.

46. "Lefcourt Marlboro Building, New York City," *Architecture and Building* 62 (May 1925): 42–43, plates 107–108.

47. Victor A. Bark Jr. designed several buildings for Lefcourt both during his partnership with Erhard Djorup and in independent practice. Bark was born in New York to Swedish parents; see United States Census, 1920, ED 1331.

48. For Buchman & Kahn and their buildings, see Jewel Stern and John A. Stuart, *Ely Jacques Kahn, Architect: Beaux-Arts to Modernism in New York* (New York: Norton, 2006).

49. Charles F. Noyes, "Cites Garment Men in City's Realty Growth," *Women's Wear Daily*, October 11, 1929.

50. "Lefcourt Says Apparel Trade Zone Will Expand," *Women's Wear*, October 14, 1927.

51. Taylor, "Master Builder," 247.

52. "His Real Estate Creed" reports that the lease was worth "more than a million dollars"; "Lefcourt Buildings Investment Large" provides a value of half a million dollars.

53. Lists of tenants and their field of merchandise appear in an advertisement for the Lefcourt Realty Corporation, "A Guidepost for Discriminating Buyers," *Women's Wear Daily*, October 27, 1931.

54. Conditions in the men's wear industry through 1922 are discussed in detail in Benjamin M. Selekman, Henriette R. Walter, and E. J. Couper, "The Clothing and Textiles Industries," in *Regional Survey of New York and its Environs*, vol. 1B (New York: Regional Plan of New York and Its Environs, 1925), 30–49.

55. *Lefcourt City*, 15.

56. $10,00,000 Lefcourt Building for Clothing Industry," *New York Times*, September 26, 1926; "First Step in Establishing New Clothing Centre," *Real Estate Record and Builders Guide* 120 (September 1927): 7; "Here Lefcourt May Build New Clothing Mart," *Women's Wear*, November 18, 1925; "Plans New Centre for Clothing Trade," *New York Times*, November 19, 1925; Stern and Stuart, *Ely Jacques Kahn*, 121–123.

57. Kenneth Murchison, "Mr. Murchison of New York Says—Hebrew Architecture," *Architect* 12 (July 1929): 456.

58. "In Justice to Mr. Lefcourt," *Architect* 13 (October 1920): 21, 23.

59. "A. E. Lefcourt Dies Suddenly at 55," *New York Times*, November 14, 1932.

60. For the Lefcourt-National Building, see "40-Story Skyscraper for Fifth Avenue," *New York Times*, January 25, 1928; "Lefcourt-National Building, New York," *Architecture and Building* 61 (May 1929): 137, plates 88–92; "Lefcourt-National Building, New York," *Architectural Record* 67 (April 1930): 341, 348–349; and "Lefcourt-National Building, New York," *Architectural Forum* 52 (June 1930): 843–844.

61. "World's Tallest Bldg. Planned by Lefcourt," *Women's Wear Daily*, October 4, 1929. In 1930 Lefcourt erected the eleven-story Lefcourt-Alan Building on the site as a memorial to his recently deceased son; Lefcourt soon defaulted on his land lease and the building became known as the Brill Building; see Christopher Gray, "Streetscapes: The Brill Building; Built with a Broken Heart," *New York Times*, January 3, 1910; and Matthew A. Postal, *Brill Building Designation Report* (New York: Landmarks Preservation Commission, 2010). A drawing of the planned skyscraper appears in *Lefcourt City*, 30.

62. "Lefcourt Retires from Presidency," *Wall Street Journal*, August 8, 1930; "Trade Shocked."

63. The case was settled in late 1932, shortly after his death; see "Normandie Suit Settled," *New York Times*, December 31, 1932.

64. Poore, "Skyscraper Builder." Lefcourt made a similar boast in 1924 in Stewart, "Half Your Brain," 67.

65. *Lefcourt City*, 6; "Wills for Probate," *New York Times*, December 15, 1932.

66. "Impressive Tribute Paid to Lefcourt," *Women's Wear Daily*, November 15, 1932.

67. For a discussion of discrimination written at the time, see Heywood Broun and George Britt, *Christians Only: A Study of Prejudice* (New York: Vanguard, 1931).

68. Italians, primarily represented by the extended Paterno family, were also heavily involved in high-end apartment house development.

69. Abraham Schepper, "Jews as Builders of New York," *American Hebrew*, July 4, 1913, 23.

〜

CHAPTER 4

Success from Scrap and Secondhand Goods

JEWISH BUSINESSMEN IN THE MIDWEST, 1890–1930

Jonathan Z. S. Pollack

Bernard Horwich lived a life that defines the Yiddish term "macher." Born in the Suwalki *gubernia* on the western edge of the Russian Empire, Horwich came to Chicago around 1880. During his time in Chicago, Horwich founded the Order Brith Abraham, the largest mutual-aid society for Russian Jews; served as the first president of the Order Knights of Zion, a Chicago-based Zionist society that was the first Zionist group in the United States; and helped create the Federated Jewish Charities of Chicago, bringing small, financially unstable organizations together under a more professional umbrella. At the same time that Horwich developed Chicago's Jewish organizations and philanthropies, he also served as the president of several Chicago banks, and he was appointed Cook County election commissioner, the first Jew to hold that position.[1]

Horwich's professional and commercial achievements prompt one to ask how this Jewish immigrant, at that time, managed to reach such prominent positions. Horwich's entry in the 1924 *History of the Jews of Chicago* yields no clue, other than to say that he turned his business over to his son while pursuing these philanthropic ventures. Horwich's son's biography in the same volume yields equally scant information, only than to say that Arthur Horwich worked for his father after a couple years at Northwestern University and that the younger Horwich also followed his father into a bank presidency and Jewish philanthropic work.[2]

A 1942 form letter, apparently sent by Arthur Horwich to scrap dealers around the country, provides one possible answer:

Dear Sir:

CATTLE HAIR!

CATTLE TAILS!

Have you any, Sir?

If you now can sell them, then to our firm refer;

We are always buying—in lots both big and small—

and are prepared to pay top market price for all.

Let us have your offers, and how you make your sales,

that is, the way you put up, count and select your Tails.

Let us know the quantity, and when you'll ship the lot,

We'll try to do the business on all the Hair you've got.

Yours truly,

THE HORWICH VITKIN COMPANY

BY: A. N. Horwich

The firm's stationery promotes them as "manufacturers of HAIR," and "buyers of horse tails, cattle tails, horse hair, cattle hair, and hog hair." At the bottom of the letterhead is a drawing of a building that appears to take up a city block, encompassing a five-story office building and a huge factory, with trucks and train cars moving in and out of it.[3]

The Horwich family is a great example of an overlooked "Jewish" occupation—dealing in scrap materials. Although Bernard Horwich discusses his career in the hide and hair business briefly in his autobiography, referring to how operating a business in that line prepared him to do the same once he had settled in Chicago, other chroniclers of Chicago's Jewish community were apparently squeamish about naming the exact nature of Horwich's business. Despite the unnamed source of the Horwich family fortune, the sums involved were obviously quite large, enabling the Horwich family to become important leaders in Chicago's Jewish community.[4]

Despite the dominance of Jewish entrepreneurs in the scrap business—Jews were said to own 90 percent of scrap-iron businesses and virtually all of the nonferrous scrap metal, scrap paper, cotton rag, wool rag, and scrap rubber businesses by 1929—academic literature on the Jewish presence in this field is extremely light. A 1941 study of Detroit's Jewish economy focuses on scrap dealers, and several historians have attempted studies in cities where some of those peddlers handled scrap. Research on the geography and economics of the scrap industry does not mention the industry's Jewish flavor. Environmental historian Carl Zimring has examined scrap from an environmental-history perspective, portraying the scrap business as the first recycling industry. Zimring has also examined scrap yards as examples of Americans' ambivalence toward consumption and waste, positing that the United States is a throwaway society that is, nonetheless, squeamish about that which is thrown away. Although Zimring mentions the Jewish and Italian ethnicity of some entrepreneurs who built and operated scrap yards, his main focus is an environmental and cultural history of scrap, focusing on the largest national firms and scrap-metal trade associations. Zimring's work is a major improvement in the scholarship beyond the handful of industry histories written by trade associations in the scrap business and scrap CEO's who've written vanity press histories of their own enterprises. Although the latter works are rich on detail and help explain how a wrecked car, for example, becomes processed into different types and grades of scrap metal, they lack a broader historical context and tend to downplay the Jewish roots of and Jewish contributions to this business.[5]

The Horwich family trajectory, from highly motivated entrepreneurs in the first generation to university-educated professionals in the second generation, is representative of many Jewish families in this business during the late nineteenth and early twentieth centuries. The family's philanthropy makes their story even more of a proud tribute to the accomplishments of American Jews. What demands closer examination is the economic niche in which the Horwich family prospered—scrap materials.

Due to the disdain for materials thrown or given away, defined as "secondhand," "scrap," or "junk," and repurposed for profit by Jewish entrepreneurs, a metonymic slide from "junk" to "Jews" created a stigma on the people engaged in these economic endeavors. Though dealing in scrap, secondhand, and surplus materials could be profitable, the economic advantages carried social risks.[6] In addition to a negative association with money lending, dating back centuries, dealing in scrap and secondhand materials also compelled entrepreneurs to deal with items that other people had discarded. Anthropologists who study how cultures make decisions about what constitutes "wastes" or other discarded goods conclude, as one would expect, that people who deal in some way with discarded goods and materials, or who live in proximity to them, are placed on a low level socially. In a similar vein, rhetoricians describe a "metonymic slide," in which the public's emotions and affects can be stirred to equate people with unpleasant characteristics.

From the perspective of Jewish entrepreneurs, however, reupholstered furniture, discarded hides, scrap paper and metals, and military surplus goods represented a possible source of income. Like Jewish entrepreneurs who made a living in other fields, dealers in scrap practiced a kind of "entrepreneurial bricolage"—making do with the materials at hand and creating networks in a new and growing industry. The creation of Jewish networks in the American scrap business, and the age-old suspicions that these networks raised, is similar to other self-created Jewish business networks. In the nineteenth century Jewish clothing and dry goods dealers built networks of wholesalers, retailers, and peddlers. In the twentieth century free-loan societies served as proto–credit

unions that provided material assistance to Jewish entrepreneurs and reinforced intra-Jewish ties.[7]

Although there had long been a small trade in scrap metals, by the 1880s, the
beginning of large-scale Jewish migration from Eastern Europe, the demand
accelerated. For the next sixty years, the scrap business was a classic example
of an immigrant-centered entrepreneurial niche. This concept, studied in
detail by sociologists such as Edna Bonacich, Ivan Light, and Stephen Gold, is
structured around a consistent formula: because new technologies create new
jobs, some kind of dirty, low-status work needs to be done. Immigrants who
have been entrepreneurs in other countries come to the United States, and the
new arrivals do not define "desirable" and "undesirable" jobs in the same way
that native-born Americans do. These factors, taken together, create an ethnic
niche economy. Members of the ethnic group who carve out a particular niche
tend to continue working in the niche for one to three generations, until newer
technologies make the niche obsolete or until subsequent generations adopt
native-born attitudes and leave the business.[8]

The Jewish niche economy of the scrap business was an integral, though
overlooked, part of the hide and leather, paper, and steel industries across the
United States. As these industries were an especially strong part of the "rust
belt" economy of the northern Midwest/Great Lakes states, the Jewish presence
in the scrap business was especially important for the formation and growth of
Jewish communities in these areas.[9]

Although the trade in secondhand goods and scrap has been identified with
Jews for centuries, scholars have seldom highlighted the Jewish role in these
fields, and Jewish families who have participated in these fields have often
downplayed their history in this particular economic niche.[10] For these reasons,
the history of midwestern scrap dealers is critical to the annals of American
Jewish history, serving both as an example of "communalist" and "dispersionist" approaches to American Jewish history. Studying the history of Jewish
scrap dealers helps us understand the role of commerce in shaping individual
Jewish communities or the Jewish life of an entire region. At the same time, the
history of Jewish participation in the scrap industry gives us insight into Jewish
entrepreneurs' role in contributing to local and regional industrial growth.[11]

The zigzagging nature of the demand for and availability of these commodities is a classic example of the risky nature of many "Jewish" enterprises, in the
United States and abroad. The importance of "handshake deals" and informal
lines of credit are a critical part of the scrap and secondhand businesses, as they
have been historically important to other Jewish businesses across time and
place.[12] Examining the role of scrap and secondhand businesses in the Midwest
and, within that, the discrete geographic area of Madison, Wisconsin, allows
us to see how entrepreneurs in these areas built Jewish communities from their
business connections.

EVOLUTION OF THE SCRAP BUSINESS ECONOMY:
HIDES, RAGS, IRON, AND OTHER METALS

As a working definition, the term "scrap business" generally describes the collection, storage, brokering, and sale of discarded materials that have potential for reuse or repurposing. Materials collected as scrap, for the purposes of this essay, include animal hides and skins, paper and rags, old iron and steel, and nonferrous metals such as copper and aluminum. Secondhand goods, such as car parts, used furniture, and government surplus, also fit into this definition of "scrap," as they were often collected alongside the first group of scrap materials and separated out to be sold more or less "as is." Collection and dumping of household trash, though, as it does not have the capability to be reused or recycled, does not fall under this essay's definition of scrap.

In the United States, the collection of scrap materials began with peddlers, who had been a fixture of American Jewish economic activity since the early 1800s. While traditional peddling required peddlers to knock on strangers' doors and urge them to purchase the random items that the peddler was carrying that day, "collecting junk" reversed the roles of buyer and seller. By bringing the hides, skins, rags, paper, and metal they collected to a dealer who sorted, graded, and brokered the material, peddlers were a source of important raw materials used in tanneries, paper mills, and steel mills. Peddlers would inquire about their customers' apparently discarded materials—old furniture, rusting farm implements, stacks of rags or newspapers—and offer to buy them for a small sum of money, or even trade them for new dry goods from their packs. Frequently, the customers who possessed the scrap items refused payment or trade for them, even offering on occasion to help the peddler load the items onto a cart or truck to be hauled away. Many peddlers preferred to be in the position of offering to buy unwanted items from customers, rather than trying to sell potential customers goods that they might not want.[13]

From the initial point of acquiring scrap materials, peddlers would sell their goods to entrepreneurs, then known as "junk dealers," who dealt in many of these scrap materials. The smallest yards, and those operating in areas that had few scrap businesses, were called "country shippers"; they collected and sorted scrap materials and shipped them to retail dealers, who specialized in one or more types of scrap materials. For materials that could be classified into grades, like hides, rags and papers, and metals, retail dealers sorted and assigned the classifications. Wholesalers bought from retailers and sold the fully processed materials to mills and factories that used scrap as a raw material in the production of leather, paper, and steel.[14]

In addition to scrap that needed extensive classifying and processing, scrap dealers also separated out materials that, with little or no repair, could be resold to customers at a price below what new products would cost. As part of a diverse business in "junk," peddlers, country shippers, and retailers would often deal in used furniture and clothing, used auto parts, government surplus, and the merchandise of bankrupt stores. As these ventures dealt with the same kinds of risks and rewards as other scrap dealers—an uncertain supply of salable material, the ability to buy unwanted items at rock-bottom prices yet still make a profit, and a less-than-savory reputation among much of the general public—it is appropriate to examine these enterprises as part of a broader examination of scrap.

Collecting scrap materials for reuse has always been part of industry. For centuries, metalsmiths melted down old metals to reuse it in new craftwork. Paper was made from old rags until huge demand for paper made it more feasible to make pulp out of "virgin fibers," or trees. The open-hearth method of steelmaking, which grew in popularity after 1900, made it possible for steel mills to use a higher percentage of scrap metal to "new" metal (forged from iron ore) to create steel. The later adoption of electric-furnace steelmaking allowed an even higher ratio of scrap metal to iron ore. An obstacle to paper or steel mills obtaining scrap was finding steady sources of scrap materials. Only the largest paper mills, steel mills, and packinghouses could afford to run their own "home" scrap collection; smaller firms relied on entrepreneurs who collected, processed, and sold their scrap for a regular fee.[15]

There was a clear hierarchy in the scrap business among Jewish dealers. The hide business was the least desirable line. Dealers in hides would gather skins, hair, and bones from slaughterhouses, store and cure them for a year, and sell them to tanneries, glue manufacturers, brush makers, cobblers, upholsterers, and other industries. The earthiness of working with dead bodies, the stench of this particular scrap material, and the huge supply prompted most all-purpose scrap dealers to drop this line as soon as they were able to do so.[16]

Nonetheless, Jews were well known as intermediaries in the hide business. By the early twentieth century, the major slaughterhouses were processing and selling their own hide and skin byproducts. So-called packer hides commanded a high price, due to their automated processing and uniform quality. However, small slaughterhouses, located in towns and rural areas across the United States, often depended on Jewish scrap dealers to process and sell their hides. For many small slaughterhouse owners, it seemed uneconomical to spend much effort processing hides, then studying the commodity markets to ascertain the best time to sell them, so Jewish entrepreneurs filled the gap. In other rural, cattle-ranching societies such as South Africa, Jews also dominated the hide business.[17]

Papermaking also relied on the collection, sorting, and sale of rags. In Europe, repairers and dealers in old clothes, many of whom were Jewish, would encounter clothing that was too damaged to repair. Although no one would willingly wear rags, paper mills needed a steady supply of rags for papermaking. As a result, secondhand clothing dealers also dabbled in rag collection. As happened to other entrepreneurs in the scrap industry, rag dealers' close contact with discarded materials gave them a dirty image. Although paper mills in the United States used more wood pulp for papermaking than European mills did, the fluctuating need for rags kept scrap-paper dealers in business supplying this industrial commodity.[18]

Recycling has always been part of metalworking. In steelmaking, the earliest processes required a great deal of iron ore, but over the course of the nineteenth century, new steelmaking technologies allowed the use of higher ratios of recycled steel to iron ore. As open-hearth steelmaking came to replace steel mills using the Bessemer process, the demand for scrap metals continued to accelerate, though at an erratic pace, through the mid-twentieth century. The existence of thousands of scrap yards, from small piles of metal in a residential backyard or storage shed, to wholesale yards that covered acres of railroad or waterfront property, meant that the scrap-metal markets operated with imperfect knowledge of the total supply of the scrap metal available for sale at any given time. More lucrative than scrap iron, nonferrous metals became an important category of scrap that was collected and processed in many yards. Copper and aluminum, though subject to price fluctuation like other commodities, generally yielded more money per pound than scrap iron did, so nearly all scrap-metal dealers collected as much copper as they could.[19]

SCRAP, SECONDHAND, AND SURPLUS FIRMS IN THE WORLD OF "JEWISH BUSINESS"

The idea of some businesses being especially "Jewish" is enduring and often problematic. On one hand, it seems awkward to give into stereotyping and assume that lines of business that include many Jewish entrepreneurs are, in some way, Jewish businesses; on the other, due to centuries of restriction, Jews understandably gravitated toward certain fields and away from others, even when discrimination was not an issue.[20]

Jewish dealing in scrap materials began with the quintessential position in European economies for Jews: money lending. Because people pawning their goods for a loan often deposited used and damaged goods, then became unable to make the payments necessary for them to redeem their possessions, Jewish moneylenders had to repair the goods to sell them on the open market. Jewish entrepreneurs' involvement in the sale of secondhand furniture and clothing resulted from the prevalence of clothes and furniture among the items that Europeans pawned. As a result of the connections between secondhand goods and money lending, by the late 1600s Jews in Italian cities dominated the trade in secondhand goods. In France, large-scale Jewish participation in this trade continued through the nineteenth century.[21]

~~Thanks to this long~~ historical ~~association~~ between Jewish merchants and secondhand goods, when peddlers acquired what we now call "postconsumer" scrap paper and metal, they were viewed as participants in a Jewish business. Beyond the networks of families and compatriots that brought peddlers to the upper Midwest, immigrant-settlement agencies such as the Industrial Removal Office (IRO) also saw the scrap business as a desirable economic niche for otherwise unskilled immigrants without personal connections to the job market. The IRO, which sent Jewish immigrants from New York City to cities and towns across the United States, with a particular focus outside the East Coast, had the goal of "removing" Jewish immigrants from the crowded, tubercular ghettos of the Lower East Side to remedy worker shortages in cities in the growing United States. IRO leaders sought cooperation from leaders of Jewish communities large and small in placing skilled, semiskilled, and unskilled workers, typically in factory jobs. However, relatively few Jews "removed" from New York were content with factory work. Even though factory owners were willing to employ Jews, few owners understood Jewish workers' desire to observe Shabbat and other holidays. Conversely, Jews who owned scrap yards could connect with even the greenest immigrants and could put non-English-speakers to work collecting and sorting scrap materials. Jews who found work through the IRO in scrap yards often stayed in the towns where they were sent, unlike many workers who took factory jobs.[22]

A Case Study of Madison, Wisconsin: Scrap Dealers, Crime, and Philanthropy in the Transformation of a Jewish Business Niche

Like many midwestern cities, Madison had a small German Jewish community that had settled there in the mid-nineteenth century and had dwindled to a few families by 1890. Jewish peddlers canvassed the area frequently, and several of those peddlers settled in Madison to get into the "junk business." Samuel, Isaac, Albert, and Solomon Sinaiko came to Madison after brief sojourns in other Wisconsin cities and bought a former coal yard on the Illinois Central railroad tracks at the edge of the heavily Italian and Jewish Greenbush neighborhood. By 1900 there were roughly forty Jewish households in Madison; that number nearly doubled by 1907, thanks to the dedication of a synagogue in 1906. In 1909, roughly twelve years after the Sinaiko family opened its scrap yard, the local newspaper called Samuel Sinaiko the "King of Greenbush." Around that time the Sinaiko yard made between $100,000 and $140,000 per year, equivalent to between 2 and 3 million per year in 2009 dollars.[23]

The Sinaikos, and their cousins, the eight Sweet brothers, were the founders of the Russian Jewish community in Madison. They were active in the Madison chapter of the Independent Western Star Order, a mutual-aid society that was the first Jewish organization in Madison's Russian Jewish community in 1903, and they became leaders in Agudas Achim, the Orthodox synagogue that began a year later. The Sinaiko yard became a magnet for new immigrants seeking work. In addition to hiring numerous relatives and fellow immigrants from Kapule, Minsk, local IRO agents suggested that prospective newcomers to Madison contact the Sinaikos if they were unable to find employment elsewhere. Like department-store owners before them, by the early twentieth century, the most successful scrap dealers had become major employers of their fellow Jews.[24]

This successful tale of Jewish immigrants' upward mobility carried a dark side as well. At the confluence of scrap, "shadiness," and Jewish charitable traditions lies the story of Louis Lotwin, a scrap-yard worker and nephew of Charles Lotwin. Twenty-nine-year-old Louis Lotwin came to the United States in 1904 from Kapule, Minsk, the same shtetl where the Sinaikos and a majority of Madison's Jewish community originated. His earliest whereabouts are unknown, but by 1911 he had moved to Madison and opened the Vienna Bakery, the city's first kosher bakery. By 1914 Lotwin had sold the bakery to one of his workers and left Madison. For at least some of the next ten years, he lived in Menomonee, Wisconsin, working for his uncle's scrap yard and secondhand store. By late 1923 Lotwin had returned to Madison, taken out his first papers for citizenship, and settled into a job at the Sinaiko scrap yard.[25]

On the morning of January 31, 1924, Lotwin was shot on his way to work. He identified his assailant, but the men whom the police arrested on Lotwin's lead were let go without coming to trial. Although the police and FBI determined that there was insufficient evidence to try them for Lotwin's murder, the two men accused, Alexander Karachoon and William Bagdenow, shed light on the underside of the scrap business in the 1920s.

Karachoon had robbed Lotwin of eighty-three dollars in 1915 and had served a year in the Green Bay reformatory as punishment. In the intervening years, Karachoon had drifted around the country, evading the World War I draft and passing bad checks, before returning to Madison by 1924. Bagdenow, who seems to have been an acquaintance of Karachoon's, had worked at the Sinaikos' yard before Lotwin returned to town and took his job. Although both seemed to tell stories of despising Lotwin to acquaintances in late-night card games, neither could be decisively linked to the shooting. Lotwin's killer was never found.[26]

Lotwin lingered for ten days in a Madison hospital. His will originally left his estate to his father and siblings in Russia, but on his deathbed he amended it to designate his uncle, Charles Lotwin, who had been visiting him during his days in the hospital, as sole executor. Though it is possible to trace Louis Lotwin's career only as a baker, laborer, stableman, and scrap-yard foreman, he managed to amass a $12,000 estate ($151,000 in 2009 dollars), mostly in the form of property and stocks. Louis Lotwin's attorney, Samuel B. Schein, implored him to leave specific directions in his will, but Lotwin repeatedly refused, stating, "My uncle will do what is right." The state claimed that Charles Lotwin had coerced his nephew into changing his will, but on appeal, the Wisconsin Supreme Court found that he had not placed undue pressure on his strong-willed nephew. Following a promise he had made while living with them in Menomonee, Lotwin's estate paid for his cousins to attend the University of Wisconsin, where they excelled, graduating with degrees in medicine and law.[27]

Aside from their true-crime value, what do Lotwin's stories tell us about Jews in the scrap business? The details of Lotwin's life tell us that he ran with a tough crowd; this was probably a result of his life as a single man, drifting from one job to another. Much of the evidence used to apprehend the suspects in his murder came from "secret" messages (probably written in Russian) and heated discussions stemming from late-night card games involving Jewish and Russian scrap-yard workers. When in Madison, Lotwin lived in the Greenbush neighborhood, while Jews with longer residence in the city (and the money to do so) had begun to leave it for more respectable neighborhoods farther west. In addition to being Madison's single largest Jewish neighborhood and the home to its synagogue, kosher butchers, and kosher bakery, Greenbush was predominantly Italian, and it was common knowledge that bootleg liquor was easy to obtain there—as long as one was willing to run the risk of hit-and-run assassination. The spot where Lotwin was shot was also the site of several other killings during the 1920s; the others involved known bootleggers of Italian ancestry, and the spot came to be known as "Death Corner."[28]

Followers of Madison's police-blotter reporting were not the only observers to link scrap dealers to illegal activity. Progressive Era reformers seized on "junking" (selling scrap items, like hunks of metal or bottles) as contributing to the corruption of young people. A pamphlet titled "Junk Dealing and Juvenile Delinquency" lays out the case for strict regulation of scrap peddlers and dealers. The authors, affiliated with the Juvenile Protective Association of Chicago, studied how scrap peddlers and a few dealers depended on young boys to steal or otherwise obtain scrap materials for them, which they would then buy cheaply and sell to larger dealers for a profit. In their condemnation of scrap dealing, the authors cite multiple sources who affirmed that scrap dealers were exploiting children and introducing them to a life of crime.[29]

Finally, the matter of Louis Lotwin's will illustrates the downside of mixing family and business. Attorneys for the State of Wisconsin, led by attorney general Philip LaFollette, tried to demonstrate that Louis Lotwin's occasional disdain for his uncle's cheapness proved that, had he been healthy, he never would have agreed to hand his estate over to this man he disliked. Testifying for Charles Lotwin, Samuel B. Schein, the attorney who drew up the revised will, and the only Jewish attorney in Madison at that time, claimed that he warned Louis Lotwin of the way that his revisions would look to a less trusting public. Lotwin pressed on with the revision anyway.[30]

The Lotwin story reminds us that the scrap business, especially in the early twentieth century, was largely a family business, in addition to being a heavily Jewish one. Although the family connections meant employment for people who could not obtain jobs elsewhere, the downside of scrap's close identification with Jewish families is that the less savory side of the business also reflected badly on Jewish communities.

Lotwin's employers, the Sinaiko brothers, used their reputation and success to rise above connections to their former employee and other negative connotations. By the early 1920s the Sinaikos had diversified their enterprises to include a coal and wood dealership, two gas stations, a flour and feed store, and a retail grocery store. Isaac Sinaiko, in particular, had begun to work with his wife, Sarah, in charitable causes in Madison, within and outside the Jewish community. By the 1920s entrepreneurs in the scrap business, and their wives, began to "clean" the "dirty work" of the scrap business by becoming involved in charitable work in the American fashion. Sarah Sinaiko served as an officer in the Jewish charitable organization called the Queen Esther Society, as well as on the citywide Associated Charities public-welfare board. Sam Sinaiko and the Sinaiko Brothers firm also contributed to Associated Charities, and Isaac Sinaiko sold one of his rental properties to the charity, which became Madison's first settlement house. Sarah Sinaiko also served the Associated Charities as a "friendly visitor," investigating potential public-aid recipients in the city's Jewish community.[31]

By building the largest scrap business in the city and cultivating relations with the wider community of Madison business leaders, the Sinaikos received an exemption from zoning regulations that harmed smaller dealers. In 1918 the Madison city council began entertaining zoning regulations that would limit where scrap dealers could store their materials before shipping it on to larger yards. The Sinaikos' yard was one of the few that fell within the proposed scrap-dealing zone. Many of the Jews in the Greenbush neighborhood at least dabbled in scrap from time to time, and some stored significant piles of scrap in their small back yards. At hearings in 1920 scrap dealer Nochum (also known as Nick or Nathan) London told the city council, "You might as well kill me if you are going to stop my business." He went on to describe how scrap dealers who paid good money for discarded rags and paper enriched the local economy and should not be punished for their business. City attorney William Ryan claimed no prejudice against scrap dealers; rather, he felt compelled to regulate the trade because of complaints that the small scrap yards were unsanitary and that the businesses were operating on Sunday. Of course, the latter point was one of the main reasons that Orthodox Jewish immigrants had entered the scrap business, unlike retail merchants, scrap dealers could close on Saturday and work Sundays.[32]

SCRAP BUSINESS GENEALOGIES AND THE
DEVELOPMENT OF AMERICAN JEWISH COMMUNITIES

Scrap-business networks did not operate in a vacuum. In addition to the sheer numbers of Jews who would have defined themselves as "scrappers," "junkers," and the like, the industry was crucial to Jewish-owned businesses that used scrap materials. Scrap dealers' involvement in Jewish charitable works further solidified the links between the scrap business and American Jewish life.

Jewish networks in the scrap business extended outside of scrap yards themselves. Jewish entrepreneurs who began in the scrap business but chose not to continue in it, or who chose not to deal in scrap materials at all, occasionally started businesses that relied on scrap dealers to obtain, sort, and grade their raw materials. In Madison, the Kailin family's soap works would have depended on bones collected and processed by family members and other Jews in South Madison, an unincorporated settlement just outside the city limits. The Kailins, and their relatives the Tobenkin family, made brooms, which often used animal hair gathered from slaughterhouses by dealers in that sort of scrap. The Shapiro family, who made mattresses, would have stuffed them with rags and cotton scrap. The Sinaiko family moved from scrap metal into selling coal and oil. The fuel business required the same kind of railroad-fronted property that scrap did and, like scrap, offered great opportunities and risks. The opportunities that existed in the scrap business, both for building one's own family business as well as creating networks with other Jewish entrepreneurs, did not stop at the end of business hours. Commercial networks, with the scrap business at their hub, became the foundation of Jewish communities across the Midwest.[33]

From 1900 to 1920 the diminishing, though still important, concentration of Jews in the scrap business is visible in Madison's census records. In 1900 a total of 23 of the 30 Jewish households in the city had at least one member selling, peddling, or working with scrap materials. Ten years later, 48 of the 84 Jewish households had at least one member in scrap. By 1920, although thirty-eight people still worked in scrap-related occupations, the number of households had grown to 183, so fewer families had someone working in scrap yards. However, the yards that remained were larger and much more profitable than the small backyard scrap piles common in households of the immigrant generation.[34]

In larger communities Jewish families in the scrap business were often the cornerstone of Jewish institutions. The builders of Madison's first Orthodox synagogue were the Sinaiko brothers, four of whom were in the scrap business when the shul was built. The Sinaiko brothers were also charter members of Madison's B'nai B'rith King David Lodge, founded in 1908. Scrap dealer Morris

Heifetz and his sons and grandson have been directors of Madison's Hebrew Free Loan Society down to the present day. Families that owned scrap yards were also central to the development of Beth Israel Center, the Conservative successor congregation to the first Orthodox shul, and to Madison's Chabad House. Wives of scrap-yard owners were active in local chapters of Hadassah and the National Council of Jewish Women.[35]

In southern Wisconsin, scrap merchants were cornerstones of the local Jewish communities in ways that depended on the size of the Jewish community in question. In towns that had only a few resident Jewish families, one of those families, down to the present, was often a scrap dealer. As a result, Jewishness was correlated to "junk," and individual Jewish families had to make the decision to either fight that stereotype by becoming a joiner and networker par excellence or largely withdraw from local society and seek social opportunities in nearby towns.[36]

In a break with the traditional association between Jews and liberal or radical politics, scrap dealers seem to have held moderate to conservative political views. Only two founding members of Madison's Workmen's Circle chapter had any connection to the scrap business, and they were peddlers who quickly left that line of work or who left Madison all together. Scrap dealers' politics seem to have been more opposed to government regulations than the views of Jewish business owners in other fields, especially as the twentieth century progressed. While other Jews were sounding the earliest alarms about the rise of fascism in Europe, scrap dealers were selling huge volumes of scrap metal to Italian steel mills, which were then working closely with the fascist Mussolini government.[37]

Scrap-yard owners and their families, then, give us an alternative model for the idea that socialism helped teach Jewish immigrants how to be American. The argument, advanced by Tony Michels and others, states that socialist concepts of solidarity extended into other forms of Jewish organization. Rather, the scrap business is an example of conservative, small-town ideas creating a particular form of Jewish community life, more akin to the lodge-hall model of community building described by Daniel Soyer.[38]

SCRAPPING THE SCRAP BUSINESS:
THE DECLINE OF A JEWISH ENTREPRENEURIAL NICHE

Many scrap yards were two-generation businesses. Immigrants, as stated previously, began collecting, processing, and selling scrap at a time of rapidly increasing demand for scrap materials and of new technology to facilitate those processes. Additionally, during the pre-1924 period of large-scale Jewish migration to the United States, many industries, even those that required only semi-skilled labor and minimal English fluency, did not hire Jews on a regular basis.

In these contexts, plus the possibility of scrap allowing great financial success, scrap looked like a good deal to Jewish immigrants of the late nineteenth and early twentieth centuries. The work ethic of this generation prompted many immigrant scrap-yard owners to work in their businesses until their deaths.

The following generation also looked to scrap as the key to a stable future. Barriers to full Jewish participation in society continued, and arguably increased, from the early 1920s to the mid-1940s. Sons of scrap-yard owners (scrap, as "dirty work," was considered unsuitable for women, generally speaking) who attended or graduated from college put their new skills to work in the family firm. Few engineering firms hired Jewish engineers, so Jewish civil engineers and metallurgists used their skills to boost the family business. Few corporations hired Jewish attorneys as in-house counsel, nor did major corporate-law firms. As a result, newly minted Jewish attorneys turned their knowledge of the law to help their family firms negotiate increasingly complicated zoning and building codes, as well as laws passed to monitor dealers' businesses. Jews who couldn't secure other business opportunities, of course, could come home and apply their accounting, management, or financial skills to the family business.[39]

By the third generation, the barriers to full Jewish participation in the economy had faded. The top colleges and graduate programs and the most prestigious law firms and corporations dropped their quotas and restrictions on Jewish students and hires, so working in a gritty family business was harder to justify than obtaining a job in a clean office, with a window view of something more glamorous than a scrap yard. Coupled with the increasing technology required to run a successful scrap yard, and wildly fluctuating prices for scrap commodities, the majority of small family yards were either purchased by a few large conglomerates or simply folded altogether. By the twenty-first century, scrap was no longer as visible a "Jewish business" as it had been even thirty years before.

JEWISHNESS AND THE MAKING OF THE
AMERICAN SCRAP INDUSTRY

From the scrap business' roots in immigrant business networks and the traditional Jewish economic niche of peddling, to the growing un-Jewishness of scrap in the late twentieth century, the scrap business follows the trajectory of other "Jewish businesses." Clothing, show business, retail stores—all of these formerly "Jewish" occupations have lost their "Jewishness" to many people, Jewish and non-Jewish alike.

But during its early twentieth-century heyday, the scrap business resembled other Jewish businesses. Like show business, scrap businesses operated at the margins of respectability.[40] Small, immigrant-run scrap yards were accused of trafficking in stolen goods, corrupting children, violating the Christian Sabbath, and fouling the urban atmosphere by virtue of the "dirty work" of collecting, sorting, processing, and shipping scrap materials.

Successful scrap dealers, as commodity brokers, rely on the imperfect knowledge of their competitors to be successful. Keeping quiet about the materials in one's yard, as well as one's contacts for scrap metal, lent the scrap business a kind of secrecy similar to the opacity associated with Jewish credit networks in the nineteenth century. The family nature of many scrap yards, and the fractures within those families, made it hard to know when scrap yards owned by people with the same name were branches of the same firm, or bitter rivals who competed with each other. Behind-the-scenes networks like family connections or Jewish free-loan societies allowed Jewish scrap entrepreneurs to bypass banks and the public scrutiny they required. As in other Jewish business networks, this opacity led to suspicion of "dirty dealing," both in a figurative and literal sense, due to the nature of scrap as trade in discarded materials.[41]

But through charitable works, both within and outside Jewish communities, the most successful families in the scrap-metal business managed to "clean" their reputations and become respected industrialists. In line with their status as small-town business leaders, scrap dealers also present us with a little-studied view of Jewish American politics: Jewish free marketeers, who revel in the rags-to-riches stories that American capitalism depends on.[42]

The story of scrap also reveals an important part of American Jewish business history—the displacement of traditional business networks by academic networks. Young Jews increasingly see college and postgraduate connections, through academic and internship mentors, as more relevant sources of advancement than family members, in-laws, and compatriots. Although the scrap business requires the same kinds of academic training as other commodity businesses, other fields of business are seen as "cleaner" and therefore more desirable.

Finally, the history of the Jewish exit from the scrap business raises some important questions about Jewish identity on the continuum of insiders and outsiders in American society. Jewish scrap-yard owners through the twentieth century were proud of their track record of employing people who faced employment discrimination elsewhere. Jews employed other immigrants, African Americans, Latino migrant workers, and ex-convicts of all backgrounds in scrap yards and were proud of their efforts to employ people who were denied a chance to prove themselves elsewhere. But members of these groups have not, to any large degree, come to dominate the twenty-first century scrap business. Like Jewish storekeepers in African American neighborhoods through the twentieth century, there seems to be a combination of acceptance and distance that characterizes the relationships between Jewish owners and a multiracial workforce. This relationship characterizes the awkwardness between

American Jews and other distinct ethnoracial groups in the United States down to the present day.[43]

Jews who created enterprises in the scrap, secondhand, and surplus goods industry often dealt in discarded goods as a last resort. Over time many businesses in this area came to serve important niches in twentieth-century America: as sources of inexpensive clothing and furniture, plus raw materials for important industries, especially in the steel and paper-manufacturing areas of the Midwest. In many communities, Jews in the scrap business built synagogues and other Jewish institutions, and the nature of their business compelled them to stay when other storeowners and professionals moved on. In small towns, Jewish scrap dealers and their families were often the only Jews in town and held the honor and burden of representing Jewishness to their gentile neighbors. Despite dealing in commodities that had been cast aside by others and earning a measure of public scorn from some local leaders, the dealers who remained in the business continue to fulfill a valuable economic niche as recyclers, selling necessary scrap materials to industries around the world.

NOTES

1. Hyman L. Meites, *History of the Jews of Chicago*, facsimile ed. (Chicago: Chicago Jewish Historical Society, 1990), 151.

2. Ibid., 638.

3. Arthur N. Horwich to Chas. Lotwin, November 11, 1942, Chas. Lotwin and Son Papers, folder 2, Menomonee Area Research Center, Wisconsin Historical Society (hereafter WHS), Madison; capital letters in original.

4. Bernard Horwich, *My First Eighty Years* (Chicago: Argus Books, 1939), 102, 134, 215–220.

5. S. Joseph Fauman, "The Jews in the Waste Industry in Detroit," *Jewish Social Studies* 3 (1941): 41–56; Albert S. Carlson and Charles B. Gow, "Scrap Iron and Steel Industry," *Economic Geography* 12 (1936): 175–184; Gerald Alfred Gutenschwager, "The Scrap Iron and Steel Industry in Metropolitan Chicago" (master's thesis, University of Chicago, 1957); Claire B. Kendrick, "Steel Scrap: Meeting the Metallic Demand of the Steel Industry" (PhD diss., Pennsylvania State University, 1991); John William Maher, "Retrieving the Obsolete: Formation of the American Scrap Steel Industry, 1870–1933" (PhD diss., University of Maryland, 1999). Carl Zimring's works are his dissertation, "Recycling for Profit: The Evolution of the American Scrap Industry" (PhD diss., Carnegie-Mellon University, 2002); "Dirty Work: How Hygiene and Xenophobia Marginalized the American Waste Trades," *Environmental History* 9 (2004): 80–101; and *Cash for Your Trash: Scrap Recycling in America* (New Brunswick, NJ: Rutgers University Press, 2005). Existing memoirs and biographies of scrap dealers and dealers in materials with close ties to the scrap business are Don Gale, *Bags to Riches: The Story of I. J. Wagner* (Salt Lake City: University of Utah Press, 2007); William Ungar, *Only in America: From Holocaust to National Industry Leadership* (Jersey City: KTAV Publishing House, 2005); Leonard Tanenbaum, *Junk Is Not a Four-Letter Word* ([Cleveland, OH?]: privately printed, 1993); and Bernard Goldstein, *Navigating the Century: A Personal Account of Alter Company's First Hundred Years*, with William Petre (Chantilly, VA: History Factory, 1998). Most overviews of the scrap industry have been produced by industry associations and are not traditional scholarly works. Two examples are Edwin C. Barringer, *The Story of Scrap* (Washington,

DC: Institute of Scrap Iron and Steel, 1954); and Charles H. Lipsett, *Industrial Wastes and Salvage* (New York: Atlas, 1963).

6. For information on how societies define and deal with "waste," see Michael Thompson, *Rubbish Theory: The Creation and Destruction of Value* (Oxford: Oxford University Press, 1979); and Mary Douglas, *Purity and Danger: An Analysis of Pollution and Taboo* (London: Routlege and Kegan Paul, 1966). I am grateful to Susan Friedman for introducing me to the concept of the metonymic slide. Jenny Edbauer Rice, "The New 'New': Making a Case for Critical Affect Studies," *Quarterly Journal of Speech* 94, no. 2 (May 2008): 200–212, provides a good overview of this field.

7. Arcadius Kahan, *Essays in Jewish Social and Economic History* (Chicago: University of Chicago Press, 1986), 6–17; Ted Baker and Reed E. Nelson, "Creating Something from Nothing: Resource Construction through Enrepreneurial Bricolage," *Administrative Science Quarterly* 50, no. 3 (September 2005): 329–366; for Jewish credit networks, see Elliott Ashkenazi, *The Business of Jews in Louisiana, 1840–1875* (Tuscaloosa: University of Alabama Press, 1988); and Shelly Tenenbaum, *A Credit to Their Community: Jewish Loan Societies in the United States, 1880–1945* (Detroit: Wayne State University Press, 1993).

8. Edna Bonacich, "Middleman Minorities and Advanced Capitalism," *Ethnic Groups* 2 (1980): 211–219; Robert Cherry, "American Jewry and Edna Bonacich's Middleman Minority Theory," *Review of Radical Political Economics* 22, no. 2–3 (1990): 158–173; Barry R. Chiswick, "Jewish Immigrant Skill and Occupational Attainment at the Turn of the Century," *Explorations in Economic History* 28 (1991): 64–86; Ivan Light and Steven J. Gold, *Ethnic Economies* (San Diego: Academic Press, 2000). For a more historical example of this theory in action, see Joel Perlmann, "Beyond New York: The Occupations of Russian Jewish Immigrants in Providence, R.I., and in Other Small Jewish Communities, 1900–1915," *American Jewish History* 72 (1983): 369–384.

9. For data on Leavenworth, Kansas; Colorado Springs, Colorado; Oswego, New York; Oshkosh, Appleton, and La Crosse, Wisconsin; Modesto, California; Lafayette, Indiana; Jackson and Kalamazoo, Michigan; and Danville, Illinois, see Lee Shai Weissbach, *Jewish Life in Small-Town America: A History* (New Haven: Yale University Press, 2005), 109–111; for "junk collecting" by Jews in rural New England, see Michael Hoberman, *How Strange It Seems: The Cultural Life of Jews in Small-Town New England* (Amherst: University of Massachusetts Press, 2008), 103–116; for Johnstown, Pennsylvania, see Ewa Morawska, *Insecure Prosperity: Small-Town Jews in Industrial America, 1890–1940* (Princeton, NJ: Princeton University Press, 1996), 53–54.

10. A recent exception is Adam Mendelsohn, "Respinning an Old Yarn: Jews and the International Trade in Used Clothing," *AJS Perspectives* (Fall 2009): 14–17.

11. See David Hollinger, "Communalist and Dispersionist Approaches to American Jewish History in an Increasingly Post-Jewish Era," *American Jewish History* 95, no. 1 (March 2009): 1–32, for the definitions of these terms. Hasia R. Diner, among others, has traced the importance of business for the history of Jewish communal life; see "Buying and Selling 'Jewish': The Historical Impact of Commerce on Jewish Communal Life," in *Imagining the American Jewish Community*, ed. Jack Wertheimer (Waltham, MA: Brandeis University Press, 2007), 28–46.

12. For the importance of trust as a business practice identified with Jewish merchants and brokers, see Francesca Trivellato, *The Familiarity of Strangers: The Sephardic Diaspora, Livorno, and Cross-Cultural Trade in the Early Modern Period* (New Haven: Yale University Press, 2009), 10–20. Derek Penslar, *Shylock's Children: Economics and Jewish Identity in Early Modern Europe* (Berkeley: University of California Press, 2001), 144–158, explores ambivalence among Jews and non-Jews toward Jewish economic connections; for similar sentiments in the United States, see Rowena Olegario, "That Mysterious People: Jewish Merchants, Transparency, and Community in Mid-Nineteenth-Century America," *Business History Review* 73, no. 2 (Summer 1999): 161–189. This "handshake

deal" approach to business results in contractual agreements that are legally unenforceable; see Thomas M. Palay, "Comparative Institutional Economics: The Governance of Rail Freight Contracting," *Journal of Legal Studies* 13, no. 2 (June 1984): 265–287; and "Avoiding Regulatory Constraints: Contracting Safeguards and the Role of Informal Agreements," *Journal of Law, Economics, and Organization* 1, no. 1 (Spring 1985): 155–175.

13. For more discussion of Jews and peddling in the United States, see Hasia R. Diner, "Entering the Mainstream of Modern Jewish History," *Southern Jewish History* 8 (2005): 1–30; for peddlers as the first Jews in small cities and towns, see Weissbach, *Jewish Life*, 96–98. For a fictionalized treatment of peddling and junk collecting, likely based on Madison scrap dealers' experiences, see Elias Tobenkin, "Old Iron," *Our World* (August 1925): 87–90. The experiences of Sol Levitan, another one-time Wisconsin peddler, appear in Alfred R. Schumann, *No Peddlers Allowed* (Appleton, WI: Nelson, 1948), 37–49; for a look at how peddlers from Jewish and other backgrounds upset traditional gender relations, see Lu Ann Jones, "Gender, Race, and Itinerant Commerce in the Rural New South," *Journal of Southern History* 66 (2000): 297–308.

14. Zimring, *Cash for Your Trash*, 12–58, explores how this supply chain worked from a peddler and scrap-dealer perspective.

15. Barringer, *Story of Scrap*, 72–85; Joe Eskenazi, "Junkyard Jews: Your Trash Is Their Treasure," Jweekly.com, August 20, 2004, http://www.jweekly.com/article/full/23446/cover-story-br-junkyard-jews/; Zimring, *Cash for Your Trash*, 12–36; Tom McCarthy, "Henry Ford, Industrial Ecologist or Industrial Conservationist? Waste Reduction and Recycling at the Rouge," *Michigan Historical Review* 27, no. 2 (Fall 2001): 52–88; William T. Hogan, *The Steel Industry in a Period of World-Wide Challenge and Fundamental Change, 1946–1971*, pt. 6 of *Economic History of the Iron and Steel Industry in the United States* (Lexington, MA: Lexington Books, 1971), 1528–1529.

16. Barbara Lorman, interviews, Fort Atkinson, Wisconsin, October 20 and November 9, 2007; Jan Loeb, interview, Madison, Wisconsin, September 19, 2007 (in the author's possession); *Built on Scrap*, directed by Jonathan Z. S. Pollack (Madison, WI: Lapinsky and Sons/Ambrose Media, 2008), DVD; Merrill A. Watson, *Economics of Cattlehide Leather Tanning* (Chicago: Rumpf, 1950), 25, 93–94.

17. John A. Arnold, *Hides and Skins* (Chicago: Shaw, 1925), 120–121, 124–129, 111–112, 205–206.

18. Harry Wasserman, "Tailoring," in *Economic History of the Jews*, ed. Nachum Gross (Jerusalem: Ketem, 1975), 194–195; Gary Bryan Magee, *Productivity and Performance in the Paper Industry: Labour, Capital, and Technology in Britain and America, 1860–1914* (Cambridge: Cambridge University Press, 1997), 105–110.

19. Zimring, *Cash for Your Trash*, 30–34, 52–55; see also Gutenschwager, "Scrap Iron," 2–19.

20. For a broader overview of Jewish discomfort with defining subjects that involve Jewish people as "Jewish," see Tony Michels, "Communalist History and Beyond: What Is the Potential of American Jewish History?" *American Jewish History* 95, no. 1 (March 2009): 61–71.

21. Harry Wasserman, "Secondhand Goods," in Gross, *Economic History*, 266–269; Zosa Szajkowski, "Notes on the Occupational Status of French Jews, 1800–1880," *Proceedings of the American Academy for Jewish Research* 46/47 (1979–1980): 547–548.

22. Correspondence between IRO removals and Jewish community leaders around the United States that deals with successful placements in scrap yards appear in Robert Rockaway, *Words of the Uprooted* (Ithaca, NY: Cornell University Press, 1998), 50, 55, 56, 121–122, 151–152. Specific cities include Ellwood and Huntington, Indiana; La Crosse, Wisconsin; and Chicago, Illinois.

23. Madison city directories for 1900 and 1907; Manfred Swarsensky, *From Generation to Generation: The Story of the Madison Jewish Community* (Madison, WI: privately

printed, 1955), 22–34; Sam Sinaiko, oral history, September 6, 1955, WHS; "Romance of the Sinaiko Family," *Wisconsin State Journal*, October 22, 1909, Frank Custer Research Papers, box 48, WHS; relative worth was calculated using Consumer Price Index and GDP deflator calculators for the United States, "Seven Ways to Compute the Relative Value of a U.S. Dollar Amount: 1774 to Present," MeasuringWorth.com, 2011, http://www.measuringworth.com/uscompare.

24. Sam Sinaiko, oral history; Fannie A. Weinberg to Isidore Frank, September 5, 1917, Industrial Removal Office records, box 66, folder 19, American Jewish Historical Society Archives, New York; "Jews Organize," *Wisconsin State Journal*, November 11, 1903, Frank Custer Research Papers, box 31, WHS. Of the fifteen charter members of the Madison chapter of the Independent Western Star Order who appear in the 1904 Madison city directory, ten worked in scrap businesses.

25. Madison city directories for 1911 and 1914; *Dane County Declarations of Intention*, vol. 12, 1923–24, Dane County Circuit Court, Dane series 88, box 52, folder 9, WHS; "Employe of Sinaiko Is Latest Victim," *Capital Times*, January 31, 1924, 1.

26. Wisconsin State Reformatory record for Alexander Karachoon, WHS; *Capital Times*, February 11, 1924, 1 and 6.

27. *Capital Times*, February 11, 1924, 1; May 19, 1924, 1; May 20, 1924, 4; May 23, 1924, 2; calculation from "Seven Ways"; Will of Lotwin, Lotwin, Appellant, v. Harper, Public Administrator, Respondent, Supreme Court of Wisconsin, 186 Wisc. 42; 202 N.W. 151; 1925 Wisc. LEXIS 203, decided February 10, 1925; *Badger* 43 (1929), 91, *Badger* 44 (1930), 104, and *Badger* 46 (1932), 112, in University of Wisconsin Archives, Madison, WI.

28. Stuart D. Levitan, *1856–1931*, vol. 1 of *Madison: The Illustrated Sesquicentennial History* (Madison: University of Wisconsin Press, 2006), 221–225; *Capital Times*: January 31, 1924, 1; February 9, 1924, 1; February 11, 1924, 1, 6.

29. Harry H. Grigg and George E. Haynes, *Junk Dealing and Juvenile Delinquency* (Chicago: Juvenile Protection Association, [1919?]).

30. Will of Lotwin.

31. Madison city directory, 1921; a clip file in the Edith Sinaiko Frank Papers at WHS details the full extent of Sarah Sinaiko's charitable work in Madison during the 1910s and 1920s. The Sinaikos' work for Associated Charities can be found in Family Service Papers (Dane County), box 1, folders 1, 4; and box 2, folder 1, WHS. In 1915 the Jewish Central Committee of Madison, led by Louis B. Wolfenson, a Wisconsin professor of ancient languages and the son of a scrap dealer, came into being to take care of indigent Jews. At this point, Jewish involvement in the Associated Charities, as board members and clients, diminished. See Family Service Papers, box 2, folder 4.

32. The *Wisconsin State Journal* ran small, intermittent mentions of the zoning controversy from 1918 to 1920. The resolution is unclear, but the London family maintained a scrap yard at their home through the 1950s (Nadine Goff, personal communication, October 20, 2007). See, in particular, "Junkmen Plead to Avert 'Ruin,'" *Wisconsin State Journal*, September 18, 1920, 8. London's fellow speakers at the meeting, Rubin Mazursky, C. H. Halperin, and Nathan Paley, were, like him, members of the Orthodox Agudas Achim synagogue. See Agudas Achim records, WHS. Ten years later, according to the 1929 Madison City directory, Mazursky was no longer living in Madison, London had no occupation listed, Halperin owned an auto-parts business, and Paley continued to run a scrap yard.

33. Madison city directories for 1900, 1907, 1914, and 1921; U.S. federal census reports for Madison, 1900, 1910, 1920.

34. Information based on Madison results of U.S. federal census reports from 1900, 1910, and 1920.

35. Swarsensky, *From Generation to Generation*, 41–48, 67–93; "Record of Voters Participating in the Election of Delegates to the Twentieth World Zionist Congress [1937?]," Hadassah Papers, WHS; Madison City directory, 1937.

36. U.S. federal census records for 1910 and 1920 Crawford, Richland, Lafayette, Green, Iowa, Columbia, Rock, Dane, Jefferson, and Marquette counties indicate that a large percentage of small-town residents born in Russia, Jewish or Yiddish-speaking, were involved in the scrap business in some way, whether as buyers, dealers, or peddlers. Towns include Baraboo, Belleville, Beloit, Blanchardville, Boscobel, Brodhead, Cazenovia, Columbus, Cuba City, Darlington, DeForest, Dodgeville, Edgerton, Evansville, Fall River, Fitchburg, Fort Atkinson, Janesville, Jefferson, Kilbourn City, Lake Mills, Lodi, Lone Rock, Monroe, Montello, Montfort, Mount Horeb, Muscoda, New Glarus, Oregon, Packwaukee, Palmyra, Platteville, Prairie du Chien, Prairie du Sac, Portage, Richland Center, Rio, Sauk City, Shullsburg, Soldiers Grove, Spring Green, Stoughton, Sullivan, Sun Prairie, Watertown, and Westfield. Accessed November 2010, http://www.ancestrylibrary.com. See also Lorman interview, October 20, 2007.

37. For an individual firm's political orientation, see Louis ͦorman Papers, WHS. Louis's son Milton, who worked in the firm with him and took it over when he died, represented the Fort Atkinson area in the Wisconsin State Assembly. His wife, Barbara, also served in that capacity. Both were moderate Republicans. For information on scrap yards' international business during the 1930s, see Zimring, *Cash for Your Trash*, 87–89.

38. Tony Michels, *A Fire in Their Hearts: Yiddish Socialists in New York* (Cambridge, MA: Harvard University Press, 2005); Daniel Soyer, "Entering the 'Tent of Abraham': Fraternal Ritual and American Jewish Identity, 1880–1920," *Religion and American Culture* 9, no. 2 (1999): 159–182.

39. Zimring, *Cash for Your Trash*, 112–113; Milt Lorman also followed this path; see also Lorman Papers, WHS; for other examples, see Jan Loeb, interview, September 19, 2007.

40. Neal Gabler, *An Empire of Their Own: How The Jews Invented Hollywood* (New York: Crown, 1988), remains the most accessible and succinct source for this phenomenon.

41. For a readable account of the edgy, scandal-prone history of commodities futures markets, see David Greising and Laurie Morse, *Brokers, Bagmen, and Moles: Fraud and Corruption in the Chicago Futures Markets* (New York: Wiley and Sons, 1991), 41–103.

42. Most of the writing on Jews and free-market economics deals with macroeconomics and conservative foreign policy. See, for example, Suzanne Klingenstein, "'It's Splendid When the Town Whore Gets Religion and Joins the Church': The Rise of the Jewish Neoconservatives as Observed by the Paleoconservatives in the 1980s," *Shofar* 21, no. 3 (Spring 2003): 83–98; see also *American Jewish History* 87, no. 2–3 (1999), a special issue devoted to Jews and American conservative movements.

43. For examples of employment of black and Latino workers in scrap yards, see Tanenbaum, *Four-Letter Word*, 163–171, 263–267; also clippings in Lorman Papers, WHS, and William Lorman, interview, November 9, 2007 (in the author's possession). For a more general perspective on the complicated relationship between Jews, blacks, and economic niches, see Eric L. Goldstein, *The Price of Whiteness* (Princeton, NJ: Princeton University Press, 2006), 75–79, 142–145, 161–164.

CHAPTER 5

Despised Merchandise

AMERICAN JEWISH LIQUOR ENTREPRENEURS AND THEIR CRITICS

Marni Davis

In 1910 Isaac Wolfe Bernheim published his memoir, recounting his journey from Jewish immigrant rags to Kentucky bourbon riches. He arrived in the United States at the age of eighteen with a few dollars in his pocket, and by forty he was one of the wealthiest men in Louisville—an internationally renowned whiskey distiller, as well as a local civic leader and an important figure in national Jewish organizations. Life in the liquor industry had served Bernheim spectacularly well. Yet he'd come to rue his choice of livelihood. "If I had to choose my occupation over again," he mused, "I should prefer to engage in some other line of trade, but we are all creatures of circumstance."[1]

Bernheim's ambivalence toward the liquor business in 1910 should come as no surprise: his industry was currently under siege. After decades of struggle and marginal political relevance, the national movement to remove alcohol from the American consumer marketplace had gained adherents by the millions and supporters in powerful places. A wave of statewide total prohibition laws was sweeping through the South; between 1907 and 1909 six states had passed "dry" legislation intended to ban beverage alcohol within their borders, and several more seemed to be headed in the same direction. Ever-greater numbers were swayed by prohibitionist claims that liquor entrepreneurs constituted a powerful and devious political cabal. The epithet that antialcohol reformers had long hurled at the trade, "the liquor evil," besmirched elite distillers of up-market liquor as well as proprietors of rough and dingy whiskey saloons. The "anti-liquor craze," as Bernheim called it, showed no signs of abating anytime soon, and the growing "hysteria" had "left a costly scar on our business."[2]

Another development, one that he didn't mention in his autobiography, likely added to Bernheim's unease: the emergence of an anti-Semitic strain within the antialcohol movement. As the battle over alcohol commerce intensified at the turn of the century, prohibitionists voiced suspicion of Jewish alcohol entrepreneurs in particular, claiming Jewish "domination" and "mastery" of the American liquor business. *McClure's Magazine* suggested that the prospect of Jewish control over alcohol commerce posed a singular menace to American culture, calling readers' attention to "the acute and often unscrupulous Jewish type of mind which has taken charge of the wholesale liquor trade in this country." Journalists and politicians sympathetic to the prohibition movement declared that "Jews who were directly or indirectly interested in the liquor traffic" sought to obstruct anti-alcohol legislation, which suggested that Jews undermined the democratic process and the well-being of the communities they lived in for the sake of their own enrichment.[3]

Though terms like "mastery" and "domination" overstated the point, it was undoubtedly true that Jewish immigrants and their descendents had gravitated toward the liquor business all over the country. In Bernheim's Louisville, for instance, where Jews accounted for no more than 3 percent of the city's population, between 20 and 25 percent of local liquor entrepreneurs were Jewish; they were prevalent rather than dominant, but still, without question, a visible presence. In many other centers of American liquor production and distribution, Jews found the liquor trade to be a similarly attractive and reliable economic niche: according to national trade journal *Bonfort's Wine and Liquor Circular,* Jewish entrepreneurs owned five of the fifteen biggest whiskey-rectifying businesses in late nineteenth-century Cincinnati.[4] Even in locales where alcohol remained small relative to other industries, Jews were frequently a conspicuous group within it. Furthermore, for reasons as rooted in their politics and their cultural practices as in their entrepreneurial interests, American Jews consistently aligned with the "antis" (as in "antiprohibition") or the "wets" (as opposed to the "drys"). They maintained their principles, and their presence in the alcohol trade, as the prohibition movement gained force.

The ideological divide revealed by American debates over prohibition went far beyond mere disagreements over drinking itself. When Americans argued about alcohol commerce, they were voicing their attitudes toward capitalism and the competing demands of individual rights and the public good in a free-market society. Was the alcohol industry to be valued as a force for economic dynamism and growth? Was its presence in American cities and its popularity among immigrant groups a benign symptom of cultural diversity? Did the rights of individual drinkers, no matter how deleterious their habit, outweigh communal responsibility for public health, safety, and morality? Prohibitionists declared no, on all counts. By their assessment, alcohol debased everything it touched, bringing nothing but economic exploitation, political corruption, domestic misery, and moral decay.[5]

These negative attitudes toward alcohol commerce overlapped, and eventually intertwined, with animosity toward Jewish commercial conduct. During the early twentieth century, a period of rising anti-Semitism, their communal involvement in the alcohol traffic seemed to confirm suspicions about Jewish economic behavior. Accusations that Jews had monopolized a controversial commodity and were aggressively distributing and promoting an immoral product mirrored broader concerns about their presence in the American economy. A new cast of villains emerged in prohibitionist rhetoric: the wealthy arriviste Jewish distiller and wholesaler; the Jewish saloon keeper and liquor store owner who served economically and socially marginalized communities; and, after the Eighteenth Amendment gained the force of law in 1920, the Jewish bootlegger. The conflict over alcohol commerce exacerbated American anti-Semitic sentiment, because anti-Semitism and prohibitionism provided parallel ideological settings for Americans to express alarm about economic stratification, the increasingly urban and commercial nature of the American economy, and the erosion of white Protestants' political and cultural dominance. By the time Bernheim voiced his own personal regrets, Jews found that they were not only on the losing side of the national debate but that they were distrusted, even vilified, for their entrepreneurial engagement in the liquor trade.

Why were Jews drawn toward the American alcohol trade in the first place? Historians and social scientists who study the relationship between ethnic identity and occupational choice in the United States propose two ways to understand communal economic trends. Cultural interpretations give greater attention to an ethnic community's premigrational traditions and experiences. For those who adhere to this theoretical framework, an ethnic group's socioeconomic proclivities are largely determined by its collective heritage—by the values, traumas, and other metaphorical baggage immigrants bring with them alongside their physical belongings. Contextual analyses, on the other hand, look to the structural circumstances, the opportunities presented and the hindrances confronted, in an ethnic group's new site of settlement.[6]

In the case of Jewish immigrant alcohol purveyance, both were true. Jewish entrepreneurs were drawn to the American alcohol trade by their culture as well as their context. Jewish culture and history partly delivered them into the business, since they were linked to alcohol production and consumption by ancient rabbinic directive: the dietary regulations of kashrut require Jews to use wine in their religious rituals and forbid consumption of wine produced or even handled by non-Jews.[7] Though these restrictions were primarily intended to prevent certain kinds of conviviality between Jews and gentiles, they had the added effect of generating an occupational niche.[8] If Jews were to have the wine they needed, they had to oversee and control every step of its production and purveyance, from the harvesting of the grapes to the raising of the kiddush cup. Jews have made wine and sold it to both their own and other religious communities since the biblical era. Their familiarity with wine production led them into the production of other intoxicating beverages as well. Centuries before the Common Era, prominent members of Persian Babylon's Jewish diaspora community brewed beer from barley and dates. Jews' experience in the wine trade, and the lack of proscription against alcohol in Jewish religion and culture, also served them well in Islamic Spain and North Africa during the Middle Ages, where prevailing interpretations of the Koran proscribed practicing Muslims from having any contact with alcohol. Muslims who drank wine despite religious prohibitions relied primarily on Jewish merchants and vintners as their suppliers.[9]

In medieval and early modern Christian Europe, where Jewish landownership was often restricted by church or state edict, Jews continued to own vineyards and to maintain viticultural practices. When they were barred from owning land and could not grow their own crops, Jews transitioned to market intermediary roles, importing and exporting alcohol as well as the raw materials that went into the production not only of wine but also of beer and distilled liquor. They acted as middlemen and brokers, purchasing agricultural products in bulk and making them available to alcohol producers elsewhere or moving the finished product between manufacturers and faraway retailers and wholesalers. This socioeconomic activity, which found them frequently trafficking in timber, cattle, sugar, spices, and textiles, as well as alcohol, situated Jews centrally in the creation of commercial markets and, it might be said, in the development of modern capitalism, in both urban centers and in the rural countryside.[10]

Eastern European Jews developed an especially potent connection to the alcohol trade. In 1496 the Polish monarchy granted an exclusive monopoly for the production and sale of alcohol to its nobles. Having already leased the collection of public revenue in the form of taxes and customs duties to Jews (a contractual relationship known as an *arenda*), the nobility allocated this concession to Jews as well. After Russia took possession of Poland's eastern provinces in the eighteenth and nineteenth centuries, alcohol production and purveyance was one of the few occupations available to Jews in the Pale of Settlement; as historian Simon Dubnow has written, "the right of propination, exercised mostly by Jews on behalf of the nobles, proved a decisive factor in the economic and . . . social life of Russo-Polish Jewry."[11] For a few liquor merchants this trade proved quite lucrative.[12] But most Jewish alcohol entrepreneurs engaged the Russian liquor trade on a smaller scale, often as rural tavern keepers and distillers. According to one estimate, fifty thousand Jews managed taverns in the Russian Polish countryside in the late 1700s, and an 1870 census determined that Jews operated 190,000 taverns, in addition to 89 percent of the distilleries and 74 percent of the breweries, in Kiev and provinces to the west.[13]

Though Jews' cultural heritage and premigration experience raised the possibility of group proclivity toward alcohol commerce, their long-standing transnational history in the trade would have mattered little in an environment where alcohol was not a commodity in much demand. But Americans made and drank a lot of alcohol. Observers from both the United States and Europe expressed amazement (and frequently dismay) at the ceaseless flow of liquor in American culture—in business dealings, at political gatherings, and in the home, where it was consumed by all family members, including women and children.[14] Over the course of the nineteenth century, even as temperance activists, and then the prohibition movement, created a culture of abstention among white native-born evangelical Protestants, drinkers continued to far outnumber teetotalers. The number of alcohol producers and purveyors increased accordingly, as did the quantity of alcohol produced. Between 1850 and 1890 national beer consumption swelled from 36 million gallons a year to 855 million gallons, and Americans upped their consumption of distilled liquors (mostly domestically produced whiskey) from 66 million gallons of in 1875 to just shy of 100 million gallons in 1900.[15]

Jews joined the droves of Americans, both immigrant and native born and of all religious and ethnic backgrounds, who made a living by indulging the national thirst for intoxicating beverages. They participated in all aspects of alcohol's production and distribution, as distillers, rectifiers, brewers, vintners, wholesalers, and retailers. But most gravitated toward whiskey commerce. The context of American wine production, which was too minuscule an industry in the United States to attract many entrepreneurs at all, kept Jews from engaging that sector in significant numbers. Though the brewing industry employed thousands, and by the end of the century tens of thousands, American breweries' hiring practices privileged workers from German immigrant communities.[16] Furthermore, the "tied-house" saloon system, which established a direct line of supply between brewers and beer retailers, removed the intermediary—a position that Jewish entrepreneurs would have been likely to seek—from beer distribution.[17]

The American whiskey trade, by contrast, offered Jewish immigrants an occupational niche that was both culturally familiar and contextually promising. Like the Scots-Irish immigrants credited with creating the American whiskey industry when they settled on the midwestern frontier, Jews could bring to bear the distilling skills and experience they had gained in their countries of origin. But an additional factor drew Jews into the whiskey business: American whiskey production was neither vertically nor horizontally integrated in any absolute sense, and the industry never developed a direct distribution system like the breweries did. Though extremely volatile, the relative openness of the whiskey trade thus offered opportunities not only for manufacturers and retailers but also for aspiring market intermediaries.[18]

Jews joined the whiskey trade at every level, moving grains and flavorings to manufacturers, distilling and rectifying liquor, wholesaling it to liquor stores and saloons, and selling it by the bottle and the glass. As Jewish entrepreneurs established themselves in these occupations, they created local entrepreneurial clusters, which expanded their cohorts and extended into other sectors of the liquor trade. Jewish distillers often sold their wares to Jewish liquor wholesalers, who in turn supplied product to Jewish saloon keepers. These in-group commodity chains intensified the allure of the liquor trade, since a site where a cohort of Jewish whiskey dealers was already in business offered employment opportunities for newcomers.[19] Though the surest line to a job was through family ties, employers also looked beyond their immediate families and toward the broader local Jewish community, for apprentices and partners. "WANTED," announced an advertisement in a Louisville Jewish publication in 1901: "Three Jewish young men to represent a leading whiskey house. Need have no experience but must be first class, tiptop salesmen and come well recommended." Pittsburgh's *Jewish Criterion* published a similar ad in 1902.[20]

After a period as a "drummer" or a clerk, employees often opened their own concern with their former boss's blessing. These networks were of mutual benefit to both parties: by supplying stock to former employees turned independent entrepreneurs, one wholesaler could generate a flock of businesses. The family and business networks created by both Solomon Levi and Julius Freiberg, each of whom established whiskey distilling and wholesaling firms in Cincinnati before the Civil War, serves as an example. Solomon brought his brothers Herman and Leopold into the business and then hired several members of their family's younger generation as traveling salesmen and clerks. He then spun the younger men off into their own businesses and served as their main suppliers. Julius Freiberg opened a whiskey rectifying house with Levi Workum, a native-born Jew who was already engaged in the liquor trade. He, too, hired sons, nephews, and sons-in-law and then set them up as independent wholesale businesses. All told, S. Levi & Brothers and Freiberg & Workum together added at least seven more Jewish-owned liquor wholesaling concerns to Cincinnati's cluster.[21]

Local cohorts were further fortified by regional networks, which not only connected Jewish businessmen to one another but also created ties between Jewish communities. Some Jewish distillers and wholesalers extended their business pursuits beyond a single location. An ambitious family might establish offices in multiple cities and create regional networks of relatives working together in their trade. Whiskey distiller and wholesaler Ferdinand Westheimer of St. Joseph, Missouri, sent his sons to Louisville, Cincinnati, and Baltimore to open affiliated branches in each city. The Jacobs brothers of Georgia did the same, maintaining the home office of their wholesaling business in

Atlanta and opening branch offices in Chattanooga, Tennessee, and Girard, Alabama.[22] This centrifugal business practice increased the number of cities where Jews took up the trade, offered newcomers a greater number of entry-level job opportunities, and demonstrated the possibility of success to other Jewish immigrants who aspired to self-employment.

Business strategies such as these enhanced the structural circumstances that drew Jewish immigrants into this line of work and help to give an explanation for the presence of clusters of Jewish liquor entrepreneurs in cities and towns all over the United States. Even with the benefit of these business networks, however, and even where they came to constitute a significant and visible portion of a local liquor industry, Jewish whiskey dealers remained a minority in that trade. The animosities that prohibitionists and their allies cultivated toward Jewish liquor entrepreneurs, therefore, require further explanation.

———

In 1885 the *Chicago Daily Tribune* reported a courtroom appearance by an Irish immigrant named Ellen Sullivan. She had been in that courtroom many times before, according to the *Tribune*, always as a defendant accused of drunken and disorderly behavior. But in this instance she was there as a witness for the prosecution. The police had arrested two "Jews who keep saloons," and the city was charging them with the crime of "selling liquor to habitual drunkards." Sullivan testified that saloon proprietor Bloom Harris had hired her to scrub his establishment's floor, paying her a nickel and five glasses of "vile five-cent whisky." Mark Rosenberg, who owned another saloon nearby, had allowed Sullivan to barter her shoes for a drink. Both men were made to pay a fine, and Sullivan, her "features bloated and distorted by excessive drinking," was returned to the prison, where she had been incarcerated for public inebriation.[23]

The *Tribune* was generally sympathetic to the growing movement to restrict the liquor traffic in the United States, and their account of Harris's and Rosenberg's trial voiced several of that movement's concerns.[24] The article characterized Sullivan as the very picture of the debased immigrant drunkard, a role frequently assigned to the Irish in American discussions of the national "liquor question." That she was a member of the "gentler sex" made her inebriated condition even more shocking. Her dipsomania spoke to her own moral deficiency, but it wasn't her fault alone: as the charges against the saloonists indicated, in the eyes of the court they had callously misused Sullivan and profited from her weakness. Furthermore, just like the *Tribune* had associated Sullivan's drunkenness with her ethnic identity, the paper also connected Harris's and Rosenberg's behavior to their ethnoreligious affiliation. They were keepers of "Jew saloons"—proprietors of an especially noxious sort of drinking establishment where, according to the *Tribune* the year previous, "the most poisonous of vile liquor is retailed at cheap rates."[25]

Criticism of Jewish saloon keepers and their business practices emerged concomitantly with two developments in American society. First, the American alcohol industry expanded with astonishing speed during the late nineteenth century. Saloons had proliferated aggressively: the number of barkeepers and saloon keepers reported in the 1890 census was nearly ten times the number from 1870.[26] Thickets of saloons sprouted seemingly overnight in industrial towns, and urban immigrant neighborhoods hosted multiple saloons on every block. While some of these enterprises were intended for a middle-class or even an elite clientele, offering well-appointed furnishings, opulent hand-carved mahogany bars, and even a reading room, the businesses that garnered prohibitionists' horrified attention of were usually of a m..h grimmer sort. At their worst, they were miserable settings where customers drank themselves into states of stupefaction or belligerence on low-quality beer and liquor while engulfed in the stench of vomit and urine. Prohibitionists warned, not with-out cause, that saloon keepers aimed to relieve their patrons of as much of their paychecks as possible, even if it left workers without any money to bring home to their families. Gambling rings and prostitutes frequently used saloons as their headquarters. In short, temperance and prohibition reformers were responding to a genuine problem in American culture.[27]

Second, the growth of the American Jewish population during mass immi-gration from the Pale of Settlement transformed the American Jewish commu-nity from primarily central European in derivation to, by the early twentieth century, eastern European in its majority. Because of their history in this trade, as well as the American context where a saloon was often a cheap and easy business to open, Russian and Polish Jewish immigrants were drawn to jobs that placed them behind a bar. Some chose locations in Jewish neighborhoods; an 1890 study of the occupational choices of Jews in New York's Lower East Side counted 248 saloon keepers among them—a number nearly equal to the number of Hebrew teachers in the quarter, though a mere fraction of the 9,595 Jewish tailors.[28] But Jewish saloon keepers were more likely to set up their busi-nesses in locations where they attended to a primarily non-Jewish clientele. For eastern European Jewish immigrants accustomed to a culture where Jews frequently sold alcohol to gentiles, this was a familiar entrepreneurial choice. Deborah Weiner's study of Jewish life in Keystone, West Virginia—a small but booming coal-mining town with a regionally famous red light district—points to this tendency: in 1898 five of Keystone's ten Jewish entrepreneurs were saloon keepers.[29] In Leadville, Colorado, where around two hundred Jews lived at the turn of the century, seventeen Jewish men had at some point in their residence there run a retail drinking establishment.[30] And in Atlanta, Geor-gia's, Decatur Street saloon district, recent Russian Jewish immigrants owned twenty-five of the fifty saloons on the main drag in 1905.[31]

These two developments—the augmented presence of Jews among American liquor venders, especially as saloon keepers who retailed alcohol to non-Jews, alongside heightened anxiety in American politics and culture about the role of alcohol consumption—combined at a moment when Americans were increasingly likely to express concerns about Jewish economic behavior. Accusations that Jews were a grasping and mercenary people whose commercial activities betrayed their essentially self-serving disposition were, of course, not new. Such insinuations have been part of the American Jewish experience since the continent was colonized: European colonial settlers came from religious and national cultures that regarded Jews as economic parasites and Jewish economic behavior as inimical to the common good. American anti-Semitism grew as Jewish immigrants became increasingly visible as a commercial presence in American life.

Any discussion of economic anti-Semitism, however, must recognize that Jewish commercial success garnered praise from some Americans too, even as it incited resentment and suspicion from others. Generally, as historian John Higham pointed out, economic anti-Semitism in the United States was "blurred by a lingering respect."[32] Occasions where anti-Jewish policies officially curtailed Jewish economic activity—such as General Ulysses S. Grant's Order 11, which accused Jews of war profiteering and expelled them from the military district under his command in 1862—were uncommon. Compared to Jews' socioeconomic experience in Europe, anti-Semitism, though alienating and distressing, interfered only minimally with American Jews' ability to conduct their businesses.[33] In this respect, Jews' experience in the American alcohol trade, even when it provoked anti-Semitic sentiment, offered a dramatic contrast to their experience in eastern Europe, where suspicion of Jewish tavern keepers and distillers directly influenced Russian state policy on several occasions.[34]

Nevertheless, economic anti-Semitism's underlying assumptions influenced the prohibitionist view of Jewish alcohol entrepreneurship at the turn of the century. When the *Chicago Tribune* suggested that "Jew saloons" were uniquely malignant, for instance, it intimated that Jewish saloon keepers selfishly capitalized on deprivation in the city's immigrant slum, accumulating profits where "the crowded tenements empty forth their horde of night-prowlers and thieves" and "drunkards and outcasts go staggering along the sidewalk."[35] Such language aligned with claims, which were pervasive in American society, that Jews' elemental nature led them to become purveyors of vice who eagerly derived commercial gain by even the most vile means. In New York City, urban reformer Frank Moss came to similar conclusions: "The criminal instincts that are so often found naturally in Russian and Polish Jews" were reflected in both their economic behavior and their leisure activities, he wrote in 1898. Moss pointed to the Lower East Side as proof, describing the neighborhood as "dotted with disreputable saloons and disorderly houses," where drunken behavior and prostitution "were carried on without concealment and in open defiance of law and decency." Jewish "dive-keepers," he concluded, facilitated most of the area's criminal and morally reprehensible behavior.[36]

Moss wasn't entirely wrong about the role that some Jewish-owned saloons played in the Lower East Side's underground economy. Their presence in the neighborhood also attracted the concerned attention of Jewish communal leaders who were troubled by the unseemly and illegal activities, especially gambling and prostitution, taking place in some of these establishments.[37] But saloons in Jewish neighborhoods were not regarded as problematic because of the alcohol consumed there, since both Jews and gentiles assumed that Jews rarely drank to excess. The Committee of Fifty, which was tasked between 1893 and 1905 with investigating the role liquor and the saloon played in American society, referred to Jews as "a most abstemious race" and remarked that "saloons flourish among nationalities like the Jews in New York, which are noted for their moderation."[38]

For most critics of Jewish alcohol purveyors, Jews who served alcohol to other Jews did not pose a problem. It was when they served alcohol to non-Jews that they became a cause for concern. Jewish saloon keepers and liquor distributors who sold alcohol in non-Jewish environments received especially intense scrutiny, because they were suspected of exploiting and corrupting their customers for their own commercial gain.

Such accusations had international antecedent in eastern Europe, the point of origin for millions of recent Jewish immigrants. Russian and Polish government officials and religious leaders had long insisted that Jewish taverners and distillers exploited the rural peasantry's dipsomaniacal tendencies, ruining them financially and rendering them unfit for productive labor. A report from Minsk to the czar in 1797 explained peasant poverty as the fault of "landowners [who] keep Jews under leases in taverns in their villages. . . . By selling liquor to the peasants on credit . . . [the Jews] lead them into squalor and make them incapable of engaging in agriculture." Though this formulation held the nobility who leased liquor concessions to Jews partially responsible, the Jews who served the drinks were regarded as the more malevolent presence.[39]

American critics of Jewish alcohol entrepreneurs made similar accusations. Jews who sold alcohol to gentiles were denounced for acting on behalf of a political and economic elite, transferring revenue from the pockets of the people to the coffers of the corrupt and reaping wealth for themselves in the process. A Methodist minister and prohibition advocate claimed as much in 1886, when he singled out Atlanta's Jewish community for obstructing local efforts to restrict alcohol commerce. Antiprohibitionist businessmen had mobilized to protest against liquor legislation, and "all Jerusalem respond[ed] to their call," he wrote. "Stein, Goldstein, Bernstein, and all the other Steins" were working on behalf of prohibition's enemies, he warned, implying that their politics were motivated by cupidity; Jews followed the gentile leaders of the antiprohibition faction, "surrender[ing] their religious and racial prejudices," because they feared that prohibition would ill-serve them financially.[40] Again, two decades later, after the Georgia legislature passed a statewide prohibition law, a different Methodist minister declared victory over the "flat heeled, flat nosed, course [sic] haired, cross eyed slew footed Russian Jew whiskey venders whom the old Georgia politicions [sic] have licened [sic] to poison our boys."[41]

Both of these clergymen viewed Jews' commercial relationship to alcohol through the prism of a populist variant of American prohibitionist ideology. The populist movement that emerged after the Civil War offered a critique of Gilded Age structures of business organization, such as monopolies, mergers, vertical and horizontal integration, and the dreaded "trust." Increased bureaucratization and centralization of the American economy, populists insisted, had concentrated manufacturing and monetary power into the hands of too few economic actors. Powerful interests had already bought off politicians and newspaper editors, this theory continued; they owned the banks, the land, and the means of production, and now the citizenry was on the verge of enslavement. The People's party, launched in 1892 to act as the populists' national political organization, raged against this state of affairs in their foundational Omaha Platform: "The fruits of toil of millions are boldly stolen to build up colossal fortunes for a few," they declared, "and the possessors of these, in turn, despise the republic and endanger liberty."[42]

Contemporary ideas about Jewish economic behavior fit within populism's vision of the struggle between the powerful and "the people." When Jews appeared in the populist narrative, they were often cast either as members of the economic plutocracy or as those who did the plutocracy's bidding. This was, in part, a response to Jewish immigrants' visibility as commercial intermediaries between agricultural producers and the market, which rendered them odious in the eyes of those who regarded them as the enemy of the American farmer. Among those populists whose politics were intertwined with their religious faith, Christian beliefs additionally reinforced distrust of Jews. For American Protestants—especially those who interacted with Jews only in commercial contexts—stereotypes of Jews as urban nonproducers and price manipulators became entangled with the New Testament story of the money changers Jesus chased out of the temple. Accusations that Jews were responsible for the crucifixion, and Christian imagery of Judas's betrayal of Jesus for thirty pieces of silver, strengthened suspicions that Jews conspired to exploit gentiles and undermine the United States as a Christian nation.[43]

Though scholars agree that the image of the Jewish economic actor in the American imagination placed Jews well outside the circles of populist sympathies, they have come to a range of conclusions about the pervasiveness and

potency of populist anti-Semitism. Some historians insist that Jews barely
registered in populist consciousness, and the use of crucifixion imagery and
invocation of names like "Rothschild" and "Shylock" were "colloquialisms
that had no real reference in their minds to the Hebrews."[44] Others who have
investigated the image of the Jew in the populist imagination dismiss such
assertions, pointing to the unequivocally anti-Semitic rhetoric employed by
movement leaders such as Ignatius Donnelly and William "Coin" Harvey.
When Donnelly wrote "in the evil conditions made by bad laws, the Jews alone
thrive," they contend, he oriented Populist thought toward Jew-hatred.[45]

Taken as a whole, however, the populist movement cannot conclusively be
described as either indifferent or hostile toward Jews. Populist anti-Semitism's
precise measure, if such a thing can be ascertained at all, differed from place
to place and varied depending on how local leaders regarded and talked about
Jews, among other factors. When assessed in the aggregate, American populists
can best be described as ambivalent toward Jews, and in this respect they were
like most Americans at the turn of the century. Even when anti-Jewish sentiment did surface in populist rhetoric, it remained of minor consequence to
their overall political platform.[46]

Nevertheless, as Richard Hofstadter wrote of populist anti-Semitism, "it is
one thing . . . to say that this prejudice did not go beyond a certain symbolic
usage, quite another to say that a people's choice of symbols is of no significance."[47] For populists who declared Jews to be inimical to the interests of the
American people, anti-Semitic assumptions that Jews were a foreign and
exploitative element in American economic life mapped onto both populist
suppositions about "money power" and Christian anti-Semitism's economic
undercurrents. Claims of a Jewish conspiracy bespoke the broader concerns of
those bewildered by modern capitalism's effect on their lives. The fact that most
farmers and small-town residents knew Jews only as merchants and creditors
(whom they were likely to resent) and as biblical figures (whom they regarded
as rejecters of the Lord) deepened their suspicion that Jews were an alien and
malevolent force in the American economy. Jews became a symbol, a stand-in
for complex and discomfiting socioeconomic dynamics; characterizing these
changes as a conspiracy hatched by Jewish capitalists and intermediaries was a
way to regain some amount of comprehension and control.[48]

The populist movement collapsed at the turn of the century, after its leaders
suffered defeat in several elections and most populists joined (or rejoined) the
Democrats. Yet populism's propensity for conspiracy theories, for assuming
that a powerful cabal schemed against the national interest, remained embedded in American political culture. It also became a formidable force in prohibitionist ideology. Prohibitionists found much that was convincing in populism's
assessment of the relationship between "money power" and "the people."[49] They
absorbed and tapped into populist anxieties about the concentration of capital

and the exploitation of labor and consumers, shifting their attentions away from the movement's antebellum concentration on the individual drinker or seller and redirecting their political and ideological assault against the business itself. Prohibitionists insisted (not incorrectly, in some cases) that the beer and liquor traffic conspired against the public good for its own enrichment, pointing out that like the "robber barons" of other industries, American alcohol industrialists sought to minimize competition and control prices by consolidating production, monopolizing avenues of distribution (as breweries did with the tied-house system of saloon sponsorship), and employing any other instrument in their reach to increase profits.[50]

Prohibitionists influenced by populist interpretations of politics and economic power constructed a narrative that pitted the virtuous democratic citizen against the soulless corporate oligarch in a battle of good against evil. As was often true of populism, prohibitionist ideology flourished in places where Protestant church networks facilitated political activism and attracted Protestants whose politics were imbued with millenarian eschatology—a belief that political, economic, and social reform would help to bring about God's kingdom on earth.[51] Prohibitionists insisted that their own efforts were squarely on the side of both God and the American people while their opponents sought to undermine Christian and American values and subjugate citizens for economic gain. "Like the Populists," historian Michael Kazin has written, "foes of the saloon seemed convinced that Mammon was dominating man, and only their movement could right the balance."[52]

All of these tendencies can be seen in a pamphlet published in the early 1890s by Rezin B. Wasson, the treasurer of Wayne County, Ohio. Wasson was protesting a bond recently issued by the state to fund the building of an agricultural research institution in his county. He used the pamphlet as occasion to unleash a barrage of invective at Jews, whose involvement in the bond matter, he suggested, illustrated their general economic tendencies. "Upon a little reflection," Wasson stated, "the most casual observer will concede that the Jews have ruled the christian [sic] world since the beginning of its era by the use of gold and silver." (This was precisely the kind of language used by populists for whom Jewish economic behavior loomed large.) He tied Jewish corruption of politics and the economy to their controlling the beer and liquor industries: Jews "invested large sums of money in breweries," he wrote, and they strong-armed secretary of state James G. Blaine "to drum up the beer trade" for themselves. Jews purchased local real estate through bond issuances, Wasson continued, and used it for the "beer brewery business" and "whiskey distiller[ies]." In addition, Jews "find little difficulty in getting good prohibition Editors [sic]" to tilt their newspapers' reporting so that it favored antiprohibitionist politics.[53]

Wasson's anti-Semitic rage, at least as articulated in his pamphlet, had no discernibly specific object; he spoke primarily of "the Jew," rather than of any particular Jews, and if he had someone in mind he did not say so. Certainly, the prominence of Jews in the liquor industry throughout the region, in addition to Jews' animosity toward prohibition, could well have made a negative impression on him. Perhaps the presence of several of Peoria's Jewish distillers in what came to be known as the "Whiskey Trust"—an agreement among a collective of midwestern industrial distillers to control prices and production, for which John D. Rockefeller's Standard Oil served as a model—angered him as well, although the ethnic affiliation of these distillers, such as Joseph B. Greenhut and Adolph Woolner, was not publicly discussed until several decades later.[54] It's possible, too, that he was an acolyte of James Coxey, the Ohio populist leader and organizer of the 1894 "Coxey's Army," who founded the viciously anti-Semitic populist newspaper *Sound Money*.[55] Whether the connection between Jews, alcohol, and political power was, for Wasson, abstract and associative or concrete and responsive to specific events, his pamphlet demonstrates how populism's socioeconomic concerns, especially when it came to Jewish economic behavior, shaped antialcohol ideology and rhetoric and shows how anxieties about economic power, the liquor industry, and Jewish influence became intertwined.

———

Through the end of the nineteenth century, with the exception of occasional outbursts (such as Wasson's toxic rant or the *Chicago Tribune*'s spotlighting of Jewish-owned saloons), observers who noted the Jewish presence in alcohol commerce also often commented on Jews' reputation for moderate drinking practices. This suggests that Jews' personal comportment still made more of an impression on the prohibitionist imagination than did their commercial activities. An 1890 local color piece in *Harper's Weekly*, which remarked on the prevalence of alcohol entrepreneurs in downtown Manhattan's densely populated Jewish quarter, expressed admiration for Jewish habits of alcohol consumption: "Wine-shops and drinking places are common, though intemperance is rare. I see no tipsy man in the whole quarter."[56]

This changed during the first decade of the twentieth century, as concerns about alcohol and the presence of Jews in the American economy combined with yet another anxiety: the resilience of the color line. With growing frequency, alcohol's enemies mentioned Jews not as admirably moderate in their alcohol consumption but as suspect in their commercial practices, especially when they sold alcohol to African American men. This version of prohibitionist anti-Semitism emerged as a response to events in the South, where the twentieth-century prohibition movement had its first string of significant victories. This energized the national antialcohol movement, especially the Anti-Saloon League. Their successes in the South inspired them to reconfigure their national strategy, which moved antialcohol activists closer to their ultimate goal: an amendment to the U.S. Constitution that prohibited the manufacture and sale of beverage alcohol. The passage of statewide prohibition laws in several southern states proved to be an important turning point in the trajectory of the American prohibition movement. In addition, these developments presaged a shift in both local and national attitudes toward Jewish alcohol entrepreneurs.

The event that set these developments in motion occurred in Atlanta, where, as has already been noted, Jewish immigrants, mostly recent newcomers from eastern Europe, owned and ran many of the saloons and alcohol retail outlets in the Decatur Street district. By 1900 all of the counties that surrounded Atlanta had gone dry. A wet island suspended in a legislatively bone-dry sea, the city—and especially the Decatur Street district—attracted significant traffic from miles around. The neighborhood was something of a tourist attraction for "slummers," middle-class whites who, as historian Chad Heap has written, wanted to visit and observe "socially marginalized urban neighborhoods and the diverse populations that inhabited them."[57] Some city boosters promoted Decatur Street as a site where visitors could observe and enjoy the local culture. Northerners of "wealth and refinement" visited the dance halls and drinking establishments on the street, "being desirous of getting a correct insight of the negro in all his social phases"—which, apparently, included watching dances such as "the quadrille, the buck and the hoochee coochee."[58]

But a growing number of middle-class Atlantans denounced the "Decatur dives." Despite the fact that white middle-class businesspeople, journalists, and politicians enjoyed the street's less reputable offerings on occasion—including and especially Mayor James Woodward, whose public intoxication and patronage of brothels scandalized the city—local newspapers focused on the neighborhood, and especially its main drag, as a locus of lower-class depravity.[59] The forms of leisure Decatur Street made available to unemployed and underemployed "loafers," they insisted, inhibited productivity, kept the city from reaching its full economic potential, and acted as a drag on Atlanta's collective moral standards.

Decatur Street also posed a threat to the color line. Besides the fact that it was one of the city's few sites of dense immigrant settlement, the saloons, restaurants, gambling rooms, and dance halls of "Rusty Row" drew black and white people from all over the city and the outlying countryside every Saturday night. These establishments were segregated by race, but when the "white only" and "colored only" businesses disgorged their patrons, the neighborhood provided space—from public streets to back-alley brothels—for blacks and whites, men and women, to engage in a spectrum of unsavory and illicit activities. Moral reformers denounced the interracial drinking, gambling, and other forms of depravity available in the district, declaring that Decatur Street's recreations muddied the racial boundaries that divided and defined every aspect of southern life.

By 1900 concerns about race and the color line most differentiated the southern prohibition movement from its northern and western variants. Middle-class southerners, both black and white, had come to the conclusion that liquor provoked racial conflict. Working-class men were more vulnerable to the demoralizations of liquor, prohibitionists argued, and had a greater tendency to get at each other's throats than did "respectable folk." Prohibitionists and other Progressive Era reformers all over the New South confidently asserted that limiting the availability of alcohol and saloon settings to both black and white men of the "lower levels" would reduce the number of race riots and lynchings in the region.[60]

Race mixing and racial conflict among the lower classes, however, were only part of the problem. Middle-class southern whites feared, above all else, the availability of alcohol to African American men. Class-based arguments for the abolition of the liquor traffic were mostly drowned out by white claims that black men were incapable of controlling their desire for alcohol. Just as northern prohibitionists of the previous century had said of Irish immigrants, southern progressives insisted that a black man's unquenchable thirst rendered him a helpless pawn of the liquor industry. Gaining access to the franchise, by this analysis, had done the freedman no favors, since his vote was so easily corrupted by an industry that debased him and used him for its own self-interested purposes. Southern prohibitionists suggested that one way to end liquor commerce was to disfranchise black men and purge the electorate of liquor power's instrument. This would serve the general good and, one southern prohibitionist insisted, was intended "in consideration of the true welfare of the negro race."[61]

But southern whites who called for a ban on alcohol commerce were not really interested in protecting black men from "liquor power" or from their own worst impulses. In the imagination of the white southerner, a drunken black man was always a rapist in the making, and the object of his lust was invariably a white woman. Limiting black men's access to alcohol, prohibitionists argued, would not only protect southern white womanhood but also diminish the incidence of lynchings and race riots, since it would eliminate what white middle-class reformers saw as their root cause: black sexual depravity fueled by liquor.[62]

In Atlanta, anxieties about race, sex, and alcohol came to a head in September 1906, after several months of incendiary reportage from the local papers. Throughout that summer's gubernatorial primary season, each candidate strove to outdo the other in demands for black subjugation. The *Journal*, the *Constitution*, and the *Evening News* relentlessly enumerated lurid details of assaults on local white women by "black brutes." Reporters and editors shamelessly exaggerated their dispatches; an incident in which a white woman looked out her window and saw a black man standing on her lawn, for example, was reported as an assault.[63]

All summer and into the fall, the press and local reformers blamed Decatur Street dives for fueling the epidemic of sexual violence. "These clubs and dives are hot-beds of crime," the *Journal* insisted; "much of the recent outlawry on the part of the negroes is attributable directly to the influence of the places." As if the availability of limitless amounts of liquor wasn't bad enough, according to news reports, there was also the matter of the "pictures of nude white women that for some time have adorned the walls of negro dives."[64] Images of lovely and voluptuous ladies—lily-white and in various states of undress—in fact adorned the walls of all kinds of saloons and drinking clubs, all over the nation; then, as now, marketers of alcoholic beverages relied heavily on erotically suggestive images of feminine flesh to sell their product. When these racy advertisements appeared in drinking establishments catering to white men of means, only antialcohol activists expressed outrage. When used to sell liquor to black men in the South, they inspired a consensus among whites that such images, when consumed along with the merchandise being advertised, directly inspired black men to rape white women.

On September 22 the day's newspapers blared headline after headline: "THIRD ASSAULT"; "ANGRY CITIZENS IN PURSUIT OF BLACK BRUTE"; "CLEAN OUT THE DIVES." Five black men were arrested for working in black-only saloons decorated with portraits of nude white women, and the city's police chief requested that the city council refuse liquor licenses to twenty-six saloons and restaurants that catered to an African American clientele. A Methodist minister and official for the Georgia branch of the Anti-Saloon League, which had been organized in 1904, insisted that the connection between Decatur Street's saloons, black men, and rape was as clear as could be. "Tank him up on booze," he warned, "and the black brute makes toward a white woman." As a case in point, in the *Constitution* recounted a black man's defense for assaulting a white woman: "Judge I don't remember a thing that happened last night. . . . I got drunk with another negro and the last thing I remember was when I was in a barroom on Decatur Street."[65] That evening, a mob of several thousand white men stormed the Decatur Street neighborhood and brutally attacked its black denizens. The rioters smashed saloon windows, drank what they found inside, and then spread throughout the city in a spree of random assaults on black people and black-owned businesses. By the time calm was restored two days later, dozens of black Atlantans had been murdered and scores more injured.[66]

Georgia prohibitionists responded to the riot by redoubling their efforts. Liquor had caused the violence, they insisted; drunken blacks had committed the "unspeakable" crime, and drunken whites had exacted vengeance. The only solution was to outlaw alcohol, for the sake of citizen safety, economic progress, and national reputation. In the summer of 1907, after less than a year of postriot prohibitionist agitation, the Georgia House of Representatives easily passed a statewide prohibition measure and Governor Hoke Smith signed it into law.[67] Georgia's newfound consensus on the need to restrict alcohol consumption and regulate behavior—a significant shift from long-standing southern inclinations against government regulation of white men's personal liberties—reached far beyond the state's borders. Georgia's outlawing of the sale or production of alcohol signaled the beginning of a series of prohibitionist successes in the South. By the end of the decade, Alabama, Tennessee, Mississippi, and North Carolina had passed similar legislation; by 1915 West Virginia, Arkansas, and South Carolina were dry as well.[68] Prohibition had come to be embraced by white southerners who regarded it as a crucial progressive and prosperity-bringing reform.

As the southern debate over prohibition escalated, northern observers—journalists from muckraking publications, most frequently—reported and commented on the movement. Their analyses usually gave an account of the issue that resembled white southerners' version, focusing on the relationship between alcohol commerce, black criminality, and racial tensions. Those who investigated the southern alcohol trade, specifically, noticed the activities of Jewish liquor dealers in the region, especially in racially and economically marginalized neighborhoods. Prevailing stereotypes of Jewish entrepreneurs as economically unscrupulous, in combination with their presence in a disreputable and despised commercial sector, provoked accusations that Jews were a major part of the South's liquor problem. But in the context of the Progressive Era "New South," these allegations, which implied that Jews represented a malevolent and alien presence in the region, were amplified by the suggestion that they were traitors to the white race and, perhaps, themselves insufficiently white.

In the turn-of-the-century South, where the black/white divide was most assiduously policed, intimations about Jews' racial status played a role in the growth of anti-Jewish feeling. Eugenicists and others who claimed scientific expertise on the topic of racial identity and human heredity suggested that Jews from the Pale of Settlement, as well as other recent European immigrants such as Italians and Slavs, were of lower racial status than northern Europeans. Race theorists of the day gave precedence to phenotypic characteristics, such as hair texture or skin color and suggested an ancestral link between Jews as a "Semitic" people and Africans. Jewish immigrant storekeepers' seeming indifference to Jim Crow customs further heightened white southern skepticism about Jews' capacity to assimilate into the region's white culture. Since the nineteenth century Jewish immigrant peddlers and storeowners had acquired a reputation for interacting more intimately with black customers than native white entrepreneurs would, even using honorifics like "Mister" in conversation with black customers—transgressive behavior, by white supremacist standards. Whether Jews treated blacks in this manner because of their own experiences with oppression or out of ignorance of (or indifference to) southern social norms, their failure to sufficiently differentiate between their white and black customers gave southern whites cause to worry that Jewish economic practices blurred the precision of the racial divide in potentially dangerous ways.[69]

Concerns about Jewish alcohol purveyance in the South first emerged during Georgia's debate over statewide prohibition legislation. These accusations were initially oblique, but suggestive. Within a day of the riot's conclusion, the editorial board of the *Journal* made clear that they abhorred the white saloon keepers who sold alcohol to black men. "Let it be understood," they wrote, "that the white man who sells or gives away liquor to a negro is an enemy of his own race, an enemy of society, an enemy of law and order." An article in the *Constitution* a week after the riot angrily described the blurring of the color line in Decatur Street's drinking establishments: "Some of the saloon men allow the negroes to curse them, applying the vilest epithets, while they in turn call the negroes 'mister' and speak of them as gentlemen."[70] Neither remark was directed at Jews specifically, though they made use of older accusations often made against Jewish salesmen in southern shops.

Two of the most widely read national muckraking magazines of the Progressive Era soon published essays on the riot, and both essays pointedly mentioned the presence of Jewish saloon keepers in the Decatur Street district. *Harper's Weekly* described the neighborhood as "the very worst part of Atlanta" and "the hatching-place of negro criminals." Author Thomas Gibson noted that "white men—mostly foreigners, Russian Jews and Greeks—run many of the saloons, pawn shops, and restaurants which cater to the negro trade." Like the *Journal*, Gibson had nothing but contempt for such businessmen. "As to white foreigners who cater to negro trade and negro vice in this locality," he contended, "it is left to the judgment of the reader which is of higher grade in the social scale, the proprietors or their customers."[71]

An essay on the riot and its aftermath in the *American Magazine* followed in April 1907. Journalist Ray Stannard Baker described Decatur Street as "the worst section of the city." Though blacks and whites drank together in some parts of the South, Baker explained, on Decatur Street their saloons were segregated, and he offered two photos of Atlanta saloons: Abram Abelsky's and Michael Cohen's. "Many of the saloons for negroes were kept by foreigners, usually Jews," read the caption.[72] While Baker's mention of Jewish saloon keepers on Decatur Street was less vitriolic and accusatory than Gibson's, their shared observations suggested that Jews were among the riot's causal factors.

Of all of the Jewish alcohol entrepreneurs whose commercial relationship to southern blacks inspired alarm, Lee Levy received the most attention. Levy was born in New York City to central European Jewish immigrants, had moved to Gainesville, Texas, and started a liquor wholesale business there by 1900. Within a few years he moved to St. Louis, Missouri, where he and his business partner, a German Jewish immigrant named Adolph Asher, established a wholesaling concern that distributed liquor throughout the Mississippi Delta region.

Levy became nationally known in 1908, after a series of articles by Will Irwin in *Collier's Weekly* described a terrible crime in Shreveport: a young white girl named Margaret Lear had been murdered, allegedly by a black man named Charles Coleman. Within a week of Lear's death, Coleman had been tried and executed by the state. But "the real murderer of Margaret Lear" had gone unpunished, Irwin insisted. "What if he wears a white face instead of a black," he asked his readers. "Would you grease a rope for him?" The true villain, according to Irwin, was not Coleman, but Lee Levy, since Coleman supposedly had been drinking Levy's "nigger gin" (as Irwin called it) when he assaulted Lear. There was no way for Irwin to know precisely what Coleman had been drinking, or whether he'd been drinking at all. But Levy's gin was cheap, popular, and available in "every low Negro dive in the South," Irwin wrote. As if the product wasn't already scandalous enough, its brand name—"Black Cock Vigor Gin"—was undisguisedly suggestive, and its packaging featured an illustration so racy that in 1908 Levy and Asher were convicted of sending obscene materials through the mail. Irwin's inclusion of Levy in the story shifted attention away from the alleged perpetrator, and even away from the attack itself. In Irwin's estimation, Levy held primary responsibility for the violence done to young Miss Lear, since his liquor, and its obscene packaging, had inspired the assault.[73]

Irwin's series on race and alcohol in the South had a far-reaching impact. Tennessee prohibitionists picked up the story of Levy's gin as that state was fighting over sumptuary legislation. "The liquor dealers of Tennessee at this very time are selling to negroes Lee Levy and Co.'s gin," Nashville's dry newspaper insisted; "they are selling it in Chattanooga. They are selling it in Memphis. They are selling it in Nashville." Prohibition activists brought bottles of Levy's gin around the state, displaying the risqué label to scandalized audiences. Within the year Tennessee had passed a statewide prohibition law of its own.[74]

Irwin's investigation of Levy's business identified two other liquor wholesaling and manufacturing concerns: Bluthenthal and Bickert of Atlanta, and Dreyfuss and Weil of Paducah—the latter of which claimed in their own advertising to be "the most widely sold brand in the South." Irwin took them at their word.[75] All four of these men were Jewish. Though he did not mention their religion or ethnicity, he was far more explicit about the Jewish relationship to alcohol commerce in a piece on the liquor industry's propaganda methods, where he profiled the editors of a Jewish weekly magazine in St. Louis called the *Modern View*. This small magazine also published an advertising circular underwritten by the city's brewing industry. When asked whether it was odd for a Jewish publishing firm to be so closely tied to the beer trade, one editor (whose "pockets bulged with anti-prohibition propaganda," according to Irwin) took a staunchly proalcohol position on the matter: "We are a Jewish religious weekly, and the Jews are opposed on moral grounds to prohibition." Irwin quoted another employee of the *Modern View*: "We are anxious to press its sale in every town of the South where the prohibitionists are contesting the ground."[76]

Irwin presented Jews who advocated against prohibition in the region as a danger to the well-being of the South, and as acting on behalf of their own self-interest and benefit. They acted as a defensive guard for southern distillers, saloon keepers, and liquor wholesalers, Irwin suggested, at just the moment when the South most desperately needed this flow of liquor to be stanched. As national magazine readers absorbed this image of the immoral and self-interested Jewish alcohol entrepreneur, similar accusations surfaced in Georgia's statewide prohibition debate when a prohibitionist from Columbus, Georgia, declared in a local board of trade meeting that "Jews and whiskey men" were responsible for blocking antiliquor legislation. When the Jewish businessman currently serving as president of the Columbus board of trade protested this "attack upon the Jews as a people," the prohibitionist responded that the president was unqualified to lead that organization, since he "was not a representative of the Christian people of the city, as he was a Jew."[77]

Accusations that Jews were alien to southern society and demands for Jewish exclusion from the southern mainstream would have consequences far beyond the regional prohibition debate. Southern anti-Semitism arguably reached its apex in 1915, when Leo Frank was lynched twenty miles outside of Atlanta. But the accusation first made against Leo Frank in 1913—that as a Jewish man he posed a threat to the sexual purity of southern white women—had in fact been present in both southern culture and in national press coverage of the South for nearly a decade. Such insinuations first emerged in Atlanta in 1906, spread throughout the South in the decade that followed, and revolved specifically around the presence of Jews in the southern alcohol trade.

———

In 1925—five years into the nation's "noble experiment" with total prohibition—American Jewish Committee president Louis Marshall expressed sentiments similar to Isaac Wolfe Bernheim's fifteen years previous. "I have no doubt," he wrote in a private communication, "that on examination it will be found that a very large percentage of wholesale liquor dealers" before the passage of the Eighteenth Amendment "were Jews. The business of that time was at least lawful," he continued, "though I always regretted that Jews were engaged in that business to as great an extent as they apparently were."[78] It had been a trying five years for American Jewish leaders, who were regularly scandalized and dismayed by incessant reports of Jewish participation in bootlegging networks. Making matters worse, the Volstead Act, which codified the parameters of prohibition law, allowed beverage alcohol to be made and sold for religious ritual use. By 1925 the Prohibition Bureau had determined that rabbinic authorization and sacramental wine stores were "the chief sources of the illicit liquor supply."[79] When industrial titan, prohibition advocate, and anti-Semitic propagandist Henry Ford declared, "the Jews are on the side of liquor and always have been," he insinuated that American Jewry's longtime ties to alcohol commerce rendered them fundamentally incapable of abiding by the tenets and values of American society.[80]

Jews were not the only ethnic group targeted by prohibitionists for their role in alcohol production and purveyance. Irish and Italian Catholics also received criticism, as did Germans, whose dominance of the American brewing industry inspired a brutal spasm of nationalistic anti-German sentiment in the years leading up to World War I.[81] But enmity against Jewish alcohol purveyance had its own singular and distinctive lineage, in which economic anti-Semitism stimulated anxieties about American Jews' role in industrial expansion, urban growth, and ethnoracial tensions at the turn of the century.

NOTES

Parts of this chapter appear in my book *Jews and Booze: Becoming American in the Age of Prohibition* (New York: NYU Press, 2012); they are reprinted here with the kind permission of NYU Press.

1. Isaac Wolfe Bernheim, *The Story of the Bernheim Family* (Louisville, KY: Morton, 1910), 62–63.

2. Ibid.

3. Burton J. Hendrick, "The Jewish Invasion of America," *McClure's Magazine* 40 (March 1913): 154; George Kibbe Turner, "Beer and the City Liquor Problem," *McClure's Magazine* 33 (September 1909): 537; John Foster Fraser, *The Conquering Jew* (New York: Funk and Wagnalls, 1915), 108–109; "Columbus Men Publish Cards," *Atlanta Constitution*, July 15, 1907, 7.

4. Freiberg & Workum, Hoffheimer & Company, Elias Block & Company, S. Levi & Brothers, and Henry Block & Company, *Bonfort's Wine and Liquor Circular*, February 3, 1875, 296.

5. On the prohibition movement of the late nineteenth and early twentieth centuries, see, for example, Jack S. Blocker Jr., *Retreat from Reform: The Prohibition Movement in the United States, 1890–1913* (Westport, CT: Greenwood, 1976); Gaines M. Foster, *Moral Reconstruction: Christian Lobbyists and the Federal Legislation of Morality, 1865–1920* (Chapel Hill: University of North Carolina Press, 2002); John J. Rumbarger, *Profits, Power, and Prohibition: Alcohol Reform and the Industrializing of America* (Albany: State University of New York Press, 1989).

6. See Shelly Tenenbaum, "Culture and Context: The Emergence of Hebrew Free Loan Societies in the United States," *Social Science History* 13, no. 3 (1989): 211–236. Social scientists of the early twentieth century famously tended toward cultural interpretation: see the work of Max Weber and Werner Sombart on the economic behavior of Calvinist Protestants and Jews, respectively. For a more recent cultural interpretation of immigrant socioeconomic behavior, see Kerby A. Miller, *Emigrants and Exiles: Ireland and the Irish Exodus to North America* (New York: Oxford University Press, 1985). In the late twentieth century, contextual scholars countered what they saw as "an often simplistic form of cultural determinism" (Tenenbaum, "Culture and Context," 212). See, for instance, Stephen Steinberg, *The Ethnic Myth: Race, Ethnicity, and Class in America*, 3rd ed. (Boston:

Beacon, 2001). For a recent example of work that regards claims for Jewish socioeconomic premigrational experience as of secondary importance, see Eli Lederhendler, *Jewish Immigrants and American Capitalism, 1880-1920* (Cambridge: Cambridge University Press, 2009). Ewa Morawska has received much praise for weaving these two interpretive frameworks together in her books on eastern European immigrants in western Pennsylvania. See *For Bread with Butter: The Life-Worlds of East Central Europeans in Johnstown, Pennsylvania, 1890-1940* (Cambridge: Cambridge University Press, 1985); and *Insecure Prosperity: Small-Town Jews in Industrial America, 1890-1940* (Princeton, NJ: Princeton University Press, 1996).

7. The exception to this rule is kosher wine that has been made *mevushal* through boiling or, more recently, flash pasteurization. Cooked wine is unfit for "idolatrous" use, according to Jewish law, so if gentiles handle mevushal kosher wine it does not become unkosher.

8. Scholar David Kraemer has found archival evidence of rabbinic approval of wines produced and handled by non-Jewish monotheists—by Muslims in particular—during the medieval period. Such leniencies were not universally granted, however, and concerns about the ability of alcohol to dissolve cultural boundaries remained a matter of rabbinic debate. *Jewish Eating and Identity through the Ages* (New York: Routledge, 2007), 129-132.

9. Salo W. Baron and Arcadius Kahan, *Economic History of the Jews* (New York: Schocken Books, 1975), 20-21, 132-133; Jane S. Gerber, *Jewish Society in Fez, 1450-1700* (Leiden, Holland: Brill, 1980), 180-182; *Medieval Islamic Civilization: An Encyclopedia*, vol. 1, ed. Josef W. Meri (London: Routledge, 2006), s.v. "Alcohol."

10. Baron and Kahan, *Economic History*, 107-113, 226-228, 257-260; Jerry Z. Muller, *Capitalism and the Jews* (Princeton, NJ: Princeton University Press, 2010), 82-93; Sheilagh Ogilvie, "The European Economy in the Eighteenth Century," in *The Eighteenth Century: Europe 1688-1815*, ed. T. C. W. Blanning (Oxford: Oxford University Press, 2000). On transregional trade networks (both Jewish and otherwise) and the development of early modern capitalism, see Fernand Braudel, *The Structures of Everyday Life* and *The Wheels of Commerce*, vols. 1 and 2 of *Civilization and Capitalism, 15-18th Century* (New York: Harper and Row, 1981-1982), 1:138-230, 2:153-168.

11. Simon Dubnow, *History of the Jews in Russia and Poland from the Earliest Times until the Present Day*, trans. I. Friedlaender, 3 vols. (Philadelphia: Jewish Publication Society of America, 1918), 1:67; Gershon David Hundert, "Comparative Perspectives on Economy and Society: The Jews of the Polish Commonwealth—a Comment," in *In and out of the Ghetto: Jewish-Gentile Relations in Late Medieval and Early Modern Germany*, ed. R. Po-Chia Hsia and Hartmut Lehmann (Washington, DC: Cambridge University Press, 1995), 103; John Doyle Klier, *Russia Gathers Her Jews: The Origins of The "Jewish Question" In Russia, 1772-1825* (Dekalb: Northern Illinois University Press, 1986), 15.

12. Benjamin Nathans, *Beyond the Pale: The Jewish Encounter with Late Imperial Russia* (Berkeley: University of California Press, 2002), 40-44; Michael Stanislawski, *Tsar Nicholas I and the Jews: The Transformation of Jewish Society in Russia, 1825-1855* (Philadelphia: Jewish Publication Society of America, 1983), 173-174.

13. Baron and Kahan, *Economic History*, 136; Hans Rogger, *Jewish Policies and Right-Wing Politics in Imperial Russia* (Berkeley: University of California Press, 1986), 127.

14. On antebellum American drinking culture, see W. J. Rorabaugh, *The Alcoholic Republic: An American Tradition* (New York: Oxford University Press, 1979).

15. Though the number of retail alcohol dealers increased in absolute terms between 1870 and 1900, there were a few downturns in the trade during the period. The total number of retail dealers registered with the Bureau of Internal Revenue fell from 197,000 in 1886 to just fewer than 135,000 in 1891. By 1900, however, more than 201,000 retailers were registered. Despite downswings in retail outlets, the amount of alcohol consumed continued to rise fairly steadily, which suggests that retailers were, on average, dispensing larger quantities of alcohol at the end of the century than they had previously. On beer

consumption, see Norman Clark, *Deliver Us from Evil: An Interpretation of American Prohibition* (New York: Norton, 1976), 55. On liquor consumption and retail dealers, see Jack S. Blocker, "Consumption and Availability of Alcoholic Beverages in the United States, 1863–1920," *Contemporary Drug Problems* 21 (Winter 1994): 636–637, 642–643.

16. According to the U.S. Census from the year 1890, of the 20,362 workers currently employed by American breweries, 13,302—more than half of the total—were German immigrants. It is highly likely that thousands of native-born brewery employees were descendants of German immigrants and members of German American communities. *Eleventh Census of the United States: 1890*, vol. 2 (Washington, DC: U.S. Government Printing Office, 1892), 305, 486. On the American brewing industry, see Maureen Ogle, *Ambitious Brew: The Story of American Beer* (Orlando, FL: Harcourt, 2006).

17. Perry R. Duis, *The Saloon: Public Drinking in Chicago and Boston, 1880–1920* (Urbana: University of Illinois Press, 1983), 25–29.

18. Gerald Carlson, *The Social History of Bourbon: An Unhurried Account of Our Star-Spangled American Drink* (Louisville: University Press of Kentucky, 1963); Amy Helaine Mittleman, "The Politics of Alcohol Production: The Liquor Industry and the Federal Government, 1862–1900" (PhD diss., Columbia University, 1986).

19. Charles Dellheim discusses the "demonstration effect," which can help explain "the existence of clusters of Jews within the same economic sector" in "The Business of Jews," in *Constructing Corporate America: History, Politics, Culture*, ed. Kenneth Lipartito and David B. Sicilia (London: Oxford University Press, 2004), 231.

20. Louisville Young Men's Hebrew Association, advertisement, *Twice-a-Month*, February 1, 1901, 7; Advertisement, *Jewish Criterion*, 15, no. 20 (October 24, 1902), 7.

21. Solomon Levi's nephews Henry Bernheim, Jacob Oppenheimer, and Reuben Levi, and Leopold's son-in-law Simon Hirsch all operated their own wholesaling businesses, as did another unrelated Levi employee, Louis Klein. Barnett Robert Brickner, "Jewish Community of Cincinnati: Historical and Descriptive" (PhD diss., University of Cincinnati, 1933), 254–256; Manuscript Census for the Year 1870, Cincinnati, Hamilton County, Ohio; S. Levi & Bros., Ohio, 82:6–7, and Hirsch & Loewenstein Wines Liq & Cigars, Ohio, 88:205, and all Klein & Bernheim, Ohio, 85:119, from credit report volumes, R. G. Dun & Company Collection, Baker Library, Historical Collections, Harvard Business School, Cambridge, MA. Freiberg nephews include Herman Freiberg, Sigmund Freiberg, J. and A. Freiberg, and Solomon and Simon Klein. *Universal Jewish Encyclopedia*, ed. Isaac Landman, 10 vols. (New York: Universal Jewish Encyclopedia, 1941), 4:434–435; Charles Frederic Goss, *Cincinnati: The Queen City*, 4 vols. (Chicago: Clarke, 1912), 3:862–867; Max Burgheim, *Cincinnati in Wort und Bild*, trans. Stephen Farrelly (Cincinnati: Burgheim, 1888), 465–467; Freiberg & Workum et al., *Bonfort's Wine and Liquor*, 296; *Williams' Cincinnati Directory* (Cincinnati, OH: Williams, 1900).

22. On the Westheimer family, see *Telegraph* (St. Joseph, MO), April 4, 1996, 1–3; Milton Westheimer, "Gold in Them Thar Hills," unpublished autobiography, Robert C. and Jean Westheimer Rothenberg Family Papers, MSS 684, box 15, American Jewish Archives, Cincinnati, Ohio. On the Jacobs brothers, see the Joseph Benjamin Jacobs Papers, MSS 165, Ida Pearle and Joseph Cuba Community Archives of the William Breman Jewish Heritage Museum, Atlanta, GA.

23. "Selling Liquor to Drunkards," *Chicago Daily Tribune*, March 14, 1885, 8.

24. Duis, *Saloon*, 63; John Kobler, *Ardent Spirits: The Rise and Fall of Prohibition* (New York: Da Capo, 1973), 97, 113.

25. "Among the Slums," *Chicago Daily Tribune*, June 21, 1884, 11.

26. *Ninth Census of the United States: 1870*, vol. 3 (Washington, DC: U.S. Government Printing Office, 1872), 834; *Eleventh Census*, 2:304.

27. Historians who have taken seriously the concerns and demands of the American antialcohol movement include Clark, *Deliver Us from Evil*; James H. Timberlake,

Prohibition and the Progressive Movement, 1900–1920 (Cambridge, MA: Harvard University Press, 1966); Barbara Leslie Epstein, *The Politics of Domesticity: Women, Evangelism, and Temperance in Nineteenth-Century America* (Middletown, CT: Wesleyan University Press, 1981).

28. Moses Rischin, *The Promised City: New York's Jews, 1870–1914* (New York: Harper and Row, 1970), 272.

29. Deborah Weiner, "The Jews of Keystone: Life in a Multi-cultural Boomtown," *Southern Jewish History* 2 (1999): 6.

30. Thanks to William Korn for his genealogical research on Leadville (personal communication, in the author's possession).

31. *City Directory of Atlanta, Georgia* (Atlanta: Foote and Davies, 1905). To determine whom among Decanter Street's Atlanta's alcohol purveyors were Jews, the following sources were used: Manuscript Census for Atlanta, Fulton County, Georgia, 1870–1910; U.S. Census Manuscript, Ward 4, ED 61, Atlantic City, Fulton County, Georgia; Interment records of Oakland Cemetery and Westview Cemetery, both in Atlanta, Georgia; Steven Hertzberg, *Strangers within the Gate City: The Jews of Atlanta, 1845–1915* (Philadelphia: Jewish Publication Society of America, 1978); Janice O. Rothschild, *As But a Day: The First Hundred Years, 1867–1967* (Atlanta: Temple, 1967), 11–19; Hebrew Benevolent Congregation Membership Questionnaires, at Cuba Archives and Genealogical Center at the William Breman Jewish Heritage Museum.

32. "On the favorable side, the Jew commonly symbolized an admirable keenness and resourcefulness in trade," historian John Higham has written, but "in another mood, keenness might mean cunning; enterprise might shade into avarice." John Higham, *Send These to Me: Jews and Other Immigrants in Urban America* (New York: Atheneum, 1975), 121–122.

33. On Grant's Order 11, see Hasia Diner, *A Time for Gathering: The Second Migration, 1820–1880* (Baltimore: Johns Hopkins University Press, 1992), 158–160; Leonard Dinnerstein, *Anti-Semitism in America* (New York: Oxford University Press, 1994), 32–33. Dinnerstein's book is the best known and most commonly referenced scholarly monograph on American anti-Semitism. Other important works that engage the topic in its broadest terms are David A. Gerber, ed., *Anti-Semitism in American History* (Urbana: University of Illinois Press, 1986); John Higham, "Social Discrimination against Jews in America, 1830–1930," *Publications of the American Jewish Historical Society* 47, no. 1 (1957): 1–33; Louise A. Mayo, *The Ambivalent Image: Nineteenth-Century America's Perception of the Jew* (Rutherford, NJ: Fairleigh Dickinson University Press, 1988); Carey McWilliams, *A Mask for Privilege: Anti-Semitism in America* (Boston: Little, Brown, 1949); Robert Rockaway and Arnon Gutfield, "Demonic Images of the Jew in the Nineteenth Century United States," *American Jewish History* 89, no. 4 (2002): 355–381. For a sociological interpretation of economic anti-Semitism spanning back to the ancient period, see Werner J. Cahnman, "Socio-Economic Causes of Antisemitism," *Social Problems* 5, no. 1 (1957): 21–29.

34. Baron and Kahan, *Economic History*, 134–137; Nathans, *Beyond the Pale*, 40–44; Stanislawski, *Tsar Nicholas I*, 173–174.

35. "Among the Slums," 11.

36. Frank Moss, *The American Metropolis from Knickerbocker Days to the Present Time: New York City Life in All Its Various Phases*, vol. 3 (New York: Fenelon Collier, 1897), 166–167.

37. On the Jewish criminal element in early twentieth-century New York and efforts to eradicate it, see Jenna Weissman Joselit, *Our Gang: Jewish Crime and the New York Jewish Community, 1900–1940* (Bloomington: Indiana University Press, 1983).

38. *The Liquor Problem: A Summary of Investigations Conducted by the Committee of Fifty, 1893–1903*, (1905; repr., New York: Arno, 1970), 125–126. For a critical assessment of the Committee of Fifty, see Rumbarger, *Profits, Power, and Prohibition*, 89–101. On

American Jewish claims of moderate drinking habits, see Marni Davis, "No Whisky Amazons in the 'Tents of Israel': American Jews and the Gilded Age Temperance Movement," *American Jewish History* 94, no. 3 (2008): 143–173.

39. Klier, *Russia Gathers Her Jews*, 87.

40. "The Liberal Club," *Atlanta Constitution*, July 31, 1886, 8; August 15, 1886, 7.

41. J.N.T. Cawhern, "Souvenir of Georgia's Victory," Anti-Semitism File, American Jewish Historical Society, New York. Also cited in Hertzberg, *Strangers*, 162.

42. When spelled with an uppercase "P," Populism here refers only to the Populist party, more correctly known as the People's party, which was founded in 1892. A lowercase "p" refers to populism as a political and ideological system taken up by a wide range of political actors, including the Grangers, Farmers' Alliances and other radical agrarians, advocates of the free coinage of silver, and those workers' advocates, such as the Knights of Labor, who aligned themselves with causes such as public ownership of utilities, a graduated income tax, and opposition to the gold standard. Two well-regarded works of scholarship on the history of populism/Populism in the United States are: Lawrence Goodwyn, *Democratic Promise: The Populist Moment in America* (New York: Oxford University Press, 1976); and Michael Kazin, *The Populist Persuasion* (New York: Basic Books, 1995). For a useful and thought-provoking inquiry into populists' attraction to the movement and its ideologies, see James Turner, "Understanding the Populists," *Journal of American History* 67, no. 2 (1980): 354–373. The quote from the Omaha Platform is in Richard D. Heffner, ed., *A Documentary History of the United States*, 7th ed. (New York: New American Library, 2002), 235–239.

43. Rockaway and Gutfield, "Demonic Images," 378–381; Gerald Sorin, *A Time for Building: The Third Migration, 1880–1920* (Baltimore: Johns Hopkins University Press, 1992), 52–55.

44. See, for example, Frederic Cople Jaher, *Doubters and Dissenters: Cataclysmic Thought in America, 1885–1918* (London: Free Press of Glencoe, 1964), 135; Norman Pollack, "The Myth of Populist Anti-Semitism," *American Historical Review* 68, no. 1 (1962): 76.

45. Ignatius Donnelly, quoted in Dinnerstein, *Anti-Semitism*, 48–50.

46. See Higham, *Send These to Me*, 124–132; Kazin, *Populist Persuasion*, 296n38; Mayo, *Ambivalent Image*, 128–132.

47. Richard Hofstadter, *The Age of Reform* (New York: Vintage, 1955), 80.

48. Richard Hofstadter famously defined the populists by their tendency to see themselves as not merely oppressed but oppressed "consciously, continuously, and with wanton malice by 'the interests.'" Hofstadter, *Age of Reform*, 70. He claimed that the populists were unconsciously driven by "status anxiety"—by fear, inspired by downward economic mobility, that they were losing control of American culture and of their own future—toward paranoid and irrational visions of political and economic power struggles. This interpretation of the populist *mentalité* has been criticized since Hofstadter first offered it in 1955; his critics accuse him of having been overly influenced by McCarthy-era anxieties of his own.

49. Sociologist Joseph Gusfield has written that both populism and prohibitionism attracted those who suffered from "a sense of economic and political powerlessness" and who either feared or had experienced a decline in economic and cultural status. Gusfield made use of Hofstadter's "status anxiety" framework, claiming that prohibitionists, like populists, viewed their adversaries from an irrational, paranoid perspective and interpreted their opponents' successes as evidence that "the people" were victimized by a corrupt political and economic system. To be fair, this assessment would certainly describe neither every prohibitionist nor every populist. It does, however, point to the uncontroversial fact that both groups feared that the nation was being steered off track by powerful, malevolent forces. Joseph R. Gusfield, *Symbolic Crusade: Status Politics and the American Temperance Movement* (Urbana: University of Illinois Press, 1963), 94–102.

50. On the alcohol industry's more corrupt practices, see Ernest E. East, "The Distillers' and Cattle Feeders' Trust, 1887–1895," *Journal of the Illinois State Historical Society* 45 (1952): 101–123; Daniel Okrent, *Last Call: The Rise and Fall of Prohibition* (New York: Scribner, 2010), 29–34; Austin Kerr, *Organized for Prohibition* (New Haven, CT: Yale University Press, 1985), 12–34.

51. On populism's religious commitments, see Bruce Palmer, *"Man over Money": The Southern Populist Critique of American Capitalism* (Chapel Hill: University of North Carolina Press, 1980), 24–25, 126–137. On those of turn-of-the-century prohibitionists, see Blocker, *Retreat from Reform* (Westport, CT: Greenwood, 1976), 82–88; Kazin, *Populist Persuasion*, 82–96; and Timberlake, *Prohibition*, 4–17.

52. Kazin, *Populist Persuasion*, 92. For a similar analysis of southern prohibitionists' hatred of "liquor power," see William A. Link, *The Paradox of Southern Progressivism, 1880–1930* (Chapel Hill: University of North Carolina Press, 1992), 39–49.

53. Rezin B. Wasson, "Wasson Experiment Station Bulletin," n.d. (in the author's possession). For more on Wasson and the Ohio Agricultural Experiment Station, see Christoper Cumo, *A History of the Ohio Agricultural Experiment Station, 1882–1997* (Akron, OH: Midwest, 1997), 51.

54. The combine was originally called the "Distillers' and Cattle Feeders' Trust," so named because they also dealt in cooked grain mash, a waste product of alcohol distilling commonly used as livestock feed. The trust was organized in 1887 and included sixty-five distilleries at its peak; it briefly dominated the American whiskey industry, producing two-thirds of the nation's whiskey during the years it was in operation. Though the Illinois Supreme Court declared the trust to be an illegal combination in restraint of trade in 1895, the industry continued to undergo reorganization and consolidation. In 1902 the Distillers Securities Corporation, an outgrowth of the dissolved trust, became the nation's leading producer and distributor of liquor by purchasing and consolidating several large distilleries and alcohol-marketing firms. Alfred D. Chandler, "The Beginnings of 'Big Business' in American Industry," *Business History Review* 33, no. 1 (1959): 10–11; William L. Downard, *Dictionary of the History of the American Brewing and Distilling Industries* (Westport, CT: Greenwood, 1980), 128–129, 213–214; East, "Cattle Feeders' Trust," 17–20.

55. Many thanks to Dr. Rebecca Edwards for suggesting this possible connection between Wasson and Coxey.

56. "Of a Friday in the Jewish Quarter of New York," *Harper's Weekly* 34, no. 17 (April 19, 1890): 306.

57. Chad Heap, *Slumming: Sexual and Racial Encounters in American Nightlife* (Chicago: University of Chicago Press, 2009), 2.

58. "Down in the Dance Halls on Decanter Street," *Atlanta Constitution*, August 6, 1900, 5; "Beattie's Dive on Decanter Street," *Atlanta Constitution*, July 13, 1902, A29.

59. Clifford Kuhn, Harlon Joye, and E. Bernard West, *Living Atlanta: An Oral History of the City, 1914–1948* (Athens: University of Georgia Press, 1990), 172.

60. Timberlake, *Prohibition*, 119–120.

61. Quote is from John E. White, "Prohibition: The New Task and Opportunity of the South," *South Atlantic Quarterly* (January–October 1908): 136.

62. David F. Godshalk, *Veiled Visions: The 1906 Atlanta Race Riot and the Reshaping of American Race Relations* (Chapel Hill: University of North Carolina Press, 2005), 47–51; Denise A. Herd, "Prohibition, Racism, and Class Politics in the Post-Reconstruction South," *Journal of Drug Issues* 13 (1983): 84; Joel Williamson, *The Crucible of Race: Black-White Relations in the American South Since Emancipation* (New York: Oxford University Press, 1984), 209–233.

63. David E. Ruth, "The Georgia Prohibition Act of 1907: Its Proponents and Their Arguments" (honors thesis, Emory University, 1984), 63.

64. *Atlanta Journal*, September 22, 1906, 1.

65. Ibid.; *Atlanta Evening News*, September 22, 1906, 1; *Atlanta Constitution*, September 22, 1906, 1; Godshalk, *Veiled Visions*, 52. On the founding of the Georgia branch office of the Anti-Saloon League, see the *Atlanta Constitution*, March 6, 1904, 4; April 18, 1904, 3.

66. The Atlanta Race Riot of 1906 has received a great deal of scholarly attention in recent years. David Godshalk's book has already been referenced. Other works include Mark Bauerlein, *Negrophobia: A Race Riot in Atlanta, 1906* (San Francisco: Encounter Books, 2001); and Gregory Mixon, *The Atlanta Riot: Race, Class, and Violence in a New South City* (Gainesville: University Press of Florida, 2005).

67. Frank Foxcroft, "Prohibition in the South," *Atlantic Monthly* (May 1908): 628; Ruth, "Georgia Prohibition Act," 79–97.

68. Michael Lewis, "Access to Saloons, Wet Voter Turnout, and Statewide Prohibition Referenda, 1907–1919," *Social Science History* 32, no. 3 (2008): 381.

69. Eric L. Goldstein, *The Price of Whiteness: Jews, Race, and American Identity* (Princeton, NJ: Princeton University Press, 2006), 75–85; Jeffrey Melnick, *Black-Jewish Relations on Trial: Leo Frank and Jim Conley in the New South* (Jackson: University Press of Mississippi, 2000), 33. Other essays on Jewish commercial activity in the South, and specifically to African American patrons, include Arnold Shankman, "Friend or Foe? Southern Blacks View the Jew, 1880–1935," in *Turn to the South: Essays on Southern Jewry*, ed. Nathan M. Kaganoff and Melvin I. Urofsky (Waltham, MA: American Jewish Historical Society, 1979), 105–123; Clive Webb, "Jewish Merchants and Black Customers in the Age of Jim Crow," *Southern Jewish History* 2 (1999): 55–80.

70. "Selling Liquor to Negros," *Atlanta Journal*, September 26, 1906, 5; "Some Atlanta Saloons That Are Dens of Vice," *Atlanta Constitution*, September 30, 1906, 2.

71. Thomas Gibson, "The Anti-Negro Riots in Atlanta." *Harper's Weekly*, October 13, 1906, 1457–1459. Also cited in Hertzberg, *Strangers*, 161.

72. *American Magazine*, quoted in Ray Stannard Baker, *Following the Color Line: American Negro Citizenship in the Progressive Era* (New York: Doubleday, Page, 1908), 35.

73. Will Irwin, "Who Killed Margaret Lear?" *Collier's*, May 16, 1908, 10; United States v. Lee Levy and Adolph Asher, U.S. District Court (E.D. MO. 1908). Trial records generously made available to author by Daniel Okrent. See also Okrent, *Last Call*, 44–46.

74. Paul Isaac, *Prohibition and Politics* (Knoxville: University of Tennessee Press, 1965), 147–149.

75. Will Irwin, "More about 'Nigger Gin,'" *Collier's*, August 15, 1908, 27–30.

76. Will Irwin, "Tainted News Methods of the Liquor Interests," *Collier's*, March 13, 1909, 30.

77. *Atlanta Constitution*, July 15, 1907, 7.

78. Louis Marshall to Sieg Natenberg, November 9, 1925, box 1597, Louis Marshall Collection, American Jewish Archives.

79. Leo Sack, "The Sacramental Wine Scandal," *American Hebrew*, March 20, 1925, 571.

80. "How Jews Gained American Liquor Control," *Dearborn Independent*, December 17, 1921, reprinted in Henry Ford, *Aspects of Jewish Power in the United States*, vol. 4 of *The International Jew: The World's Foremost Problem* (Dearborn, MI: Dearborn Independent, 1922), 7–18.

81. Charles Thomas Johnson, *Culture at Twilight: The National German-American Alliance, 1901–1918* (New York: Lang, 1999), 142, 150–158; Ogle, *Ambitious Brew*, 172–173; Okrent, *Last Call*, 101.

CHAPTER 6

Blacks, Jews, and the Business of Race Music, 1945–1955

Jonathan Karp

"Race" music was a term employed by the recording industry in the years 1920 to 1950 to describe commercial music made by blacks for blacks. Between 1945 and 1955 many of the most significant companies specializing in race music (or "rhythm and blues," as it later came to be known) were owned or co-owned by Jews. These were independent ("indie") labels that exploited the vacuum left by the "majors," the established music corporations, in servicing the black record market. They included such influential labels as King in Cincinnati; Savoy in Newark; Apollo, Old Time, and Atlantic in New York; Chess and National in Chicago; and Specialty, Aladdin, and Modern in Los Angeles, as well as many others of lesser stature and duration. The men, and occasionally women, who ran these companies were Jewish entrepreneurs, businesspeople first and foremost, only sometimes with a previous strong interest in and deep knowledge of black music. Although the successful ones came to take the music seriously, to the point of making detailed studies of its commercial qualities, their activity was driven by money, not aesthetics. In true Adam Smithian fashion—that is, out of self-interested motives—they provided black musicians with unprecedented opportunities to record and acquire fans. But they also almost invariably exploited black artists who were doubly vulnerable: individually as musicians lacking in independent capital and collectively as members of a subordinate racial caste in a still largely segregated society.

If the story of these business pioneers is a morally ambiguous one, the morality tale so often central to accounts of the music business is only part of the story. A related but distinct aspect is the matter of how and why Jewish entrepreneurs succeeded to a comparatively greater degree than black ones in a business whose initial market was almost exclusively African American. A further issue is the extent to which the label owners represented a creative force in their own right, not just in the Schumpeterian sense of innovative entrepreneurship but also in the artistic sense of making creative contributions to the development of American popular music. Finally, the topic of what constituted the label owners' Jewishness cannot be ignored; if these men and women tended to be infrequent attendees at synagogue, they nevertheless evolved a kind of Jewish subculture, one in which Yiddish provided a part of the code and where business networks followed ethnic patterns not just within a single generation but over the course of many. In what follows I address all of these issues: how the market for rhythm and blues music evolved, the relation of race music to black capitalism, the ways in which Jewish entrepreneurs capitalized on this niche, and the complex character of the resulting relations between Jewish owners and black artists.

The Birth of Rhythm and Blues

The race industry reflected the emergence of new styles in black popular music. What became known as rhythm and blues evolved out of a trimmed down, ensemble-based jazz band sound synthesized with the blues music of blacks who had recently migrated from rural parts of the South to cities such as New Orleans, Houston, Memphis, New York, Detroit, Chicago, Cincinnati, and Los Angeles. Although there were many different styles of race music—the "boogie woogie" of the 1930s and the raucous "jump blues" of the 1940s, the subdued "club blues" played by piano-based trios with gentle crooning vocalists and the sweet a cappella–style "doo wop" prominent in the mid-1950s—the following brief description of one record serves to convey a sense of the genre's qualities as a whole.[1] A good deal of information can be gleaned, for instance, from the grooves of a 1949 release by jump blues master Louis Jordan. His "Beans and Cornbread" was among the last in a series of hits with his group, the Tympany Five, that had helped to redefine postwar black popular music, with songs such as "Choo Choo Ch'Boogie," "Saturday Night Fish Fry," "Knock Me a Kiss," and "Ain't Nobody Here But Us Chickens." Although these records were released on Decca, one of the "majors" (along with RCA-Victor, Columbia, Mercury, and Capitol), they were linked to the indie phenomenon through their producer, Milt Gabler, who, as we will see, was an important figure in the history of the independent label phenomenon.

Jordan, who both wrote and performed "Beans and Cornbread," was an Arkansas-born musician who had played alto sax and sung with the Chick Webb Orchestra during the mid-1930s (Ella Fitzgerald was the singer in the band). His creation of the Tympany Five in 1940 (always spelled with a "y" and in many incarnations including up to seven musicians) corresponds to the decline of this era. Most big bands had catered to both white and black audiences, albeit almost always in a segregated fashion. In contrast, small groups like Jordan's were targeted more narrowly to the African American market. Although Jordan built on the aural foundation of such groups (retaining a horn section and piano-based rhythm section), his music updated older band styles by stressing a distinctive, frenetic shuffle beat, one that utilized "dotted eighth notes and sixteenths," as producer Gabler described.[2] The honking sax that introduces the song suggests a layer of continuity between Lindy bands such as Lionel Hampton's and the "honky tonk" style of 1950s tenor-led ensembles of Earl Bostic, Jimmy Forrest, and Red Prysock. This was neither the classic blues of 1920s singers like Bessie Smith, nor the rural acoustic blues of the Mississippi Delta; rather it was urban dance music played for black ex-GIs and factory workers, secretaries, and seamstresses. It was good-time music with an optimistic feel, performed in roadhouse clubs, dance halls, and theaters for a mobile (both physically and socially), automobile-owning crowd.

The lyrical themes also differed from those of the preceding era. The music was for newcomers, sometimes nostalgic for and sometimes contemptuous of the country life left behind—yet always self-conscious about the distance in space and time from the rural South and its mentalities. "Beans and Cornbread," like so many Louis Jordan songs, reflects this new urban spirit, one that pokes gentle fun at the old peasant ways. The mock gospel urgency of the vocal performance, its call-and-response punctuation, builds to an exuberant church choir resolution. Its secularized gospel feel is also anticipatory of the "soul music" approach taken a decade later by Ray Charles and Sam Cooke. Finally, though softened with humor, the message of "Beans and Cornbread," as with so much of Jordan's music, is serious: the song's wit is born of a new assertiveness in postwar African American consciousness determined to put an end to segregation and racial enmity. Beans and cornbread (i.e., blacks and whites), must learn to stop their squabbling, because, "like liver and onions," "like bagels and lox," "they go hand-in-hand."[3]

Milt Gabler's presence during the recording points to the business side of contemporary race music. Although this was music geared to an exclusively black market, there was an important connection between its emergence and patterns of white consumption. In the late 1930s a crop of mostly white jazz aficionados was eager to find jazz and blues 78s that had been made years earlier during the first wave of race-music recordings in the 1920s, the period of Louis Armstrong, "Blind Lemon" Jefferson, Alberta Hunter, and Bessie Smith. Throughout the pre-Depression period, labels such as Gennett, Okeh, Paramount, Bluebird (a subsidiary of Victor), and Vocalion (a subsidiary of BBC-Brunswick) had recorded these and scores of lesser-known musicians for the African American market.

These original race records (the "race" categorization was first employed by Okeh in 1923) were sold by mail order, by Pullman porters on train journeys or stops along the way, and at local general stores in rural communities. By the late 1930s most were out of print, having vanished when the labels that produced them dissolved during the Depression.[4] With music becoming increasingly commercialized, listeners—conspicuously white ones—who craved an earlier, purer sound became interested in locating these old recordings. Fellow jazz fans with an entrepreneurial bent, men such as Gabler, Herb Abramson, Bob Thiele, Lester Koenig, Alfred Lion, Norman Granz, Bob Weinstock, Jac Holzman, Ahmet and Nesuhi Ertegun, Manny and Seymour Solomon, and Orrin Keepnews, all of whom were eventually indie jazz label owners, began to organize the market. Gabler was among the first, selling used jazz 78s out of his father's electronics shop in midtown Manhattan. A true pioneer, he established Commodore Records in 1938, named after the shop that he co-owned with Jack Crystal (the father of comedian Billy Crystal) on 42nd Street between Lexington and Third Avenues. A year earlier another small label, Varsity, had been created by Eli Oberstein, a music industry veteran and former recording engineer for Victor. Varsity and Commodore both specialized in reissuing jazz and blues from the 1920s and early 1930s, the kind of music collectors had been doggedly hunting out in used furniture shops but which these small labels now made available in freshly minted form through reissues and custom pressings.[5] In fact, the reissue business proved profitable enough to capture the attention of majors such as RCA-Victor and Decca, which, through the acquisition sprees of an earlier era, had acquired the catalogs of the old race labels. Thus, by the early 1940s, with the reissue market slipping away to the majors, Gabler decided to concentrate on recording contemporary artists, beginning with musicians such as Eddie Condon, who was then spearheading a Dixieland revival, nostalgically recreating the jazz style of New Orleans.[6] Although Dixieland was hardly music attuned to current African American tastes, Gabler's creation of an early indie label set a notable precedent. Once the new race music sound began to emerge, in part through Gabler's own productions of Louis Jordan on Decca, some of Gabler's associates and disciples (many of them Jewish) would follow suit by starting their own indie labels.[7]

Meanwhile, dramatic changes were shaking up the industry as a whole. The trade organization of music publishing—the American Society of Composers, Authors, and Publishers (ASCAP)—had excluded most jazz, blues, country (or "hillbilly" as it was then called). In 1940 ASCAP attempted to double royalties for the live performance of its copyrighted material. Radio broadcasters, long resentful of ASCAP's demands, responded by forming an alternative and friendlier organization, Broadcast Music Incorporated (BMI). Since ASCAP represented most of the established composers who wrote in the Tin Pan Alley tradition, BMI was forced to take on representational duties for significantly more jazz, blues, and hillbilly songwriters. But when broadcasters played BMI music on the air, particularly the recorded music for which musicians were paid no royalty, it provoked the wrath of another powerful organization, the American Federation of Musicians (AFM), which between August 1942 to November 1944 banned its members from recording in the studio or performing live on the air.[8]

The fact that many of the early race labels emerged amid the recording ban underscores the furtive, at times illegal, character of the industry's origins (which some would argue was never to disappear). Yet in retrospect there appears to have been no other way that indie labels could have achieved a foothold, since employing various deceptions to violate the ban was precisely what enabled the indies to gain a head start on the majors in the emerging market for rhythm and blues. The strike (along with a wartime rationing of shellac, an essential ingredient for making 78 records as well as munitions), had led to a momentary shift in the majors' recording priorities. Not only did corporations such as RCA and Columbia release fewer records, but they now focused their resources on vocalists, a category not covered by AFM contracts. This concentration ushered in a golden age for singers such as Bing Crosby, Frank Sinatra, Nat "King" Cole, and Rosemary Clooney and put another nail in the coffin of big bands. But it also distracted the majors from the increasing popularity of race and hillbilly recordings. Even when the strike and the war ended, the majors (with the exception of Decca) were slow to pick up the slack. So much money was being made from mainstream stars like Sinatra that the majors were prepared momentarily to forgo the dynamic niche markets, which in 1950 still amounted to only about 15 percent of all U.S. record sales, although these were expanding rapidly.[9]

The dynamism of the race industry was the result of two additional developments. First, the increasing availability of television was forcing radio to concentrate more on the local than the national market, including the broadcasting of music designed to meet the demands of nearby communities and advertisers.[10] It was in this period that African American disk jockeys like Al Benson in Chicago, or white ones like Los Angeles's Hunter Hancock, gained a foothold, pioneering an early version of "top 40" radio for black audiences.[11] Second, the World War II and Korean War periods had coincided with and significantly contributed to a dramatic demographic restructuring of African American life. The decades-long Great Migration of southern blacks really constituted a great urbanization, in which African Americans gradually ceased to be an overwhelmingly rural population. Farm mechanization back home and military production in the North, opening up new industries and jobs to blacks, fueled a major shift in population. During the war years well over a million blacks left the South. Areas where previously only small black communities had existed now acquired sizable ones, particularly on the West Coast.

In the decade of the 1940s the number of blacks in California increased by 272 percent.[12] As exemplified in Louis Jordan's recordings, these migrants brought with them both a nostalgic yearning for the rural folk culture they left behind and a hunger for fresh interpretations of that culture that befit the new circumstances. And though still poor and beset by a host of social and economic problems, urban blacks increasingly had money to spend. In 1939 black males earned 41 percent of what white males earned, but by 1947 that figure had climbed to 54 percent. During the Korean War (1950–1953) the median gap in income among blacks reached a historical low point.[13] Consumerism was thus essential to African Americans' reshaping of their cultural inheritance in the racially segregated cities where they increasingly lived.

But who would record and market the music that was being performed in the bars and nightclubs of Maxwell Street in Chicago, Central Avenue in Los Angeles, and 125th street in Harlem? To put the question otherwise: why did Jewish rather than African American entrepreneurs succeed in filling this vital niche? Indeed, the music business can serve as a laboratory for the comparison of post–World War II Jewish and African American entrepreneurial activity. For surely here, if anywhere, conditions would seem ripe for the successful proliferation of African American small businesses. As noted, race records had been made since the early 1920s, but until the advent of Motown in the 1960s black businesses never played a prominent role in serving the African American record market. Even with Motown's rise and subsequent to it, black companies would not achieve dominance in the rhythm and blues, soul, or hip-hop fields. The notable instances of black ownership—the Black Swan label in the early 1920s, Duke/Peacock and Vee-Jay in the 1950s, Motown in the 1960s, and Def Jam in the 1980s and 1990s—underscore the rule that successful black labels have always been the exception. This is the case despite the fact that African Americans are clustered in the popular music business as musicians, talent scouts, and producers and that blacks form an internal ethnic market that a black record label would presumably be best equipped to service. Yet in the postwar decades, and especially during the race period of 1945–1955, it was Jewish entrepreneurs who far more consistently and successfully managed the business of black popular music.

A number of recent books and articles have addressed the prominent role played by Jews in the history of American popular music, with a special focus on black-Jewish relations. Building on research into how nineteenth-century immigrant groups like Germans and Irish deployed racial mimicry (often in the form of blackface minstrelsy) to establish and affirm their own whiteness, these studies see the Jews' use of black musical forms as a form of appropriation that was ultimately aimed at successful assimilation. As Ralph Ellison succinctly put it, "the darky act makes brothers of us all"—that is, of all who at the end of the show can remove the blackface makeup to reveal white skin underneath.[14] However compelling, this interpretation of white ethnic participation in minstrelsy needs to be supplemented with other explanatory models of immigrant interactions with blacks, particularly with regard to black-Jewish relations. It cannot, for instance, account for the persistence over many decades of a similar pattern of black-Jewish relations in the pop music industry. Why, one might ask, did Jews dominate not only the music song-writing and publishing industry of Tin Pan Alley's golden age in 1895–1925, in which "coon songs," ragtime, and jazz were prominent song genres, but also the independent race and rhythm and blues record labels of the period 1945–1955, and even (albeit to a lesser extent) the labels specializing in rap and hip-hop music of the 1980s and 1990s? If one adopts the cultural studies model described earlier, in which successive immigrant groups paradoxically prove their whiteness by mastering black music as a rite of passage into the mainstream, then a successfully assimilated group like Jews should long ago have lost any need for a black musical connection. Yet this has clearly not been the case, since the phenomenon of a racial mimicry of blacks on the part of a segment of the American Jewish population has continued over decades and generations. The cultural studies model suffers from historical shortsightedness. It tends to treat American Jews as a tabula rasa, and either succumbs to the worst caricatures of the "lachrymose conception" of European Jewish history (treating their victimization as the Jews' only distinctive cultural characteristic) or else ignores the earlier history of Jews altogether, as if beyond religious differences they were essentially indistinguishable from any other European immigrant group.

One of the most neglected aspects of modern Jewish history is Jews' economic experience. Historically Jews have differed from blacks (as well as from the bulk of immigrant Irish, Italians, and Slavs) not just ethnically, culturally, and religiously, but economically as well. The majority of blacks during the nineteenth century were agricultural laborers (whether as slaves or nominally free) with important but small segments in skilled crafts, business, and the professions. European Jews, in contrast, were not peasants, however persecuted or impoverished. Many, particularly from central and eastern Europe—the source of most nineteenth- and early twentieth-century immigration—had long experience as middlemen, commercial agents, brokers, franchisers of tax and revenue operations, peddlers, old-clothes dealers, pawnbrokers, jobbers, and, of course, as artisans, teamsters, and unskilled laborers.[15] Though many of the Jewish immigrants to the United States were poor, they retained skills and a cultural outlook attuned to entrepreneurship and mobility—even when they were professed socialists.[16] This socioeconomic difference contributed to the eventual emergence of a "black-Jewish" alliance, since throughout the first half of the twentieth century, Jews and African Americans were not usually in direct competition for the same jobs.[17] Racial restrictions, on the one hand, and anti-Semitism, on the other, surely reinforced existing structural differences between the two groups and ensured that blacks would have limited access to entrepreneurial activities, while Jews would be overrepresented in them. But Jews' rapid upward mobility in the United States was not caused by their acquisition of "whiteness," as so many recent treatments have claimed; rather, it was purchased through the rapid restoration of their middlemen capacities.[18]

BLACK-OWNED LABELS

To be sure, black capitalism has had a far more robust history in the United States than many commentators have recognized. Racist or romantic assumptions that rural blacks were too natural, pastoral, and innocent to engage in hard-nosed business activity ignore the reality that the black community, even under slavery, always had its share of entrepreneurs. This fact has been obscured in part because many of the leading black spokesmen (including historians) were hostile to capitalism even when they supported black economic nationalism. While blacks might strive for economic self-sufficiency, insisted W.E.B. Du Bois, they would also eschew "the old, individualistic, laissez faire method."[19] In fact, most blacks were not ideologically opposed to free enterprise. Even a rough analogy between rural blacks and European peasants in no way precludes entrepreneurship, for peasants have demonstrably proven capable of mastering the market operations of the countryside.[20]

The era of increasing urbanization, moreover, ushered in by World War I, created what one recent historian of black business in the United States has labeled a "Golden Age," lasting to the Great Depression.[21] Segregation in the urban setting created a circumstance in which blacks had no alternative but to attempt to construct their own separate communities as mirror images of white society.[22] With severely limited resources, African Americans sought to replicate the financial, commercial, civic, and recreational institutions of the country as a whole, including insurance companies, real estate agencies, taxicab services, hotels, hospitals, and the like. At the micro level, blacks created tens of thousands of small businesses, including countless barbershops, beauty parlors, and shoe repair operations.[23] On a far larger scale were the business empires of Madame C. J. Walker, and later John H. Johnson and Arthur G. Gaston. In fact, there were few categories of enterprises not created and conducted by blacks, whether in retail, clothes manufacture, mining, even munitions.

Thus, the tragedy of black capitalism is not that it was never attempted (it has been continuously so) but rather that its achievements have been so fleeting, and its effects on the economic well-being of black Americans so limited. At the peak of the "Golden Age," black enterprises employed only around 2 percent of African Americans. Moreover, the fragility of many of these businesses made them disproportionately vulnerable during the general economic collapse of the Great Depression. Well over half of the black retail stores existing in 1927 were gone by 1933. Of the sixty-four black banks in 1912, only a handful remained at the Depression's onset.[24] While in the postwar years this picture improved significantly, the overall pattern remained the same. In the race-music era, while blacks on average had more disposable income than ever before, black business did not grow in kind.

Structural obstacles, preeminently de facto and de jure racism, surely accounted for much of this weakness. As Juliet E. K. Walker has observed, despite the fact that blacks responded to residential segregation by creating their own financial and commercial institutions, they could do nothing to prevent white businesses from penetrating black markets and competing directly with these same black businesses. By the 1920s white trade journals began to show an awareness of black consumer spending power, as was the case, for instance, with the race records produced by Okeh and Paramount.[25] White businesses benefited from comparatively greater capitalization and efficiency. Even when black consumers felt insulted by white merchants, or expressed a commitment to race solidarity, the presence of white businesses, their ability to offer credit, greater variety, and convenience, put African American enterprises at a competitive disadvantage. From the standpoint of a black capitalism, the opportunity for entrepreneurship presented by *residential segregation* was offset by the reality of *commercial integration*, which tended to benefit the white businesses situated in the ghetto.[26]

Despite these handicaps, blacks played a role in brokering race music from the start. In the 1910s, to cite just one example, the Quality Amusement Corporation emerged to provide bookings for the black vaudeville circuit in major East Coast cities and as far west as Chicago, as historian Ted Vincent has described. But while the corporation was a pioneer, theater owners soon came to prefer its larger and more effective white competitor, the Theater Owners' Booking Agency.[27] Similarly, while the black-owned and highly race-conscious record company Black Swan released a number of successful blues records in the early 1920s (by performers such as Alberta Hunter and Ethel Waters), its product was in no way superior from a commercial or aesthetic point of view to that of Okeh or Gennett (white family-owned firms that evolved out of the piano and furniture industries).[28] These white companies could hire the black musical expertise they needed to compete. So while Black Swan's recording director was the well-known jazz musician Fletcher Henderson, Okeh employed the equally adept Clarence Williams and Perry Bradford.

After Black Swan's demise in 1924, the Paramount furniture company bought up its catalog of master recordings and hired a black college graduate, J. Mayo Williams, to run its Chicago race records outfit. Though no musician and certainly no admirer of race music prior to joining the company, Williams possessed a keen ear and considerable business savvy. Indeed, he has been described as the most successful A&R man in the early history of the blues (i.e., artist and repertoire, which at the time included duties of overseeing the song selection, musical arrangements, and recording operations).[29] Yet his own stab at record company ownership, despite having the financial backing of investors from Gennett, was short-lived. His Black Patti Records began and folded in 1927, and thereafter Williams resumed his career as a talent scout and recording expert for white companies (initially Brunswick and later Decca). For a black man at the time, Williams was well paid, with commissions for individual recording sessions as well as revenue from in-house music publishing. Given the especial risks that black business ownership involved, following his one abortive effort, Williams likely felt no pressing need to strike out again on his own.

Like Williams's Black Patti, most of the numerous black-owned record companies of the 1940s and 1950s led short lives. In many cases they proved successful in identifying and nurturing future stars, only to lose them to white labels. Usually pure self-interest was at work: artists had a logical reason for assuming that a white label was more likely than a black one to take their careers to a higher plateau. For instance, in the wake of his 1950 hit, "Two Years of Torture," Percy Mayfield shifted from black entrepreneur John Dolphin's Record-in-Hollywood label to Jewish label owner Art Rupe's Specialty Records.[30] Another example is Ray Charles's early career at Jack Lauderdale's Swing Time (previously Down Beat), a label he would soon flee to join the white-owned Atlantic.[31]

A further disadvantage was inadequate capitalization—a crippling defect for many black labels. The indefatigable Bob Geddins, a seminal figure in the history of West Coast blues music but a perpetually hapless businessman, could rarely benefit from the fine records he cut because he lacked the means to advertise and distribute them. Not surprisingly, a number of his discoveries, such as bluesmen Lowell Fulson and Jimmy McCracklin, eventually lost patience.[32] Similarly, Walter "Dootsie" Williams, another West Coast black record entrepreneur, barely had the resources to distribute the Penguins' epic 1954 hit "Earth Angel," and quickly lost the group to Mercury.[33] To be sure, distribution proved the Achilles heel for countless labels, both white and black. In the lucky case of a hit record, these labels could not afford to press sufficient numbers of copies until the invariably delinquent distributors paid them for the ones already sold. The distributors would cough up once the pressed records were available and ready to ship. The catch-22 could be averted only if a label had access to credit, which was a traditional weakness of black enterprise in general.

This pessimistic evaluation of the black labels deserves qualification, however. First, as music historians readily point out, business failure is not always incompatible with aesthetic success. That is, in each of the instances cited earlier, by boosting important artists early in their careers, black labels were able to make signal (if brief) contributions to the evolution of rhythm and blues.[34] Second, if success is measured in terms of durability, or even of mere survival, rather than only in large profits and persistent hits, then the verdict on black labels would have to include numerous such successes. Although they might not have been able to compete with white- and Jewish-owned labels, they could still find a niche within a niche by serving more peripheral markets (regional musical styles without national appeal, or less current styles of gospel music and blues).[35] Third, the tiny elite of black labels that did make it to the top of the race industry—Don Robey's Duke/Peacock label out of Houston and Vivian and James Bracken's Vee-Jay out of Chicago—were able to do so by virtue of their location, musical and business perspicacity, and, especially in the case of Robey, ruthless determination. In fact, while Vee-Jay's glittering roster and proven hit-making formula could not prevent the company from eventually going bust, Robey's consistently effective management, his diverse repertoire of genres, and tough business stance, kept his company aloft until his death.

If Robey possessed brutal qualities associated with the worst of the white record moguls, he had other advantages that made him unique among black record entrepreneurs of the time. He wisely exploited the steady if unspectacular market for gospel records to keep him afloat between pop hits, and he demonstrated savvy in fending off competitors through the courtroom. With the talents of company lawyer Irving Marcus, Robey acquired the Memphis-based, white-owned Duke label in 1953 and won a precedent-setting lawsuit against Sam Phillips's Sun Records, which Robey accused of "copycatting" his big hit, "Hound Dog." Contrast Robey's successful suit with that of a white small label entrepreneur, Al Patrick, who owned Supreme Records in Los Angeles. Though on merit both Duke/Peacock and Supreme evidently had equally strong cases, Robey had the wisdom to sue merely another fledgling indie. Patrick, in contrast, went after Decca, a major label with deep pockets.[36] The result: Stewart's suit bankrupted Supreme, while Robey's helped him to fend off rapacious competitors. A final example of Robey's discipline was his ability to resist the temptation to which so many other owners of successful regional labels succumbed, that of shifting operations to glamorous but highly competitive entertainment capitals such as New York and Los Angeles. Robey's Houston, like New Orleans, Nashville, Memphis, and later Motown's Detroit, had a blues-soul sound all its own and a bevy of local talent to draw on.[37]

Thus the advantages enjoyed by white- and Jewish- over black-owned labels were considerable but not insuperable. Astute management and good luck are the sine qua non of all small businesses. Given the cutthroat competition of race labels, in which a novice's mistake could prove fatal, previous business experience was often indispensable as well. Like Don Robey, the black label owners who made it all possessed such experience. Otis and Leon René, who in 1942 founded in Los Angeles one of the earliest rhythm and blues labels,

Exclusive, came from an entrepreneurial tradition in the black artisan class. Their father had been a brick contractor, both brothers had attended black colleges, and Otis had owned a pharmacy during the Depression to supplement his brothers' song-writing activities.[38] Similarly, Berry Gordy's father owned painting and plastering businesses, as well as the Booker T. Washington Grocery Store, attesting to the family's ideological as well as practical dedication to black enterprise.[39] Another early black label in Los Angeles, Dootsie Williams's Dootone, emerged out of his earlier music-publishing business. Music publishing was a field in which black entrepreneurship had laid down firm roots, going back to the various firms housed in New York's Gaiety building during the 1920s and even earlier to W. C. Handy's publishing concerns in the 1910s.[40] These cases underscore the importance of entrepreneurial experience, from learning from past failures to achieving eventual label success.

Most black labels that fit this bill started from record retail operations. Indeed, it is hardly surprising that many black as well as white labels began as extensions of record stores (or appliance and dry goods shops, which frequently sold some records). Among these were the aforementioned Milt Gabler's Commodore, Herman Lubinsky's Savoy, Glen Wallichs's Capitol, Syd Nathan's King label, Bobby Robinson's Red Robin, the Brackens's Vee-Jay, John Dolphin's Hollywood, and later Berry Gordy's Tamla/Motown. Record shops, like disk jockeys, were effectively partners of indie labels, the latter providing retailers with free merchandise in return for promotion, information, and even the calculated inflation of sales figures to radio stations or trade journals.[41] Record stores were frequent sponsors of radio programs (they might even run a program on the premises) and through labels and disk jockeys maintained close contacts with musicians and performers. Chances are, the idea of making records has crossed the mind of every record store owner at one time or another.

While black-owned record retail outfits were plentiful, the extraordinary prominence of Jewish retailers underscores the competitive advantages possessed by Jews, not least of all the advantage of timing. Jews, well entrenched in American cities by the first quarter of the twentieth century, often had well-established retail operations in the very locales in which black immigrants had settled more recently. This is likely why a high percentage of Jewish race labels developed in Los Angeles and Oakland, cities where only relatively small numbers of blacks had resided before the war. But even where black communities had been long established, for example, in New York and Chicago, Jewish retailers exceeded black ones in scale of their operations and in their durability. In fact, retail was historically one of the weakest areas of black capitalism, a fact that seriously reduced the chances that black labels could achieve parity, let alone domination, of the black record market.[42] As mentioned, because of its links to record distribution and promotion, knowledge of retail practices and connections to mom-and-pop stores were especially critical to small label success.

In contrast, exposure to the merely the musical side of a label operation, either through performance or "A&R" work, rarely led to successful label ownership. Such was the case with black A&R man Henry Glover of Glover Records, Johnny Otis's Dig label, black deejay Al Benson's Parrot, black singer Syl Johnson's Shama, and former Specialty producer Harold Battiste's race-conscious AFO (All for One) label. It was not enough to know music, the market for it, and the methods of making hit records (as these men surely did). Sales techniques, distribution networks (critical for the success of any indie), continuous rationalization of the production process, that is to say, the mastery of operations that applied not just to music but to all businesses, were equally essential. This is underscored by the failure of labels started by veteran Jewish A&R men too, such as Fred Mendelsohn's Herald, and Lee Magid's Central label.[43] Still, there appears to have been a larger proportion of black than Jewish labels that evolved from A&R and performance backgrounds, and conversely a higher proportion of Jewish-owned labels launched from businesses that lay fully or partly outside of music altogether.

JEWISH-OWNED LABELS

In contrast to some of the black labels, none of the important Jewish ones in the period 1945–1955 evolved out of an owner's earlier career as a musical performer, and only rarely during the 1940s did a previous career in songwriting lead to Jewish label management (though by the late 1950s the shift from composer to owner would become more common).[44] Instead, one might speak of two principal Jewish label-owner "types" during the race-music era: first, the aficionados of jazz and blues, like Gabler, and, second, the business owners with little or no previous interest in black music, like Herman Lubinsky or Al Green. But what is extraordinary is the degree to which a large number of individuals in both categories were able to succeed at the record game. This was likely the case because even many of the Jewish jazz aficionados possessed previous business knowledge, either acquired on their own, from parents (as the case of Milt Gabler suggests), or from close contacts with Jews in various spheres of the entertainment business. Like Gabler, Bob Weinstock, the creator of Prestige Records, started out with a jazz specialty record shop. Alfred Lion, cofounder of Blue Note Records, was an executive for a German import/export firm, who took time off during his business trips to New York to scrounge for rare 78s. Fellow jazz collector Herb Abramson was a dental student prior to becoming a producer for Al Green's National label in Chicago, but his wife Miriam was an experienced accountant and financial manager.[45] The father of Elektra Records founder Jac Holzman was a physician, but many of his patients were in the record business. Their example inspired the doctor's teenage son. "I took my Bar Mitzvah money and decided I would start a record company," Holzman recalled.[46] Norman

Granz, who worked as a film editor when he began promoting jazz concerts, grew up in his family business, a department store that went under during the Depression. Combining practicality with idealism, Granz once described his career goals in descending order of priority as "to make money, to combat racial prejudice, and to present good jazz."[47] These examples suggest that the division between the Jewish jazz aficionados who set up businesses to conserve and control the music they loved and those who established indies from more purely capitalist motives was one of degree rather than kind.

Jerry Wexler's career illustrates how the two sides could readily blend. Eventually, a senior partner with Turkish-born Ahmet Ertegun in Atlantic Records, Wexler started out as a disciple of Milt Gabler, hanging out at the Commodore Records shop on 52nd Street, endlessly exchanging information about the jazz recordings of the 1920s. But (as with Gabler himself), despite pledging his devotion to jazz, it was black pop music that would form the actual substance of his future livelihood. Here, however, a further Jewish business stronghold supplied the connection. When Wexler, the product of a poor but culturally middle-class family in Washington Heights, was just starting out, there were any number of signs pointing him in the direction of a career in race records. He had before his eyes not merely the Commodore shop, owned by the son of a Jewish immigrant electronics retailer, but also the "Jewish" industry of Tin Pan Alley. Like the record labels of the 1940s, the popular music-publishing industry of the early twentieth century had been dominated by Jewish-owned firms. Among the most important were M. Witmark and Sons; Shapiro-Bernstein; Marks and Stern; Snyder, Waterhouse, and Berlin; Charles K. Harris; Harry Von Tilzer; and Jerome Remick.[48] Wexler followed a path that had been laid out by preceding generations of American Jews, figures like Monroe Rosenfeld and Julius Witmark, who progressed from music journalism to song plugging, and thence to song publishing, and, by the postwar years, to label ownership.

Wexler was first a song plugger for the old Tin Pan Alley house of Leo Feist, and then a columnist for *Billboard*, where he covered the New York Tin Pan Alley beat (at that time headquartered uptown at Brill Building, some twenty blocks north of its original home on 28th Street):

> I'd start at the Brill Building (1619 Broadway) . . . home of 1000 tunesmiths and assorted hustlers. From the top floor, I'd work my way down, poking my head into every office, nosing around for news. I'd jump over to 11th Avenue, down around 34th Street, where the record jobbers, distributors, and jukebox roughnecks operated. A lot of these guys were ex–cigarette machine bosses, a few were mobbed up, and they all had stories to tell.[49]

Through his city beat, Wexler learned the music business from song manufacturing to sales, from mob-controlled vending-machine operations to payola dispensed by publishers and record labels for jukebox and radio play. By 1952 he was ready. He joined Atlantic Records as a junior partner—a label cofounded by the son of a Turkish diplomat, Ahmet Ertegun, and veteran record man Herb Abramson in 1947. Both were jazz fanatics and both disciples of Milt Gabler. The Gabler connection to which we have referred again and again was important for both symbolic (mentoring) and practical (financial) reasons. When Atlantic had been on the verge of its first rhythm and blues hit, Stick McGhee's "Drinking Wine, Spo-Dee-O-Dee," the fledgling operation nearly collapsed because the partners lacked the funds to press more records. But in Atlantic's case, in contrast to the examples of Bob Geddins and Dootsie Williams, the necessary capital managed to arrive in time. The source: a loan from Milt Gabler.[50]

Indeed, if Wexler was torn between the competing domains of the aficionado and the entrepreneur, it was Gabler who pointed the way toward a workable compromise. In 1941 Jack Kapp, the president of Decca Records, had hired Gabler to work as an in-house producer, not of its jazz but of its race record division. As noted, Decca was the only major label of the period that entered early and seriously into contemporary race production. Kapp had been a race record man himself back in his days with the Brunswick label in the 1930s. When he took over Decca he brought in his black assistant from Brunswick, J. Mayo Williams, to record blues. Gabler had inherited Williams's old position (it was Williams who persuaded Kapp to sign Louis Jordan), working with black musicians to craft race-music hit records while devoting his Commodore label exclusively to the recording of noncommercial jazz, a condition strictly imposed by Kapp.[51] Gabler's many hits with Jordan on Decca suggested to Wexler, Ahmet Ertegun, and others like them that musical love and money making were not mutually exclusive:

> [Ahmet and I] could have developed a label along the lines of Blue Note, Prestige, Vanguard or Folkways, fastidious documentarians of core American music. Bobby Weinstock, Alfred Lion, Moe Asch, Orrin Keepnews, Manny Solomon and the other keepers of the flame were doing God's work. Ahmet and I, however, didn't feature ourselves as divinely elected. We weren't looking for canonization; we lusted for hits.[52]

In light of Wexler's comments and experiences, we can begin to formulate some general conclusions about Jews and the business of race music. Jewish domination of the race-music industry grew partly out of earlier ethnic business penetration into pop music publishing, as well as jazz record retail and reissue labels, not to mention theater management and booking agencies, such as the venerable William Morris Agency. These various arenas comprised informal Jewish networks which, though devoid of any conspiratorial quality, afforded individual Jews "ins" into fields through which race record production might become possible. As sociologist Michael Billig has observed, for the Jewish kid growing up in Brooklyn or the Bronx, it was not unusual to know someone who was or had been in the popular music business, someone whose Jewishness, however remote or alienated, still functioned as proof that a career in "the biz" was feasible or perhaps even natural for someone like himself. A Christian kid growing up in Oklahoma, Billig conjectures, would be unlikely to feel a similar sense of connection, to know to whom to turn or how to break in.[53] One can go further: even a black kid growing up in Harlem, perhaps acquainted with a number of musicians, interested in business, and well informed about the history of black music in America, would probably lack the personal business connections, lessons, and skills imbibed from those with experience, as well as the self-confidence afforded to his Jewish counterpart by virtue of the history of Jewish business achievement in entertainment and popular music. In fact, the unspectacular record of blacks in the business end of the music business could serve as a discouragement. J. Mayo Williams once hypothesized that the demise of Black Swan Records in 1924 had dissuaded many blacks from pursuing music entrepreneurship. In both the black and Jewish cases, then, awareness of group business history was a factor in determining prospects for future success.[54]

This leads to a further hypothesis about the relationship between race, business, and identity formation. Jews attracted to the black mystique may have sought escape from their own ethnic heritage through immersion in the culture of a hipper "other," but such empathy did not mean sharing in any debilitating anxieties that blacks may have felt over their capacity to succeed in business. As Wexler recalled,

> I had always known white Negroes, not pretenders or voyeurs but guys who opted to leave the white world, married black women, and made Harlem or Watts their habitat, such as Milton Mezz Mezzrow, author of the white Negro's bible, *Really the Blues*; Teddy Reig, the 300-lb soul man who managed Count Basie and Chuck Berry; Symphony Sid Torin . . . , Johnny Otis . . . [and] Monte Kay, bebop impresario, manager of the Modern Jazz Quartet, whose kinky coif might well have been the first Jewfro in hair fashion history.[55]

All of these men spoke and acted "black," yet made their living from *managing* black musicians. In this regard, Jews could combine the best of both worlds. They could think of themselves as aesthetically black yet entrepreneurially Jewish, certainly a potent combination in a world of race record enterprise. This point is often missed by scholars who address the question of "how Jews became white folks in America." The reality is that many Jews in the race-music business had no wish to become fully white. The interdependency between their identification with the culture that black music made possible and the knowledge and skills that enabled them to merchandize it required that they maintain a delicate balance. In light of their frequent disdain for the traditional markers of Jewish religion and national identity, the inevitable question of what made these individuals Jewish can be answered only if one views them as comprising a distinctive black-Jewish subculture, one in which business itself, doing business with black music, making and marketing hits with like-minded Jews, *was* the self-consciously Jewish component of their psyches. The frequent sprinkling of Yiddishisms in their patois was not inconsistent with a quasiblack identity. Yiddish symbolized the language of business *and* of the street. Thus Wexler's own formula of white negritude, like that of many of the most successful Jewish record men, was to stop short of full conversion.

But there existed another type of Jewish "white Negro," one whose proximity to blacks was less psychological and more social or class-based. This was a figure hinted at by Wexler's earlier reference to "the record jobbers, distributors, . . . jukebox roughnecks," and ex–cigarette machine bosses, some of whom were mobbed up. These individuals weren't aficionados who haunted used furniture stores in search of vintage 78s of King Oliver's Creole Jazz Band or the Mississippi Sheiks. Instead, they were the men and women who owned the used furniture stores in black ghetto neighborhoods, found the records lying inside phonograph cabinets, took note of the black customers' record purchases, and calculated that their own entrepreneurial niche lay in creating records directly for such a market. This category includes figures such as Herman Lubinsky in Newark; Syd Nathan in Cincinnati; Leonard and Phil Chess in Chicago; Bess Berman of Harlem's Apollo Records; Al Green of National; Morris "Moishe" Levy, founder of Roulette Records from the Bronx; Al Silver, president of Herald Records in Newark; and Hy Weiss of Old Town Records. While their routes to race music varied, instructive patterns can be discerned: furniture sales, especially used furniture in which records were commonly stored, was sometimes a trajectory to label ownership; manufacturing of materials like varnishes was another, since it might lead to the leasing or ownership of record-pressing plants, which in turn afforded contact with the record distribution business, possibly culminating in label ownership.[56] Both liquor and—as was frequently the case—jukebox distribution could also serve as launching pads.

It was liquor that provided the stepping stones to eventual record label fortunes for Leonard (Lazer) and Phil (Feivel) Chess, who grew up on the South Side of Chicago. Sons of a junk dealer (the Wabash Junk Shop, on 2971 South State), Leonard used his savings to purchase a liquor store in the predominantly black neighborhood of Chicago. Since the store was equipped with a jukebox, Chess soon recognized the business advantages of encouraging customers to linger, play music, even dance. In 1946 he opened a bar proper, the Macomba Lounge, now offering live music for the black clientele. Macomba was a neighborhood hangout but also a spot frequented by prostitutes, drug dealers, musicians, and a handful of white customers, a number of whom were

Jews connected to Chicago's indie record circuit, such as Charles and Evelyn Aron. With perceptive awareness of the tastes of his black customers and plenty of connections with Jews who could impart information on how it was done, Leonard's transition from store owner to impresario to record producer and label owner was nearly seamless.[57]

Both the haphazard paths to label ownership and the seeming inevitability of Jews traversing them were described by A&R man Lee Magid in an interview with music historian Arnold Shaw. Magid's remarks demonstrate that a Jewish kid determined to break into the business, if persistent enough, would usually find mentorship. "I used to hang around the studio," recalled Magid, "and Al Green showed me all the detail stuff—with the union, the contracts, the W-2 forms, deductions." Magid's description also makes clear that for tough, enterprising Jews like Green, label ownership capped the difficult climb out of the ghetto, creating the possibility of riches as well as a legacy to pass on:

> Sylvia Langler was the secretary with the company and later married Al Green, the father of Irving Green, who ran Mercury Records for years. But this Al Green was not the Al Green who ran The Flame Bar in Detroit. This Al Green was originally from Chicago where he was a union organizer of the painters. He came from a rough, rough school.[58]

Of course, in the record business the old neighborhood was never really far behind. As a new and unregulated niche industry renegotiating the boundaries between white and black worlds and tied in with nightclubs, liquor, and jukebox distribution, the race-music business was ripe for mob penetration.[59] One of the most notorious cases was that of Morris "Moishe" Levy. Orphaned at four months, a delinquent at nine, a runaway at thirteen, Levy picked up odd jobs as gofer and chauffeur for nightclub mobsters in New York. By the age of twenty Levy had enough mob connections to facilitate his acquisition of a major Manhattan nightclub, in fact what would become one of the most famous jazz clubs in the world, Birdland on 52nd Street. Levy soon began picking up the contracts of black entertainers, with clauses affirming his ownership of the copyright to songs first performed in his clubs. Protests from artists were met with violence and intimidation. Employing such methods, he rapidly established his own record companies, such as Roulette, but mostly operated by acquiring existing labels, consuming their publishing catalogs and then running them into the ground.[60] He was a parasite, albeit a colorful one, not to be confused with such equally tough but genuinely pioneering figures as Nathan and Lubinsky, or the Chess brothers in Chicago, or the Bihari brothers and Art Rupe in Los Angeles.

The Biharis came from Hungary and wound up in Oklahoma with a farm implements business, which then led to appliance sales and radios, with son Jules branching out into jukebox distribution in Los Angeles (a business then virtually synonymous with West Coast mobster Mickey Cohen), fueling the inexorable push into record production. Syd Nathan's path was more serpentine: born in Cincinnati, Nathan quit school at thirteen, found work in an amusement park demonstrating radios, then supplying jukeboxes. Later he opened a dry goods shop on West 5th Street, which intersected the neighborhoods populated by recent migrations of poor whites from Appalachia and poor blacks from Georgia and Alabama. "During the war," Nathan recalled, "records were hard to get, and I naturally thought of a brilliant idea, that I could get some hillbilly singers and cut some records, and somebody would press them for me." The casualness of Nathan's account obscures the real secrets behind a successful label, such as his own. Nathan once quipped that "all you need to get into the record business is a desk, a telephone, and an attorney."[61] Yet Nathan launched King not only with years of retail and merchandizing experience behind him but with a twenty-five-thousand-dollar loan from his parents, all of which he put to good advantage.[62] A brilliant businessman, Nathan was among the few indie owners prior to Motown to bring about a high degree of vertical integration. Eventually, King Records combined in-house pressing facilities, a house band to support many of its acts in the studio, and, crucially, its own distribution network.[63]

In contrast to figures like Gabler, Ertegun and Wexler, for men like Nathan and Green, interest in black music was merely incidental; the commodity attracted them not in itself but because of its ready access and salability. As Leonard Chess indelicately phrased it, "If shit is gold, we'll sell shit." Be that as it may, with an abundance of talent and intense competition, survival in the business depended on making quality hit records, and even some of the pure capitalists among the label owners developed good ears. Herb Abramson's characterization of his former boss, Al Green, as a "guy who knew and cared nothing about music," could not be applied to a Chess or even a Syd Nathan.[64] Art Rupe (aka Goldberg), founder of Specialty Records in Los Angeles, provides a good example of a man who came into race music purely out of business motives and yet developed a connoisseur's musical tastes. Though he would retrospectively claim a childhood devotion to gospel music, having heard it wafting from the windows of a church in the McKeesport, Pennsylvania, of his youth, Rupe actually started his career in the Hollywood film business, only later deciding that the record industry would be more receptive to fresh blood. After losing money in a label that specialized in middle-of-the-road pop music, Rupe decided that he needed to find "an area neglected by the majors and in the process [take] the crumbs off the table of the recording industry." Determining that this meant race music, he proceeded to investigate its properties in true scientific fashion. He withdrew two hundred dollars from the bank and made the rounds of black-owned record shops lining Central Avenue, purchasing disks along the way. His purpose was twofold: first, realizing that the black record shop owners, lacking credit, were entirely ignored by the majors, he hoped to establish a network of retail outfits that would be only too happy to promote his own product. Second, he intended to listen systematically to his purchases so as to divine, with pencil and stopwatch in hand, the secret formula for making hits. In both these strategies Rupe succeeded. Specialty became a pillar of West Coast rhythm and blues.[65]

BLACKS AND JEWS IN THE BUSINESS

Rupe's calculated approach to a passionate music leads to the final component of this study of blacks and Jews in race music. Although Jewish involvement in race records is not a story about Judaism, Jewish politics, or even, overtly, Jewish identity, it is at the very least a contribution to the history of black-Jewish relations. Having reviewed some of the factors that led to the relatively greater success of Jews than blacks in the contemporary music business, it remains to be seen what effect this differential exerted on the mutual perceptions of the two communities. While here too there was no simple formula, one thing is clear: the black-Jewish relationship in the music industry had a hierarchical or class, as well as a racial and religious, dynamic. Black musicians and A&R men were most often the Jews' employees who only occasionally managed to become their competitors. One who did, former Specialty A&R man Harold Battiste, expressed the view of many African American musicians that the label owners were businessmen and exploiters who knew little and cared less about the music, outside of its cash value. In forming his own all-black label, AFO, in the late 1950s, Battiste asked his fellow blacks why "that cat Rupe . . . should . . . sit in his ass; can't even keep time to the music, and he becomes a wealthy man—and all of us [blacks] are beggin' for rent money." Battiste then exhorted blacks to "own it yourself!"[66]

Some musicians, of course, echoed Battiste in seeing the owners as excellent businessmen but musical incompetents. Rhythm and blues pioneer Etta James's recollections are fairly typical in this regard: "None of the Biharis really had any taste in music. . . . [They] couldn't even pat their feet to the beat. So they hired guys like Maxwell Davis and Johnny Otis to run their music department."[67] James's remarks suggest that it was the white owners' ability to exploit the wealth of musical knowledge possessed by such black A&R men as Battiste, Henry Glover at King, Ralph Bass at Savoy, Jesse Stone at Atlantic, Dave Bartholomew at Imperial, Bumps Blackwell at Specialty, Willie Dixon at Chess, or Ike Turner at Modern that made them parasitical, almost Shylockian figures. Of course, this ignores the fact that a number of the top A&R men and producers were themselves Jews: Teddy Rieg, Fred Mendelsohn, Lee Magid, and, in a sense, Milt Gabler and Jerry Wexler too.[68] But if the charge of musical theft, as implied in James's accusation, misses some of the ambiguities of an industry in which whites and Jews often did make important musical contributions, the ubiquitous accompanying charge of financial theft seems in itself incontrovertible. What especially rankled was the common practice among label owners (who generally had their own in-house publishing firms) of listing their own names as authors or coauthors of their artists' hit songs. Such appropriation was built into the owner-performer or even the owner-songwriter relationship, since American copyright law dictated that an employer had proprietary rights to the compositions of their hires.[69] (The earlier reference to Morris Levy's appropriation of publishing rights to songs *performed* in his clubs appears as an extension of this principle to the point of absurdity.)

Beyond such loopholes, illegality seems to have pervaded the industry as a whole. Fraud, bribery (in the form of payola), numbers juggling, tax evasion, and other forms of book cooking were inseparable from the business. Bernard Besman, the Detroit founder of Sensation Records and local distributor for the Biharis' Modern label, exaggerated only slightly when he claimed, "Everybody in the record business was crooked. Everybody. I don't care how big they are." Naturally, Besman was careful to add, "I'm not talking about me, I don't count."[70] His comment, however, reflects an unfortunate historical reality: scrupulous honesty in the record business would have been suicidal. In exasperated response to accusations that he had stolen musicians' royalties, black record label owner Don Robey once asked, "How can these ignorant sons of bitches think I owe them money because they hear their record on the air? Hell, I paid the deejays to play it!"[71] It appears that like the Christian myth of original sin, the music business entered the world corrupted. As harmonica player Eddie Burns once theorized, since the race-music industry was born illicitly amid the AFM recording strike, it perpetually bore the mark of its original sin:

> What happened was them Jews found a way to record blues musicians and people like that, but your contract wasn't worth the paper it was written on. But they had a way of settin' these dates when they released the stuff, saying it was recorded back then [i.e., before the ban]. So a lot of blues people got in on the deal, which mean that you automatically was gonna get a screwin' because it wasn't legal in the first place.[72]

Such rip-offs and shenanigans make characterizing the exact nature of black-Jewish collaboration treacherous. What is clear is that the race record phenomenon was not merely art, not merely music—it was at least equally business as well. Records were constructed with careful attention to current fashion, with an awareness of the functioning of the industry as a whole, with an eye toward promotion, and, if the label was going to thrive, even with attentiveness to maintaining an artist's relationship over time with a specific audience, with a particular market and fan base. Musical purism, therefore, was antithetical to the interests of everyone involved, while formula, insofar as it introduced an element of stability into a world of high-stakes gamble, was integral to the industry's health. Jewish businessmen helped to hone the commercial qualities of rhythm and blues music, to package and merchandize it effectively, and thereby accelerate its emergence as *the* popular music of America. That the capitalist enterprise of rhythm and blues entailed the exploitation of artists—white and black alike—is a fact of life; that the industry was also built on a foundation of racial inequality, however, is its historical tragedy.

While the Jewish label owners clearly took advantage of African American musicians' powerlessness within a segregated society, their own economic self-interests also demanded a degree of transcendence of overt race hatred. This often led, not just the liberals like Gabler and Wexler, but also the tough guys like Levy and Nathan to demonstrate a form of white negritude of their own, as a consequence of their total involvement in the business of making black music. "Just think of it," remarked *Billboard* journalist Johnny Sippel, "Paul Reiner of Black and White Records, Herman Lubinsky of Savoy, Fred Mendelsohn of Regent, Leonard Chess of Chess and Art Rupe of Specialty—all of them became so profoundly enmeshed in Rhythm and Blues that they literally changed color. And all of them happened also to be Jewish."[73] Whether or not they "literally" changed color, their jobs and attitudes were not simply those of most whites in segregated and increasingly suburbanized America. According to B. B. King, "Jules Bihari didn't show the prejudice or reserve of many white men of that era. He hated segregation and paid it no mind, crossing the color line like it wasn't there." Of course, in a sense, the indies' business depended on the existence of a segregation or racism that required that it be white entrepreneurs, in most cases, that recorded, marketed, and profited from rhythm and blues. Segregation and racism did not create Jewish pop music entrepreneurship, but it considerably facilitated Jews' penetration and exploitation of the black pop niche. This fact epitomizes the ambiguity of Jews in the business of race music as a whole. "The Biharis," insisted King, "were Jewish people who loved recording and selling black music."[74] Crossing boundaries was therefore a function of and necessity for the indies' success. As Syd Nathan's assistant at King put it, "In many ways [Nathan] was a remarkably open-minded man. He perceived this wonderful notion of American music as not being segregated into different styles, but one big cross-ethnic whole. He did that because it was a way to make money."[75]

Yet the very success of the indies in crossing boundaries proved to be their undoing, even if their collective death would be a protracted one. Inadvertently, through recording R&B and promoting it to black record buyers, they had helped make race music popular among *white* listeners, and this, also inadvertently, provided a powerful impetus to the search for white musicians who could sing and play rhythm and blues music. In 1954 Milt Gabler applied the lessons he had learned over many years with Louis Jordan, to accent the sound of country and western singer Bill Haley, resulting in the watershed rock 'n' roll hit "Rock around the Clock." Although many Jewish indie labels soldiered on after the advent of rock 'n' roll—and some even enjoyed their greatest successes after that date—they were no longer functionally unique. Both major and indie labels now signed black artists, and both now pushed white rock and rollers as well.

What seems surprising is that to the present day the music business retains much of its character as a black-Jewish affair. The love of the game, the lifestyle, the extensive network of connections over the course of generations continues to feed this peculiar American subculture of "non-Jewish Jews" or Jewish "white Negroes." As for the blacks, the relationship with Jews is now too enduring to forget, too disturbing to forgive, yet too intimate to dissolve. Questions of art and business, black capitalism and Jewish entrepreneurship continue to swirl, long past the time when social scientists might have prophesied their irrelevance. In fact, the troubled symbiosis between the two groups reflects a common devotion to the music, albeit at times from differing perspectives, and a compatibility born of a functional division of labor, significantly modified and blurred in recent decades but with important elements still intact.[76] Blacks and Jews, no longer allies, but not exactly enemies either, appear almost to have gotten used to each other at last. As Magnificent Montague, the black disk jockey for whom Jews were "just about the only white people who gave me a break in this business," recently wrote, "We knew . . . from dealing with Jewish merchants in black neighborhoods and from being ripped off by Jews in the record business, that there were as many sinners as saints in this marriage, yet still we recognize the kinship."[77] Or, as Louis Jordan once put it, "beans and cornbread, they go hand-in-hand."

NOTES

1. Still the most valuable general history of rhythm and blues, with much attention to both musical and business aspects, is Arnold Shaw, *Honkers and Shouters: The Golden Years of Rhythm and Blues* (New York: Macmillan, 1978). Important aspects of the history are covered in Charles Kiel, *Urban Blues* (Chicago: University of Chicago Press, 1966); Mike Rowe, *Chicago Breakdown* (London: Edison, 1973); Robert Palmer, *Deep Blues* (New York: Penguin, 1981); and Charlie Gillett, *The Sound of the City: The Rise of Rock and Roll* (New York: Pantheon, 1983).

2. John Chilton, *Let the Good Times Roll: The Story of Louis Jordan and His Music* (London: Quartet, 1992); Shaw, *Honkers and Shouters*, 64.

3. Perhaps this interpretation accounts for the song's presence on the soundtrack of Spike Lee's 1992 biopic *Malcolm X*.

4. Robert M. W. Dixon and John Goodrich, *Recording the Blues* (New York: Stein and Day, 1970).

5. Ibid., 100–103; Dan Morgenstern, "Recording Jazz," in *The Oxford Companion to Recorded Jazz*, ed. Bill Kirschener (New York: Oxford University Press, 2000), 474.

6. "Milt Gabler," *New Yorker*, March 1946.

7. For further biographical information on Gabler, see the memoir by Billy Crystal, *700 Sundays* (New York: Time-Warner, 2005), 31–37.

8. Reebee Garofalo, "Crossing Over: From Black Rhythm and Blues to White Rock 'n' Roll" in *Rhythm and Business: The Political Economy of Black Music*, ed. Norman Kelley (New York: Akashic Book, 2002), 113–117.

9. Michael Lydon, *Ray Charles: Man and Music* (New York: Riverhead, 1998), 68.

10. Garofalo, "Crossing Over," 118–119.

11. William Barlow, *Voice Over: The Making of Black Radio* (Philadelphia: Temple University Press, 1999).

12. Ben Wattenberg, interview, "The First Measured Century," PBS, August 2008, http://www.pbs.org/fmc/segments/progseg8.htm; more generally, see Nicholas Lemann, *The Promised Land: The Great Migration and How It Changed America* (New York: Knopf, 1991).

13. Gart Galen and Roy C. Ames, *Duke/Peacock Records: An Illustrated History with Discography* (Milford, NH: Big Nickel Productions, 1990), 22. Ben Wattenberg, interview.

14. Quoted in Michael Rogin, *Blackface, White Noise: Jewish Immigrants in the Hollywood Melting Pot* (Berkeley: University of California Press, 1996), 49.

15. Arcadius Kahan, *Essays in Jewish Social and Economic History* (Chicago: University of Chicago Press, 1986), 107; Yoav Peled, *Class and Ethnicity in the Pale: The Political Economy of Jewish Workers' Nationalism in Late Imperial Russia* (New York: St. Martin's Press, 1989), 115.

16. Daniel Soyer, "Class Conscious Workers as Immigrant Entrepreneurs: The Ambiguity of Class among Eastern European Jewish Immigrants to the United States at the Turn of the Century," *Labor History*, 42, no. 1 (2001): 45–59; but compare Eli Lederhendler, *Jewish Immigrants and American Capitalism, 1880–1920* (New York: Cambridge University Press, 2009).

17. Arnold Shankman, *Ambivalent Friends: Afro-Americans View the Immigrant* (Westport, CT: Greenwood, 1982), 136.

18. But compare Lederhendler, *Jewish Immigrants*, who denies that this upward mobility was outstanding or rooted in European legacies.

19. W.E.B. Du Bois, signed editorials in *Crisis*, July 1917, December 1920.

20. See Tom Scott's introduction to *The Peasantries of Europe: From the Fourteenth to the Eighteenth Centuries* (New York: Longman, 1998).

21. Juliet E. K. Walker, *The History of Black Business in America: Capitalism, Race, Entrepreneurship* (New York: Macmillan, 1998).

22. Rayford Logan, *The Negro in American Life and Thought: The Nadir, 1877–1901* (New York: Collier Books, 1965).

23. Timothy Bates, *Black Capitalism: A Quantitative Analysis* (New York: Praeger, 1973), 10.

24. Charles Johnson, ed., *The Economic Status of Negroes: Summary and Analysis of Materials Presented at the Conference on the Economic Status of the Negro* (Nashville: Fisk University Press, 1933), 14, 36–37; Raymond Walters, *Negroes and the Great Depression: The Problem of Recovery* (Westport, CT: Greenwood, 1970), 214, 225.

25. Dixon and Goodrich, *Recording the Blues*, 9–10.

26. Here I owe much to the analysis in Walker, *History of Black Business*, 213–215.

27. Ted Vincent, *Keep Cool: The Black Activists Who Built the Jazz Age* (London: Pluto, 1995), 61.

28. David Suisman, "Co-workers in the Kingdom of Culture: Black Swan Records and the Political Economy of African American Music," *Journal of American History* 91, no. 1 (March 2004): 41–52. Suisman credits a number of factors for Black Swan's demise: "ill-timed capital expansion," intense competition due to initial race-music success, and the growing popularity of radio, which temporarily undercut the record market.

29. Stephen Calt, "The Anatomy of a 'Race' Music Label: Mayo Williams and Paramount Records," in Kelley, *Rhythm and Business*, 101.

30. J. C. Mann, "Recorded in Hollywood/Hollywood Records—An R&B Split Personality," *Jamm-Upp E-zine* 8 (August 2008): http://home.earthlink.net/~jaymar41/RIH.html.

31. As Charles acknowledged in his autobiography, Lauderdale had nurtured his youthful talent and given him freedom to grow as a solo recording act, but the cash-strapped label was forced to sell Charles's contract to the better-financed Atlantic at the time that "Brother Ray" was poised to explode. Ray Charles and David Ritz, *Brother Ray: Ray Charles' Own Story* (New York: Dial, 1978), 131.

32. Shaw, *Honkers and Shouters*, 248–252.

33. The Doo-Wop Society of Southern California, accessed August 2009, http://www.electricearl.com/dws/buck_ram.html.

34. David Sanjek, "One Size Does Not Fit All: The Precarious Position of the African American Entrepreneur in Post–World War II American Popular Music," *American Music* 14, no. 4 (Winter 1997): 535–562.

35. Detroit's Joe von Battle (JVB Records) made a respectable (if not entirely legal) business recording artists outside of their exclusive contracts and pirating the tapes to various labels. J. C. Marion, "JVB Records," *Jamm-Upp E-zine* 12, accessed August 2008, http://home.earthlink.net/~jaymar41/jvbrecords.html; Charles Shaar Murray, *Boogie Man: The Adventures of John Lee Hooker* (New York: St. Martin's Press, 2000), 143. And by relying increasingly on black comedy records, "Dootsie" Williams's Dootone managed to survive for well over a decade without having any major stars on its roster. Shaw, *Honkers and Shouters*, 266. A number of black labels, moreover, seem to have adjusted to the role of functioning as entry-level outfits, as was the case, for instance, with Bobby Robinson's various labels, Red Robin, Fire, and Fury.

36. J. C. Marion, "Forgotten Sessions—Part 2," http://home.earthlink.net/~jaymar41/labels_2.html.

37. On Robey, see the excellent treatment by Galen and Ames, *Duke/Peacock Records*.

38. Shaw, *Honkers and Shouters*, 130.

39. Brian Ward, "'All for One, and One for All': Black Enterprise, Racial Politics and the Business of Soul," in Kelley, *Rhythm and Business*, 145.

40. Vincent, *Keep Cool*, 53.

41. Nelson George, *The Death of Rhythm and Blues* (New York: Pantheon, 1988), 76.

42. Walker, *History of Black Business*, 215.

43. Mendelsohn created Herald in 1950, sought investment from New York record-pressing plant owner, Al Silver, who quickly bought him out and maintained the company for fifteen years before back payments and penalties to the IRS forced him to give up the company. Shaw, *Honkers and Shouters*, 450–460; "Al Silver," accessed August 2008, http://www.rockabilly.nl/references/messages/al_silver.htm.

44. One thinks, for instance, of labels owned or run by the song-writing team of Jerry Lieber, Mike Stoller, Herb Alpert, Phil Spector, and Bert Berns. See Michael Billig, *Rock 'n' Roll Jews* (Nottingham, UK: Five Leaves, 2000), 61–112.

45. Charlie Gillett, *Making Tracks: Atlantic Records and the Growth of a Multi-Billion-Dollar Industry* (New York: Dutton, 1974), 23, 117; Herb Abramson obituary, *Billboard*, November 1999.

46. "Jac Holzman, The Man, the Music, The Doors" (reprinted from *The Doors Collectors Magazine*), accessed August 2009, http://www.cinetropic.com/janeloismorris/interview/holzman/.

47. Peter D. Goldsmith, *Making People's Music: Moe Asch and Folkways Records* (Washington, DC: Smithsonian Institution Press, 1998), 167–68.

48. Isaac Goldberg, *Tin Pan Alley: A Chronicle of Popular Music* (New York: Unger, 1961), 108–109; David Suisman, "The Sound of Money: Music, Machines, and Markets, 1890–1925" (PhD diss., Columbia University, 2002), 53–56.

49. Jerry Wexler, *Rhythm and the Blues: A Life in American Music* (New York: Knopf, 1993), 67.

50. Lydon, *Ray Charles*, 87.

51. Ashley Kahn, liner notes to *Billy Crystal Presents: The Milt Gabler Story*, Verve Records B000391100, 2005, compact disc; Chris Ingham, *Billie Holliday* (London: Unanimous, 2000), 19; Chilton, *Good Times Roll*, 73.

52. Wexler, *Rhythm and the Blues*, 91.

53. Billig, *Rock 'n' Roll Jews*, 93.

54. Calt, "Anatomy," in Kelley, *Rhythm and Business*, 90.

55. Ibid.

56. For example, Al Silver of Herald Records, Al Green of National, and Max and Sol Weiss of Fantasy.

57. Nadine Cohodas, *Spinning Blues into Gold: The Chess Brothers and the Legendary Chess Records* (New York: St. Martin's Press, 2000), 5–32.

58. Lee Magid, quoted in Shaw, *Honkers and Shouters*, 359.

59. The mob took control of the jukebox business around the same time that race labels were getting starting, in the immediate postwar years. See Marc Eliot, *Rockonomics: The Money behind the Music* (New York: Watts, 1989), 44–45.

60. On Levy, see Frederic Dannen, *Hit Men: Power Brokers and Fast Men inside the Music Business* (New York: Vintage, 1991), 31–57.

61. Syd Nathan, quoted in Rick Kennedy and Randy McNult, *Little Labels—Big Sound: Small Record Companies and the Rise of American Music* (Bloomington: Indiana University Press, 1999), 61.

62. D. K. Peney, ed., "History of Rock n' Roll, 1954–1963," accessed August 2009, http://www.history-of-rock.com/king_records_two.htm.

63. See John Hartley Fox, *King of the Queen City: The Story of King Records* (Chicago: University of Illinois Press, 2009).

64. Herb Abramson, quoted in Gillett, *Making Tracks*, 23.

65. Eric LaBlanc, "Art Rupe and Specialty Records," http://www.island.net/~blues/arupe.htm; Daniel Wolff, *You Send Me: The Life and Times of Sam Cooke*, with S. R. Crain, Clifton White, and G. David Tenenbaum (New York: Quill, 1995), 73–76; Shaw, *Honkers and Shouters*, 179–184; for a fuller portrait of Rupe, one emphasizing his aesthetic sophistication as well as his commercial acumen, see Peter Guralnick, *Dream Boogie: The Triumph of Sam Cooke* (New York: Little, Brown, 2005), 65–73, 113, based largely on Billy Vera's liner notes booklet for the CD box set *The Specialty Story* (Berkeley, CA: Specialty Records, 1994), 4412.

66. Harold Battiste, quoted in Sanjek, "One Size," 553.

67. Etta James and David Ritz, *Rage to Survive: The Etta James Story* (New York: Da Capo, 1998), 51.

68. In his memoir, Billy Crystal writes that his uncle, Milt Gabler, cowrote or wrote numerous hit songs, including "Choo Choo Cha Boogie," "Rock-a-Bye Your Baby," "Danke Schoen," "Three Coins in the Fountain," "Volare," and "Red Roses for a Blue Lady." At the same time, Gabler's manner in the studio, at least with jazz musicians, was to give them freedom to play as they wished. "Listen. Who am I to tell them how to play this? After all, this is jazz, America's only true art form." Crystal, *700 Sundays*, 35–37.

69. Garofalo, "Crossing Over," 127.

70. Bernard Besman, quoted in Murray, *Boogie Man*, 136.

71. Don Robey, quoted in Galen and Ames, *Duke/Peacock Records*, 94.

72. Eddie Burns, quoted in Murray, *Boogie Man*, 110.

73. Johnny Sippel, quoted in Shaw, *Honkers and Shouters*, 343.

74. B. B. King and David Ritz, *Blues All Around Me: The Autobiography of B. B. King* (New York: Avon, 1996), 141, 140.

75. Quoted in Kennedy and McNult, *Little Labels*, 63–64.

76. Nelson George, *Hip Hop America* (New York: Penguin, 1999), 57–58, 84–85; Alex Ogg, *The Men behind Def Jam: The Radical Rise of Russel Simmons and Rick Rubin* (London: Omnibus, 2002). Black-Jewish relations in the music business over the course of generations and between eras requires scholarly investigation, particularly to sort out continuities and differences.

77. Magnificent Montague, *Burn, Baby! Burn! The Autobiography of Magnificent Montague*, with Bob Baker (Urbana: University of Illinois Press, 2003), 82.

‿◠

Jews, American Indian Curios, and the Westward Expansion of Capitalism

David S. Koffman

Like dozens of young Jewish entrepreneurs who migrated to the burgeoning towns and cities, farms and homesteads, near American Indian reservations and allotments, or to the in-between places in the shifting zone known as the American western frontier in the second half of the nineteenth century, Julius Meyer forged a life and made a living as an American Indian trader, and eventually one as an American Indian curio dealer. He left Bromberg, Prussia, in the early 1860s, and when he arrived in Omaha shortly after the U.S. government created Nebraska Territory, he began trading trinkets from his brother's jewelry and cigar store for American Indian "beads, moccasins, wampum pouches, tomahawks, bows and arrows, petrifications, and peace pipes."[1] Meyer opened his "Indian Wigwam" in the early 1870s and ran it until the end of the century. He came to be known to the local Pawnees as "Curly-headed white chief who speaks with one tongue," apparently for his exemplary honesty, and was reputed to speak Ponca, Omaha, Winnebago, Pawnee, and Sioux in addition to English and German. He eventually led a delegation of Native leaders to the Paris Exposition in 1889 and boasted of his close bonds of friendship with Standing Bear, Red Cloud, Sitting Bull, and other Native American leaders whom he paid to pose with him in a series of portraits taken over several years.[2] He became, according to a journalist in 1909, "a master merchandiser of the Indian to white society."[3]

Julius Meyer was among the thousands of Jews who rushed west to exploit the commercial opportunities that accompanied homesteading, mining, and the newly interconnecting trade routes. The contours of Meyer's relationships

Figure 7.1. Julius Meyer seated above Native Americans. American Jewish Archives, PC 2980, N.2535, Nebraska State Historical Society, Omaha.

with Native Americans provide a colorful example of Jewish economic agency in the emerging American West during the last decades of the nineteenth century and the early decades of the twentieth, and the extent to which Jewish mobility rode, in part, on their interactions with Native Americans.[4] In many ways, Meyer was emblematic of westward migrant Jews more generally, whose meteoric commercial success was made possible by the collusion of capitalism and colonialism. Immigrants and laborers migrated to the geographic margins of American economic life, where they incorporated the marginal peoples who inhabited them into larger capitalist structures. Jewish peddlers reached into new territories and helped bring Native Americans into the nation's developing market economy.[5]

As members of a merchant minority, Jews spread American capitalism by extending its reach across three boundaries. First, Jewish immigrant merchants engaged new players, Native Americans, in the United States' evolving commercial system. Second, these merchants linked economic networks from urban metropolises to rural geographies that had yet to be included in America's nationwide capitalist purview. Finally, Jewish traders helped create new markets for a new commodity, curios, objects that originally had little to no concrete value outside of their Native American communities. In inventing this new market, Jewish merchants played active parts in the expansion of not just American capitalism but American colonial expansion.

Jews enjoyed speedy upward mobility from their first arrival in the American West in the 1850s. Though plenty of Jewish migrants, like other whites in the West, considered Native Americans a barrier to their immigrant aspirations for settlement and integration, enterprising merchants among them saw opportunities for productive exchange. Generally, Jewish men came to the frontier alone. They sought places in the West and found people to trade with based on their material needs. Many western Jewish peddlers traded with Native Americans for a short time in their fledgling business careers. When they had accrued enough capital, Jewish entrepreneurs tended to move on to larger enterprises and establish themselves in the larger towns and cities that had sprung up within a few decades. Jews enjoyed not just staggering economic mobility in the West but speedy social integration and a significant voice in civic and political life.[6] During the first segment of the male immigrant experience in the West, American Indian–related commercial activity formed a seedling stage in career mobility.

A small portion of these businessmen entered the curio industry, a subset of American Indian trading that involved the buying and selling of moccasins, totem poles, headdresses, baskets, rugs, and the like—objects that symbolized American Indians themselves. A market for these heritage objects exploded in the last two decades of the nineteenth century, after Native Americans ceased to pose a serious threat to the colonial settlement project.[7] The period of the most intense collecting of Native artifacts on the rural periphery coincided with the tremendous growth of museums of all kinds in urban centers in the late nineteenth century, as museum and collections scholars have well noted, when "national, civic, and academic pride had combined with governmental aid to science and culture, and more particularly with an enormous outpouring of capitalist philanthropy, to bring about the foundation or expansion of an incredible number of institutions devoted to the exhibiting of scientific and artistic objects."[8]

The American Indian heritage market bundled all the material objects that indexed "Indianness" as an essential ingredient to their value, financial, social, and otherwise.[9] It included ethnological specimens for anthropological museums sprouting up across the United States, Canada, and Europe; "relics" for the antiquities trade; sculptures and crafts for the emerging fine art market for Native works; and a wide swath of objects sold in the booming tourist market.[10] The industry was, according to the scholar and director of the Wheelwright Museum of the American Indian, Jonathan Batkin, "the public aspect of a lopsided barter system in which dealers mined Native communities for artifacts that were later converted into cash."[11] Stimulated by widely held romantic notions of a vast, untamed wilderness, it was built on the subjugation of indigenous peoples of the American West and their internment on reservations. Jewish participation in the curio trade, and in American western commercial growth more generally, clearly benefited Jewish immigrants themselves, but the role they played as agents of economic expansion had a more ambiguous impact.

The occupational profile of Jews in the West during the last third of the nineteenth century served expansion's end and contributed to the particular articulation expansion would have in the United States, that is, one closely linked with the championing of capitalism.[12] Simply doing what Jews often did to make a living, namely, peddling and engaging in merchant exchange, gave a positive valence to small-scale enterprising and helped Jews feel a part of a bigger story of civilizing or "winning" the American West. Commercial intercourse provided Jews not just a vehicle for settling in a new land but a seismic shift in Jews' position within their new national context. As the historian William Toll has noted, "for Jewish men, the merchant role in the American West enabled them and their families in a single generation to move from medieval artisanship and itinerant merchandising to the highest civil status."[13] Pursuing their material betterment harmonized with the essence of the American expansion project.

A number of historical and economic forces positioned Jews to pioneer and participate in the American Indian trade generally, and the curio business specifically. The lure of the pioneer spirit that figured romance, adventure, and an exoticism unknown to Jews in the places from which they emigrated, motivated some to seek business and settlement opportunities in the West.[14] More prosaically, having migrated from the German provinces and from eastern Europe for the promise of plenty the American West offered, many Jews had been pushed out of seaboard cities by limited or limiting employment opportunities and found themselves on the margins of trade.[15]

In the 1870s and 1880s capital-intensive enterprises such as cattle ranching and mining surged in New Mexico, Arizona, Texas, and much of the Southwest and brought capital and power from outside the region into its sphere. From the time of the region's mid-nineteenth-century boom, patriarchs of influential Jewish families in New Mexico, such as the Zeckendorfs, Ilfelds, Jaffas, Freudenthals, and Letchers, established themselves through their overwhelmingly Jewish business networks as merchandisers, wholesalers, and financiers, often securing major provision contracts for the military and for government-run American Indian reservations.

The Spiegelbergs, one of the most powerful Jewish families in the Southwest, for example, founded their fortune on government contracts to ship goods to and from American Indian reservations in New Mexico.[16] The Polish Jewish immigrant Louis Fisher dealt in hides, pelts, and wool, and, along with Louis

Gold and his uncle Joseph Hersch, "El Polaco" won grain contracts with the U.S. Army as it fought American Indian wars through the 1850s. These contracts provided them with the funds and access to Native American producers they would later use in the 1870s and 1880s to build regional curio businesses. In the 1870s Louis Gold and his son Jake received American Indian trading licenses from Santa Fe County, enabling them to procure pottery directly from the Pueblos to provide for a larger commercial market well beyond New Mexico. A local newspaper reported in 1894 that Gold's "rapidly expanding business procured items from hundreds of self-employed agents with pack animals, journeying throughout remote and isolated areas of New Mexico, Arizona, and Colorado, trading German-town tools and brightly colored prints of saints for old blankets and pottery."[17]

Merchant-class immigrant Jews on the vanguard of industrialization, as well as poorer peddling Jewish immigrants who made their living off the commercial opportunities that came with the expanding railroad infrastructure and the mining industries, helped shift the balance of land and power ownership away from Hispanics and American Indians between the 1880s and the 1910s.[18] Many Jewish traders became involved in American Indian trading, and in the curio business in particular, due to prior participation in complementary markets such as provisions sales, furs, hides, gold dust, land and oil speculation, small crafts, and hotels.

The U.S. government had enabled this commercializing and settling process. It established the Office of Indian Trade in 1806 as a subdivision of the War Department to control American Indian trade throughout its territories.[19] Until 1822 the office operated trading houses, the so-called factory system, to facilitate the safe settlement of whites on frontier lands for trouble-free commerce. After 1822 it provided licenses to traders and prescriptions of conditions for private trade.

American Indian trade attracted Jewish merchants from the earliest arrival of Jews in the western United States, where they participated in the capitalist colonial process as allies of the state throughout the nineteenth century.[20] Dozens of Jewish trading enterprises dotted the frontier. They supplied American Indian reservations with foodstuffs and general merchandise through state-backed contracts. Michael Elhart, a Dutch Jew, for example, engaged in trade with the Creek Indians under government contract in Georgia, while the government of Alabama supported Abraham Mordecai's American Indian trade along the banks of the Alabama River in the first years of the nineteenth century.[21] In 1852 the English Jewish brothers Samuels ran an American Indian trading post at Taylor falls, on the Minnesota side of the St. Croix River, some twelve miles from the trading post of another Jewish trader, Isaac Marks.[22] The Jewish merchants who won contracts to furnish goods to American Indian traders exchanged letters with the superintendent of Indian Trade in the

Figure 7.2. Rose Brothers Indian fur traders. American Jewish Archives, PC 3705, Nebraska State Historical Society, Omaha.

1870s, 1880s, and 1890s. Preoccupied with the details of payments and goods rendered, these letters revealed that Jewish traders had regular contracts with the federal government and that the state tried to exercise control over its American Indian traders in its efforts to protect its wards against exploitative business interests, including some Jewish merchants.[23]

Jewish curio dealers provide a particularly rich subset of the commercial encounters between Jews and American Indians because they not only worked as economic integrators of Native Americans but also acted as cultural mediators, translators, and intermediaries in white consumptions of "Indianness." They sold physical proxies of their American Indian clients to white buyers. Quite consciously, Jewish curio dealers branded themselves, alternatively, as American Indians' custodians, fighters, friends, and sometimes even as near American Indians themselves, to increase the visibility and desirability of the items they aimed to sell. The Jewish traders who helped invent the curio market made a profitable living from the American Indian heritage trade as new economic agents in a national economy that had an increasing number of non-functional cultural products available for purchase. American Indian sellers and manufactures, white buyers, and Jewish intermediaries helped create the category and context for American Indian items as commodities, consumable by non-Natives.

In Santa Fe, New Mexico, the hub of the Southwest curio business, the first generations of dealers included a significant number of Jews, including Wolf Kalisher, Samuel Snow, Caspar Behrendt, Marcus Katz, Isadore Meyerowitz, Abe Cohn, Emil Strauss, Albert Rose, Elias and Henry Laupheimer, Mark Cohn, Bernard Wolf, Isaac Isaacson, Samuel Strauss, and Joseph Sondheimer. Scores of other Jewish merchants dotted the West Coast and the western territories in Oklahoma and Nebraska, Utah and Nevada, Arizona and Wyoming.[24] The Northwest coast, most of it Canadian, had a similar network of Jewish entrepreneurs who cornered the curio business out of its hub in Victoria, British Columbia, during these same late nineteenth-century decades.[25] Abraham A. Aaronson, John J. Hart, Jacob Isaac, Samuel Kirschenberg and his partner Fredrick Landsberg, all Jews, owned and operated almost all of the major companies active in the curio business on Johnson Street in Victoria.[26] At least sixteen Jews listed themselves as "Indian traders" in Victoria business registers.[27] By the 1860s Jewish tobacconist and fur trader Meyer Malowanski, along with his Croatian partner Vincent Charles Baranovich, had developed one of the largest fur-trading businesses on the coast by establishing a chain of posts from Bella Bella to southern Alaska.[28] The fur boom busted in the 1880s, and in its wake, money migrated to the tourist market. Businessmen such as Malowanski and Baranovich refitted ships and shifted laborers who had once served the fur trade to the tourism industry, as companies like the Alaska Commercial Company arranged and promoted this new form of business.[29] Entrepreneurs such as the brothers Levy, the brothers Shirpser, David Hart, and Mike Cohen helped grow the nascent curio and tourist industries.[30]

These Jewish traders helped invent their respective regional curio industries, encouraging commodity manufacturing from American Indian territories. They provided access to American Indian objects for non-Native buyers and markets across the United States by cultivating demand for such objects and erecting channels for their distribution, primarily tourist shops and mail-order catalogs. Dealers spread American Indian artifacts across the continent into the homes and the imaginations of thousands of non-Indians, as indicated by the business registers from traders' shops, such as Gold's Free Museum from the 1890s, which recorded the names and addresses of the tourists who bought souvenirs.[31] Dealers leveraged enthusiasm for American Indian items and the concomitant increase in demand for tangible objects that might embody the figure of the American Indian and distributed them into fashionable city homes in America's urban centers as decoration, tourist souvenirs, adventure memorabilia, and objects suited for playing American Indian. Whether as home decor or props for children's play, the objects themselves fed America's

appetite for the imaginary American Indian. Once in the hands of white consumers, curios inevitably embodied more of the imagined than the real Native
Americans.[32]

Merchants sold American Indian artifacts not just to domestic consumers
and tourists but to natural history and ethnology museums across the country
and ocean, widening the scale of the curio market to international scope. Large
institutions purchased collections and presented them as objects of visual and
educational consumption, further incorporating previously marginal people
and places into a national and international marketplace. Moving these objects
from trading posts to museums transformed curios into specimens of science
displayed alongside exhibits of other indigenous peoples, or exhibitions of
America's natural history, its geology, flora and fauna. It also collapsed the
geographic and cultural distance between the frontier and the western world's
largest urban centers. Victoria, British Columbia's John J. Hart, for example,
sold curios not just to middle-class tourists and mail-order consumers in
small towns across the United States and Canada, but to the World Columbian
Exposition in Chicago in 1893. He also sold a significant collection to the German Jewish immigrant anthropologist Franz Boas.[33] Abraham A. Aaronson
likewise sold artifacts to the American Museum of Natural History in New
York City, the Ottawa Field Museum, and the Royal Ontario Museum in
Toronto.[34] Aaronson sold eighty-five carvings to collector Leigh Morgan Pears-
all, whose collection eventually made it to the University of Florida.[35] Frederick
Landsberg sold collections to the University of Pennsylvania in 1900, the Field
Museum in Chicago in 1903 and 1904, the Milwaukee Public Museum, and
in 1904 and 1905 the New York Museum of the American Indian. The Royal
Ontario Museum in Toronto acquired his remaining stock when his curio shop
closed in 1908. Jacob Isaac arranged a shipment of Tsimshian and Nisga articles
from the Nass and Skeena Rivers to the Indian commissioner Israel W. Powell,
who had acted as a collector for the American Museum of Natural History and
helped assemble the American centennial exhibition in Philadelphia. Finally,
Jake Gold sold curios to Adolph Bandelier, the early twentieth-century scholar
of the Southwest, who acquired a portion of Gold's "magnificent collection of
Indian goods" for the folk art museum in Berlin.[36]

Jewish curio merchants expanded capitalism not just by including new players or by providing access to American Indian commodities for buyers far from
American Indian territories. They helped create new demand; they created
a new market for items that had not had prior commercial value. Merchants
used several marketing strategies in their catalogs, shops, print advertisements,
and the photographs they arranged, to sell the curio objects themselves and to
nurture the development of this new market. Accounting for these marketing
strategies goes some distance in explaining, specifically, how dealers invented

these commodities and created demand for them by tapping into the broader social imagination that figured American Indians into its national consciousness. Merchants developed alternate personae for presentation to white customers, reflecting competing ideas of the American Indian that might sell. The dealer dressed as an antique curator, an ethnologist, a scholar of natural history, a cultural rescue worker, or a salvager of ancient cultures that might soon be lost to the modern world.

Curio dealers from the Southwest, Pacific Northwest, and the Great Plains sold wholesale to one another to mix together pan–American Indian collections valued by customers.[37] They bundled together West Coast Haida totem poles, Southwest Navajo blankets, and Plains Sioux headdresses, for example, clearly unconcerned about whether or not their white consumers paid attention to the cultural specifics of various Native peoples and artifacts. In search of opportunities, Jewish merchants unwittingly provided the material basis on which a consuming white public absorbed ideas about Native Americans. Jake Gold marketed himself as a purveyor of American Indian heritage objects from not just the Southwest but nationwide.[38] H. H. Tammen and W. G. Walz of El Paso, Gold's Jewish competitors, mimicked Gold's catalogs, selling packages of goods as collections including one, for example, of "pottery, Apache Soap Weed Basket, a Pueblo Idol, a bow, arrows, Beaded moccasins, an Indian drum, a buckskin shirt, Indian necklace, a raw hide canteen, Apache war club, mounted bird, a pair of old Spanish spurs . . . all labeled and carefully shipped."[39] Other catalogs organized their curios by tribe: Uncompaghre, White River Ute, Sioux, Piute, Crow, San Carlos, Apache, Zuni, Navajo, Cochita, and others.

Marketing curios as "relics" or antiques provided another sales strategy that pulled both purse strings and cultural strings. The ability to tie an object to a bygone era of the "primitive" past increased a curio's sale price and endowed it with an aura of that certain *something* that modern civilization had lost.[40] Prior to 1910 Tammen published at least thirteen full-length catalogs and at least four supplements in color for mail-order sales from "The H. H. Tammen Curio Co." established in 1881 in Denver, Colorado, most of which echoed this type of nostalgia. One, called "Western Echoes," from 1882, made American Indian objects into stand-ins for the ancient aboriginal American past, somehow both lost to the West but still located there.[41] These "echoes," supposedly embodied as artifacts, could be purchased, owned, and kept. Likewise, "Gold's Free Museum and Old Curiosity Shop" sold "old stone vessels and pottery from the Cliff Dwellers of New Mexico." Gold promoted not just his wares but New Mexico itself as the "richest field in the world of antiquities and historical curiosities." His marketing strategy associated American Indian curios with his global competitors' exotica and relics from other dying civilizations around the globe. Gold elevated American Indian objects above all, and then excoriated his customers' ignorance, hoping to convince them to buy a piece of the U.S. past:

Americans—always comparatively ignorant of their own great nation—
travel the earth over in search of novelties less marvelous than abound in
New Mexico. . . . The undersigned has known and been known by the people
of New Mexico for 27 years. He is familiar with their country, their customs
and their languages. His collectors are all the time gathering curios from the
remotest parts of the Territory where the stranger could not penetrate. There
is no archeological treasure which does not come to his hands, from relics of
the Stone Age to the implements used by the aborigines of to-day. All articles
are genuine, and it is well known by New Mexican travelers that each article
can be bought more cheaply from him than from the Indians themselves.[42]

Boasting of his own credentials as a master of American Indian country, customs, and languages, and his collectors' furtive access to zones otherwise forbidden to white men, Gold claimed to have been the intermediary for all local
artifacts, a custodian of archaeological treasures, hoping to convince buyers to
bypass even Native sellers themselves.

If the remote past, "relics from the Stone Age," offered a certain appeal, so too
contemporary ethnological accuracy, "the implements used by the aborigines
of to-day," as Gold's catalog worded it, provided an effective marketing strategy
merchants designed for domestic and institutional collectors.[43] Gold's catalog of
"Curios from the Ancient Mounds and Ruins in the Salt River Valley, Arizona,"
advertised for sale "many curious Articles used by the Modern Indians of Arizona and New Mexico." His 1893 advertisement pitched an "extremely low price
asked for this collection [which] places it in the power of any college, public
institution and many private collectors to become the owner of it."[44]

A related strategy leveraged the idea of the West's natural landscape as a
point of sale. Calling himself a "Purveyor of Natural History," Tammen, known
in Denver as an amateur mineralogist, eventually built one of the largest curio
businesses in the country, growing out of a business enterprise in which he
and a partner sold inks, stereoviews, and photographs of western landscapes.[45]
One curio catalog emphasized the link between nature and the American
Indian curio, listing a collection of "wood, slate, stone carving, basket-woven
articles, wearing apparel, and miscellaneous section including doctors' aprons,
Wampooms, used by the Indians as money, carved spoons, recreation games,
paint, shells, bracelets, sperm-whale, bear, beaver, seal and other animals' teeth,
tom toms of different sizes." As this wares list shows, curio dealers brought
together all kinds of commodities, including medical, domestic, music, and
play objects, and linked them seamlessly with objects of nature like wood, slate,
shells, animal teeth, stones, and materials. Presenting themselves as natural
historians, dealers capitalized on the popular associations between American
Indians with nature in order to sell wares to urban consumers eager to bring
natural exotica into their homes.[46] It also allowed Jewish merchants to present

VIEW OF MR. F. LANDSBERG'S INDIAN CURIO COLLECTION, VICTORIA, B.C.   Published by T. N. Hibben & Co., Victoria, B.C. No. 54

Figure 7.3. Frederick Landsberg's Indian curio collection, Victoria, B.C. Jewish Museum and Archives, L.01008, British Columbia.

themselves as knowledgeable of, and connected to, the land, countering the persistent image that they suffered estrangement from land.

Casting themselves as educators, ethnographers, and natural historians provided dealers further opportunities for improved sales. Their supposed specialized, esoteric, or arcane knowledge offered potential buyers the sense that the newly available objects for purchase might embody this knowledge. Morris Moss, an English Jewish trader on the Northwest coast, fashioned himself an "expert" on the Natives around Bella Coola.[47] Frederick Landsberg published a pamphlet that advertised what he called "The Largest Stock of Curios on the Pacific North West," which included pseudoethnographic discussions of American Indian mythology, the history of the totem pole, legends and traditions of Alaskan Indians, and a terse study of Ne-kil-stlass, "The Creator-The-Raven God." Other dealers emphasized the ritual power still attached to "Indian Idols" to enhance their desirability. "The Idols are made by the Cochita Indians in New Mexico," ran one advertisement, "and until recently have been worshiped by them as gods. Nothing surpasses them as an ornament for mantle pieces or brackets, and their extreme oddity makes them a valuable curiosity. . . . Should you desire any . . . write, as they are hard to obtain and not always in stock."[48]

The marketing strategies from Jewish curio sellers ought to be seen within the larger context of the Jews' economic position in the West, particularly the

Figure 7.4. Advertisement, "British Columbia and Alaska Indian Bazaar," ca. 1860. Jewish Museum and Archives, L.08766, British Columbia.

Southwest. Jewish firms dominated the newly American New Mexico economy from the 1860s to the 1880s so significantly that a one-time dean of the University of New Mexico School of Business Administration, William Parish, argued that German Jews effected nothing less than a "commercial revolution" there.[49] The historian Hal Rothman concurred, arguing that "*extranjero* [foreign] merchants, German-Jewish émigrés prominent among them, constituted the merchant class [of New Mexico in the 1880s], which played the dominant role in capital formation, intermarried with local people, and traded extensively [and] possessed the goals of an individualist mercantile culture." Rothman stressed that this domination resulted from the asymmetrical power relations between different groups on the frontier, not just Native Americans. He argued that "the colonial nature of trade in the peripheries of the Southwest gradually transferred agriculturalists' tangible assets to merchants."[50]

Native Americans had been either forcibly encouraged to become agriculturalists by the Dawes Act of 1887, designed to produce "surplus land" upon which further settlement and commerce could take place, or forced onto reservations with limited opportunities for acquiring capital.[51] Part of the process of frontier conquest involved commodifying and monetizing the land itself.

Along with many other whites, Jews gained from the broad commercial trans-formation of colonized territory, which had been supported by capital, law, and military, and which dislocated native populations to make living room for European and American settlers.

By the early 1880s frontier traders, Jews among them, had brought many tribes of Native Americans into cash economies that connected them with merchants and to larger markets, as the railroads and lines of credit linked rural outposts to commercial city centers.[52] Jewish merchants took some measure of pride in believing they had taught Native Americans to be better capitalists and therefore better Americans. Expanding capitalism to new participants in the economy of the West provided Jews social capital on top of the actual capital gained from commercial exchange with American Indians.

To both Jews and non-Jews, trading in American Indian items could be seen as a kind of missionizing for capitalism. One *Boston Hebrew Observer* article described how American Indians learned to become more savvy buyers over time, admiring their abilities to learn capitalism's logic. A *Los Angeles Times* piece praised Hopi traders as "Indian Jews," describing their trading acumen in detail and claiming that the Hopi "are natural traders of the keenest sort, against whom visitors from neighboring tribes have no chance whatever."[53] These kinds of articles cast Jews as educators for capitalism or models for commercial activity, and Jews tended to embrace the mantle. Indeed, Jews hoped to show their fellow white but Christian neighbors that the patriotic pursuit of civilizing and Americanizing the American Indian did not require Christianization. Rather, the spirit of capitalism alone, to which Jews strategically laid claim, could bend outsiders into insiders in the American cauldron.[54] The civic repercussions of Jews' efforts at making a living in this wild West also helped to counter anxiety Jews had of themselves as underproductive siphons of more natural primary producers such as mining or agriculture. Being a part of the commercial transformation of empty land, inhabited only by the uncivil, meant participation in the expansion process as well as a means to the practical end of mobility. Of course, commercial expansion and the extension of the frontier both formed key elements in the West's conquest.

Jewish curio men were not shy about casting themselves as conquering colonist to further promote their industry. "Subduing" American Indians, as nineteenth-century western Jewish memoirists frequently put it, allowed civilization and commerce to bloom in its wake; curios appeared to customers as the salable plunder of the conquerors.[55] J. J. Hart, for instance, promoted himself by championing his filibuster past in Nicaragua under General Walker before he migrated up the West Coast and established himself as a merchant trader fifty yards from the American Indian reserve near Comox. He sold liquor illegally to Haida and Tsimshians for fur, silver, and gold work from skilled Native artisans and eventually ran an American Indian curio business in Victoria from

1880 until his death in 1900.[56] Listed as a pawnbroker at the British Columbia and Alaska Colonial and Indian exhibition in 1886, "Wild Dick" Aaronson told the British press he was "in charge of B.C. Indian curios," clearly modeling himself on the Wild West show character "Wild Bill" Hickok. Dressed in buckskin, he fibbed that he was "employed to hunt the recalcitrant Indian to his forest retreat," pushing back Indians, killing them, and selling the booty to white consumers of white bravado and anti-Indian sentiment.[57]

Jews in the West, more generally, expressed pleasure in the power they found as fellow white settlers helping civilize the frontier, enjoying what they saw as a reversal of fortune from their subordinate position in Europe. Turn-of-the-century Jewish settlers proudly celebrated the Jews among them who engaged in American Indian trades for advancing not just capitalism but American colonial expansion. By the close of the nineteenth century, western Jewish immigrant memoirists and reporters highlighted Jews' business acumen, their service to civilization, and the credit they deserved for either clearing American Indians from the path of settlement expansion or incorporating them into settlement's commercial orbit. They aimed to articulate to the non-Jewish world that it owed the western Jews a debt of gratitude for "subduing the Apaches, permitting us [settlers] now to live in peace," as one Arizona memoirist put it.[58] Journalists and local Jewish history writers would routinely reproduce this rehearsal of Jewish contribution with remarkably little variation.[59] Jews in Alaska, Minnesota, and Wyoming served the country by advancing capitalism in their local counties in much the same way. Likewise, over time, Jews in the 1860s, 1870s, and 1890s presented themselves as heroes in the same noble project of transforming new lands into economically and commercially viable civic spaces. In 1894 Isaac Goldberg, an Arizona pioneer trader, characterized Jewish traders as standing at the cutting edge of the "irrepressible advances of conquering civilization."[60] This process represented, according to those who hoped to write Jews into the center of American history, the most significant gift that Jews made to the development of the nation.

Frontier trading among American Indians meant more than eking out a living at the margins. It meant transforming the economically backward European Jewish subcitizen into a heroic agent of American nation building. Not only might a living be made through commercial intercourse with Natives, but as new immigrants during the era of mass migration, Jews decidedly cast their commercial achievements as proof of their utility to the larger project of nation forming.

The marketing strategies that Jewish merchants such as Meyer on the Great Plains, Gold in the Southwest, or Hart on the Pacific Northwest used to promote the curio business obfuscated the primary action of the industry. By helping invent and supply a new market for whites to buy "Indianness," the curio trade brought new players into intercontinental cash relations and thus helped incorporate Native Americans into the expanding commercial structure. It also commodified Indianness. Curio sellers thus sold more than American Indian objects. They sold the idea of the American Indian, flexible enough to include a range of meanings. By helping create and foster a new commodities market that specifically laid claim to American Indian heritage, American Jews helped extended capitalism's reach to peoples that had lay outside the national economy.

The curio trade, and the Jews that plied it, helped the expansion of American capitalism not just by including new players in the system but by absorbing new geographies and new lands—and the resources on those lands—into the national economy as well. It helped Americans appropriate land on which mass development in the West depended, for it helped perpetuate myths about American Indians as alternately disappearing, recalcitrant, and otherwise uncitizenlike. Jews, along with other American-born whites and immigrants, clearly benefited from western expansion, much of it reliant on the very Native producers, consumers, and laborers who suffered systemic land loss. Although it remains a minor factor in the juggernaut of development, attention to the curio trade and Jews' involvement in American western expansion more generally reveals ways that culture and commerce collude in the colonial story of the "winning of the West."

NOTES

I would like to express my gratitude to the anonymous readers of this article for their helpful feedback.

1. Susan Ludmer-Gilebe, "Box-Ka-Re-Sha-Hash-Ta-Ka from Nebraska," *Toledo Jewish News*, July 1929, 18.

2. Julius Meyer, store in Omaha, c-2284; posed with Indians, N-2535; Indian wigwam store, n-2538, d-403; Julius Meyer with Red Cloud, Sitting Bull, Swift Bear, and Spotted Tail, n.2536; Julius Meyer with Chief Standing Bear, 29752, n2534; all in Picture Collection 2980, American Jewish Archives, Cincinnati, OH.

3. *Omaha Morning Bee*, May 11, 1909, cited in Carol Gendler, "The Jews of Omaha," *Western States Jewish Historical Quarterly* 5, no. 3 (April 1973): 217; Mel Marks, *Jews among the Indians: Tales of Adventure and Conflict in the Old West* (Chicago: Benison Books, 1992).

4. Peddling and post trading became sites not just of commercial exchange but of interethnic encounter. Jewish merchants understood their interactions with American Indians in frontier towns as fundamental to their immigration-integration narratives. In the retellings of personal and communal Jewish history, trading with American Indians became a mark of privileged status. Jews made use of Indians as practical tools as well as cultural foils for their vision of themselves as civic builders of America, owning-class whites, and masculine frontiersmen. The subject is taken up in greater detail in David S. Koffman, "The Jews' Indian: Native Americans in the Jewish Imagination and Experience, 1850–1950" (PhD diss., New York University, 2011).

5. Hasia Diner, "With Packs on Their Backs: Jewish Peddlers, Immigrants, and the Discovery of New Worlds" (paper presented at the Jews and American Capitalism Conference, Columbia University and New York University, March 3, 2008).

6. Kenneth Libo and Irving Howe, *We Lived There, Too: In Their Own Words and Pictures—Pioneer Jews and the Westward Movement of America, 1630–1930* (New York: St.

Martin's; Marek, 1984); Ava Fran Kahn, *Jewish Life in the American West: Perspectives on Migration, Settlement, and Community* (Los Angeles: Autry Museum of Western Heritage; Seattle: University of Washington Press, 2002); Jeanne E. Abrams, *Jewish Women Pioneering the Frontier Trail: A History in the American West* (New York: New York University Press, 2006); Ellen Eisenberg, Ava Fran Kahn, and William Toll, *Jews of the Pacific Coast: Reinventing Community on America's Edge* (Seattle: University of Washington Press, 2009).

7. Leah Dilworth, *Imagining Indians in the Southwest: Persistent Visions of a Primitive Past* (Washington, DC: Smithsonian Institute Press, 1996).

8. Roland W. Hawker, "The Johnson Street Gang: British Columbia's Early Indian Art Dealers," *British Columbia Historical News* 22, no. 1 (1989): 11. See also Leah Dilworth, *Acts of Possession: Collecting in America* (New Brunswick, NJ: Rutgers University Press, 2003); Jane I. Guyer, *Peripheral Markets and the Purchase of Museum Collections in Early Colonial Equatorial Africa* (Boston: African Studies Center, 1992); Sally Price, *Primitive Art in Civilized Places* (Chicago: University of Chicago Press, 1989); and Enid Schildkrout, *The Scramble for Art in Central Africa* (New York: Cambridge University Press, 1998).

9. Art historians, anthropologists, and historians of Native America have understood the production and sale of American Indian cultural commodities in various ways. Critics of capitalism have bemoaned the commodification of everyday goods and ceremonial artifacts, with particular emphasis on the loss of cultural meaning during this transformation. The curio trade has been examined from the perspective of the collectors, focusing in some cases on the accumulation of wealth by Americans, increased leisure time, and Victorian sensibilities—that is, on the cultural changes brought about by advancing industrial capitalism. Others have focused on the colonial aspects of the trade in which curios or "grotesques" contributed to the discourses of power and control between the strange and the familiar and on the systems of belief that "projected the American anti-self onto Indian tribes" Patricia Fogelman Lange, "Nineteenth-Century Cochiti Figurines: Commodity Fetishes," *Museum Anthropology* 19, no. 1 (1995): 39–44. Still other scholars have attended to the economic processes that transformed American Indian culture. Some of this work emphasizes the experiences and consequences of exploitation, and some emphasizes Native people's agency in the operations. Ruth Phillips, introduction to *Unpacking Culture: Art and Commodity in Colonial and Postcolonial Worlds*, ed. Ruth B. Phillips and Christopher B. Steiner (Berkeley: University of California Press, 1999), 4. Finally, scholars have also considered the curio from the perspective of the invention of the tourist "Indian" and the invention of place-bound tourism. See, for example, Eliza McFeely, *Zuni and the American Imagination* (New York: Hill and Wang, 2001); Hal K. Rothman, *Devil's Bargains: Tourism in the Twentieth-Century American West* (Lawrence: University of Kansas Press, 1998).

10. Though these are different markets with varied distribution networks and final consumer destinations, and are ultimately made up of objects with meanings that differ on account of the various discursive worlds to which they belong, for my broader purposes in this argument I am treating them as one bundled market, irrespective of market segmentation. For a similar use of these objects bundled together, see Kate C. Duncan, *1001 Curious Things: Ye Olde Curiosity Shop and Native American Art* (Seattle: University of Washington Press, 2000).

11. Jonathan Batkin, "Some Early Curio Dealers of New Mexico," *American Indian Art Magazine* 23, no. 3 (1998): 69.

12. William G. Robbins, *Colony and Empire: The Capitalist Transformation of the American West* (Lawrence: University Press of Kansas, 1994); William Cronon, *Nature's Metropolis: Chicago and the Great West* (New York: Norton, 1991); William Cronon, George Miles, and Jay Gitlin, eds., *Under an Open Sky: Rethinking America's Western Past* (New York: Norton, 1992).

13. William Toll, "The Jewish Merchant and Civic Order in the Urban West," in Kahn, ~~Jewish Life, 83.~~

14. See, for example, Floyd S. Fierman, *Guts and Ruts: The Jewish Pioneer on the Trail in the American Southwest* (New York: Ktav, 1985); Kahn, *Jewish Life*.

15. Hasia Diner, *Hungering for America: Italian, Irish, and Jewish Foodways in the Age of Migration* (Cambridge, MA: Harvard University Press, 2001); Hasia Diner, *The Jews of the United States, 1654–2000* (Berkeley: University of California Press. 2004).

16. See Floyd S. Fierman, *The Speigelbergs of New Mexico, Merchants and Bankers, 1844–1893* (El Paso: Texas Western College Press, 1964). Astonishingly, Flora Spiegelberg left a confession that Willi, her husband, purchased an American Indian orphan in 1905, whom the family named Joseph, educated, and raised. Spiegelberg Family Papers, Small Collections 11853, American Jewish Archives, Cincinnati, OH.

17. Henry Russell Wray, "A Gem in Art," *Weekly New Mexico R··iew* (1894), p. 4, col. 6

18. Rothman, *Devil's Bargains*, 97.

19. Letters, MS, RG 75, Office of Indian Trade, Letters Sent, vol. B, Records of the Bureau of Indian Affairs, National Archives, Washington, DC, reprinted as "John Mason to Jacob Marks, 1811" and "John Mason to Ben Sheftall, 1813," in *The Jews of the United States, 1790–1840: A Documentary History*, vol. 1, ed. Joseph L. Blau and Salo W. Baron (New York: Columbia University Press/Jewish Publication Society of America, 1963), 112–115. The political reality of this history is that the process was by no means a straightforward or simple matter of the state paving the way for commerce at the expense of Native agency or interests. See David Andrew Nichols, *Red Gentlemen and White Savages: Indians, Federalists, and the Search for Order on the American Frontier* (Charlottesville: University of Virginia Press, 2008).

20. American Indian trade also attracted Jews in the East in the seventeenth and eighteenth centuries. Jacob Lumbrozo, a Portuguese Jewish planter, physician, and fur trader in the palatinate of Maryland, earned a commission to trade with American Indians as early as 1665. Jacob Lumbrozo file, GF 639, folder 1, American Jewish Archives, Cincinnati, OH. Levy Solomons resided among and retained interests in mercantile enterprises with American Indians from Michilimackinac to the Gulf of St. Lawrence and down the Hudson River in the 1770s and 1780s. Joseph Jacobs and Clarence I. de Sola, "Solomons, Levy," in *Jewish Encyclopedia* (London: Funk and Wagnall, 1906). By supplying dry goods and foodstuffs to both American Indians and the military as it roved about the frontier, Aaron Levy helped develop the commercial infrastructure of Northumberland County, Pennsylvania. Cyrus Adler and Abraham S. W. Rosenbach, "Levy, Aaron," in *Jewish Encyclopedia*.

21. See in Blau and Baron, *Jews of the United States*, 847, 852; on Elhart see *Letters of Benjamin Hawkins, 1796–1806, Collections of the Georgia Historical Society* (Tuscaloosa: University of Alabama Press, 2003), 9, 169, 258, 476, in Blau and Baron, *Jews of the United States*, 986.

22. Cyrus Adler and Ephraim Deinard, "Minnesota," *Jewish Encyclopedia*.

23. See letters from Louis Rosenbaum, dated June 30, 1876, from Las Cruces, New Mexico; the Spiegleberg brothers in Santa Fe, throughout the summer and fall of 1875; D. Bernard Koch of Santa Fe in March 1897; and Zadok Staab in January 1875. Microfilm Records, 1875–1880, roll 24, cabinet 59, drawer 10, T1, New Mexico Superintendent of Indian Affairs, Department of Interior, National Archives.

24. See, for example, Eileen Hallett Stone, *A Homeland in the West: Utah Jews Remember* (Salt Lake City: University of Utah Press, 2001); Benjamin Kelson, "The Jews of Montana," pts. 2–5, *Western States Jewish Historical Quarterly* 3, no 4 (1971): 227–242; Benjamin Kelson, "The Jews of Montana," pt. 1, *Western States Jewish Historical Quarterly* 3, no. 2 (1971): 113–120.

25. Helen Akrigg and G. P. V. Akrigg, *British Columbia Chronicle: Gold and Colonists* (Vancouver: Discovery, 1977); Cyril Edel Leonoff, *Pioneers, Pedlars, and Prayer Shawls: The Jewish Communities in British Columbia and the Yukon* (Victoria: Sono Nis, 1978).

26. Hawker, "Johnson Street Gang," 10–14.

27. Among those signatories included the Jewish merchants Lewis Levy, W. Cohn, Joseph Boscowitz, Morris Dobrin, Abraham Martin, Abraham Israel of the firm Martin and Israel—Indian Traders, Abraham Frankel, Hyman Copperman, Julius Seitz, Nathan Solomon, owner of "The Indian Store," Aaron Oldenburg, Leopold Blum, Lewis Goldstone, Samuel Myers, Henry Nathan, and Jules Friedman. Ibid.

28. Christopher J. P. Hanna, "The Early Jewish Coastal Fur Traders," *Scribe: Journal of the Jewish Historical Society of British Columbia* 19, no. 1 (1999): 9–14.

29. *Victoria Evening Express*, September 9, 1864, 3.

30. Christopher J. P. Hanna, "Mike Cohen: 'King John of the Red House,'" *Scribe: Journal of the Jewish Historical Society of British Columbia* 19, no. 1 (1999): 29–34.

31. Batkin, "Early Curio Dealers," 68–81.

32. Philip, J. Deloria, *Playing Indian* (New Haven, CT: Yale University Press, 1998); Rayna Green, "The Tribe Called Wannabee: Playing Indian in America and Europe," *Folklore* 99, no. 1 (1988): 30–55; and Jay Mechling, "'Playing Indian' and the Search for Authenticity in Modern White America," *Prospects* 5 (1980): 17–33. The last sentence contains the language of Robert F. Berkofer Jr., *The White Man's Indian: Images of the American Indian from Columbus to the Present* (New York: Knopf, 1978).

33. Boas's Jewishness is subject to a growing scholarly discussion. See Douglass Cole, *Franz Boas: The Early Years, 1858–1906* (Seattle: University of Washington Press, 1999); Regna Darnell, *And Along Came Boas: Continuity and Revolution in Americanist Anthropology* (Amsterdam: Benjamins, 1998); Jeffrey David Feldman, "The Jewish Roots and Routes of Anthropology," *Anthropological Quarterly* 77, no. 1 (2004): 107–125; Gelya Frank, "Jews, Multiculturalism, and Boasian Anthropology," *American Anthropologist* 99, no. 4 (1997): 731–745; Leonard Glick, "Types Distinct from Our Own: Franz Boas on Jewish Identity and Assimilation," *American Anthropologist* 84 (1982): 545–565.

34. Douglas Cole, *Captured Heritage: The Scramble for Northwest Coast Artifacts* (Seattle: University of Washington Press, 1985).

35. Sarah H. Tobe, "Victoria's Curio Dealers," *Scribe: Journal of the Jewish Historical Society of British Columbia* 19, no. 2 (1999): 15–18.

36. Jonathan Batkin, "Mail-Order Catalogs as Artifacts of the Early Native American Curio Trade," *American Indian Art Magazine* 29, no. 2 (2004): 40–49.

37. Jonathan Batkin, "Tourism Is Overrated: Pueblo Pottery and the Early Curio Trade, 1880–1910" in Phillips and Steiner, *Unpacking Culture*, 282–297.

38. Batkin, "Early Curio Dealers."

39. Batkin, "Mail-Order Catalogs."

40. The American Indian curio boom ought also to be seen within the context of booming markets for other exotica—Japanese and Chinese antiques and curios, African heritage objects, and relics from ancient defunct empires. See, for example, David Lowenthal, *Possessed by the Past: The Heritage Crusade and the Spoils of History* (New York: Free Press, 1996).

41. Batkin, "Mail-Order Catalogs."

42. Catalogue of Gold's Free Museum, 1889, ZC54 889go, Beinecke Rare Book and Manuscript Library, Yale University, New Haven, CT.

43. For example, Black Hills Retail Catalogue 12, Est. 1884 (1911): *Indian Relic and Curio Establishment*, L. W. Stilwell Wholesale and Retail, Deadwood, SD, ZC35 911LW, Beinecke Rare Book and Manuscript Library.

44. "Curios from the Ancient Mounds and Ruins in the Salt River Valley, Arizona," 1893, Catalogue of Collection of Curios, ZC56 893dy, Beinecke Rare Book and Manuscript Library.

45. An October 1881 article about a topical remedy called Saint Jacob's Oil, in which Tammen was quoted, described him as "a well-known and reliable collector of Colorado

curiosities." *Rocky Mountain News* 8 (1881): 43; Martin Padget, "Claiming, Corrupting, Contesting. Reconsidering 'The West' in Western American Literature," *American Literary History* 10, no. 2 (Summer 1998): 378–392.

46. Catherine Albanese, *Nature Religion in America: From the Algonkian Indians to the New Age* (Chicago: University of Chicago Press, 1990); and Roderick Nash, *Wilderness and the American Mind* (New Haven: Yale University Press, 2001).

47. Sarah H. Tobe, "New Frontiers," *Scribe: Journal of the Jewish Historical Society of British Columbia* 19, no. 2 (1999): 10.

48. Quoted in Batkin, "Early Curio Dealers."

49. William J. Parish, "The German Jew and the Commercial Revolution in Territorial New Mexico, 1850–1900," *University of New Mexico Sixth Annual Research Lecture* (Albuquerque: University of New Mexico, May 1, 1959). Parish made no mention of these Jews' business with Native Americans, nor of profiting from the broad transformation in Native American economics, politics, geography, and culture that their business affected.

50. Rothman, *Devil's Bargains*, 82.

51. I am not implying that Native Americans lacked economic agency. Scholars are quick and right to point out that Native Americans took active roles as cultural and economic agents in their own right, and as they became more thoroughly involved in cash economies, trade became increasingly commercial, while the barter system fell out of use. Bruce Johansen, ed., *The Encyclopedia of Native American Economic History* (Westport, CT: Greenwood, 1999).

52. Cronon, *Nature's Metropolis*, pt. 3, "The Geography of Capital."

53. "Indians Trading," *Boston Hebrew Observer* 1, no. 21 (1883); "Decay Hits Oldest Town," *Los Angeles Times*, September 24, 1924.

54. This argument was often made implicitly rather than explicitly. It is significant, however, given that the "missionary spirit" was at the heart of much American Indian relations. Though Jews were excluded from harnessing this missionizing spirit, they nonetheless adopted an adapted version of it that removed religion from the equation.

55. Samuel H. Drachman, "Arizona Pioneers and Apaches," May 4, 1855, handwritten reminiscences, AJA MC 649, folder 8, box 13, American Jewish Archives, Tucson, AZ.

56. Victoria Directory and *Victoria Times* advertisement, in *Scribe: Journal of the Jewish Historical Society of British Columbia* 19, no. 1 (1999): 9n28.

57. *British Colonist*, August 10, 1866, 3, quoted in Hawker's "Johnson Street Gang," 11.

58. Drachman, "Arizona Pioneers and Apaches."

59. Personal, familial, local, state, and popular western Jewish history writers reproduced this narrative of frontier Jews from their earliest arrival in the Americas. Ruth Arnfeld describes Pittsburgh's Jewish American Indian trading "Founding Fathers," as "pioneers [of] vision and faith," the "men of good will" who transformed the frontier from a dangerous place of raw wild, to the great cities of American life." "Jews in America Tradition: Some of Pittsburgh's Own Founding Fathers," *Jewish Criterion*, September 11, 1942, 30–31. Harold Sharfman exaggerated that the trading activities of Joseph Simon, David Franks, Heyman Levy, and Levy Andrew Levy "helped shape Indian policy and opened much of the Trans-Appalachian West to commerce and settlement," and that Heyman Levy of New York, "the leading Indian trader of his day," along with Abraham Mordecai and his Indian wife, "dominated the trade of the lower Mississippi Valley." *Jews on the Frontier* (Chicago: Regnery, 1977).

60. Isaac Goldberg, "An Old Timer's Experiences in Arizona," *Arizona Historical Review* 2 (October 1929): 90–91. First published in 1894 in San Bernadino, California, SC 4010, American Jewish Archives, Cincinnati, OH.

PART III

Jews and the Politics of American Capitalism

༄

CHAPTER 8

The Multicultural Front

A YIDDISH SOCIALIST RESPONSE
TO SWEATSHOP CAPITALISM

Daniel Katz

In 1934 two competing May Day parades in New York City drew two hundred thousand participants and spectators. The mood was both festive and tense throughout the city. Riots had erupted in France and Ireland in recent days; the Nazis were taking elaborate precautions to prevent any communist demonstrations in Berlin; Newark, New Jersey, banned the socialists from marching; and police in Queens, New York, brutally suppressed an illegal march of communists the night before. Nearly two thousand heavily armed police monitored both marches and both rallies at Union Square and Madison Square.[1] In this highly charged moment, during which general strikes across the country were building and being led by various communist and Marxist parties, both of the major radical marches and rallies in New York emphasized the multicultural as well as the anticapitalist dimensions of their revolutionary movements.[2] Through songs, placards, banners, and speeches at the Union Square rally, the communists expressed their commitment to racial and ethnic inclusion. The *New York Times* reported, "There were Negro, Chinese and Japanese speakers proclaiming the solidarity and unity of aim of all working men to overthrow the capitalist system and set up a soviet of America."[3] Uptown, near Columbus Circle, the Dressmakers' Local 22 of the International Ladies' Garment Workers' Union (ILGWU) assembled in Central Park to march down Broadway, led by their manager, Charles "Sasha" Zimmerman, to join the Socialist Party demonstration in celebration of a stunning organizing victory six months earlier. Photographs from the march show members riding on and marching alongside a horse-drawn float that unified themes of multiculturalism, labor militancy, and antifascism. In the center of the float, in place of a May Day pole, a single, upright fist clenched ribbons held at the other end by white and black members. Crowned by a rendering of the Western Hemisphere, the medallion on the right flank reads, "THE POWER OF LABOR LIVES IN ORGANIZA-TION AND MILITANCY." The central slogans proclaims, "WORKERS OF 32 NATIONALITIES UNITED: DRESSMAKERS UNION *Local* 22, ILGWU" and "ONE ARMY UNDER ONE FLAG FIGHTING FOR ONE CAUSE—THE CAUSE OF LABOR." The horse drawing the float is draped with a banner reading, "DOWN WITH NAZISM."[4]

Like the podium speakers in the communist rally, the image created by Local 22's float reflected the interracial and international revolutionary sensibilities that form a familiar narrative for historians of American labor and the Left. But a second look at the photographs reveals something different from what scholars have assumed about the militancy underpinning the rise of industrial labor in the 1930s. Union members are dressed in traditional peasant and village costumes from eastern, northern, and central Europe, the Middle East, Spain, Mexico, South America, and the West Indies. At a time that few historians of multiculturalism noticed any appreciable movement embracing multiple ethnic identities, one of the most prominent local unions in the

Figure 8.1. Local 22 members constructed this May Day float in 1934 to illustrate the links between multiculturalism, union militancy, and anti-Nazism. File 15, box 1, collection 5780/14p, ILGWU Papers, Kheel Center for Labor-Management Documentation and Archives, Martin P. Catherwood Library, Cornell University.

country broadcasted not only its diverse membership but the diverse cultures those members brought to the militant wing of the labor movement.[5] The point was made repeatedly over the next several years, as in Local 22's fondness for an interracial collage of members' faces in a broadside that read "A UNION OF MANY CULTURES."[6]

Over the past two decades, labor historians who have investigated the rise of the industrial labor movement in the 1930s have concluded, in varying degrees, that class consciousness increased among first- and second-generation immigrant industrial workers as their ties to ethnic working-class communities weakened or transformed. In his study of French Canadian and Franco Belgian textile workers, Gary Gerstle saw an increasing class consciousness among workers

Figure 8.2. The ILGWU used this collage frequently in the mid-1930s. After the August 1933 strike, Local 22 boasted that it represented workers from thirty-two nationalities, including Jewish, Italian, Spanish, and African American. *Growing Up: 21 Years of Education with the I.L.G.W.U., 1917–1938* (New York: Wolff, 1938). From the private collection of Daniel Katz.

who in the 1920s felt "a deep ambivalence . . . about their ethnic heritage."[7] He argues they adopted a "working-class Americanism" in the 1930s, forging a new ethnic identity that appropriated the broad political and cultural movements of assimilation in the 1920s for the movement of mass unionization of the 1930s. Lizabeth Cohen argues that the Congress of Industrial Organizations' "culture of unity" appealed to workers across ethnic lines in part because American mass culture supplanted the institutions of atomized ethnic neighborhoods.[8] In both of these formulations, mass American culture, not multiple ethnic cultures, was responsible for working-class solidarity. But the Dressmakers' celebration of ethnic cultural difference illustrates a phenomenon—evident throughout the Jewish Left, including socialists and communists—that cuts against the grain of this narrative. In this essay, I argue that in response to the systems of social and cultural oppression that accompanied Jewish workers' experiences under capitalism in Russia and the United States, revolutionary Jews constructed a peculiar form of cultural socialism, which survived into the 1930s just in time to help build a multicultural and industrial labor union.

YIDDISH SOCIALISM IN RUSSIA

Jewish workers' encounter with capitalism, first in Russia, then in the United States, was accompanied in different ways and to different degrees by the subordination of ethnic cultures, including and especially Jewish cultures. The same economic, political, and social forces that pushed millions of Jews to emigrate from the Russian Empire from the 1880s to the 1910s engendered a revolutionary movement among Jews living in Russia and throughout the diaspora. Following the assassination of Czar Alexander II in 1881, the Russian state issued the May Decrees, enforcing new restrictions on Jewish domicility, education, and employment and reinforcing older limits that had been relaxed in recent decades. With a series of legislative orders, the czarist state forced Jews to move back to the shtetls and urban ghettoes within the Pale of Settlement. The law prohibited Jews from owning land. They could not vote, sit on a jury, or sue non-Jews for civil damages. State authorities severely curtailed Jewish admission to universities and relegated Jews to a few spots in Russian gymnasiums.[9] State-sponsored schools offered classes solely in the Russian language as a means to break down ethnic cultural identity among children. Jews in large part refused to send their children to Russian schools and developed both religious and secular Jewish schools within the Pale of Settlement.[10] Thus, the institutions of education became arenas of cultural conflict between czarist efforts to control the economic, political, and social mechanisms of the empire on one hand, and Jewish nationalist resistance to those efforts on the other.

By the late 1890s perhaps six hundred thousand Jews labored in industry under brutal conditions, largely for Jewish employers. One historian noted, "a

17–18 hours working day was usual" among hatters, tailors, and shoemakers in small villages and cities "under horrifyingly unhygienic conditions . . . and rewarded by appalling low wages."[11] They suffered "hunger in the fullest meaning of the word, sweating-system, shrunk chests, lifeless eyes, pale faces, sick and tubercular lungs."[12] When workers, including many employed by Jewish manufacturers, sought to organize, the Russian state came down hard on the side of employers, crushing unions, often violently, and putting union leaders in prison.[13] So, for the Jewish socialists who came to revolutionary consciousness in the 1880s and 1890s, the czarist state that restricted education, blocked paths to the professions, and relegated Jewish industrial workers to lives of poverty and toil wore a Jewish face. And Jewish revolutionaries responded by constructing a Jewish working-class–based ethnic identity.

While Jews suffered under harsh conditions, the Russian Empire also suppressed other minority cultures within its borders. In the early 1880s revolutionaries of various nationalist movements began to form multinational parties, encouraging a united front against the czar. Over the course of the next two decades, a Yiddish cultural movement grew among revolutionaries dedicated to reaching into the factories and workshops of Russian Jewish workers throughout the world. Among the most prominent thinkers and activists, Chaim Zhitlowsky worked in a multiethnic Russian revolutionary movement predicated on a form of multinational state building that he and other European philosophers referred to as *national cultural autonomy*.[14]

Jewish nationalist ideas formed in the 1890s within the currents of international debate over the status of ethnic-minority groups that were situated or migrating by the millions within and between states and empires. Efforts to reconcile the presence of diverse ethnic groups with the construction of a singular state occupied government leaders, philosophers, and political essayists in Europe and the United States from the late 1890s through World War I. Zhitlowsky, while concerned primarily with Russian Jewry, participated in European social-democratic movements and shared key ideas with Austrian Marxists. Karl Renner, who two decades later assumed the office of the first prime minister of Austria, wrote a seminal essay in 1899 called "State and Nation," in which he proposed one of the innovative reforms embraced by social democrats for the Austro-Hungarian Empire. Renner argued for a form of national-cultural autonomy in which minority ethnic communities within the empire would have proportional representation throughout several levels of government, in addition to territorial representation. Individuals would choose their national affiliation regardless of territory, and an additional legislature would be composed of representatives from national cultures.[15] The proposal sought to ensure that minorities were not overwhelmed by territorial majorities and that such issues as education and cultural affairs would be controlled by national groups. As historian Jack Jacobs notes, the Austro-Marxists were influenced heavily by the writings of Franz Kursky, who addressed the question of national groups within Austria-Hungary prior to Renner's work.[16] Kursky was a member of the General Jewish Workers' Union in Lithuania, Poland, and Russia, or the Bund, a secret revolutionary organization of Jewish radical intellectuals and workers to struggle for socialism and promote civil rights for Jews within the territories controlled by the Russian czar.[17]

In a later essay Renner argued that the formal constitution of national groups within the empire was a matter of necessity. "If one wants to make a law for nations, one must first create the nations. . . . Unless nationalities are constituted it is impossible to create national rights and eliminate national dissension."[18] Renner's ideas go well beyond tolerance fo ethnic cultural differences. For the integrity of the state, he insisted that national groups form structures for national cultural autonomy, even if people are not demanding it. Renner's contemporary and future deputy, Otto Bauer, expanded on Renner's themes in "The Question of Nationalities and Social Democracy," published in 1907. Bauer argued that "national autonomy is a necessary goal of the proletarian class struggle," thus articulating a view favored by the left wing of European social-democratic parties, in which national cultural autonomy was seen as a function of revolutionary resistance to capitalism.[19]

Those same ideas of ethnic cultural nation building were evident among the most prominent Jewish revolutionary groups. In 1897 several Jewish socialist groups gathered to form the Bund, which advocated the formation of unions, political parties, and self-defense militias to protect the general Jewish population. The Bund adopted Yiddish socialism, or Yiddishism, when Chaim Zhitlowsky joined in 1898, as the principle idiom of revolutionary Judaism.[20] Zhitlowsky, a founder of the Russian Socialist Revolutionary Party, explained the centrality of Yiddishism to revolutionary thought in a series of articles he wrote for the Bund journal in 1898 and 1899. He argued that Jews could effectively struggle for socialism only from a position of equality as an autonomous nation within a multinational socialist movement.[21] He advocated for an entire cultural reorientation among Jewish intellectuals and workers. "Everything he will achieve in art and science will be brought out in Yiddish, and Yiddish culture and Yiddish education will grow continuously and will become a formidable force that will bind together as one not only the educated people with the folk, but also all Jews from all countries."[22]

For Yiddish socialists then, revolution, ethnic culture, and education were intertwined.

YIDDISH SOCIALISTS IN NEW YORK

Russian Jews, who engaged in the most intense period of revolutionary thought and action in the empire, from the late 1890s to the beginning of the 1905

Russian Revolution, came to New York ready to apply Yiddish socialist principles, as they reinvigorated and founded institutions in the Jewish labor and
socialist movements. The conditions of American capitalism were different
than in Russia. Jews did not suffer state-sponsored or state-tolerated pogroms,
and political freedoms before World War I allowed for greater degrees of dissent. But work and living conditions were brutal nonetheless. The mass production of the sewing machine during the decades after the Civil War made it
possible for a significant number of skilled Jewish tailors to open workshops,
often in the overcrowded apartments in which they lived. Typically, these
petty entrepreneurs employed a few workers, including family members and
boarders, in overcrowded, poorly ventilated sweatshops. Large manufacturers
employed jobbers, or intermediaries, to parcel out bundles of clothes, divid-
ing various stages of garment production among several tenement workshops.
The sheer number of immigrants, coupled with the deskilling created by the
division of labor, meant that jobbers forced sweatshop bosses to compete
with one another. The "cutthroat capitalism" that characterized the sweatshops created tremendous instability in the industry and misery among the
workforce. The system drove wages down to starvation levels, demanded that
workers and owners alike work long hours, employed children, fed myriad
diseases, and forced workers to fend for themselves during prolonged periods
of unemployment.[23]

After the turn of the twentieth century, spurred by municipal electricity
infrastructure and innovations in electric sewing machine technology, industrialists began to build modern garment factories to take advantage of the
massive influx of cheap Jewish and Italian labor. Reformers hailed the better
lighting and ventilation in what seemed to be far more humane workplaces than
the sweatshops, but the young women who constituted the factory workforce
experienced speedups facilitated by modern machinery and suffered numerous
managerial abuses, including sexual harassment.[24] More, infamous garment
manufacturers resorted to violence and public humiliations to break strikes,
including the hiring of gangsters and prostitutes to beat down women picket-
ers. Manufacturers' disregard for workplace safety was brought to the world's
attention when 146 women and men burned or jumped to their death during
the Triangle Shirtwaist factory fire in 1911.[25] In New York City, as in Russia, the
face of the oppressor in the sweatshop and the modern factory was most often
another Jew, sometimes a compatriot. Again Russian Jews found themselves in
a ghetto. But their concentration in the Lower East Side allowed Jews to form
labor unions, fraternal societies, newspapers, and political organizations that
were mutually supportive and bound together by the growing socialist movement dedicated to fighting back in the war against garment manufacturers.

Separate and interdependent at the same time, various institutions centered
in the Jewish Lower East Side of Manhattan—such as the United Hebrew

Trades, the *Jewish Daily Forward*, the Workmen's Circle fraternal society, the Rand School for Social Science, and the ILGWU—cultivated activists, advocates, and leaders. Members, students, readers, and leaders of these institutions overlapped extensively. Jews who were attracted to the whole panoply of radical movements, including anarchism, and later communism, formed rival institutions. At the same time, for some Jewish leaders, progressive political movements and politicians in the United States, particularly in New York, held out some hope that the state could act as an agent of reform. Still, Jewish workers continued to suffer unpredictable employment, long hours, low pay, unhealthy workplaces, and employers who hoped to divide the workers by race and ethnicity. Time and again, the ideas of national cultural autonomy, articulated by philosophers like Chaim Zhitlowsky, proved to be powerfully effective tools when Jewish unionists were faced with the problems of building a cohesive and militant union among workers of different racial-ethnic cultural groups.

The leading visionary of education in the ILGWU was Fannia Cohn, a Russian Jewish revolutionary with close ties to Zhitlowsky's Russian Socialist Revolutionary Party. She was born in Minsk, Russia, in 1885, joined the party in 1901, and immigrated to New York in 1904 at the age of nineteen after a brother was almost killed in a pogrom.[26] In the United States, Cohn joined the Socialist Party, went to work in the garment shops and set out to organize her coworkers.[27] From 1918 until 1935 she designed and oversaw the ILGWU educational programs, and she was the most critical link between Yiddish socialists before World War I and the multicultural educational movement that underpinned the rise of the ILGWU and the Congress of Industrial Organizations in the 1930s.

MULTICULTURAL EDUCATION IN THE ILGWU

From the earliest days of her union work, Fannia Cohn was concerned with the cultural and linguistic divides between the Jewish majority and the significant Italian minority in the garment trades workforce. In 1908 Cohn met Rose Schneiderman, another Russian Jew, during a white goods workers' strike and bonded with her over a similar style of organizing. In a strategy that Cohn and others would perfect over the years with respect to other racial-ethnic groups, Schneiderman went to the heart of the Italian women's community and began to work with a local priest in Brooklyn to identify potential leaders among the workers. She worked to create the same ethnic institutional supports in the Italian community that Jewish women workers enjoyed. At her suggestion, the New York Women's Trade Union League hired an Italian-speaking organizer to appeal to Italian professionals to back the strike. Cohn was similarly sensitive to the ethnic diversity in the industry and sought ways to join the various communities. Her concerns were not only that there was a language barrier that existed between these women workers but that Italian as well as Czech, Polish, Slavic, and Arab women had very different cultural experiences with unions. Most worrying, she felt that many of the workers from rural areas, principally the Italian and Slavic women, had no experience with trade unions.[28]

For Cohn, the solution to these problems was an integrated program of educational, social, and cultural activities, which she first created in ILGWU Local 41 in 1913, that encouraged workers to trust one another in spite of cultural differences. They learned to think about their participation in the union as a long-term strategy of attacking the capitalist system rather than just a means to improve their immediate working conditions and standard of living. Louis Friedland, who for a time directed the educational programs in the ILGWU under Cohn, wrote in 1919 that worker education should transform the "spirit" as well as the "aim" of all education and be integrated with all aspects of workers' lives. He wrote about the "inspiring task" of preparing workers for social change. "For the time will come when the workers—all of them, hand and brain workers, will unite to control industry."[29] Union members learned to trust that the union was not another institution trying to suppress their language or denigrate their culture. Local 41 created separate Jewish and Italian branches to accommodate workers' distinct language needs and cultural interests. Both branches conducted musical entertainments and popular lectures, while the local union sponsored programs that included parties and a series of monthly dances. It was a form of union organization that touched members not only in the shops but also in their homes, in their communities, and with their families.[30]

Cohn and other organizers' fears that Italian workers would not join the union or participate fully proved to be unfounded. Italian men and women joined the union at levels commensurate with Jews in the 1910s, so much so, that they began to demand their own local unions to conduct meetings in Italian, instead of Yiddish or English, to create their own recreation programs, and to assert their own political voice.[31] After some initial resistance, in 1916 the ILGWU leadership created Local 48 for the Italian cloak makers, and in 1919 they formed Local 89 for the Italian dressmakers to allow them a measure of autonomy. The structure resonated with Yiddish socialists convinced of the necessity of national cultural autonomy, and since many Italian garment workers worked in shops owned by Italians, separate Italian locals devoted to the nuances of labor-management relations in an Italian cultural context made practical sense.

By 1920 the ILGWU had more than one hundred thousand garment workers in its ranks. Though a majority of members were Jewish, more than a third were Italian. Union leaders heralded the end of the sweatshop in New York City and other major garment centers in the United States. Union contracts established good wages, reasonable working hours, and sanitary working conditions. However, from the mid-1920s through the early 1930s, the ILGWU suffered a

steady decline in membership and a weakening position in the garment industry. Members of the nascent Communist Party—formed from groups that split
off from the Socialist Party in 1919 and left-wing members of the IWW—vied
for control of local unions with more moderate anarchist and Socialist Party–
affiliated union leaders. The rivalry grew to mutually destructive proportions.
Communists and anticommunists condemned one another and battled in the
courts and on the streets.[32] In addition, garment manufacturers pushed back
against the union and supported the open shop, antiunion movement of the
1920s by segmenting the production process into subcontracted shops and
hiring members of various racial-ethnic groups, principally black and Spanish-
speaking workers, in an attempt to divide the workforce.

Nevertheless, Jewish leaders reached out to black leaders and nonunion
black workers. At the 1920 ILGWU convention, President Schlesinger submit-
ted a report that observed the increase of young black women who had "begun
invading" the ladies' garment trades over the preceding few years in New
York, Baltimore, Philadelphia, and Chicago. Black women were first "used by
employers as a club against the organized workers in the shops." But, the report
went on, the idea of unionization had spread among these workers, and blacks
were joining the union in increasing numbers. Union officers explained the
black workers' affinity for the ILGWU this way: "The friendly attitude of the
members of our locals towards them, the fact that they have treated the colored
women in a friendly and equitable spirit, has aided materially in revealing to
the negro women workers where their true interests lie."[33] In addition, the
General Executive Board expressed a desire to educate black garment workers
and by 1929 hired Floria Pinkney, a black activist associated with A. Phillip
Randolph and a protégé to Fannia Cohn, to organize black women.[34] Union
leaders touted the donations they made to the *Messenger*, founded and edited
by Randolph, president of the Brotherhood of Sleeping Car Porters, as one way
to support the organizing of black workers in the ILGWU. This pattern follows
the experience that many ILGWU members had when, as recent immigrants,
they found their way to unions through reading the *Jewish Daily Forward*.

Into the 1930s some sweatshop bosses, including Jewish employers, continued to preferentially hire non-Jewish workers. In her first job interview in 1931,
Amelia Bucchieri was asked by the boss, who was Jewish, if she was Catholic.
She was, and she believed that was why she was hired. Her suspicions were con-
firmed when she got to know her coworkers. One Jewish coworker who wore a
crucifix told her, "If I don't wear a cross, I'll never have a job."[35] The suppression
of Jewish ethnic identity was one of many tools employers used to keep workers
scared and suspicious. The task for union organizers, then, was as much about
reinforcing ethnic pride as it was to instill respect for ethnic difference.

Jewish unionists throughout the political Left responded to these challenges through a constellation of educational programs that supported Yiddish

culture and appealed to the multiple racial-ethnic cultures of new garment workers. In the early and mid-1930s, Jewish union and radical political leaders in the Socialist and Communist Parties, as well as a host of smaller left-wing parties and groups, continued to appeal to the Yiddish culture of their coethnics and reached out to members of racial-ethnic groups through cultural mechanisms. The Communist Party, whose leadership was dominated in New York City by first- and second-generation Russian Jews in the 1930s, focused heavily on interracial organizing, just as their socialist counterparts did.[36] They sponsored athletic leagues and dances and owned a retreat on the Hudson River, Camp Unity, in which blacks and whites mixed easily. Across the nation, including the South among black workers, communists formed study groups, organized picnics, and adapted religious hymns at meetings. They also sent activists to the Workers' School in New York, and they sent children to the Young Pioneer camps.[37]

With meager budgets, Fannia Cohn kept educational programs alive in the ILGWU from the mid-1920s to the early 1930s. She consistently expressed key multicultural themes in educational literature and in reports to the union and the American Federation of Labor.[38] She developed curricula, produced plays and pageants, and programmed events at the union's retreat, Unity House, to celebrate the strength of ideas found in the diversity of cultures in the union. Referring to the experiences of union members in these programs, she wrote,

> They heard how other workers, members of other races, speaking other languages, also struggled for many years; how they attempted to get more joy and happiness out of their miserable existence; how their attempts to unite for common interest were met with persecution and oppression from the ruling classes; and how, in spite of it all, they too succeeded finally in winning the improved conditions which prevail today, and in raising society to a higher level.[39]

These sentiments of cultural pluralism were critical in creating a vision that treated racial-ethnic diversity as a strength rather than a divisive barrier.[40] But the educational programs did not serve to increase the numbers of members directly. Rather, they prepared activists for opportunities to organize and, just as importantly, to hold onto those members who did enter the union's ranks.

EDUCATION AND THE REBIRTH OF THE ILGWU

After nearly a dozen years of general decline in membership and internecine warfare that all but bankrupted their union, the Great Depression took an exacting toll on garment workers as sweatshop conditions returned. But, in a matter of weeks during the summer of 1933, ladies' garment workers in New York quite suddenly reversed course, as the dressmakers led a general strike and the industry's workforce was nearly completely unionized in New York City and the surrounding metropolitan market. New York dressmaking manufacturers were unprepared and readily signed two-year contracts that reestablished reasonable pay and working conditions. By September the ILGWU had grown fivefold to more than two hundred thousand members, nearly doubling the number that joined the union at the previous height of its power in the early 1920s. The New York Dressmakers' Local 22 alone multiplied nearly tenfold to thirty thousand members during the August strike.[41] The ILGWU membership also encompassed a greater diversity of cultures than ever before. In addition to the Jewish and Italian workers that made up the majority of the union members, the Jewish-led union organized more than four thousand black and more than three thousand Spanish-speaking workers in those few weeks.[42]

The abrupt expansion of the ILGWU presented leaders with the challenges of rebuilding the union's infrastructure and inculcating union novitiates before they drifted away from the organization. More than any other unit of the ILGWU, the Dressmakers' Local 22 confronted the concerns regarding the new membership. Zimmerman was concerned that young women in their teens and twenties who generally had no experience with unions now made up the majority of the membership. Union leaders also had to contend with a labor law so weak that labor-management agreements were essentially unenforceable without shop-floor militancy. The recently passed National Industrial Relations Act provided no mandatory mechanism to settle contract disputes.[43] Members who worked in isolated shops, with an average of thirty-one members, had to be ready to report violations, strike, and picket in support of other members' strikes. New members had to learn how unions organized workers, formulated demands, and articulated those demands. They had to learn how to exercise the power of an organized workforce to win everything from pay raises and shorter hours to safe work conditions and a reasonable work pace and how to establish systems to enforce concessions won from the employer. Hundreds of union members had to be trained as shop-floor leaders who could represent coworkers in grievances, monitor contracts, and lead workers out on strike when necessary. Some had to learn English, and many needed to become public speakers. As leaders, they would have to rally coworkers to action without having been veterans of such actions themselves. And workers from many different racial-ethnic cultures had to learn to trust one another.

To meet these goals, union architects returned to the education programs, pioneered by Fannia Cohn, which had succeeded so well in the past, to teach political ideals, encourage social cohesion, and develop union leadership. Jewish union leaders like Zimmerman and Cohn, whose ideas were shaped and inspired by the revolutionary movements in Russia and the socialist foundations of Jewish American institutions, promoted programs that celebrated the variety of ethnic cultures among the membership and strengthened the trust between workers of different racial-ethnic groups. These programs that emphasized multiculturalism and radical movement building became the linchpins that held the union together.

Several local unions created educational programs in late 1933 and early 1934. Within months of the August strike, thousands of union members and their families enrolled in classes, athletic programs, dramatics, orchestras, and choirs sponsored by local unions and to some extent by the International union's educational department. At the height of these programs in the 1936–1937 academic year, more than twenty-two thousand union members and their kin enrolled in classes, groups, or teams that met at least once a week. Tens of thousands more attended concerts, pageants, festivals, and parades or visited Unity House. But Fannia Cohn's greatest influence was felt in the Dressmakers' Local 22, as Zimmerman adopted her ideas with zeal.

Zimmerman announced the formation of Local 22's educational department in late November 1933 under the direction of his friend and close political ally, Will Herberg. Like Zimmerman, Herberg was a key leader among the small Lovestone faction that was expelled from the Communist Party in 1929. In the most ambitious local education program in ILGWU, Herberg established seven education centers around the city and gave special attention to programs aimed at the thousands of black and Spanish-speaking workers who had recently joined the ILGWU.[44] Local unions formed athletic teams and the International union organized leagues that included teams from various socialist institutions for union members and their families to develop local and International union identities.[45] Especially during periods of mobilization, the union used sites of recreational activities to educate and recruit members for organizing and strike-related responsibilities.[46] These programs were steeped in revolutionary culture and politics, through institutional links to the other institutions of the Jewish labor and socialist movements.

Echoing the ideas of national cultural autonomy found in Yiddish socialist thought as well as Renner's "State and Nation," Local 22 created a local union branch in which blacks in Harlem could gather to make political decisions and explore their identity as African American trade unionists. In addition, the local union opened branch offices in neighborhoods all around New York City, including an East Harlem branch for Spanish speakers. At the same time, black and Spanish-speaking members also participated in most of the programs offered by the local and the International union in their main centers in the midtown Manhattan Garment District. Local unions encouraged each racial-ethnic group to sponsor elaborate balls and festivals that provided opportunities to demonstrate group identity, foster ethnic pride and cultivate leadership.[47]

For Fannia Cohn, Charles Zimmerman, Will Herberg, and local union leaders who embraced this form of radical working-class cultural pluralism, education meant more than teaching ordinary union members to function within the complex organization of the union, to assume leadership in union affairs, and to develop a trade-union consciousness that encouraged loyalty to the ILGWU and the labor movement. To them, education also meant developing a class consciousness that imagined a socialist society eclipsing the misery and exploitation inherent in the capitalist system. They believed that workers needed both practical and theoretical education in militant unionism, particularly regarding shop-floor struggle. Beginning in 1934 Will Herberg attracted some of the leading radical theorists of the socialist and labor movements to teach in the program. Educators from the Rand School of Social Science, the New School, and Columbia University taught economics, trade-union theory, Marxist analysis, and history to thousands of ILGWU members.[48] Themes that ran through many of the course outlines included such shop-floor issues as the piece rate, explained in the context of capitalist exploitation.[49] From the standpoint of various academic disciplines, instructors encouraged workers to be vigilant in holding the line against even the smallest incursion by employers on workers' control and power.

Socialist theories of culture were discussed in the classrooms and theaters of the Rand School for Social Science, an important institution supported by the Socialist Party, the Workmen's Circle, and socialist-led unions such as the ILGWU, the Amalgamated Clothing Workers of America, and the Brotherhood of Sleeping Car Porters. ILGWU officers such as Fannia Cohn and general organizer Frank Crosswaith taught at the Rand School, ILGWU local unions sent officers to training classes there, and many ILGWU events were held at the school. In 1934 a group of students from the Rand School formed the Rebel Arts Group to produce plays, music, and murals exploring the intersection of art and revolutionary ideology. Many ILGWU locals used Rebel Arts materials in their own literature. And several ILGWU dramatic groups participated in a two-day labor drama festival held at the New School for Social Research in April 1935, along with the theater groups from the Rebel Arts, the Young Circle League, and the Brookwood Labor College.[50]

In the founding issue of the Rebel Arts Group's cultural magazine *Arise*, it averred that the new magazine

> will take sides in the class struggle—the side of the working class. It will be a cultural forum for artists in all fields who are eager to contribute to the great movement of workers of hand and brain which fights for the conquest of society for the benefit of the masses. Realizing that art is a weapon, and should be used by workers for the working class, *Arise* will wield that weapon for the toiling masses along the whole cultural front—graphic arts, photography, literature, the drama, the dance, music, criticism.

Arise argued that the socialist artist is a "class conscious fighter" who "is with the victims of capitalist brutality and fascist savagery. He is with all of the oppressed proletarians whose dreams are shattered on the rocks of a cruel system and whose children are starving in the midst of the superabundance that made inevitable the want of many."[51] The Rebel Arts Group explained the relationship of arts and politics for the movement of which Local 22 was a part. The plays and outings organized by Local 22 activists emphasized the plight of exploited workers under capitalism. Through these experiences Local 22 officers and activists, as constituents of a militant socialist movement, sought to expose the culpability of capitalism in fanning the flames of racial discord among workers.

In May 1934, at the start of the International union's convention, ILGWU president David Dubinsky and the General Executive Board of the ILGWU demonstrated their support for black members in a dramatic fashion. When the union delegates arrived for the first day of the convention, they found that the hotel they originally reserved refused entry to the black members of the delegation. The entire body of convention delegates, several thousand strong, marched out of the hotel into the Chicago streets and into a hastily reserved hotel that would accommodate them.[52] In all, there were in fact only a handful of black delegates present in Chicago, but union leaders intended the move to show the thousands of black members back home that the union would go to great lengths and expense to insist on their equal status.

Later in 1934 Dubinsky turned to Frank Crosswaith, a well-known black organizer in the socialist labor movement, to lead the International's efforts to organize black workers.[53] A powerful speaker and a prolific writer, Crosswaith had helped to organize the Brotherhood of Sleeping Car Porters. Crosswaith supported the development of a race consciousness in the Socialist Party and urged leaders to become acquainted with black newspaper editors and to sponsor forums on issues important to black people. He urged Socialist Party leaders to develop structures that addressed needs peculiar to blacks, similar to those programs in the Communist Party, such as a black news service.[54] Crosswaith was the principal ILGWU spokesperson for blacks and addressed numerous union meetings, conventions, and mass rallies. His articles in *Justice* drew attention to the progressive attitude of the Jewish unions in particular: "Those of us who are in the labor movement know that in the needle trades unions the Negro worker receives a square deal."[55] He taught classes in the ILGWU educational program, including "The Negro in American History," which followed black accomplishments and contributions. In 1935, with the backing of the ILGWU, Crosswaith founded the Negro Labor Committee, which he patterned on the United Hebrew Trades.[56]

In the Spanish section of Local 22, members listened to reports from the local and international leadership and voted on strikes, contract settlements, and political issues, all in Spanish. Union leaders also sponsored lectures and organized classes in the Spanish language on trade union principles, dance, and music.[57] The Spanish-section programs promoted ethnic identity and helped to empower Spanish workers through English- and Spanish-language classes. English classes, for example, promoted language tools without denigrating the workers' native Spanish. Through the English class, workers learned how to talk with non-Spanish-speaking members in their shops about the union and how to confront their bosses when necessary.

Carmen Rosa, though exceptional in her level of activism in the union, embodied the possibilities created by the Spanish-section programs. Rosa was born in Puerto Rico in 1906. Her paternal grandfather came to Puerto Rico from Cadiz, Spain, and died resisting the Spanish during the Spanish-American war. Her mother was an American Indian, native to Puerto Rico. Rosa married as a teenager and reluctantly moved to New York with her husband and two young children in the 1920s. After her husband left her, she went to work in the garment industry to support her family. In the 1930s she took every class offered by the union, including an English-language class. Rosa was elected chair of her shop, attended weekend union leadership courses at the Brookwood Labor College, joined the education committee of the local union, and was elected to the local union's executive board.[58]

The success of the political component of union education was apparent immediately. From 1933 to 1937, as black and Hispanic women were elevated to hundreds of shop chairperson positions and to local executive board positions, they became increasingly represented in the places where critical decisions were made. Contracts had to be enforced, but the labor law, such as it was, was no help. After the U.S. Supreme Court rejected the National Industrial Relations Act, the much stronger and more prolabor Wagner Act of 1935 would not be upheld for a few more years. Each local union, then, depended on rank-and-file vigilance in the thousands of garment shops to enforce contract provisions. Shop chair people monitored the terms of the contracts, settled disputes that arose, and recommended to the local union whether to strike if an employer was noncompliant.[59] Their role as the eyes, ears, and voice of the union in the shops was critical to the health of the union. Charles Zimmerman noted that in the two and a half months from mid-September to the end of November 1933, shop chairpeople reported more than 11,700 complaints to the union. In this period union shop chairpeople held 1,482 shop meetings, and the local union held 173 jobbers' group meetings. In one month alone the union found eight hundred shops violating the maximum hour provision of their contracts with the ILGWU.[60] In addition, students in Local 22 classes, most of whom were women, joined the Union Defenders Committees (UDC), organized to patrol shops to enforce contract provisions, especially maximum hours and restricted workdays, and to report violations by employers and complicit members.[61]

The potential for how a multicultural membership engaged in social, cultural, and educational programs could flex power muscles was realized in the

New York dressmakers' contract negotiations of 1936. The contracts negotiated during the great upsurge in membership two years earlier were set to expire on January 1, 1936. *Justice*, the ILGWU organ, reported that the United Dress Manufacturers Association presented demands—such as mandatory overtime, elimination of a minimum wage, and the freedom to discharge employees—that would have undermined the gains won in the 1933 strike. Members involved in every aspect of union activity were mobilized. In December 1935 the Local 22 Education Committee established a council representing twenty-seven sports, social, and cultural groups, with thirty-three delegates bringing the classes, athletic teams, and social clubs into the political structure of the local.[62]

Throughout January and into the middle of February 1936, *Justice* reported on the mass mobilization of the 110,000 union members employed in the New York City–area dress industry, demonstrating the integrated strategy of social and cultural programming and militant unionism. Julius Hochman, as chair of the Joint Dress Board, called a mass meeting at the Manhattan Opera House of building chairpeople and UDC members in early January to coordinate the work of all local unions in preparation for a general strike. Local 89 had already mobilized six hundred members of the Italian UDC. Manager Luigi Antonini stated, "We need vanguard groups for various union activities in peace time as well as in time of strikes. We also need defense groups against various enemies, above all the Fascists, who are trying to disrupt our unity." Local 22's UDC, formed at eleven neighborhood section meetings in December, numbered one thousand members.[63] Three successive meetings at Madison Square Garden with tens of thousands in attendance led to the settlement of contracts in February 1936, avoiding a strike. The power of the ILGWU in the mid-1930s, then, required a citizen army of union members to enforce the complicated terms of the new agreements, mobilized on the shop floor and through educational programs in the local unions.

The Welfare State and Popular Union Culture

David Dubinsky, a Russian Jewish immigrant, a former member of the Bund, and an active member of the Socialist Party, ascended to the presidency of the ILGWU in 1932. At first he supported the work of Local 22 and other local unions that launched similar educational programs. He hired new staff to coordinate programs burgeoning throughout the local unions and to expand some opportunities. Dubinsky initially turned to men who shared the dominant Yiddish socialist understanding of culture and politics. In 1934 he hired Louis Schaffer, labor editor of the *Jewish Daily Forward* and an activist in the Socialist Party, putting him in charge of recreational and cultural activities in the educational department.[64] Dubinsky also hired Gus Tyler, who had initially worked for Schaffer at the *Forward*.[65] Schaffer began to direct the cultural activities of the International educational department and was responsible for building up the union's orchestras, choruses, and theater. Schaffer in turn hired Lazar Wiener, who conducted the Workmen's Circle orchestra and chorus, to conduct the ILGWU orchestra and chorus. He continued to hold both posts throughout the 1930s and introduced a broad program of music to both organizations that included standard Yiddish music, Italian opera, Negro spirituals, and popular music. The orchestras played at union-sponsored pageants, labor rallies, and in public performances at Carnegie Hall, helping to create and publicize a multi-cultural union identity.

As the ILGWU expanded through the 1930s, in part by following garment manufacturers who tried to avoid the union by moving to other states and regions, Dubinsky wanted to broaden the image of the union. He looked to appeal to new union members from Native American stock across the country and also to mainstream cultural and political elites. In spite of his own accent and Bundist past, Dubinsky was deeply embarrassed by Fannia Cohn's radical politics and Yiddish accent as the voice of ILGWU education. He asked Schaffer and Tyler to seek out a director for the International educational department who had "general appeal."[66] Tyler suggested Mark Starr, a Welsh-born trade union educator from a coal-mining family, who was teaching at the time at the Brookwood Labor College. In 1935 Dubinsky hired Starr as director of the International's education department in a deliberate move to undermine Fannia Cohn's authority. Though Starr was nominally Schaffer's boss, Dubinsky wanted Starr to concentrate on classes and lectures, while Schaffer developed the International's work in theater and athletics.[67]

The New Deal for labor crystallized when in 1937 the Supreme Court upheld the provisions of the Wagner Act. Though the ILGWU continued to engage in aggressive organizing and contract negotiations with employers around the country, the Wagner Act helped to balance labor-management relations. The NLRA guaranteed a legal process for organizing workers into unions, negotiating for multiyear contracts and mandatory union membership, and enforcing the provisions of those contracts. For Dubinsky and Zimmerman, the war with garment manufacturers that had raged since the 1910s was over, and the U.S. government became the guarantor of the peace. For manufacturers, peace with the union offered a greater degree of stability within the industry. Both union officials and garment manufacturers developed a common interest in reducing the destabilizing influence of shop-level militancy. Dubinsky began to shift resources from the local unions to the International offices, including education funds. More programs were designed to teach active members to operate within the legal framework of labor-management relations. Radical ideas about politics, the economy, and culture began to diminish. As a result, the International union slowly abandoned the ethnic cultural programs just as they were demonstrating their greatest effect.

As Dubinsky consolidated his power in the ILGWU in the mid- and late 1930s, his view of the political possibilities of the greatly expanded ILGWU and the cultural expressions of the union's education department differed from those of visionaries like Fannia Cohn or local union leaders like Charles Zimmerman. As the ILGWU became more powerful, Dubinsky saw the opportunity for the union to become an architect in the construction of a liberal welfare state, rather than a vehicle to assume state power as had been expressed by groups such as Rebel Arts.

Indeed, Dubinsky formally abandoned all efforts to elect socialists to statewide or national offices when he helped to found the American Labor Party in 1936.[68] Socialist labor leaders formed the party, which Zimmerman and other local union leaders embraced as well, so socialists could support Franklin Roosevelt for president and Herbert Lehman for New York State governor without having to vote as members of the Democratic Party. Dubinsky saw that the ILGWU and other unions were playing a greater part in domestic and international affairs than U.S. labor had ever achieved in American history. American Labor Party leaders believed support for the liberal state meant that as unionists they had allies and sympathizers in the Roosevelt and Lehman administrations.[69] The needle trades in particular could obtain reasonable contracts without resorting to costly and disruptive seasonal strikes fought on hundreds of fronts in individual shops. Union leaders also felt reasonably sure that the state would not intervene with force on the side of employers to break the union. As the new partnership with the liberal state burgeoned, Dubinsky sought to tamp down the more political and cultural elements of Jewish revolutionary ideology, including the form of multiculturalism favored by Yiddish socialists.

As Dubinsky's political stance turned decisively more moderate, he backed Louis Schaffer with increasingly larger sums of money to help express a more conciliatory union image among the members and the general public. In 1937 Schaffer produced the ILGWU's tour de force, *Pins and Needles*, a Broadway revue that lasted for nearly four years and included three New York and two national touring companies. *Pins and Needles* was the brainchild of Schaffer, who sought to construct a public image for the union that was both politically and culturally moderate. He recruited performers for the first cast largely from the ranks of the ILGWU, though the cast also included professional actors who had tenuous links to the garment shops. The production initially had only one black cast member and included very little music derived from the ethnic cultures of the union's membership. Thousands of union members saw the play, but middle- and upper-class audiences sustained the production financially.

Pins and Needles as a cultural product represented a broader public acceptance of the union but a repudiation of dearly held values, especially for those who had internalized the sensibilities of Yiddish socialism. In the *New York*

Times, Brooks Atkinson hinted at that change when he praised several numbers written by Harold Rome: "'Doing the Reactionary' and 'Sing Me a Song of Social Significance' have done more than anything else to remove the Fannie Brice curse of 'rewolt' from the stagecraft of the labor movement."[70] Brice, the comic star of the Ziegfeld Follies, was known for her exaggerated Lower East Side Jewish accent. One of her signature skits in the mid-1930s was a satire of the radical choreographer Martha Graham, in which Brice's character cries out in a Yiddish accent, "Rewolt!" *Pins and Needles*, Atkinson was letting us know, had no such ethnic or radical political signature.[71]

The political ideology expressed in the revue, as skits were dropped and added, reflected the changes in political thinking of the ILGWU leadership and the broader Socialist Party movement. *Pins and Needles* criticized the state only mildly and numerous skits revealed declining commitments toward union militancy, ethnic and racial identity, and gender equity. The show ignored all references to race issues. And in contrast to dramatic programming in locals such as the Dressmakers' Local 22, Schaffer made no real attempts to ensure blacks and Hispanics were well represented in *Pins and Needles*. Initially, Olive Pearman was the only black person in the show, and she had only a supporting dancing role. Schaffer added more African Americans to the show only after the cast pressured him to do so, but there were no Hispanics in any of the three companies. Behind the scenes, the production of *Pins and Needles* reinforced an expanding cultural bureaucracy within the ILGWU that ignored racial injustice, assaulted ethnic and racial identity, and undermined the notions of equity fostered in the local union educational programs.

Schaffer was particularly concerned that *Pins and Needles* not be seen as upsetting local sensibilities as the show toured Chicago, San Francisco, and Los Angeles. When local customs dictated Jim Crow accommodations, Schaffer capitulated. Schaffer and his production staff repeatedly warned the cast that they would not tolerate public dissent regarding the show's management policy in these matters. In one instance he threatened cast members with dismissal for staging a walkout of a restaurant in Denver that refused Pearman service. In 1938 Schaffer and the road manager, Sam Schwartz, insisted that Olive Pearman and Dorothy Tucker, the only two African Americans in the cast then, observe the Jim Crow culture in Los Angeles hotels. Pearman and Tucker stayed in a hotel miles away from the rest of the cast when the show played in Los Angeles—this just four years after Dubinsky led an entire convention's delegation out of a segregated hotel in Chicago.[72]

The arrival of *Pins and Needles* as an emblem of the ILGWU's political and cultural liberalism came on March 8, 1938, when a truncated cast played a command performance for Franklin and Eleanor Roosevelt at the White House. Dubinsky did not tell the cast about the White House event until the day of the performance and, on behalf of the cast, refused the president's invitation to dinner after the show. According to one cast member, Dubinsky "was afraid we wouldn't know how to act, or know which fork to use." The White House production pointed up one of the dearest concessions ILGWU leaders made in building a relationship with the state and its more conservative constituents. Violating the spirit of racial equity that permeated many of the local unions, Dubinsky chose to omit Olive Pearman from the White House performance. Pearman understood why: "I was eliminated from the show because I was black."[73]

Pins and Needles opened some opportunities for African American artists. Archie Savage, a black dancer with Katherine Dunham who later performed in *Pins and Needles*, noted that "Dunham's first professional New York show was due to Schaffer. He produced her dance group's Sunday night concerts at the Windsor Theatre when *Pins and Needles* was dark."[74] Dunham later choreographed new dance numbers for *Pins and Needles*, which brought more blacks into the show. While this opportunity did celebrate black culture, Dunham and her troupe, including Savage, Randolph Sawyer, and Alice Sands, were professionals, and their entrée came at the expense of black and Spanish-speaking union members who had no access to the stage.

In general, *Pins and Needles* reflected a declining interest on the part of International officers in appealing to the ethnic and racial cultural identities of members in the union. This certainly meant playing down the presence of African Americans and ignoring Hispanics altogether, but it also meant undermining Jewish ethnicity. Louis Schaffer was intent on demonstrating to the public, through *Pins and Needles*, that the ILGWU was not an ethnically Jewish union. Schaffer and his staff persuaded actors to change their Jewish-sounding names, pressured women to surgically alter their appearance, and replaced "Jewish-looking" actors with those who appeared more northern European. At least two actors did change their names. "The press agent, Lee Mason, decided I should change my name from Hyman Goldstein to Hy Gardner. Eventually I made it legal. Sylvia Cohen became Sylvia Cahn." Many cast members were aware of Schaffer's intentions from the beginning. Al Levy, an original cast member, said, "We managed to get it across with our accents. But eventually Schaffer weeded out those people with thick Jewish accents. People who looked Jewish were also weeded out." Both Nettie Harari and Ruth Rubinstein said that Schaffer asked them to get nose jobs, and Ethel Kushner remembered that Lynne Jaffee did have a nose job during the run of the show.[75] In an echo of Amelia Bucchieri's story in which Jewish workers tried to hide their religion from Jewish bosses, Schaffer insisted that one cast member prominently wear her crucifix in performances. Ruth Rubinstein remembered that Schaffer "wanted to show that not everybody's Jewish" in the cast.[76]

CONCLUSION

The multiculturalism that was evident in the Dressmakers' float on May Day 1934 emerged out of a specific historical context that began in the nineteenth century. The czarist system linked capitalist exploitation with an ethnic cultural repression that restricted Jewish access to all forms of institutional power, including the gymnasium and university. This helps explain why when Russian Jewish socialists later founded worker-based education programs in the United States; they understood those programs to be a natural extension of Jewish radical resistance to capitalism. Jewish immigrants were able to realize their multicultural ideals while establishing unions in the needle trades because they were in the majority in the ILGWU. Union leaders with experience in Russian revolutionary movements, and steeped in Yiddish socialism, were well placed to recognize the opportunities presented by the entrance of new racial-ethnic groups in the garment industry workforce. Fannia Cohn and Charles Zimmerman saw the educational experiments work over decades and moved decisively to establish and strengthen educational programs designed to retain thousands of new workers in the 1930s. The programs thrived in New York City local unions because the core membership was Jewish and supported ideals familiar to them.

Though multicultural education prevailed for several years in the mid-1930s, neither members nor leaders in the ILGWU universally or unconditionally accepted the ideals propagated by Fannia Cohn and others. As the 1930s progressed, social and political forces that operated below the surface of the multicultural experiment helped weaken the union's commitment to the mutual embrace of ethnic cultures, especially when leaders no longer considered it critical to the health of the union. *Pins and Needles* helped to establish Dubinsky's more moderate image of the ILGWU as suited for an allied relationship with the state: critical but not militant, and certainly not radical. *Pins and Needles* reflected the newly dominant ideals in the ILGWU and the union's place in the New Deal coalition. Along with a growing rejection of socialism, leaders in the ILGWU increasingly abandoned the strategy of promoting a diverse cultural identity among the membership. The International continued to support ideas of racial integration through educational, social, recreational, and cultural activities, but within a more conservative context. The union would continue to showcase individual blacks, for example, and even support important movements for black civil rights. But the International educational program began to emphasize unanimity of culture and underplayed ethnic cultural difference.

NOTES

1. "1,500 Police Put on Parade Guard," *New York Times*, May 1, 1934; "100,000 Rally Here, with No Disorder," *New York Times*, May 2, 1934.

2. The San Francisco General Strike began on May 8, 1934, followed by the Minneapolis General Strike on May 16. The Auto Lite Strike began in April and turned bloody during

the "Battle of Toledo" in late May. For a detailed survey of these and other strikes in 1934, see Irving Bernstein, *The Turbulent Years: A History of the American Worker, 1933–1941* (Boston: Houghton Mifflin, 1970), 237–337; and Jeremy Brecher, *Strike!* (Boston: South End, 1972), 150–177.

3. "100,000 Rally Here."

4. File 15, box 1, collection 5780/14p, Martin P. Catherwood Library, ILGWU Papers, Kheel Center for Labor-Management Documentation and Archives (hereafter Kheel Center), Cornell University, Ithaca, New York.

5. For debate about the origins and nature of multiculturalism, see *American Quarterly* 45, no. 2, special issue, *Multiculturalism* (June 1993): 195–256.

6. Ryllis Goslin Lynip, *Growing Up: 21 Years of Education with the I.L.G.W.U., 1917–1938* (New York: Wolff, 1938).

7. Gary Gerstle, *Working Class Americanism: The Politics of Labor in a Textile City, 1914–1960* (Cambridge: Cambridge University Press, 1989), 59.

8. Lizabeth Cohen, *Making a New Deal: Industrial Workers in Chicago, 1919–1939* (Cambridge, MA: Harvard University Press, 1990), 99–158.

9. David H. Weinberg, *Between Tradition and Modernity: Haim Zhitlowsky, Simon Dubnow, Ahad Ha-Am, and the Shaping of Modern Jewish Identity* (New York, Holmes and Meier, 1996), 37; Henry J. Tobias, *The Jewish Bund in Russia: From Its Origins to 1905* (Stanford, CA: Stanford University Press, 1972), 7–10.

10. Weinberg, *Between Tradition and Modernity*, 51.

11. A. L. Patkin, *The Origins of the Russian-Jewish Labour Movement* (Melbourne: Cheshire, 1947), 39, 42–43, 40–41.

12. Jacob Leshczynski, quoted in ibid., 41.

13. David Dubinsky, the future president of the ILGWU, was arrested as an active Bundist in 1908 after leading a bakers' strike. See Max D. Danish, *The World of David Dubinsky* (Cleveland: World, 1957), 16–20.

14. On Zhitlowsky, see Melech Epstein, *Profiles of Eleven Men Who Guided the Destiny of an Immigrant Society and Stimulated Social Consciousness Among the American People* (Detroit: Wayne State University Press, 1965), 295–322; Weinberg, *Between Tradition and Modernity*, 83–144; Tony Michels, *A Fire in Their Hearts: Yiddish Socialists in New York* (Cambridge, MA: Harvard University Press, 2005), 125–178; Patkin, *Origins*, 153–157; and Vladimir Medem, *The Life and Soul of a Legendary Jewish Socialist: The Memoirs of Vladimir Medem*, trans. and ed. Samuel A. Portnoy (New York: Ktav, 1979), 295–298n.

15. Karl Renner, "State and Nation," in *National Cultural Autonomy and Its Contemporary Critics*, ed. Ephraim Nimni (New York: Routledge, 2005), 13–41.

16. Jack Jacobs, *On Socialists and "the Jewish Question" after Marx* (New York: New York University Press, 1992), 124–127.

17. Weinberg, *Between Tradition and Modernity*, 81.

18. Karl Renner, quoted in Joseph V. Stalin, "Marxism and the National Question," *Prosveshzhentye* 3–5 (March–May 1913), transcribed and translated by Carl Cavanaugh, accessed May 11, 2011, Marxist.org.

19. Otto Bauer, *The Question of Nationalities and Social Democracy*, trans. Joseph O'Donnell (Minneapolis: University of Minnesota Press, 2000), 258. Originally published as *Die Nationalitatenfrage und die Sozialdemokratie* (Vienna: Verlag der Wiener Volksbuchhandlung, 1924).

20. Weinberg, *Between Tradition and Modernity*, 89.

21. Emmanuel S. Goldsmith, *Architects of Yiddishism at the Beginning of the Twentieth Century: A Study in Jewish Cultural History* (Rutherford, NJ: Farleigh Dickenson University Press, 1976), 168–171.

22. Chaim Zhitlowsky, quoted in Michels, *Fire in Their Hearts,* 133.

23. Louis Levine, *The Women's Garment Workers: A History of the International Ladies' Garment Workers' Union* (New York: Huebsh, 1924), 18–23; Melech Epstein, *Jewish Labor in U.S.A.: An Industrial, Political, and Cultural History of the Jewish Labor Movement, 1882–1914* (New York: Trade Union Sponsoring Committee, 1950), 87–107.

24. Daniel E. Bender, "Too Much of Distasteful Masculinity: Historicizing Sexual Harassment in the Garment Sweatshops and Factory," *Journal of Women's History* 15, no. 3 (2004): 91–116; Nancy MacLean, "The Culture of Resistance: Female Institutional Building in the International Ladies' Garment Workers' Union, 1905–1925," *Michigan Occasional Papers in Women's Studies* 21 (Winter 1982): 17.

25. Richard A. Greenwald, *The Triangle Fire, the Protocols of Peace, and Industrial Democracy in Progressive Era New York* (Philadelphia: Temple University, 2005), 35–42, 129–153.

26. Annelise Orleck, *Common Sense and a Little Fire: Women and Working-Class Politics in the United States, 1900–1965* (Chapel Hill: University of North Carolina Press, 1995), 23.

27. Ibid., 48, 47.

28. Ricki Carole Meyers Cohen, "Fannia Cohn and the International Ladies' Garment Workers' Union" (PhD diss., University of Southern California, 1976), 56.

29. Louis Friedland, "Our Educational Aims and Problems," *Justice*, November 21, 1919; Louis Friedland, "The Bases of Our Educational Work," *Justice*, February 2, 1920, 3.

30. Susan Stone Wong, "From Soul to Strawberries: The International Ladies' Garment Workers' Union and Workers' Education, 1914–1950," in *Sisterhood and Solidarity: Workers' Education for Women, 1914–1984*, ed. Mary Frederickson (Philadelphia: Temple University Press, 1984), 43.

31. For Italian immigrant women's history and culture of militant collective action, see Jennifer Guglielmo, *Living the Revolution: Italian Women's Resistance and Radicalism in New York City, 1880–1945* (Chapel Hill: University of North Carolina Press, 2010).

32. For a detailed report of the internecine warfare among Left factions in the garment industry, see *Report of the General Executive Board to the Nineteenth Convention of the International Ladies, Garment Workers' Union* (New York: Education Department of the ILGWU, May 7, 1928), 20–135.

33. *Report to the 1920 ILGWU Convention* (Boston: Union, 1920), 50.

34. Melinda Chateauvert, *Marching Together: Women of the Brotherhood of Sleeping Car Porters* (Urbana: University of Illinois Press, 1997), 44.

35. Amelia Bucchieri, interview with author, New York, February 11, 1999. On Jewish employers who tried to undermine unionization through hiring across racial-ethnic lines, see Alice Kessler-Harris, "Where Are the Organized Women Workers?" in *A Heritage of Her Own: Toward a New Social History of American Women*, ed. Nancy Cott and Elizabeth Pleck (New York: Touchtone Books, 1979), 358.

36. Scholars of the Communist Party USA disagree on numbers, and as Harvey E. Klehr points out, the charge over the years by anticommunists and anti-Semites that Jews and Bolsheviks were the same people have complicated the discussion. See *Communist Cadre: The Social Background of the American Communist Party Elite* (Stanford, CA: Hoover Institution Press, 1978), 37–52. See also Nathan Glazer, *The Social Basis of American Communism* (New York: Harcourt, Brace and World, 1961), 131.

37. Robin D. G. Kelley, *Hammer and Hoe: Alabama Communists during the Great Depression* (Chapel Hill: University of North Carolina Press, 1990), 94–96, 99, 105; Robbie Lieberman, *"My Song Is My Weapon": People's Songs, American Communism, and the Politics of Culture, 1930–1950* (Urbana: University of Illinois Press, 1995), 14–24. The Socialist Party camps were called Pioneer Youth.

38. *Report of the Educational Department to the Nineteenth Convention of the ILGWU* (New York: Education Department of the ILGWU, May 7, 1928), 14; Fannia M. Cohn, "Twelve Years Educational Activities International Ladies' Garment Workers Union," *American Federationist*, January 1929, 110.

39. Fannia M. Cohn, "Educational and Social Activities," *American Federationist*, December 1929, 1449.

40. Horace Kallen coined the term "cultural pluralism" in *Culture and Democracy in the United States: Studies in the Group Psychology of the American People* (New York: Boni and Liveright, 1924) but began to develop his ideas in "Democracy versus the Melting Pot," *Nation* 100 (February 19 and 25, 1915).

41. "Financial Report, April 1, 1932 to April 30, 1934" (paper presented at the twenty-second Convention of the International Ladies' Garment Workers' Union, Chicago, Illinois, May 28 1934).

42. *Report and Proceedings to the Convention of the International Ladies' Garment Workers' Union* (New York: Education Department of the ILGWU, 1934). By 1937, the National Women's Trade Union League reported, the ILGWU represented between 5,517 and 6,122 blacks. This range probably reflects midseason layoffs in the downturn year of 1937 in the garment industry. See folder 12A, box 12, collection 5780/2, ILGWU Papers, Kheel Center.

43. The weaknesses of the National Industrial Relations Act regarding unionization applied across most industries. See, for example, the lack of enforcement in the textile industry in Bernstein, *Turbulent Years*, 303.

44. For a discussion of the ILGWU education programs and race relations, see Hasia Diner, *In the Almost Promised Land: American Jews and Blacks, 1915–1935* (Baltimore: Johns Hopkins University Press, 1995), 199–230. While I argue the centrality of Yiddish socialism, Diner rejects the significance of socialism to explain union leaders' motivations in reaching out to blacks and other union members.

45. Cohen, *Making a New Deal*.

46. Local 22 Education Committee Minutes, December 3, 1935, file 5, box 8, collection 5780\14, ILGWU Papers, Kheel Center.

47. "Dressmakers' International Ball," folder 9, box 2, collection MG100, Archives and Rare Books Division, Schomburg Center for Research in Black Culture Manuscripts, New York Public Library.

48. ILGWU, "Minutes of the Educational Committee of Local 22, September 4, 1935," file 11, box 2, collection 5780/15, ILGWU Papers, Kheel Center; ILGWU, "Local 22 Spring Course Guide, Spring 1935," folder 4a, box 4, collection 5780/49, ILGWU Papers, Kheel Center.

49. File 6, box 7, collection 5780/14, ILGWU Papers, Kheel Center.

50. Folder 4a, box 4, collection 5780/49, ILGWU Papers, Kheel Center.

51. *It's Coming at Last*, Vertical File, Tamiment Library, New York University.

52. *Justice*, July 1934, 10.

53. David Dubinsky to Charles Zimmerman, October 26, 1935, file 8, box 13, collection 5780/14, ILGWU Papers, Kheel Center.

54. John H. Seabrook, "Black and White United: The Career of Frank R. Crosswaith" (PhD diss., Rutgers University, 1980), 105, 106.

55. Frank Crosswaith, "Some Vital Problems of Negro Labor," *Justice*, January 1, 1935, 5.

56. Negro Labor Committee, "Minutes of the Negro Labor Committee, January 29, 1937," file 82, reel 14, box 8, Negro Labor Committee Papers, Schomburg Center for the Research in Black Culture, New York Public Library.

57. Saby Nehama, report on Spanish Activities, Local 22, ILGWU, Minutes of the Executive Board of the Dressmakers' Union Local 22, September 4, 1934, vol. 7, box 1, collection 5780/36, ILGWU Papers, Kheel Center.

58. *Our Aim*, September 1937, 3.

59. Educational Department of Dressmakers Union, "The Structure and Functioning of the ILGWU," Local 22, ILGWU, file 6, box 8, collection 5780\14, Kheel Center, 2.

60. "N.Y. Dressmakers, Local 22, At Work," *Justice*, February 1934, 19.

61. *Labor Stuff*, 1938, file 7, box 8, collection 5780/14, ILGWU Papers, Kheel Center, 8.

62. ILGWU, "Minutes of the Educational Committee of Local 22, Dec. 3, 1935," file 5, box 8, collection 5780/14, ILGWU Papers, Kheel Center.

63. *Justice*, January 1, 1936, 5.

64. Gus Tyler, interview with author, New York, July 22, 1999; Benjamin Stolberg, *Tailor's Progress: The Story of a Famous Union and the Men Who Made It* (New York: Doubleday, 1944), 294, 296–297.

65. Gus Tyler, interview.

66. Ibid.

67. Ibid.

68. David Dubinsky and Abraham H. Raskin, *David Dubinsky: A Life with Labor* (New York: Simon and Schuster, 1977), 265–277.

69. Robert D. Parmet, *The Master of Seventh Avenue: David Dubinsky and the American Labor Movement* (New York: NYU Press, 2005), 128–132.

70. Brooks Atkinson, "Garment Specialty: 'Pins and Needles,' Being a Night Out for Thirty-Two I.L.G.W.U. Members," *New York Times*, January 23, 1938.

71. Julia L. Foulkes, "Angels 'Rewolt': Jewish Women in Modern Dance in the 1930s," *American Jewish History* 88, no. 2 (2000): 233–252.

72. Nettie Harari Shrog, interview with author, New York, May 22, 2000.

73. Goldman, "Pins and Needles," 159, 155.

74. Ibid., 149.

75. Ibid., 107–108.

76. Ruth Rubinstein Graeber, interview with author, New York, January 26, 2000.

CHAPTER 9

Making Peace with Capitalism?

JEWISH SOCIALISM ENTERS
THE MAINSTREAM, 1933–1944

Daniel Soyer

The East European Jewish immigrant inclination toward socialism is well documented. For a short time in the late 1910s, the Socialist Party (SP) even became the dominant electoral force in the Jewish immigrant neighborhoods of New York. After 1920 the socialists lost their electoral power, but they continued to influence the community through their control of important institutions such as the *Jewish Daily Forward*, the Workmen's Circle, and the garment workers' unions. By 1936, looking to break out of their electoral isolation, most Yiddish-speaking socialists split from the Socialist Party after several years of bitter factional infighting. In New York the socialist Right, also known as the Old Guard, took advantage of a quirk in the election law to help form an independent party to support President Franklin D. Roosevelt and Governor Herbert Lehman without entering the corrupt and conservative Democratic Party. After the 1936 election, the American Labor Party (ALP) became a permanent party, playing an important role in the campaigns of Mayor Fiorello La Guardia and other progressive New York politicians. In 1944 the founding group split from the ALP to form the Liberal Party, which for decades performed a function similar to that of the ALP. While not strictly Jewish parties, Jews provided the bulk of the leadership, institutional support, and electoral base of both the ALP and the Liberal Party.

Through the ALP and Liberal Party, the old Jewish socialist movement thus entered the American political mainstream, helping to elect presidents, governors, and mayors. Neither party was explicitly socialist, so it is easy to see them as representing the end of Jewish ambivalence toward capitalism and infatuation with socialism. Indeed, a number of historians have argued

215

that they represented a definitive break with the Jewish radical tradition and served as mere halfway houses that eased Jewish voters' transition from the Socialist Party and radicalism to the Democratic Party and mainstream American liberalism.[1]

But in important ways there was more continuity to Jewish socialist politics than is usually recognized. True, most of New York's Jewish socialists abandoned any vision they may once have had of a sudden and decisive revolutionary transition to a new and radically different social order based on common ownership of the means of production and regulated by rational planning for the common good rather than the free market. But their reformist leanings long predated their split from the SP, which they no , took to calling the "Militant-Trotskyist Socialist Party." In their acceptance of a system based largely on private ownership and a free market, the American Jewish socialists resembled their Social Democratic comrades throughout the western world. And like their comrades on the international scene, American Jewish socialists continued their commitment to independent labor politics marked by distrust of capitalist enterprise and suffused with social values. Through the ALP and Liberal Party, Jewish socialists wove a Social Democratic strand into the fabric of postwar liberalism, contributing to the persistent liberalism of American Jewry and to the Social Democratic nature of liberalism in New York City.[2]

The evolution of Jewish socialist politics in the 1930s reflected the complexity of the Jewish position in New York's capitalist system. The Jewish economic role was distinct from that of other ethnic groups, with Jews dominating some sectors and virtually absent from others. The Jewish labor movement had taken shape in the garment industry, of course, but it was also active in other trades where Jews predominated. By the 1930s the blue-collar Jewish working class was shrinking, many Jews were moving into white-collar jobs and the professions, and Jews owned two-thirds of all businesses in New York City. Not surprisingly, many Jewish socialists reacted to these developments by seeking to enlarge their constituency beyond the narrowly defined proletariat and moderate their anticapitalism. At the same time, however, there were factors that reinforced their distrust of an unfettered capitalist system: the Jewish working class remained sizable, and many white-collar and even professional workers still retained ties to the working class, as did the owners of tiny businesses. Some white-collar workers joined unions like their garment worker parents. The Depression, which retarded upward mobility, reinforced the sense that many Jews had that the class system was arbitrary and unfair.[3]

Far from a simple capitulation to capitalism, Jewish labor politics of the 1930s and 1940s represented an expansion of the space between liberalism and socialism that historian Howard Brick has called "post-capitalism."[4] In post-capitalism, reformist socialists converged with liberals who had come to the conclusion that capitalism could neither survive on its own nor provide for social justice without significant public intervention. Post-capitalists, whether they came from liberal or socialist backgrounds, called for an extensive government-run social security system, increased mechanisms for democratic economic planning, government intervention in the market to smooth out business cycles and guide the economy in socially desirable directions, and public ownership of some industries. At the time, the Old Guard socialists saw American bourgeois liberalism and progressivism, represented most prominently by Roosevelt and the New Deal, moving toward socialism. The Old Guard's break with the increasingly isolated and sectarian SP represented a search for political relevance at a time when the mainstream was wide open, in their view, to socialist ideas and programs. At the very least, they believed, if the state was going to manage competing interests in the economy it was imperative to mobilize the working class to maintain control over the nascent organs of economic planning.

The Jewish socialists were fascinated by the National Recovery Administration (NRA). The cornerstone of the early New Deal program, the NRA was brought into being by executive order to carry out the provisions of the National Industrial Recovery Act passed in June 1933. The NRA called for industry-wide cartels that would set "codes" to regulate competition, prices, wages, and conditions in each industry. Although many radicals viewed the NRA with hostility, the Jewish socialists believed that cooperation with the NRA meant taking a stand with the working class against the capitalists, not class collaboration with the capitalist state.

This chapter looks at the emergence of the ALP and Liberal parties, and the relationship of the Jewish socialist movement with the New Deal, primarily through the lens of the *Jewish Daily Forward*, the world's premier Yiddish newspaper and America's most important socialist daily. As Melech Epstein notes, there was "no one among the old-time socialists who became so early an ardent follower of Franklin D. Roosevelt" as Abraham Cahan, the *Forward*'s longtime editor.[5] In one famous incident in October 1933, Cahan, then still a member of the SP, praised the New Deal as a manifestation of the socialist program before an audience of twenty-five thousand dressmakers in Madison Square Garden and invited Roosevelt to join the party and accept the entire socialist platform. Before a party disciplinary committee, Cahan denied having done this, at least not in earnest, and claimed that he was unfamiliar with the party stand on the NRA in particular, having been out of the country for several months. He admitted, however, that he admired the president's energy in fighting the Depression and saw the NRA as a golden opportunity for organized labor.[6] The *Forward* spoke not only for Cahan but also for other wings of the Jewish socialist movement, including the Workmen's Circle, the International Ladies' Garment Workers' Union (ILGWU), and the Jewish Socialist Verband, as they debated their positions on the New Deal, socialism, and capitalism.

Cahan was responding largely to the NRA in his speech to the dressmakers. Historians have generally viewed the NRA as a failure, and leftists then
and since have seen it as government promotion of corporate domination.[7] But
the garment unions and Old Guard socialists saw tremendous opportunity in
the NRA, especially in paragraph 7(a), which guaranteed workers the right to
organize and bargain collectively. Indeed, the ILGWU and the Amalgamated
Clothing Workers of America were among the most aggressive unions in using
7(a) to their advantage. In industries characterized by weak, mostly small
employers, both unions had long sought to play a dominant role in maintaining stability and order in their industries, and now they sought to shape the
relevant codes for the benefit of the workers. Both unions grew explosively in
the months after the NRA came into being, leading Socialist Party member and
ILGWU president David Dubinsky to support enthusiastically the NRA and,
by extension, the New Deal.[8]

Cahan and the *Forward* viewed the NRA with a little more skepticism, but
also with fascination. In addition to the opportunity it presented to the labor
movement, the NRA seemed to the *Forward* to embody values that were the
antithesis of capitalism, a system too individualistic, selfish, exploitative, and
characterized by cutthroat competition.[9] The NRA promoted cooperation
and rational economic planning under government direction, something that
socialists had long called for. Moreover, the *Forward* emphasized the NRA's
intention to raise wages and cut hours to improve the purchasing power of the
masses and encourage the creation of jobs. In October 1933 *Forward* writer
Lazar Fogelman (a graduate of Fordham University Law School) summed up
the advantages of the NRA in the eyes of the socialist Old Guard:

> The NRA has, after all, opened new broad paths for American workers. It
> has pushed American workers into the unions; it has heightened the role
> of the workers in industry; it has opened the door to planned industry, and
> therefore in the future to a planned economy in general; it has sharply posed
> the question of and raised the idea of control over economic life, an idea for
> which radicals have been fighting for years; it has underscored more sharply
> the idea of the weakness and faults of the current economic order, an idea
> that we have also been explaining and trying to pump into plugged up ears
> and minds of apathetic and backward people.[10]

The NRA thus appeared to the *Forward* to be a drastic break with American
traditions of rugged individualism and government alliance with great capitalists, and even a potential step toward socialism.[11]

The NRA as conceived by FDR was therefore proworker in the eyes of the
Forward. But the newspaper believed that business was trying to subvert the
president's progressive plan by turning the NRA into its own tool for control
over the economy. "At the same time that our capitalists sing songs of praise

for Roosevelt's recovery plan," the newspaper editorialized, "they are stick-
ing a knife in its back" by stockpiling cheap goods without implementing
the act's wage, hours, and bargaining provisions.[12] But if the capitalists could
move to seize control of the regulatory mechanism, so could the workers.
Under the NRA the state would broker among various interests; the codes
would regulate the economic life of the nation, and someone would have to
write the codes. The job at hand for socialists, according to the *Forward* and
other members of the Old Guard, was to help expand and mobilize the labor
movement to block the capitalists' designs on the agency and ensure that the
workers would have a decisive say in the development of the codes.[13]

During the first two or three years of the Roosevelt administration, however,
the *Forward* remained somewhat ambivalent toward the president and the
New Deal. On the one hand, Roosevelt's immediate reforms "opened the way
for true Socialist reforms in the future." They demonstrated that the United
States was "turning its back to individualist capitalism" and that socialism
was no longer a dirty word.[14] But, of course, socialist orthodoxy insisted that
no amount of tinkering could fix capitalism or make it just. The economic
crisis itself had proven the socialists correct in their assessment of the inherent
instability of the capitalist system. As long as President Roosevelt, with all of
his good intentions, remained within the framework of a bourgeois party and
the capitalist system, none of his reforms would do more than provide a temporary and partial salve to the deep wounds inflicted by capitalism's collapse.
The administration would not make a real revolution, the newspaper argued
early on, "first, because just as Hoover, [the New Dealers] also believe in the
rationality of the capitalist system, and, second, because the party which they
represent represents in turn the country's capitalist classes, in whose interests
it is to maintain the current system under all circumstances."[15]

The *Forward*'s ambivalence continued through the 1934 midterm election.
True, "President Roosevelt and many of the people surrounding him also speak
of the necessity of a more just and fair distribution of the national wealth," the
newspaper admitted, but they could not carry their conviction to the logical
conclusion, because they were members of a party controlled by the capitalist
class.[16] The newspaper sometimes insisted that only the Socialist Party consistently had the workers' interests at heart and offered answers to the vexing questions of the Depression. But other times, the *Forward* noted the importance of
such "semi-Left" campaigns as those of the Farmer-Labor Party in Minnesota,
the Progressive Party in Wisconsin, and Upton Sinclair's EPIC in California.
Victories by the Left and semi-Left, the newspaper argued, would demonstrate
the widespread sentiment for "a real 'new deal,' a true program to help the workers, farmers, the poor storekeepers, and other exploited classes. . . . The president
will have to take this into account."[17] Success of the Left might even lead to a
national labor party. In the meantime, socialists demanded the institution of

unemployment insurance, old age pensions, public works programs, a shorter work week, bank reform, and public ownership of utilities.[18]

In 1935 the New Deal did turn left and incorporate many of the socialist demands. By that time, the *Forward* had decided the NRA was in fact "progressive in the Socialist sense," a "step on the road that goes in the direction that strives to eradicate the capitalist system," so the newspaper saw the Supreme Court decision that ruled the NRA unconstitutional that May as a severe blow to the working class.[19] Within a month, however, the Jewish socialists' enthusiasm for the New Deal intensified with the passage of the Social Security Act and the National Labor Relations Act (Wagner Act), and FDR's proposal for a sharply progressive estate tax. The NLRA reinstated some of the most important provisions of the NRA, most notably paragraph 7(a), guaranteeing the workers' right to organize. The Social Security Act, which created government-sponsored old age pensions, unemployment insurance, disability insurance, and aid to indigent families, seemed to be a fulfillment of long-standing socialist demands. And the president's call for an estate tax showed that he shared the old socialist belief that inequality of wealth led to unfair inequalities of power. All of the new programs had shortcomings—some of them forced by the Supreme Court ruling on the NRA, some of them insisted on by conservatives within the two capitalist parties. But the important point was that FDR was enacting many of the socialists' traditional "immediate" program. It was up to them now to see to it that these laws were just the beginning of social legislation, not the end.[20]

In his adoption of socialist programs, Roosevelt was simply the leading exemplar of what the *Forward* perceived as a general convergence of liberal and socialist thought. Between 1933 and 1936 the newspaper periodically pointed to admissions by leading liberals and progressives that capitalism had collapsed and could not recover without massive intervention by the state: "The smarter [liberals], the more farsighted, are now coming to the conclusion that the present capitalist system is bankrupt and must be changed."[21] Support by Catholic bishops, cabinet secretaries, major-party politicians, AFL leaders, and liberal intellectuals for government regulation and planning with guarantees of social justice vindicated views that the socialists had long advocated and proved that although the SP was weak, socialist ideas had permeated American society and politics.[22] Even Catholic priests and Methodist ministers agreed that capitalism "toyg af tsen toyznt kapores" [was no good].[23] Within the administration itself, Left battled Right, with the Left seeking to promote "greater social justice" by making the New Deal permanent and pushing for further reform of the economic system.[24] The newspaper considered it front-page news when Attorney General Homer Cummings early on publicly proclaimed, "Socialism has become part of the social order in America and the Roosevelt administration is gradually introducing Socialism into the country's economic life." While

Democratic Party politicians objected to this characterization of the president's program, and conservatives bemoaned the New Deal's creeping socialism, the Old Guard socialists saw this as evidence that the liberal move to the left was no mere lip service.[25]

Ironically, even as socialist ideas seemed to have gained credence in wider circles than ever before, the Old Guard increasingly suspected that the Socialist Party itself was becoming an obsolete political liability. (Cahan referred to the party as a "second mortgage.")[26] Bitter factional battles fueled this suspicion, as the so-called Militants, allied with party leader Norman Thomas, gained control. In 1934 and 1935 they pushed through resolutions that seemed to the dismayed Old Guard to endorse revolutionary insurrection, massive war resistance, and the Leninist concept of the dictatorship of the proletariat. The Militants' revolutionary rhetoric offended the practical political sensibilities of the Right, which believed that if the SP was to play a serious role in American politics it was as an advocate for working-class interests within the New Deal order and as a catalyst for a farmer-labor party.[27]

The Socialist Party officially supported the creation of a national farmer-labor party, but Left and Right had different ideas of what such a party would mean. The Left seems to have hoped that a farmer-labor party would be not much different from the SP itself, with a clearly socialist program, but broader support. The Right, on the other hand, saw a farmer-labor party as a center to rally all progressive, liberal, working-class, and socialist elements against the forces of unbridled capitalism and reaction. Indeed, the *Forward* perceived the emergence of two sharply antagonistic camps vying for control of the government, and even of the administration. The progressive/liberal/socialist/working-class camp valued democracy, equality, and social solidarity.[28] The opposing conservative camp held capitalist values: individualism, competition, and inequality. As the 1936 elections approached, socialists had no choice but to take their place in the progressive camp. To try to outflank it from the left was to consign oneself to political irrelevance or, worse, to split the forces of progress and thereby aid those of reaction. While in 1935 the *Forward* sometimes complained of Roosevelt's failure to follow through on even his own most progressive positions, by 1936 the Right socialists clearly saw FDR as a member of the progressive camp.[29]

Cahan, who traveled to meetings of the Socialist International and had contact with many leading European Social Democrats, polemicized against the international socialist Left in a way that had domestic resonance. Like his European comrades in the revisionist camp, Cahan believed that socialism had to evolve with experience.[30] For the left socialists, he argued, "Socialism consists of loyalty to congealed abstract principles that they have inherited from earlier times, just as a Jew inherits an Elijah's cup." Left socialist objections to coalitions with progressive nonsocialists were a remnant of the irresponsibility of the early socialist movement. Responsible socialist leaders, on the other hand, recognized that the movement had to institute practical reforms.[31] In this light, Roosevelt started to look like the functional equivalent of moderate European socialist leaders. Cahan gathered validation for his support of Roosevelt from important socialist spokespeople and intellectuals, including Harold Laski, Leon Blum, and the long-deceased Jean Jaures.[32]

But if FDR was the leader of the progressive bloc, including its socialists, the Democratic Party, dominated by white supremacists, big-city machines, and old-line conservatives, was not part of that camp. The *Forward*'s take on the Democratic Party was informed by the political context of New York City, where large segments of the notoriously corrupt Tammany Hall machine, the dominant faction in Manhattan, never solidly backed Roosevelt or the New Deal. Of course, neither Tammany, nor the Democratic machines in the boroughs outside of Manhattan, would support the leading local exponent of New Deal reform, Mayor Fiorello La Guardia, a nominal Republican. Added to Tammany's history of corruption and the element of ethnic conflict between traditionally Irish-dominated Tammany and the Jewish socialist movement, the Democrats' relative conservatism made them an unattractive vehicle for socialist support of the president.[33] Thus, the *Forward* sought to distinguish sharply between Roosevelt and the Democratic Party. Roosevelt was in no way the Democratic Party's "spiritual and moral representative," Cahan argued. "To consider him the spiritual representative of a bourgeois party would be ridiculous."[34] The *Forward* may have exaggerated Roosevelt's differences with his party, but its rhetoric stemmed from a deeply held conviction in the necessity of independent labor political action. The Old Guard socialists aimed not only to reelect President Roosevelt and Governor Lehman in 1936 but to consolidate and extend the New Deal with greater social reforms. The Democratic Party could not be a vehicle for radical reform, so a new party was needed.[35]

The Right finally bolted the Socialist Party in the spring of 1936. Nationally, it formed the Social Democratic Federation. In New York State, though, the former socialists joined with the leaders of the garment unions (including Dubinsky, who had also just left the Socialist Party, and Sidney Hillman of the Amalgamated Clothing Workers, who had not been a party member), other labor leaders active in the CIO's Labor's Non-Partisan League, independent liberal and radical intellectuals, and disaffected New Deal Democrats, to form the American Labor Party. The *Forward*'s counsel, Alexander Kahn, and its manager, Baruch Charney Vladeck, were present at the first meeting called by Hillman to discuss the idea.[36]

In doing so, they hoped to take advantage of an unusual feature in New York election law that allowed candidates to run under the auspices of more than one party. To this day in New York, the votes that a candidate receives on multiple ballot lines are combined to give the candidate his or her total vote. A number of small parties have taken advantage of this law over the decades to support major-party candidates closest to their point of view and, thereby, to exert their influence over policy. The ultimate hope of the small parties is that they will provide office seekers with their margin of victory, thus gaining even more leverage over their policy positions and appointments. The ultimate threat that the minor parties wield is that they might field their own candidates, siphoning off votes from the major party closest to them. Very occasionally, the small parties win races on their own.

The American Labor Party thus set out in 1936 to support FDR and Governor Lehman for reelection and to push for an extension of the New Deal. The new party's platform reflected its leaders' impatience with theoretical formulations of ideology, and its short preamble contained no revolutionary vision of social reconstruction. Instead, the program declared support for practical measures that would redistribute wealth in society, including laws to enhance workers' ability to organize unions, a minimum wage, child-labor regulation, progressive taxation, and improved social security provisions. Although the ALP did not oppose private enterprise, it doubted its ability to provide for a fair distribution of resources. The party therefore called for government-run employment agencies, public housing, public ownership of utilities, and the establishment of consumer cooperatives. The ALP defined itself as a party of "the people," including not just industrial workers, but also farmers, storekeepers and other small businesspeople, white-collar workers, and professionals. Farmers aside, these were social groups well represented in the party's Jewish ethnic constituency.[37]

The *Forward* enthusiastically backed the ALP campaign. The newspaper now argued, "Socialism is not now on the agenda in America. The issue is not capitalism or Socialism, but Roosevelt and social progress or Landon and social reaction."[38] Landon represented the "old . . . capitalist logic" that insisted that those who succeeded did so because of their own talents and that those who labored all their lives and suffered poverty were simply out of luck. But Roosevelt was the first mainstream politician to say, "No, it doesn't have to be this way. A person's life must not be a crapshoot; the fate of the great masses of people must not be gambled on. We must institute some order, a system, a sense of control. We should see to it that there are no people in need and no millionaire gamblers."[39]

Although they had come to the conclusion that socialism was not on the immediate agenda, the Social Democrats of the ALP did not believe that supporting Roosevelt meant that they were betraying their socialist principles. Rather they felt that they were being realistic and avoiding the sectarian trap into which the SP had fallen. After sixty years, argued Cahan, the Socialist Party had not a single representative in Congress. No wonder socialists in Europe saw Roosevelt as their counterpart in the United States. "An ounce of practical Socialism on the spot," wrote the editor, "is worth more than a pound of Socialist theory concerning an indeterminate future."[40] If Roosevelt deserved criticism for "saving capitalism," then so did the socialist parties of Sweden, Denmark, Norway, Belgium, Czechoslovakia, and France![41] The issue, wrote *Forward* contributor David Shub, was whether the Socialist Party wanted to be a sect living in the past and working for the "oylem 'abe" (the world to come), or whether it wanted to be a real political party that influenced the direction in which the country would go.[42] In any case, Social Democratic voters did not have to vote for a capitalist party but could pull the lever for Roosevelt on the line of the ALP, a working-class party that aimed to "uproot the social evils from which we suffer, such as, for example, poverty and .ant, and insecurity concerning tomorrow."[43]

The *Forward* worked hard to convince its core constituency that they should abandon their habit of voting the Socialist Party ticket. But the sell really wasn't that difficult. In fact, the leaders were simply following the rank and file in their admiration for Roosevelt. Reporting to Cahan on a meeting of the Forward Association, *Forward* counsel Alexander Kahn wrote, "All worries that it would be awkward for the Forward to support Roosevelt and Lehman are gone. The sentiment among Labor, Socialist, and Jewish circles is beyond description. The situation has changed so radically that it would be awkward for the Forward not to support them."[44]

The question of whether or not the ALP should be a permanent independent political force was hotly debated. Democratic operatives, of course, hoped that it would prove to be a temporary expedient to reelect the president and that FDR himself would pressure its leaders to fold up shop after November. Hillman vacillated. But Dubinsky, the Social Democratic Federation, and the *Forward* urged that the ALP become a permanent political home for progressive labor, socialists, and independent radicals and liberals—perhaps even that it become the nucleus of a national political realignment or labor party.[45] The following year the ALP played an important role in the reelection of Mayor La Guardia, who left the Republican Party and enrolled as a Laborite. While on the national and statewide level, the ALP supported the Democrats, on the local level it often fused with progressive Republicans or even with the socialists. Those left in the Socialist Party apparently also agreed that socialism was compatible with support for the ALP, as the SP repeatedly sought to affiliate officially with the Labor Party.[46]

One of the socialist Old Guard's original complaints against the Militants had been the latter's willingness to make common cause with the communists. It was ironic, then, that with the inauguration of the Popular Front the communists adopted a similar political stance to that of the pro–New Deal Old Guard. On orders from Moscow, the Communist Party now sought alliances with social democrats and liberals against the imminent danger of fascism, and in

New York the American Labor Party became the perfect vehicle for communist unity with other progressive forces. After the communists lost their ballot status in 1938, communist infiltration of the ALP became even more pronounced. The SDF warned against growing communist influence in party clubs around the city, but the party leadership, in particular Dubinsky and millinery union leader Alex Rose, who was emerging as the party's most important political strategist, largely ignored the issue, perhaps because they did not want to give credence to right-wing charges of communist leanings in the party.[47]

But the Hitler-Stalin Pact of 1939 exposed the communist influence in the left wing of the party, as it quickly turned against Roosevelt, accusing him of imperialist warmongering. Although the procommunist Left snapped back into line after the German invasion of the Soviet Union, the ALP became a sectarian battleground for the next four and a half years as Left and Right fought for control. When procommunist elements, with the help of Hillman and the Amalgamated Clothing Workers of America, took control of the party in the spring of 1944, the Right split.

Very soon, the ALP's former leaders announced that they would form a new party to support FDR's bid for a fourth term and to push for a revitalization of the New Deal. The *Forward* once again gave it voice. Through Alexander Kahn, its manager and a vice chair of the new party, the newspaper also made its voice heard within party circles.[48] Kahn and the *Forward* weighed in on the new party's name and emblem. An editorial noted that the terms "Socialist," "Labor," and "Democratic" were already being used by parties on the New York State ballot and therefore unavailable according to state election law. He also argued that the word "progressive," although used often by the *Forward* to describe its allies, was discredited by its association with the isolationist Wisconsin Progressives. Kahn argued, unsuccessfully, against the use of the Liberty Bell as the new party's emblem because "a bell signified quite another thing to Jews, and therefore, should be avoided." In the end, the new group chose the name Liberal Party because it was felt that this would win the widest possible support.[49]

Like the ALP before it, the Liberal Party was a labor party. Its institutional mainstays were the International Ladies' Garment Workers' Union, led by David Dubinsky, and the United Hat, Cap, and Millinery Workers' International Union, led by Alex Rose. Although both officially vice chairs of the party, they were universally recognized as the true powers behind the throne (the chairmanship), which was always occupied by a gentile intellectual. Together with other affiliated unions, the ILGWU and the hatters provided the bulk of the money and personpower that supported the party. The intellectuals attracted to the party, including its first chair, Professor John Childs of Teachers College, were those who saw the labor movement as the heart of modern social liberalism.[50]

The Liberal Party's program, which the *Forward* called the "best, most serious, and most sensible" of any radical party ever in the United States, was social democratic in nature.[51] It emphasized the importance of government action to both spur economic development when private capital failed to take the lead and to reign in private enterprise when it acted in opposition to the public good. It also recognized that private enterprise needed to play a central role, together with government, in maintaining economic growth and prosperity. It called for an "extensive" government-sponsored low- and middle-income housing program, with proper safeguards for any who might be displaced by projects carried out under the program; universal health insurance; a state economic agency that would make socially productive investments in areas that private capital refused to touch; and expanded and improved coverage under social security, workers' compensation, and unemployment insurance. The Liberal Party also supported measures to guarantee civil rights and racial equality, including a permanent Fair Employment Practices Commission and a ban on restrictive covenants. In foreign affairs, the Liberals condemned dictatorships and imperialism of all stripes, right and left, and called for a permanent structure for international cooperation. It was not afraid to criticize Great Britain for what it saw as a revival of Britain's imperial ambitions and, in an open letter to President Roosevelt, to warn against such ambitions on the part of the United States. At the same time, the party was outspokenly anticommunist and saw the Soviet Union as a clear danger to the liberation of Europe and the world.[52]

The Liberal Party's top leaders, the former socialist Dubinsky and Labor Zionist Rose, were impatient with sectarian ideological politics—the whole enterprise represented, after all, their effort to make an impact on mainstream politics. So the Liberal Party continued the ALP's coalition electoral strategy, which meant that it most often backed candidates from the procapitalist Democratic and Republican Parties. Indeed, in the party's earliest years, many Liberals hoped to spark a realignment of national politics that would draw in many "Willkie Republicans," that is, liberal, internationalist followers of the 1940 Republican standard bearer.[53]

Nevertheless, for many of the party's backers, socialism remained an animating force, lurking right beneath its centrist surface. Some of its prominent figures had long been associated with socialist politics: Brooklyn City council member Louis Goldberg, for example, had run often for public office on the socialist ticket and continued to serve as chair of the Social Democratic Federation while he held public office as a Liberal. August Claessens, longtime socialist functionary, was also a Liberal candidate in Brooklyn.[54] The *Forward*'s own Alexander Kahn had run for office a number of times as a socialist before turning first to the ALP and then to the Liberals. In the pages of the *Forward*, it was always clear that the party's constituency included "liberals, progressives, and *socialists*" (or social democrats or democratic socialists), and the newspaper considered the Liberal Party as the latest political expression of the tradition that stretched back through the ALP and the Socialist Party to the Socialist Labor Party. Tellingly, the Liberal Party maintained informal fraternal relations with such social democratic parties as the Labour Party in Britain and the Canadian Cooperative Commonwealth Federation.

Indeed, the *Forward* dealt explicitly with the issue of socialist support for an avowedly non-Socialist Party. Before the founding convention, the newspaper called on the Liberal Party to see to it that "not private capitalist, but people's, interests determine the fate of the country. The party should not be afraid," the editorial continued, "of ideas that have until now been preached by Socialists."[55] Another editorial put it even more strongly: "Every true liberal must in the present day necessarily accept at least a part of the old Socialist program."[56] In any case, as Alexander Kahn wrote in a polemic against socialist candidate Norman Thomas, socialist support for LaFollette in 1924 proved that voting for a non-socialist candidate was not necessarily to "mekhalel sotsializm zayn" (desecrate the name of socialism). Anyone wishing to vote for Roosevelt and at the same time to vote "in the spirit of the Socialist ideal" could do both by voting on the Liberal line.[57]

So, was the Liberal Party simply a halfway house, or even a three-quarter-way house (after the ALP) for Jewish socialists on their way from socialism to the Democratic Party? The seriousness with which its leaders and members took the independence of the Liberal Party belie that idea. Despite their admiration for some of the national leaders of the Democratic Party and their willingness to ally locally with liberal Republicans, the founders of the Liberal Party viewed both of the major parties as fatally flawed. As the call to the founding convention put it, "The Republican Party is dominated by the reactionary economic interests and convictions of the great citadels of finance and industry"; with the passing of Wendell Willkie it vacillated between the "imperialistic-isolationism of industrialists and . . . agrarian isolationism." But the Democrats were little better, since "no Republican group is more viciously reactionary than the group of Southern Congressmen and Senators" who supported white supremacy and opposed labor rights.[58]

Moreover, it's clear that both parties attracted far more support than that of the former socialists that Dubinsky hoped to bring into the New Deal coalition. This is made clear by some gross election results:

Sample Presidential Election Returns for New York State:

1920: Debs (Socialist, high point): 203,201 (7 percent)
1924: LaFollette (Progressive-Socialist fusion): 474,913 (14.6 percent)
1932: Thomas (Socialist, last race before ALP): 177,397 (3.8 percent)
1936: Roosevelt (ALP): 274,824 (4.9 percent)
Thomas (Socialist): 86,897 (1.6 percent)

1944: Roosevelt (ALP and Liberal combined): 826,000+ (13.1 percent)
Thomas (Socialist): 10,553 (0.2 percent)

Sample Mayoral Election Returns for New York City:
1917: Hillquit (Socialist, high point): 145,332 (21 percent)
1933: Solomon (Socialist, last race before ALP): 59,846 (2.7 percent)
1937: La Guardia (ALP): 487,128 (21.1 percent)
(Socialists did not run candidate out of deference to ALP.)

The ALP-Liberal votes thus compared favorably to the Socialist Party's very highest points in local elections and generally exceeded them in presidential voting. If anything, these electoral results show that the ALP and Liberal Party were drawing progressive-minded voters beyond the old core constituency of the Socialist Party, and away from the two major parties. They may have even drawn former socialist voters back to an independent labor party line on the ballot after they had begun to vote for Democrats or Republicans.[59]

Certainly there was a long way from a confident prediction that the workers would institute a new social order to an argument that ideas traditionally put forward by the socialists had to inform modern liberalism. But by injecting those ideas into the political mainstream, the American Labor and Liberal Parties contributed greatly to what Joshua Freeman has called the unique post–World War II New York experiment in social democracy in one city. As Freeman argues, postwar New York liberalism had a strong socialist element, with its support for extensive networks of public housing and hospitals, its government- and labor-initiated health plans and cooperative housing projects, and its acceptance of working-class political power. Freeman downplays the overlapping ethnic and ideological differences within the labor movement, but the social democratic sensibility he describes owes much to the Jewish socialist movement.[60] During the La Guardia administration and after, Jewish socialists returned to some local power as members of the city council, commissioners, and judges. They did so not by melting into the major bourgeois parties, but by maintaining an independent, labor-oriented, progressive political presence in the American Labor and Liberal Parties.

Likewise, much of the earlier literature on postwar Jewish liberalism recognizes the socialist influence, but most of the more recent literature on the phenomenon does not. Historians have paid much more attention to Jews' liberal attitudes (or lack thereof) toward questions of race, sex, civil liberties, child rearing, cosmopolitan culture, and international affairs than they have to progressive Jewish positions on class, social justice, and economic equality. But as Tony Michels has argued, socialism was central to the east European Jewish immigrant experience and therefore formative to the political sensibilities of the community.[61] The suspicions of capitalism and the class system that inspired and infused Jewish socialism in the early years survived the collapse of the Socialist Party in the 1930s and entered the mainstream as an important strand in postwar American, especially Jewish American, liberalism. This social democratic element was most visible in New York mainly because of state election laws that encouraged the formation of minor parties.

NOTES

1. Deborah Dash Moore, *At Home in America: Second Generation New York Jews* (New York: Columbia University Press, 1981), 221; Beth Wenger, *New York Jews and the Great Depression: Uncertain Promise* (New Haven, CT: Yale University Press, 1996), 134; Irving Howe, *World of Our Fathers* (New York: Harcourt, Brace, Jovanovich, 1976), 351; Steven Fraser, *Labor Will Rule: Sidney Hillman and the Rise of American Labor* (1991; repr., Ithaca, NY: Cornell University Press, 1993), 363–364; Ezra Mendelsohn, *On Modern Jewish Politics* (New York: Oxford, 1993), 89. For the observation that Jewish radicals entered the "mainstream" in this period, see in addition to Mendelsohn, Henry Feingold, "From Equality to Liberty: The Changing Political Culture of American Jews," in *The Americanization of the Jews*, ed. Robert Seltzer and Norman Cohen (New York: NYU Press, 1995), 107, and Ira Katznelson, "Between Separation and Disappearance: Jews on the Margins of American Liberalism," in *Paths of Emancipation: Jews, States, and Citizenship*, ed. Pierre Birnbaum and Ira Katznelson (Princeton, NJ: Princeton University Press, 1995), 198.

2. Joshua Freeman, *Working Class New York: Life and Labor Since World War II* (New York: New Press, 2000). There is, of course, an extensive literature on Jewish liberalism. While older works (and more recent ones written by senior scholars) often note the connection between the Jewish socialist tradition and American Jewish liberalism, newer studies by younger scholars tend to ignore liberalism's social democratic strand. For studies of Jewish liberalism that recognize the contribution of labor and socialism, see Ben Halpern, "The Roots of American Jewish Liberalism," *American Jewish Historical Quarterly* 66, no. 2 (December 1976): 190–214; William Spinrad, "Explaining American-Jewish Liberalism: Another Attempt," *Contemporary Jewry* 11, no. 1 (Spring 1990): 107–119; Lawrence H. Fuchs, *The Political Behavior of American Jews* (Glencoe, IL: Free Press, 1956); Feingold, "From Equality to Liberty"; Nathan Glazer, "The Anomalous Liberalism of American Jews," in Seltzer and Cohen, *Americanization of the Jews*, 133–143; and Katznelson, "Between Separation and Disappearance." Among the studies that pay little attention to the labor and socialist strand in American Jewish liberalism are Geoffrey Braham Levey, "The Liberalism of American Jews—Has It Been Explained?" *British Journal of Political Science* 26, no. 3 (July 1996): 369–401; Stuart Svonkin, *Jews against Prejudice: American Jews and the Fight for Civil Liberties* (New York: Columbia University Press, 1997); Marc Dollinger, *Quest for Inclusion: Jews and Liberalism in Modern America* (Princeton, NJ: Princeton University Press, 2000); Marc Dollinger, "Exceptionalism and Jewish Liberalism," *American Jewish History* 90, no. 2 (June 2002): 161–164; Michael Alexander, "Exile and Alienation in America," *American Jewish History* 90, no. 2 (June 2002): 165–168; Michael Staub, *Torn at the Roots: The Crisis of Jewish Liberalism in Postwar America* (New York: Columbia University Press, 2002); Michael Walzer, "Liberalism and the Jews: Historical Affinities, Contemporary Necessities," *Studies in Contemporary Jewry* 11 (1995): 3–10; Anna Greenberg and Kenneth Wald, "Still Liberal after All These Years? The Contemporary Political Behavior of American Jewry," in *Jews in American Politics*, ed. L. Sandy Maisel et al. (Lanham, MD: Rowman and Littlefield, 2001), 161–193; and Stephen Whitfield, "Famished for Justice: The Jew as Radical," in Maisel, *Jews in American Politics*, 213–230. See also Ira Forman, "The Politics of Minority Consciousness: The Historical Voting Behavior of American Jews," in Maisel, *Jews in American Politics*,

141–160; and Alan Fisher, "Continuity and Erosion of Jewish Liberalism," *American Jewish Historical Quarterly* 66, no. 2 (December 1976): 322–348.

3. Wenger, *New York Jews*, 10–32; Ronald Bayor, *Neighbors in Conflict: The Irish, Germans, Jews, and Italians of New York City, 1929–1941* (Baltimore: Johns Hopkins University Press, 1978), 8–21; Joshua Zeitz, *White Ethnic New York: Jews, Catholics, and the Shaping of Postwar Politics* (Chapel Hill: University of North Carolina Press, 2007), 19. For a view that downplays Jewish distinctiveness, see Eli Lederhendler, *Jewish Immigrants and American Capitalism, 1880–1920: From Caste to Class* (New York: Cambridge University Press, 2009).

4. Howard Brick, *Transcending Capitalism: Visions of a New Society in Modern American Thought* (Ithaca, NY: Cornell University Press, 2006). See also Daniel Rodgers, *Atlantic Crossings: Social Politics in a Progressive Age* (Cambridge, MA: Harvard University Press, 1998); Doug Rossinow, *Visions of Progress: The Left-Liberal Tradition in America* (Philadelphia: University of Pennsylvania Press, 2008).

5. Melech Epstein, *Profiles of Eleven: Biographical Sketches of Eleven Men Who Guided the Destiny of an Immigrant Jewish Society* (Detroit: Wayne State University Press, 1965), 104; Melech Epstein, *Jewish Labor in USA: 1914–1952* (1953; repr., n.p.: Ktav, 1969), 244, 247; "Statement by Abraham Cahan to Forward Association," n.d., file 266, Papers of Abraham Cahan, RG 1139, Institute for Jewish Research (YIVO), New York.

6. Epstein, *Jewish Labor*, 244; "Garment 'Intrigue' Assailed at Rally," *New York Times*, October 5, 1933, 7; "Tsendlike toyznter dresmakher fayern oyflebung fun yunyon mit riziker demonstratsie in medison skver garden," *Forward*, October 5, 1933, 1, 2; "Report of Committee on Ab Cahan Speech Appointed by the City Central Committee, S.P.," n.d., file 191, Papers of Abraham Cahan, RG 1139, YIVO.

7. L. Fogelman, "Di hoypt taynes vos vern nokh itst aroysgeshtelt kegn dem N.R.A. plan," *Forward*, October 22, 1933, sec. 2, p.1. On the attitude of left historians, see, for example, Barton Bernstein, "The New Deal: The Conservative Achievements of Liberal Reform," in *Towards a New Past: Dissenting Essays in American History*, ed. Bernstein (New York: Pantheon, 1968), 263–288; Thomas Ferguson, "Industrial Conflict and the Coming of the New Deal: The Triumph of Multinational Liberalism," in *The Rise and Fall of the New Deal Order, 1930–1980*, ed. Steve Fraser and Gary Gerstle (Princeton, NJ: Princeton University Press, 1989), 4, 17–18; Howard Zinn, *A People's History of the United States 1492–Present* (New York: HarperCollins, 2003), 392–393.

8. "Prezident Dubinski bagaystert groyse masmitingen fun klouk un dresmakher in Shikago un St. Luis," *Forward*, July 4, 1933, 5; Dovid Dubinski, "Di revolutsie vos iz forgekumen in di treyds fun froyen kleyder," *Forward*, October 18, 1933, 6; Robert Parmet, *The Master of Seventh Avenue: David Dubinsky and the American Labor Movement* (New York: NYU Press, 2005), 86–93; Epstein, *Jewish Labor*, 193–206; Joseph Brandes, "From Sweatshop to Stability: Jewish Labor between Two World Wars," *YIVO Annual* 16 (1976): 62–76; David Dubinsky and Abraham H. Raskin, *David Dubinsky: A Life with Labor* (New York: Simon and Schuster, 1977), 112–115, 125–126. See also, "Industriel rekoveri gezets diskutirt bay sotsialistishn miting in rend skul," *Forward*, July 22, 1933, 4; "Di goldene gelegnhayt vos der rikoveri ekt git di yunyons tsu organizirn nit organizirte arbeter," *Forward*, August 6, 1933, 3.

9. On capitalist values, see "Di tsayt iz rayf far an enderung," *Forward*, July 1, 1933, 8; "Der gantser rikoveri–plan in gefar," *Forward*, July 10, 1933, 6.

10. Fogelman, "Di hoypt taynes."

11. "Ruzvelt's 'nyu dil' un di sotsialistn," *Forward*, July 6, 1933, 4; "Der fareynikter front fun di reaktionere fabrikantn un di komunistn," *Forward*, July 23, 1933, 4; "Der nayer radio-apil fun prezident," *Forward*, July 26, 1933, 4; "Ersht itst iz noytik di 30-shtundike arbets-vokh," *Forward*, October 23, 1933, 6. The National Industrial Recovery Act proclaimed its intention to raise purchasing power. It did not explicitly provide for a cut in hours, though it did call for their regulation. But in his speech explaining the act,

FDR did call for a shorter work week at a living wage. See "National Industrial Recovery Act 1933, FDR Presidential Library and Museum, http://www.ourdocuments.gov/doc.php?flash=true&doc=66; "Franklin Roosevelt's Statement on the National Industrial Recovery Act, June 16, 1933," National History Day, National Archives and Records Administration, http://www.fdrlibrary.marist.edu/odnirast.html.

12. "Gantser rikoveri–plan"; "Der shtiler kamf fun di groyse industrien kegn rikoveri plan," *Forward*, July 14, 1933, 6; "Der yoysher fun balebatim," *Forward*, July 20, 1933, 4; P. Lazar, "Der nayer plan ibertsugebn di N.R.A. in di hent fun di kapitalistn," *Forward*, November 11, 1933, 7; L. Fogelman, "Di en-ar-ey lebt itst iber a krizis," *Forward*, November 12, 1933, 2.

13. "Prezident Dubinski bagaystert"; "Fareynikter front"; "Vos hot Ruzvelt's prosperity-plan oyfgeton biz itst?" *Forward*, July 16, 1933, sec. 2, p. 2; "Nayer radio-apil"; "Di konvenshon fun dem idishn sotsialistishn farband in Shikago," *Forward*, September 14, 1933, 6; "Shtelung fun sotsialistishn partey tsu N.R.A. diskutirt oyf konferents in rend skul," *Forward*, December 3, 1933, sec. 2, pp. 8, 12; "Di sotsialistisher partey in dem itstikn moment," *Forward*, December 10, 1933, 6.

14. "Der sotsializm marshirt forverts," *Forward*, November 5, 1933.

15. "Ruzvelt's 'nyu dil.'" See also, "Endern oder ophshafn," *Forward*, August 23, 1933, 6.

16. "In tsvey teg arum," *Forward*, November 4, 1934, 4

17. "Elekshon ibern land," *Forward*, November 6, 1934, 10.

18. Dinstik iz elekshon un di oygn fun gantsn land zaynen gerikhtet oyf 3 steyts: Nyu York, Viskonsin, Kalifornie," *Forward*, November 4, 1934, 4; "Vi azoy ir darft haynt shtimen bay di valn," *Forward*, November 6, 1934, 4; "Di nekhtike valn," *Forward*, November 7, 1934, 6.

19. Ab. Kahan, "Di N.R.A., linke sotsialistn un di entshaydung fun suprim kourt," *Forward*, June 1, 1935, 8. See also "Nokh der N.R.A.—vos vayter?" *Forward*, May 29, 1935, 8.

20. "A groyser shrit foroys," *Forward*, April 22, 1935, 4; "Endlikh arbetsloze inshurens in Nuyork," *Forward*, April 27, 1935, 8; "Dem prezident's mesedzsh un di tsvey arbeter bils in kongres," *Forward*, June 21, 1935, 6; "Ruzvelt's radikaler mesedzsh vegn tekses oyf raykhe," *Forward*, June 21, 1935, 6; "Gen. Valdman vegn der N.R.A. antshaydung fun suprim kourt," *Forward*, June 3, 1935, 5. Still, the newspaper also ridiculed frightened capitalists who saw the "blood-red color of socialism where a normal person would barely make out the pink color of liberalism." "Sotsializm fun di ongeshrokene," *Forward*, May 23, 1935, 1.

21. "Endern oder ophshafn."

22. "A katoylisher bishof vegn dem sof fun kapitalizm," *Forward*, October 5, 1933; "Sotsializm marshirt forverts"; "Ruzvelt plant shafn 4 milion dzhabs," *Forward*, November 9, 1933, 1, 12; N. Khanin, "Rayznder gefint haynt a sakh sotsializm in der Amerikaner luft," *Forward*, April 12, 1935; "Bloyz demokratisher sotsializm brengt frayhyt tsu masn, zogt Valdman bay arbeter ring konvenshon," *Forward*, May 10, 1935, 1, 10; L. Fogelman, "Dos Amerikaner lebn aleyn hot ongefangen tsu redn mit der shprakh fun sotsializm," *Forward*, June 30, 1935, 4; "Naye verter mit alte toesn," *Forward*, January 2, 1936, 4.

23. "Di sotsialistishe shtimungen in land farshtarkn zikh," *Forward*, May 19, 1935, 4.

24. Hillel Rogoff, "Di 'rekhte' un 'linke' in Ruzvelt's administratsie," *Forward*, December 21, 1933, 4.

25. "N.R.A. a shtik sotsializm, zogt minister Komings," *Forward*, September 2, 1933, 1.

26. Abraham Cahan, quoted in Epstein, *Jewish Labor*, 244.

27. J. S. Hertz, *Di yidishe sotsialistishe bavegung in Amerike* (New York: Wecker, 1954), 311–323; Louis Waldman, *Labor Lawyer* (New York: Dutton, 1945), 259–261; "Leybor dey," *Forward*, September 4, 1933, 4.

28. L. Fogelman, "Di arbeter noytikn zikh fil mer in demokratie vi di kapitalistn," *Forward*, October 15, 1933, sec. 2, p. 3; "Di bavegung far a leybor partey in Amerike," *Forward*, July 8, 1935, 4.

29. N. Zalavits, "Ale eyntslhaytn fun Ruzvelts plan tsu shafn dzshabs far 3 milion arbet-sloze," *Forward*, May 1, 1935, 3; Reaktsionere bizneslayt fardamen reformen Runvelt vet ltst geyn links, zogt men," *Forward*, May 3, 1935, 1; P. Lazar, "Ruzvelt in zayne ershte por yor als prezident un Ruzvelt itst," *Forward*, July 21, 1935, 6; "Ruzvelt ruft ale progresive koykhes tsu kemfen far nyu-dil," *Forward*, January 9, 1936, 1; "Prezident Ruzvelt fartey-dikt nyu-dil: tshalendzsht reaktionere kegner," *Forward*, January 5, 1936, 1, 2.

30. On the evolution of revisionist Socialism into Social Democracy, see Sheri Berman, *The Primacy of Politics: Social Democracy and the Making of Europe's Twentieth Century* (New York: Cambridge University Press, 2006).

31. Ab. Cahan, "Rekhte un linke oyf der internatsionaler sotsialistisher konferents," *Forward*, October 22, 1933, sec. 2, p. 2.

32. "Forshteyer fun gantser arbeter bavegung bagrisn Ab. Kahan bay tsuzamenkunft," *Forward*, September 22, 1933, 1, 10; "Sotsialistisher partey"; "A. Kahan, "Dzshudzsh Penkin. Luis Valdman, Dszh. Miler, un N. Khanin in simpozium iber sotsialistishe fragn baym 'veker' banket," *Forward*, May 2, 1935, 1, 10; Ab. Kahan, "Farvos yeder emeser sotsi-alist darf arbetn mit ale kreftn far Ruzvelt's vidererveylung," *Forward*, October 7, 1936, 8; "Ruzvelt—di greste hofnung far demokratie," *Forward*, October 24, 1936, 10.

33. Bayor, *Neighbors in Conflict*, 30–56; Louis Eisenstein and Elliot Rosenberg, *A Stripe of Tammany's Tiger* (New York: Speller, 1966), 76–134.

34. Kahan, "Farvos yeder emeser sotsialist."

35. "Di reaktsionern fun beyde alte parteyen zaynen kegn Ruzvelt," *Forward*, January 26, 1936, sec. 2, p. 3.

36. Dubinsky and Raskin, *Life with Labor*, 265. Steven Fraser and Melech Epstein write that Abraham Cahan attended the meeting. But Dubinsky, who was there, would prob-ably have remembered if Cahan were also present. Yiddish journalist Epstein may have confused A. Cahan with A. Kahn, since in Yiddish there is only a difference of one letter between the two names. Fraser followed Epstein's account. Fraser, *Labor Will Rule*, 363; Epstein, *Jewish Labor*, 228.

37. *Program of the American Labor Party* (New York, American Labor Party, October 1936).

38. "Di reaktsionern kenen zikh nit tsuzamenredn, *Forward*, October 2, 1936, 7; "In der letster minut far di valn," *Forward*, November 11, 1936, 6.

39. Ab. Kahan, "Muz dos mentshlekhe lebn zayn a kortn-shpil?" *Forward*, October 24, 1936, 1; "Der hay-yoriker politisher kampeyn, di militantn un di Ameriken leybor parti," *Forward*, October, 1, 1936, 4, 5.

40. Kahan, "Farvos yeder emeser sotsialist."

41. "Farvos yeder arbeter un sotsialist darf hay-yor shtimen far Ruzveltn," *Forward*, October 25, 1936, 4.

42. Dovid Shub, "Farvos demokratishe sotsialistn shtitsn itst Ruzvelt," *Forward*, Octo-ber 11, 1936, 6, 7.

43. "Platforme fun leybor parti shtelt aroys arbeter rekht als hoypt punkt," *Forward*, October 1, 1936, 16; "Far vos ir zolt shtimen far Ruzvelt un Lehman oyfn tiket fun der Amerikaner leybor parti," *Forward*, October 24, 1936, 10.

44. Alexander Kahn to Abraham Cahan, September 3, 1936, file 172, Papers of Abraham Cahan, RG 1139, YIVO.

45. Max Danish, "Forward with Labor: A Permanent Party," *Forward*, October 16, 1936, 6. Fraser, *Labor Will Rule*, 363–367, 377; Epstein, *Jewish Labor*, 228; "Short History of the American Labor Party and the Liberal Party," unsigned typescript, file 3b, box 149, Dubinsky Correspondence, ILGWU Records, 5780/002, Kheel Center, Cornell, Ithaca, NY; Kahn to Abraham Cahan, September 3, 1936, file 172, Papers of Abraham Cahan, RG 1139, YIVO; Dubinsky and Raskin, *Life with Labor*, 268; Robert Frederick Carter, "Pressure from the Left: The American Labor Party, 1936–1954" (PhD diss., Syracuse University, 1965)," 13–14.

46. Norman Thomas to David Dubinsky, July 31, 1938, file 3B, box 141; Minutes, Executive Committee, ALP, March 7, 1938, file 6, box 145, Dubinsky Correspondence; "Labor Party Here Spurns Socialists, *New York Times*, November 30, 1936, 2; Carter, "Pressure from the Left," 67–68

47. Epstein, *Jewish Labor*, 231–234; Waldman, *Labor Lawyer*, 292–295; "Leaders of ALP in Battle over Red Infiltration," *New York Mirror*, May 10, 1939; ALP in Turmoil over Charges of Communist Grip," *New York Post*, May 15, 1939; "Waldman Seeks ALP Purge but Gets It Himself," *New York Post*, May 18, 1939; "Labor Party Rule by Reds Is Feared," *New York Times*, May 7, 1939; "Antonini Seeks to Expel Waldman," *New York World Telegram*, May 16, 1939; "No Reds There, Say Laborites," *Sun*, May 16, 1939, "Red Play Denied by Labor Party," *New York Times*, May 16, 1939, clippings in file 6, box 145, Dubinsky Correspondence.

48. "Officers and Executive Committee Members of the Liberal Party, Elected May 20, 1944," file 138, YIVO.

49. "Di konvenshon tsu shafn a naye parti," editorial, *Forward*, May 7, 1944; "Naye liberale partey nominirt Ruzvelt," *Forward*, May 21, 1944, clippings, file 139, YIVO; Pearl Willen to Alexander Kahn, May 31, 1944, file 137, and Alexander Kahn to Pearl Willen, June 9, 1944, file 141, Records of Forward Association, RG 685, YIVO.

50. Liberal Party, press release (text of Childs's speech), June 28, 1944, file 138, YIVO; "A vout far Ruzvelt'n afn tiket fun liberal parti hot a dopeltn vert, zogt dr. Tshaylds," undated clipping, file 139, YIVO.

51. "Di naye liberale partey," editorial, *Forward*, May 23, 1944, clipping, file 139, YIVO.

52. Liberal Party, "State Legislative Program for 1945"; "For Victory and Lasting Peace: An Open Letter to President Roosevelt on American Foreign Policy"; "The First Year of the Liberal Party," unsigned typescript, May 19, 1944; all in file 141, Flyer, "Ring the Bell on Election Day"; press release (text of Alfange's speech), June 28, 1944, file 138, YIVO.

53. Liberal Party, flyers: "Vote the Liberal Party Line, Make Your Vote Count Twice," and "People Are Asking, Why?," both in file 138; press release (text of Alfange's speech), June 28, 1944, file 138, YIVO; "1400 delegaten bay grindings konvenshon fun nayer liberaler un arbeter partey," *Forward*, May 20, 1944, clipping in file 139; "Senator Truman, kandidat far vays prezident, hot konferents mit firer fun liberal parti," undated clipping, file 139, YIVO.

54. "Sotsial demokratishe federatsie bashlist af kovenshon onteyl tsu nemen in nayer partey," *Forward*, May 15, 1944, clipping in file 139, YIVO.

55. "Di ervartete naye parti," editorial, *Forward*, April 20, 1944, clipping in file 139, YIVO.

56. "Naye liberale partey," May 23, 1944.

57. Alexander Kahn, "A brivl tsu undzere lezer fun Aleksander Kahn, menedzher fun Forverts," undated manuscript labeled "Sunday," file 137, YIVO.

58. "Convention Call," May 1944, file 138, YIVO; see also Liberal Party, press release (text of Childs's speech).

59. For election returns, see Epstein, *Jewish Labor*, 237; Chris McNickle, *To Be Mayor of New York: Ethnic Politics in the City* (New York: Columbia University Press, 1993), 37; Peter Eisenstadt, ed., *The Encyclopedia of New York State* (Syracuse, NY: Syracuse University Press, 2005), 71, 1243–1244; Kenneth T. Jackson, *The Encyclopedia of New York City* (New Haven, CT: Yale University Press, 1995), 738–739; James Hagerty, "Hillman, Liberals Share in Triumph," *New York Times*, November 9, 1944, 1. Ronald Bayor correctly sees the ALP as a *threat* to the local Democratic Party, not as an adjunct to it. See *Neighbors in Conflict*, 40–41.

60. Freeman, *Working Class New York*.

61. Tony Michels, *A Fire in Their Hearts: Yiddish Socialists in New York* (Cambridge, MA: Harvard University Press, 2005), 1, 255–259.

CHAPTER 10

༄

A Jewish "Third Way" to American Capitalism

ISAAC RIVKIND AND THE CONSERVATIVE-COMMUNITARIAN IDEAL

Eli Lederhendler

Is there a sympathetic relationship between Jews and capitalism, or at least a pattern of such relationships that, arguably, have had their apotheosis in the case of American Jewry? And if so, why are so many Jews in the United States apt to link the idea of social conscience with their Jewish heritage?

Scholars and laypeople alike have often remarked on American Jews' successes in the economic realm and have sought explanations. Some contend that success is a function of the Jews' willing conformity to American capitalist ideals: a moral equivalency between private virtue, the acquisition of skills, and personal achievement as a measure of individual worth and social esteem. Others point to the adaptability of Jews as a classic immigrant minority, especially applicable to behaviors such as risk-taking and innovation in enterprise; stability and moderation in personal affairs; and the aspiration to match, if not exceed, the accomplishments of the nation's most prestigious social sectors.[1]

Against the "conformity" or symbiotic school of thought, others view the Jews in the United States as exemplars of "exceptionalism," or, at the very least, the Jewish case is seen as occupying some distinctive position within wider American social patterns. For quite a long time—lasting to some degree until the 1960s—discrimination shaped Jewish occupational choices and mobility strategies in academic institutions, professional schools, industries, corporations, and financial institutions. Surveying the contemporary scene, the higher levels of income, education, and professional achievement observed among American Jews, as well as their record of concentrating in selected professional niches rather than dispersing across the entire occupational spectrum, continue to set them apart from other Americans. The ostensible gap between experiencing discrimination on the one hand, and enjoying a high occupational and income profile on the other, is explained most often through the "human capital" argument: Jews benefit from derivative cultural traits connected to their ethno-religious milieu, associated with a mercantile environment, and building on those traits, engage in especially intensive academic preparation to compensate for social status disadvantage.[2]

Jews, it is argued, have extrapolated from the experiences of preceding generations and applied such useful skills and habits as the handling of money as a normative aspect of everyday life; the acquisition of requisite knowledge (literacy and numeracy, for example) to facilitate economic survival; the positive evaluation placed on occupational independence (self-employment) in trade, crafts, or professions; a positive relation to "middle-class" values, including ambition, thrift, and sobriety; and adaptability, born of circumstance and honed by necessity, which enabled a low-status migrant population to thrive in newly developing occupational niches or to seek out unsuspected entrepreneurial opportunities. At the religious or theological level, attention has been drawn to aspects of rabbinic Jewish culture such as the superior value placed on learning, learnedness, and abstract thought and the legitimacy bestowed on worldly endeavors, material security, and the secular fruits of life in general.

Elsewhere, I have critiqued this line of argumentation, casting doubt on the linear, value-based affinity ostensibly detected between Jewish mores and American socioeconomic values. Were Jews indeed historically preconditioned for occupational success and economic exceptionalism? In the crucial period of Jewish immigrant arrival and occupational reintegration—in which past experience ought to have come most readily into play—their premigration skills and worldly knowledge did not constitute a clear advantage in employment. Moreover, the notion of a close elective affinity between traditional Jewish and middle-class American social values was mainly constructed in the context of the early post–World War II decades. This construct bears the earmarks of a time when the bulk of American Jewry did attain middle-class status, when cold war ideology put a premium on social conformity, and when the drive for full Jewish integration in the academy and corporate America was reaching its height.[3]

Parallel to this debate over Jews and American capitalism, and posing a distinct challenge to the thesis of a historical-cultural Jewish predilection for capitalist-mediated social behaviors, a second group of observers has focused on another conundrum of Jewish conformity or deviance: the conspicuous nature of American Jewish political liberalism. This orientation has been a stock item in Jewish public discourse since the New Deal, if not earlier. Like the quest for explaining Jewish overachievement, the inquiry associated with Jewish hyperliberalism consists of dichotomous parts. Jews in the aggregate appear to have wholly internalized an American ideology—civil liberties and egalitarianism—while at the same time they deviate statistically toward the left in a way that seems inconsistent with a culture of self-reliance and achievement, entrepreneurship, and material success.[4]

In that light, comparisons between the voting behavior of Jews and other Americans of similar income levels have highlighted the dissident political profile of the Jewish constituency. Jews, more so than others, have tended to vote Democratic; to adopt critical positions on public policy in social welfare, government spending, and the conduct of foreign affairs; and to display an entrenched opposition to hegemonic structures in society, politics, the arts, and the academy. This profile, in turn, bears some resemblance to the liberal-leftist sympathies observed among acculturated members of other modern Jewish societies: Imperial and Weimar Germany, the historical finale of Imperial Russia, Poland during the interwar period, and east European Jewish immigrant enclaves from Vienna to Buenos Aires (though these analogies suffer somewhat when we consider that very powerful right-wing trends precluded all but a liberal or left-wing option for anyone who would support Jewish integration in those societies). Typically, linkages exist between underlying Judaic values (expressed in canonical texts and communal welfare practices) supportive of social justice; Jewish "underdog" consciousness bred by generations of minority status and episodes of oppression (mainly outside the United States); and the heritage of Jewish families in America, which in many instances included labor union activism in the immigrant generations or student radicalism among second- or third-generation Jewish youth.

Just as conformity and exceptionalism have been brought into tandem with each other in the literature on Jews and American capitalism, there are those who have attempted to sublimate the polarities of Jewish social integration, ambition, and upward mobility versus Jewish liberal-left loyalties. Their contention is that Jews have an underlying interest in securing a level playing field so that they might compete more successfully and integrate more securely and that this has motivated Jewish liberal agendas. Furthermore, recent analyses offer the hypothesis that ethnocentric concerns have also fueled Jewish identification "downward" with the interests of less privileged (even stigmatized) social groups and that similarly ethnocentric interests have been chipping away for decades at an erstwhile left-liberal Jewish political culture.[5]

As noted, I have previously sought to uncouple the "Jewish success story" from the discourse of cultural predisposition and economic exceptionalism. In this essay, I want to go down the other path and to complicate the debate over the persisting American Jewish liberal-left political culture. I want to address the possibility of a third Jewish approach, one that fostered a dissenting attitude toward capitalism and eschewed cultural integration, yet also maintained a preoccupation with social justice and equity—but not from within the universalistic discourse of the left. Rather, I suggest that it could have drawn on a religiously conservative (small "c") and neocommunitarian discourse which, in its own way, challenged regnant American social and economic values.

In that sense, "Jewishness"—not other-regarding universalism—could have fueled a critique of capitalist individualism. Thus, where the secular-leftist genesis of Jewish liberalism would point to Jewish labor union activism in the immigrant generation and to liberal Democratic voting patterns in succeeding American Jewish generations, a communitarian theory would have to take account of mutual-assistance fraternalism at the grassroots level of urban Jewish life.

This, it should be stressed, is different from the institutionalized mechanics of large-scale Jewish philanthropy and social services—services that, from their inception in American cities, were placed at the disposal of a nonsectarian clientele. Organized philanthropy (both Jewish and non-Jewish) is generally not a sponsor of an anticapitalist ethos but quite the reverse: it upholds capitalist achievement as public virtue, inculcating in those who are successful a healthy desire to "do good" in society at large and so to return the benefit of self-respect and self-fulfillment to those at a lower social station.

This Jewish third way might be thought of as resembling in certain respects other critiques of capitalism that emerged from socially and religiously or culturally conservative circles in Europe and the United States. In Europe, we might recall the anticapitalist and antimaterialist slant of German *völkisch* ideology in the nineteenth to early twentieth centuries, as well as the dissent from both socialist and capitalist materialism in Catholic doctrines, as expressed in such documents as Pope Leo XIII's 1891 encyclical, *Rerum Novarum*.[6] The teachings of the church in these matters harked back to the communitarian values of a precapitalist European society and defined the task of religion as providing moral intervention in the secular sphere. That doctrine was wielded most aggressively against Marxist radicalism and sought to preempt the radical critique of capitalism by providing a doctrine of social reconciliation in its place.

In America, some Catholic reform activists and moral philosophers sought to apply *Rerum Novarum* in such a way as to support liberal reforms (minimum wage, protection of working women and children, unionization, pension rights), though taking care to root their ideas in the "natural law" perspectives on human dignity embraced by the Vatican and steering clear of class radicalism. In 1931 Pius XI issued a new encyclical, marking forty years since *Rerum Novarum: Quadragesimo Anno*. The new document, "drenched in German Catholic corporatism," as one scholar has put it, was in some ways more radical in its stance against laissez-faire capitalism—enough so that even Franklin D. Roosevelt was able to quote from it during his first presidential election campaign in 1932.[7]

Other examples would include American populist movements and ideas that arose periodically to promote a grassroots agenda of social reform, creating a politically potent counterculture quite separate from that of the American left and, indeed, often more consonant with right-wing radicalism.[8]

Was there a Jewish third way that dissented from the values of corporate America but that eschewed the language of the secular left and adhered to a socially and religiously conservative worldview? Like some of its historical counterparts, the dimensions of such an impulse among American Jews and the possible varieties of such sentiments are likely to be wide and ambiguous. They might embrace disparate voices ranging, for example, from some aspects of Mordecai Kaplan's thought—based on his ideal communitarian concepts that eschewed the materialistic culture of the business world—to the socioeconomic nonconformity displayed by some present-day sectarian (*haredi*) Orthodox groups, to some Jewish politicians, such as the populist New York mayor, Ed Koch (b. 1924).[9] This essay cannot answer the question definitively and can only suggest the desirability of further inquiry.

For the present, I would like to address a nearly forgotten, idiosyncratic work that might be imagined as a key semantic tool in the ideological arsenal of the hypothetical Jewish third way. I refer to a 673-item Yiddish lexicon of terms associated with money and its multiple applications, published in the late 1950s by Isaac Rivkind: *Yidishe gelt in lebnsshyteger, kultur-geshikhte un folklor: A leksikologishe shtudye* (Jewish Money in Lifestyle, Cultural History and Folklore: A Lexicographical Study).[10] Rivkind (1895–1968), a librarian, bibliophile, and antiquarian scholar at the Jewish Theological Seminary of America, compiled all the words and phrases used in Yiddish for specific fees, payments, taxes, donations, income, and any other form of monetary exchange. To this he added an introductory essay and a massive body of philological, historical, and literary annotation. Each entry in the lexicon is illustrated with usages and etymologies distilled from documents spanning several hundred years of Jewish life in central and eastern Europe—including *pinkasim* (communal record books), *takanot* (communal regulations), rabbinical *responsa*, modern belles lettres, journals, newspapers, oral documentation from ethnographic surveys, and business handbooks, in addition to learned sources from outside the Jewish purview (the writings of Karl Marx, for example).[11] It is, in that respect, a treasury of old knowledge gleaned by an adept of Jewish discourse in early twentieth-century eastern Europe.

Isaac Rivkind was born in 1895 in Łódz, Poland, and was educated in the Lithuanian Torah centers of Volozhin and Ponivezh (Panevezys). He was active in the religious Mizrachi Zionist movement and took part in organizing its youth wing, Tse'irei Mizrachi, in Łódz. In the immediate aftermath of World War I, he served as a member of the short-lived Provisional Jewish National Council in Poland. He traveled to the United States in 1920, intending to continue his work on behalf of the Mizrachi movement there, but lost his enthusiasm for party activities, reportedly due to the mundane character of Zionist organizational work in America. He nevertheless remained in the United States, and in 1923 he joined the staff of the Jewish Theological Seminary of America Library, where he quickly proved his professional worth and encyclopedic knowledge as a bibliophile and textual expert. He was a frequent contributor to periodicals in Yiddish, Hebrew, and English. Apart from *Yidishe gelt* he also authored a short tract in Hebrew about the origins of bar mitzvah customs (*Le'ot ulezikaron*, 1942); a treatise in Yiddish on Jewish ethical exhortations against gambling (*Der kamf kegn azartshpiln bay yidn*, 1946); a short Hebrew study on folk musicians (*Klezmorim: Perek betoledot ha'omanut ha'amamit*, 1960); and an entry on the Ponivezh community for the *yiskerbukh* (memorial volume) published in 1951 to commemorate Lithuanian Jewry.[12] All told, the scholarly and journalistic oeuvre of this bookish, somewhat pedantic, and rather obscure intellectual totaled over 350 articles, essays, reviews, biographical sketches, documents, and monographs.[13]

Rivkind opens *Yidishe gelt* by observing that Jews, as portrayed stereotypically in Christian culture, were identified with money, usury, and greed. Rivkind begged to differ, submitting his book as a brief against the Shylock stereotype. In the very first line of his book, Rivkind admitted that a popular Yiddish adage averred that "Ver s'hot di meye, hot di deye" (He who pays the piper calls the tune), but he insisted, "I do not share the belief that 'money talks'"—a characteristically American phrase that he inserted verbatim in English. Rather, he insisted, "knowledge talks," while money is merely "counted. . . . If the author 'counts' Jewish money it is for the purpose of 'recounting' what money can tell us about Jewish life" (ix). *Yidishe gelt* attempts, through mapping the language of monetary exchange in Yiddish speech, nothing less than a reconstruction of the east European Jewish social order.

Rivkind's purpose is explicitly hagiographical: namely, to portray Judaism— particularly east European Judaism and its manifestation in the culture of Yiddish—as spiritually noble and socially ennobling, precisely at that cultural site most maligned and caricatured by others. By highlighting the money motif as his focal interest, Rivkind was exploiting the weight of the contempt for "Jewish money" to achieve the opposite rhetorical effect. "Money was created," he declared, "for the sake of Judaism [*yidishkayt*]: wisdom, integrity, scholarship, generosity, charity, sanctity, compassion, good sense, and Torah" (xv–xvi). It is not the meaning of "monetary forms in Jewish expression" that he is after, but rather, "through the medium of money to plumb the way of life, cultural traditions, customs and folklore of the Jews . . . a world of piety, a world of morals, virtue and charitability, of Judaism and humanism [*yidishkayt un mentshlikhkayt*] . . . a life that was, and is no more." His lexical entries illuminate the wide variety of social uses of money in traditional Jewish society and the ethical self-control to which the gaining and spending of money were subject (ix, xiii, xli)

Rivkind's post-Holocaust portrayal of European Jewry before the destruction bears a close resemblance to Abraham Joshua Heschel's famous elegy to east European Jewry, *The Earth Is the Lord's* (1949).[14] But where Heschel's approach was to address Jewish spirituality directly, Rivkind takes the indirect path of finding the sacred at the heart of the prosaic—indeed, in the recesses of the most mundane element of all.

Among his close associates and colleagues whose help Rivkind acknowledged were: Moshe Lutsky at Yeshiva University's library, where Rivkind was able to use a collection of *pinkasim* from the Posen district, Dina Abramowicz, the legendary librarian at the YIVO Institute and an important bibliophilic authority in her own right; Rivkind's wife, Yehudit, whom he credits with providing extensive ethnographic details; and the eminent Yiddish literary critic and scholar Shmuel Niger.[15]

Rivkind's social world and discursive universe, in short, was that of the interwar generation of European autodidacts, independent scholars, and refugee intellectuals whom the unmerciful exigencies of twentieth-century history cast up on American shores and who were largely engaged in recording and preserving the destroyed Jewish culture of their youth. Preceding by a generation the formal academicization of Jewish Studies in American universities, they found their callings in and around Jewish institutions, magazines, and libraries, where they assumed the role of primary custodians or curators of an entire culture. Gathering pearls from the torn strand of wisdom in semimonastic fashion, without realistic hopes of finding many readers or even the wherewithal to publish, Rivkind's discourse on Jewish money was an act of homage and self-sacrifice whose solace lay in contemplation itself. No doubt this, too, explains the tone of elegy that pervades this book.

Rivkind's world was also one of straitened personal circumstances. In 1949 his friends and colleagues Abraham Duker and Mordechai Kosover published a bibliography of Rivkind's writings in an anniversary pamphlet they presented to him. In it they wrote, "For years, Rivkind has been leading a life bordering on penury, one of constant and protracted want. Often he lived literally from hand to mouth."[16]

These circumstances, along with the strident demurral in Rivkind's opening statement ("I do not share the belief that 'money talks'"), prompt me to suggest that *Yidishe gelt* is, among other things, the protest of a scholarly soul, raised to believe in the dignity of learning and the honor owed to the learned but having found instead a marginal place in a skinflint, "money talks" environment. American capitalism, one might say, was not kind to Isaac Rivkind, and he was not kindly disposed to the culture of American capitalism. The destroyed and idealized alternative world of grace and virtue, as portrayed through his lexicon, was Rivkind's counterimage of how society ought to be. By tapping the stream of "folk-wisdom"—the "common man," construed in the populist or *narodnik* tradition as the unimpeachable arbiter of ultimate truth—and finding there a valorization of spiritual over material concerns, Rivkind was personally vindicated in his path in life.

The book was dedicated to his grandchildren: "I have no other worldly goods to bequeath to them," he noted, underscoring his marginal status in material terms: "only a book, and a Yiddish book at that, in a language which for them is not a mother tongue, but prayerfully I hope that, with God's help, they may grow up as 'complete' Jews—the Torah-*mitzves* [religion]-and-good-deeds sort of Jews—to whom all things Jewish should be near and dear" (xii). As we will see, the mention here of an integral Judaism is by no means coincidental.

Notwithstanding the considerable personal freight borne by this ethnographic thesaurus of Yiddish money terminology, Rivkind's *Yidishe gelt* is not easily dismissed as a simple apologetic tract or a panegyric to a martyred world. Rivkind's work invites us to go over the ground once more to take stock of the changed ethical order that was entailed in some Jews' adjustment to America.

To cite an example, based on neologisms he mined from immigrant Yiddish usage, *shiveh-gelt* and *minyen-gelt* were terms invented in the United States by members of *landsmanshaften* (mutual aid societies of fellow townspeople) to create provisions in their organizational bylaws by which a member could pay a fee in lieu of actually attending in person the obligatory prayer quorum held at the home of a member in mourning (155, 256). "As is well known, the main activities of the landsmanshaften to this very day are based around their cemeteries. . . . [But] one would be hard pressed to say, to use [poet Chaim Nachman] Bialik's phrase, 'In their death they bequeathed to us the commandment of life.'[17] By no means, for did we ever hear in the old shtetl about such things as minyen-gelt and shiveh-gelt?" (xlvii). Rivkind is not just carping about the clichéd cheapening and diminution of Judaism's spiritual content under the impact of Americanization (though he was doing that, too). In a more important sense, Rivkind was exemplifying the overall issue of social solidarity as a problem in American life, under conditions that appeared to possess strongly individuating forces and were geared to a no-holds-barred competitive ideology, implying an instrumentalization or objectification of all human relations.

————

In its original context, *yidishe gelt* (*mamonam shel yisrael*) was a juridical term, derived from the Talmudic precept (Yoma 39): "The Torah 'takes pity' on Jews' money"—in other words, in matters of exchange, litigation, and jurisdiction, Jewish civil law favors the nonalienation of Jewish property. Thus, the assets or earnings of any Jewish individual are also, by extension, the corporate possession of Jewry at large, and as such ought to be conserved within the Jewish social sphere. Civil litigation between Jews, for example, ought never to be brought before gentile courts, which could easily lead to gentile confiscation and taxation. The economic realm figured as a boundary between "ours" and "theirs" and denoted socially effective barriers in trade, employment, industrial enterprise, class identification, and consumption patterns.

Rivkind, however, expanded the meaning of the concept considerably (122–126), understanding it to convey a common Jewish interest in the widest sense and, in line with that, an identifiable Jewish social ethic. This afforded him the chance to comment on the internal moral and social obligations among Jews that this entailed, including elements of social, religious, and political criticism aimed at Jews in positions of authority. Thus, Rivkind noted that nineteenth-century religious reformers and *maskilim* (proponents of the Hebrew Enlightenment) often wielded economic arguments against waste and nonproductive pursuits to good effect when they criticized existing Jewish practices and urged that they be reformed (122).

He then cited a late nineteenth-century critique of Jewish religious customs related to pre-Passover domestic arrangements, some of which obliged indigent Jewish families to discard various foods and housewares. In the passage that Rivkind cited, the author had warned, "Our Jews really ought to take into careful consideration [the valid basis] for each and every custom. . . . Is it really based on Torah law, or is it only some excess of stringency handed down by a fanatical rabbi who has no pity for the [waste of] Jews' money, for their sweat and toil?"[18]

This construction of Jewish economic ethics as based, first of all, on core-sponsibility and mutual respect, crops up in numerous other entries in the volume. This, under *melokhe-gelt* (payment for labor), we read a selection from a Jewish ethical will by Rabbi Avrohom Danzig, enjoining on his heirs the supreme importance of prompt payment to craftsmen and laborers (drawing on a biblical tenet): "Right away, as soon as the craftsman has brought you the finished item, pay him his due at once, even if it means that you yourself must borrow in order to get the cash, or even if it means [transgressing by] missing afternoon prayers while you go and secure the required money."[19]

Rivkind similarly stressed the underlying ethical foundation of mutual respect in explaining the term *sguleh-gelt* (roughly: good luck money), a phrase reportedly used among Yiddish-speaking migrants in Frankfurt-am-Main and which referred to "an anonymous gift [of coins] given by women upon leaving the *mikveh* [ritual immersion pool], as a security for good luck and healthy children." As Rivkind elaborated, "For the sake of propriety and delicacy [*tsniyes*] the money was inserted through a small slot, ensuring that both the giver and the receiver [on the other side of the wall] could not see each other" (177). Here, the married woman returning home to resume cohabiting with her spouse and the indigent receiver of alms are portrayed as equally deserving of proper human decency and dignity.

In yet a further example, in this case involving Jewish-gentile relations, Rivkind drew on a Talmudic gloss by Rashi (the renowned Jewish scholar and commentator Rabbi Shlomo Yitzhaki of Troyes, 1040–1105) to explain the meaning of *purim-gelt*: "Money collected by beadles of the community to distribute to the poor at the Purim holiday feast. . . . Jews [have also] kept this practice in order to fulfill the obligation 'to furnish the needs of Gentile poor as well as the poor among Israel.'" Rivkind commented, "Thus, even in such fearsome times as Rashi's days [the Crusades] Jews still heeded the injunction that 'for the sake of peaceful relations' [*mipnei darkei shalom*] one should also distribute Purim gifts to poor Christians, without denying deserving Jews their due" (188–189).

In bringing his book up-to-date, Rivkind also used the *yidishe gelt* motif to voice his moral opposition to the decision by the State of Israel to seek German reparations (in an agreement reached with the German Federal Republic in 1952). He opined that a Jewish state ought to be built with "our own wealth, not with blood money [*khurbn-gelt*]" (xlix–1, 122).

In short, Rivkind was arguing that the world of trade, production, consumption, domestic welfare, charity, and high fiscal policy constituted a moral realm of coresponsibility. In framing this argument in terms of an abiding heritage of Jewish social and economic ethics, authenticated lexicographically as it were, Rivkind resorted to an ahistorical procedure. Linguistic deposits along the riverbed of spoken Yiddish, deriving from various historical eras and cultural contexts, were all unearthed and pressed into service for his didactic aims. The world of traditional Judaism that he offered for inspection was an ideal construction inevitably shaped by the commemorative impulse. Moreover, it was a kind of regressive portrait, eliding to a considerable degree the extent to which Jewish society in the Yiddish-speaking milieus of east central and eastern Europe had undergone processes of urbanization, secularization, and politicization in the period between the late nineteenth century and the Holocaust. With this mythical world to refer back to, Rivkind was in possession of the cultural weapons he might need in placing a question mark over the pieties of the American way of life.

Nevertheless, Rivkind's intuitive sense that Yiddish monetary parlance in eastern Europe reflected a grammar of economic relations that was Jewish in a proprietary sense was based on a legacy of Jewish economic and civil segregation. After the 1860s, by which time Jews had largely lost their historical role and viable market function of bridging the manorial and town economies, they increasingly found themselves within the stagnating limits of a truly ethnic, subsidiary economy, where they were employed almost exclusively by other Jews. By documenting the relevant linguistic cues, Rivkind's text reveals the coordinates of the social responses demanded by a life framed by economic segregation and stagnation.

Among other matters, this meant that the costs of essential social and religious services could not be borne by regular communal self-taxation arrangements, and therefore the burden of paying for them had to be spread very thinly indeed among local householders in a regularized system of redistributive handouts. Consider, for instance, the term *khanike gelt*—which we have come to think of as meaning a gift of pocket money for children in the Chanukah holiday week. In fact, as Rivkind points out, children were "the last ones," historically speaking, "to become recipients of this gift of money" (102–105). More often than not, the beneficiaries of this modest "largesse" and similar charitable gifts, periodically distributed at holiday times, were adults in need, chiefly the very poorly remunerated teachers of young children.

Other instances involved itinerant "rabbis" visiting outlying families in rural districts to offer religious instruction and receive something for their pains and their travel expenses. The custom then spread to others, such as ritual slaughterers, cantors, beadles, and other such lower-class Jewish religious functionaries, all of whom apparently depended in part on this system of compensatory subsidies, living from one holiday to the next. As economic historian Arcadius Kahan once pointed out,

> The "culture of poverty" . . . in Eastern Europe was one of the right to charity as a birthright of a member of the community. The "culture of poverty" was also based upon the traditional belief that the affluent need charity for the salvation of their immortal souls and that the needy, providing them with such opportunities, thus participate in an equivalent exchange.[20]

––––––

Rivkind's work was, in its day, congruent with the existing body of Yiddish folkloristics and in particular the well-trodden ethnolinguistic approach, dating back to the late nineteenth century. In turn, this approach to Yiddish was rooted in the Germanic-Romantic tradition of identifying cultural values as products of a group-specific popular or national spirit (*Volksgeist*) or group mentality and associating these values with a historically unique lexical and linguistic genealogy. The linguistic strategy and its underlying outlook that relates speech to social psychology was also famously deployed in North America in the early twentieth century by Franz Boas to reshape the field of anthropology around culture, rather than race, and to preserve nonliterary, endangered tribal cultures through their spoken languages. Closer perhaps to Rivkind's own place, time, and concerns, Max Weinreich, head of the YIVO Institute (housed in the early years after the war just down the street from the Jewish Theological Seminary of America), famously propagated the importance of Yiddish-language scholarship as the main gateway to the cultural repository of Ashkenazic Jewry.

These are important considerations when we seek to explain the intellectual background of Rivkind's method and hypothesis. But in addition, and crucially, it appears that Rivkind proposed to reconstruct Jewish culture from the vantage point of its money ethic, in part, to counter the work written on that subject by Werner Sombart. This author, whose *Die Juden und das Wirtschaftsleben* (1911) was translated into English and republished in 1951 as *The Jews and Modern Capitalism*, may well be said to be the specter that hovers over Rivkind's work, for Sombart himself claimed to have delved deeply into the syntax of Jewish values and mentality to uncover their linkage to capitalist relations.[21]

Sombart, of course, was leaning on and revising Max Weber—as Rivkind did, as well—in seeing economic and behavioral outcomes as projections of culturally embedded values. Sombart's Judaism is, in the Weberian vein, a demystifying and abstract or rationalizing approach to life. This attempt to show the supposed "secret life" of Judaism as an essentialist, cultural whole, a "spirit" of capitalism that anticipated Protestantism, was tendentious enough, derived as it was from a view of Jews in their economic behavior as endemically "other" in their native European milieu. But Sombart went even further in his essentializing argument, and in this respect he leaned rhetorically on Marx, who dubbed the "spirit" of the Jews as one of "huckstering."[22] Sombart, too, caught hold of this unflattering verbal cue and consigned the worldly ethic of the Jew to an undifferentiated tradesperson category, while reserving to the non-Jewish businessperson a more positive assessment as the ideal "entrepreneur": no mere fortune hunter but a motive force in his society, a figure of social responsibility, vision, and strength of character. Ultimately, Sombart did not deny Jews a significant role in modern economic life; indeed, he affirmed them as a prime lubricating element in the transition to a modern bourgeois ethic. But he did deny them the stature of socially anchored economic agents within a structured and positive *moral* universe.[23]

Isaac Rivkind takes direct aim at Sombart's argument by offering a counterimage of Judaism as an encompassing cultural system in its own right— albeit one of a different character than the one portrayed by Sombart. Where Sombart looks at the upper bourgeoisie of west European Jewry, Rivkind parries with the poor but morally beautiful Jews of eastern Europe. Where Sombart targets the bourgeois ethic in its "Jewish" form from the point of view of its naked instrumentality, Rivkind trumps him by positing a non-instrumentalist Jewish ethos. Where Sombart abstracts supposedly Jewish values from a digest of social statistics, often garbled textual references, and sweeping generalizations, Rivkind counters with the recorded linguistic evidence of Jewish social communication.

In aiming for a corrective to the Sombart thesis, Rivkind also betrayed some elective affinities of his own as he went about portraying a vital, "integral" Judaism as an abiding national-religious society with its own social conventions.

Rivkind's Judaism may be described as religio-national-organic. He borrowed its tenor and vocabulary from a critique of modern capitalism that was fairly current in Europe in the first half of the twentieth century, perhaps especially so in Catholic Europe and, notably, in Rivkind's native Poland, where strongly nationalist elements came together with a staunchly Catholic social discourse. The comparison is offered here in a tentative vein, but I believe it has substance.

While Rivkind's work contains no hint of an overtly antiradical critique (as compared with conservative Catholic doctrine), it does argue the moral superiority of communitarian values over egoistically competitive or consumerist drives, and it clearly assigns to religion a corrective function. It construes acquiring legitimate wealth through one's own efforts as honest work, expressed linguistically as *eygn gelt* (one's own earnings; 11–13), while speculative, fraudulent, or unscrupulous use of someone else's money—*fremd gelt* or *yenems gelt*—is an ethical and religious transgression (127, 204–207). In his definition of *miskher-gelt* (profit earned from trade), Rivkind cleverly cites a passage written in 1913 by Yehoash (Solomon Blumgarten, 1870–1927), the immigrant poet, writer, and correspondent for the politically centrist Yiddish daily *Der Tog:* "Father kept trying to persuade Mother . . . that trade is a decent [*kosher*] thing . . . , but Mother stood her ground—income from trade is impure [*miskher-gelt iz treyf*]" (155).

Conservative social critic Michael Novak aptly summarized the analogous position in the Catholic intellectual camp in the modern age as coming down on the side of "personalism, community, and 'solidarism,'" against "individualism, utilitarianism, and pragmatism . . . [and was] properly, fascinated by distributive ethics."[24] Rivkind's worldview, I believe, was not far removed in social and economic terms. Socially conservative, religiously inflected, and communitarian in spirit, *Yidishe gelt* holds up to Rivkind's various interlocutors a selective image of premodern, premigration, and pre-Holocaust eastern European Jewry as a righteous society. Rivkind's book is thus not just a defense against those who would malign Jews as economic predators but is also an assertion that social virtue as such could belong only to an ideal projection of a culture now destroyed. That is surely a not-too-veiled critique of American and American Jewish life in Rivkind's day, which, as he saw it, promoted the notion that "money talks."

This entails new analytic possibilities for understanding the variety of Jewish responses to American capitalism. *Yidishe gelt* allows us to plot a possible middle ground between the two poles defined by past convention, according to which the Jewish immigrant community in the United States could conveniently be divided between the successful, upwardly mobile *nouveaux riches*—the so-called allrightniks—on the one hand, and working-class "reds" on the other. The possibility that anticapitalist, neocommunitarian ideas and resentments percolated within Jewish immigrant ranks is not farfetched. Given how little we know about the less thoroughly researched Orthodox sector, which was quite large (a quarter to a third of the Jewish population at the time) and which may have harbored precisely this kind of mindset, it is at least worth taking it seriously as a research challenge. We are liable, for example, to discover that those within the immigrant stratum who entertained such views could have supported welfare state liberalism at a later stage and perhaps influenced second-generation Jews nearly as much as did the immigrant labor radicalism more frequently cited as background to a Jewish liberal orientation.

We might also discover that the genealogy of this stratum of Jewish social thinking was not as marginal as we might think. As a central figure to modern American Judaism, Mordecai Kaplan was, I believe, a spokesperson for a neo-communitarian liberalism that chafed at American compromises, not just in religion but in social action too. Kaplan entertained populist views about the ill-gotten gains of prosperous people and toyed with the notoriety he won by occasionally expressing "radical" ideas. "As rabbi of the Jewish Center," he confided to his diary in 1919, "I am allied with the typical bourgeois Jews. I went into this alliance open eyed though with a great deal of reluctance and disgust."[25]

Later, in his seminal book *Judaism as a Civilization* (1934), Kaplan referred to the material and leisure culture of modern times as a "strain" and an "economic attack" on Judaism. Kaplan complained of the position of disadvantage occupied by Jewish life and Jewish law in the face of modern capitalism. A decade afterward, Kaplan reiterated some of his position on the need to socialize American Jews under the aegis of an "organic" Jewry that would "activate the high ethical standards transmitted in the Jewish tradition by developing specific codes and sanctions for various social and economic relationships."[26]

We are also liable, in another sense, to uncover a way of thinking about capitalism within Jewish circles that in some ways anticipated the emergence of a secular Jewish neoconservative intellectual camp, on the one hand, and a Jewish religious Orthodoxy unfazed by "faith-based initiatives" on the other.

Moreover, it is worth pursuing this line of thought in a comparative vein, with reference to the communal and family-centered approach often found to have dominated among other southern and east European immigrant groups in their transition from European villages to American mines and factories, as John Bodnar and other scholars of immigrant labor have suggested.[27]

In sum, *Yidishe gelt* affords us a way of reconsidering the scholarly agenda on American capitalism, liberalism, and the Jews. It suggests the utility of rephrasing some of the central issues, shifting from questions of exceptionalism versus symbiosis to an appreciation of multiple routes and concerns. With its subtext focused on the moral or normative challenges that immersion in American capitalism entailed, Rivkind's book gives us an inkling of how complex the emergence of an American Jewish social consciousness really has been. By sketching the possibility of a third position on economic affairs it also may help us account for certain long-term continuities from the postimmigration period to our own day.

NOTES

1. For a recent restatement of these arguments, see Jerry Z. Muller, *Capitalism and the Jews* (Princeton, NJ: Princeton University Press, 2010). Cf. David L. Featherman, "The Socioeconomic Achievement of White Religio-Ethnic Subgroups: Social and Psychological Explanations," *American Sociological Review* 36, no. 2 (1971): 207–222.

2. Thomas Kessner, *The Golden Door: Italian and Jewish Immigrant Mobility in New York City 1880–1925* (New York: Columbia University Press, 1977); Simon Kuznets, "Immigration of Russian Jews to the United States: Background and Structure," *Perspectives in American History* 9 (1975): 35–124; Stephen Steinberg, *The Ethnic Myth: Race, Ethnicity, and Class in America* (Boston: Beacon, 1981); Arcadius Kahan, *Essays in Jewish Social and Economic History*, ed. Roger Weiss and Jonathan Frankel (Chicago: University of Chicago Press, 1986); Calvin Goldscheider and Alan S. Zuckerman, *The Transformation of the Jews* (Chicago: University of Chicago Press, 1984); Calvin Goldscheider, "Immigration and the Transformation of American Jews," in *Immigration and Religion in America: Comparative and Historical Perspectives*, ed. Richard Alba, Albert J. Raboteau, and Josh DeWind (New York: New York University Press, 2009), 203–204, 207–208; Joel Perlmann, "Which Immigrant Occupational Skills? Explanations of Jewish Economic Mobility in the United States and New Evidence, 1910–1920" (working paper 181, Levy Economics Institute of Bard College, Annandale-on-Hudson, NY, 1996; Barry R. Chiswick, "The Occupational Attainment and Earnings of American Jewry, 1890–1990," *Contemporary Jewry* 20, no. 1 (1999): 68–98; Chiswick, "Jewish Immigrant Skill and Occupational Attainment at the Turn of the Century," *Explorations in Economic History* 28, no. 1 (1991).

3. Eli Lederhendler, *Jewish Immigrants and American Capitalism, 1880–1920: From Caste to Class* (Cambridge: Cambridge University Press, 2009); Lederhendler, "American Jews, American Capitalism, and the Politics of History," in *Text and Context: Essays in Modern Jewish History and Historiography in Honor of Ismar Schorsch*, ed. Eli Lederhendler and Jack Wertheimer (New York: JTS, 2005), 504–546; Lederhendler, "Jews and the Bourgeois Ethic" (paper presented at the first conference on "Jews, Commerce and Culture," Herbert Katz Center for Advanced Judaic Studies, University of Pennsylvania, April 27–29, 2009, and forthcoming in translation in *Les cahiers du judaïsme*. Cf. Eli Lederhendler, review of Jerry Z. Muller, *Capitalism and the Jews*, H-Judaic, H-Net Reviews, July 2010, http://www.h-net.org/reviews/showrev.php?id=3D30303.

4. Laurence H. Fuchs, *The Political Behavior of American Jews* (Glencoe, IL: Free Press, 1956); Werner Cohn, "The Politics of American Jews," in *The Jews: Social Patterns of an American Group*, ed. Marshall Sklare (Glencoe, IL: Free Press, 1958), 614–626; Ben Halpern, "The Roots of American Jewish Liberalism," *American Jewish Historical Quarterly* 66, no. 2 (December 1976): 190–214; Alan Fisher, "Continuity and Erosion of Jewish Liberalism," *American Jewish Historical Quarterly* 66, no. 2 (December 1976): 322–348; Arthur Liebman, "The Ties That Bind: The Jewish Support for the Left in the United States," *American Jewish Historical Quarterly* 66, no. 2 (December 1976): 285–321; Liebman, *Jews and the Left* (New York: Wiley, 1979); Deborah Dash Moore, *At Home in America* (New York: Columbia University Press, 1981), ch. 8; Steven M. Cohen and Charles S. Liebman, *Two Worlds of Judaism* (New Haven, CT: Yale University Press, 1990), ch. 5; Cohen and Liebmanidem, "American Jewish Liberalism: Unravelling the Strands," *Public Opinion Quarterly* 61 (1997): 405–430; Henry L. Feingold, "From Equality to Liberty: The Changing Political Culture of American Jews," in *The Americanization of the Jews*, ed. Robert M. Seltzer and Norman J. Cohen (New York: New York University Press, 1995), 97–118; Nathan Glazer, "The Anomalous Liberalism of American Jews," in Seltzer and

Cohen, *Americanization of the Jews*, 133–143; Geoffrey Brahm Levey, "Toward a Theory of Disproportionate American Jewish Liberalism," in *Values, Interests, and Identity: Jews and Politics in a Changing World: Studies in Contemporary Jewry*, vol. 11, ed. Peter Y. Medding (New York: Oxford University Press, 1995), 64–85; Levey, "The Liberalism of American Jews—Has It Been Explained?" *British Journal of Political Science* 26, no. 3 (July 1996): 369–401; Ira N. Forman, "The Politics of Minority Consciousness: The Historical Voting Behavior of American Jews," in *Jews in American Politics*, ed. L. Sandy Maisel and Ira N. Forman (Lanham, New York: Rowman and Littlefield, 2001), 142–160; Anna Greenberg and Kenneth D. Wald, "Still Liberal after All These Years?" in Maisel and Formanibid, *Jews in American Politics*,162–193; Tony Michels, *A Fire in Their Hearts: Yiddish Socialists in New York* (Cambridge, MA: Harvard University Press, 2005), 253, 257–259; Michael Walzer, "Liberalism and the Jews: Historical Affinities, Contemporary Necessities," in Medding, *Values, Interests, and Identity*, 3–10; Walzer, "Why Are Jews Liberal (an Alternative to Norman Podhoretz)," *Dissent*, October 2009.

5. Stuart Svonkin, *Jews against Prejudice: American Jews and the Fight for Civil Liberties* (New York: Columbia University Press, 1997); Marc Dollinger, *Quest for Inclusion: Jews and Liberalism in Modern America* (Princeton, NJ: Princeton University Press, 2000); Michael Alexander, *Jazz Age Jews* (Princeton, NJ: Princeton University Press, 2001); Michael E. Staub, *Torn at the Roots: The Crisis of Jewish Liberalism in Postwar America* (New York: Columbia University Press, 2002); Kenneth D. Wald, "Toward a Structural Explanation of Jewish-Catholic Political Differences in the United States," in *Jews, Catholics, and the Burden of History: Studies in Contemporary Jewry*, vol. 21, ed. Eli Lederhendler (New York: Oxford University Press, 2005): 111–131.

6. The text of the Rerum Novarum can be found at http://www.papalencyclicals.net/Leo13/l13rerum. See also George L. Mosse, *The Crisis of German Ideology* (New York: Grosset and Dunlap, 1964), ch. 6.

7. John T. McGreevy, *Catholicism and American Freedom: A History* (New York: Norton, 2003), 127–165; cf. Jay P. Dolan, *The American Catholic Experience* (Garden City, NY: Doubleday, 1985), 334–346. "The principal way in which bishops and priests appropriated the encyclical was as another arrow in their quiver to use in the battle against socialism" (336).

The text of *Rerum Novarum* reads, inter alia:

> Just as the symmetry of the human frame is the result of the suitable arrangement of the different parts of the body, so in a State is it ordained by nature that these two classes [labor and capital] should dwell in harmony and agreement, so as to maintain the balance of the body politic. Each needs the other: capital cannot do without labor, nor labor without capital. Mutual agreement results in the beauty of the good order, while perpetual conflict necessarily produces confusion and savage barbarity. Now, in preventing such strife as this, and in uprooting it, the efficacy of Christian institutions is marvelous and manifold. . . . There is no intermediary more powerful than religion . . . in drawing the rich and the working class together, by reminding each of its duties to the other, and especially of the obligations of justice (par. 19).

8. John D. Hicks, *The Populist Revolt: A History of the Farmers' Alliance and the People's Party* (Minneapolis: University of Minnesota Press, 1931); Richard Hofstadter, *The Age of Reform: From Bryan to FDR* (New York: Vintage, 1955); Norman Pollack, *The Populist Response to Industrial America* (New York: Norton, 1966); Sheldon Hackney, *Populism to Progressivism in Alabama* (Princeton, NJ: Princeton University Press, 1969); Lawrence Goodwyn, *Democratic Promise: The Populist Movement in America* (New York: Oxford University Press, 1976); Steven Hahn, *The Roots of Southern Populism* (New York: Oxford University Press, 1985); Robert C. McMath Jr., *American*

Populism: A Social History 1877–1898 (New York: Hill and Wang, 1993); Peter H. Argersinger, *The Limits of Agrarian Radicalism: Western Populism and American Politics* (Lawrence: University of Kansas Press, 1995); Michael Kazin, *The Populist Persuasion: An American History* (New York: Basic Books, 1995); Charles Postel, *The Populist Vision* (New York: Oxford University Press, 2007).

9. On Kaplan's desire to preach against economic exploitation and on his personal disdain for affluent congregants and in general for the world of business, see Mel Scult, ed., *Communings of the Spirit: The Journals of Mordecai M. Kaplan*, vol. 1, *1913–1934* (Detroit: Wayne State University Press, 2001), 137–138, 103: "the hard, pitiless grind of the average well-to-do Jewish business man whose life is ill-organized, empty, and futile." Cf. ibid., 73: "He was a rather clever *Baal Habayis* [i.e., *balebos*, Yiddish: householder] of the Lithuanian type, well learned for a layman. . . . at as for bringing up children Jewishly he knew as much about [it] as a cow about Sunday"; ibid., 73–74, re: Harry Fischel, a wealthy community leader and philanthropist: "Rumor has it that he engaged in some shady deals whereby he had defrauded an employer of his who was a Gentile. . . . On the whole he would be quite repellent, were it not for the animation in his face which betrays a mixture of shrewdness and intelligence. . . . In spite of these traits, however, he cannot live down the inordinate vulgarity which urges him on to elbow his way to the front, regardless of the ridicule he provokes"; ibid., 88, re: Felix M. Warburg, the wealthy banker and one of the foremost figures in Jewish philanthropic activity: "There is no doubt that he is as democratic as it is possible for one in his circumstances to be. The only misfortune is that he does not seem to me to possess the depth of character that might have rendered him a power in Jewry. He is not interested in Judaism for what it means to him but for what it might mean to the masses whom it might keep out of mischief."

10. Isaac Rivkind, *Yidishe gelt in lebnsshyteger, kultur-geshikhte un folklor: A leksikologishe shtudye* (New York: American Academy for Jewish Research, 1959). Hereafter cited in text.

11. A reference to Marx's writings occurs, for instance, in the entry: "Papirgelt" (paper money). Rivkind, *Yidishe gelt*, 186.

12. Mendl Sudarsky, Uriah Katzenelenbogen, Y. Kissin, and Berl Cahan, eds., *Lite* (New York: Kultur-geselshaft fun Huishe Yidn, 1951).

13. On Isaac Rivkind's life, see the obituary notice by Tuvia Preschel, *Proceedings of the American Academy of Jewish Research* 37 (1969): xxxii–xxxiv; Mordechai Kosover and Abraham Duker, eds., *Minha le-Yitzhak, lemalot 'esrim vehamesh shana likehunat safran biyisrael: Bibliografya shel kitvei Yitzhak Rivkind* (New York, 1949); Jacob Kabakoff, "Some Notable Bibliographers I Have Known," Rosaline and Meyer Finestein Lecture Series, 1999, http://www2.jewishculture.org/jewish_scholarship_ feinstein_ kabakoff.html.

14. Abraham Joshua Heschel, *The Earth Is the Lord's: The Inner World of the Jew in Eastern Europe* (Woodstock, VT: Jewish Lights, 1949).

15. Niger was not, in fact, terribly encouraging about the fate of Rivkind's manuscript in a world no longer interested in buying and reading this sort of scholarly achievement in Yiddish. In a letter dated May 14, 1955, Niger wrote the following pragmatic and prosaic note (tellingly ironic, given the context): "Who will print it? And once it's printed, what will I do with it? Peddle it from door to door? . . . What hope have you got with your nearly completed work, unless you want to go begging for people to sign

up subscriptions, as they used to do back in the old days? Please don't take offense if I touch on an especially sore point—our absolute disaster [*makas medine*]." Rivkind, *Yidishe gelt*, xi).

16. Kosover and Duker, eds., *Minha le-Yitzhak*, ix (English text) and 10 (Hebrew).

17. Chaim Nachman Bialik, "'Im yesh et nafshekha lada'at," a poem written in Russia in the 1890s.

18. Quoted from Moshe Aharon Shatzkes, *Der yudisher far-peysekh* (Warsaw, 1881), in Isaac Rivkind, *Yidishe gelt*, 124.

19. Avrohom Danzig, *Beys avrohom, tsavoes harov avrohom danzig, ibergezetst af ivri-taytsh 'al yedei reb yitshok hamburger* (Lemberg, 1875), quoted in Rivkind, *Yidishe gelt*, 152.

20. Arcadius Kahan, "The First Wave of Jewish Immigration from Eastern Europe to the United States," in Kahan and Weiss, *Social and Economic History*, 123–124.

21. Werner Sombart, *The Jews and Modern Capitalism*, trans. M. Epstein (Glencoe, IL: Free Press, 1951).

22. *Zur Judenfrage* (Braunschweig: Otto, 1843).

23. On Sombart's discussion of the Jews, the bourgeois spirit, and the entrepreneurial image in German society, see Paul R. Mendes-Flohr, "Werner Sombart's: *The Jews and Modern Capitalism*: An Analysis of Its Ideological Premises," *Leo Baeck Institute Year Book* 21 (1976): 87–107; Werner E. Mosse, "Judaism, Jews and Capitalism: Weber, Sombart, and Beyond," *Leo Baeck Institute Year Book* 24 (1979): 3–15.

24. Michael Novak, *The Spirit of Democratic Capitalism* (New York: Simon and Schuster, 1982), 23, 25.

25. *Communings of the Spirit*, 134. See also note 9.

26. Mordecai Kaplan, *Judaism as a Civilization* (New York: Macmillan, 1935), 34; Kaplan, "How to Envisage the Jewish Community," *Reconstructionist* 12, no. 7 (1946): 21.

27. See, for example, John Bodnar, *The Transplanted: A History of Immigrants in Urban America* (Bloomington: Indiana University Press, 1985).

༄

PART IV

Selling Judaism

CAPITALISM AND RESHAPING OF JEWISH RELIGIOUS CULTURE

CHAPTER 11

Sanctification of the Brand Name

THE MARKETING OF CANTOR YOSSELE ROSENBLATT

Jeffrey Shandler

During their period of mass immigration from eastern Europe to America, it quickly became a commonplace sentiment among Jews on both sides of the Atlantic Ocean that the United States was inimical to proper Jewish religiosity and that this new way of life was more suited to worship of the almighty dollar than of the Almighty. However, such assumptions were complicated by the phenomenon of the celebrity cantor, a fixture of American Jewish life from the 1880s through the middle decades of the twentieth century. Exemplifying the American celebrity cantor is one of the most well known Jewish clerics in the United States during the first decades of the twentieth century: Cantor Joseph (Yossele) Rosenblatt. His career, as recounted in print and documented on recordings and in films, suggests not only the possibility of being a religious Jew in the United States but also how the American marketplace could be engaged to enable new prospects for traditional Judaism. Rosenblatt's piety was not despite his fame but defined by it. Indeed, the very fact that Rosenblatt was a celebrity cantor, widely known among Jews and non-Jews alike, evinces a new kind of religiosity in the making, one that embraces rather than reviles modern capitalism, seeking to do so on terms compatible with traditional religious precepts and values.[1]

Born in Belaia Tserkov, a small town in the Russian Empire, in 1882, Rosenblatt was the son of a cantor, who early on recognized the boy's musical talents. Celebrity quickly became a fixture of his life as a musician. Young Joseph and his father spent much of the boy's youth touring small towns in eastern Europe, showing off the young singer's talents.[2] At the age of eighteen, Joseph

Rosenblatt was engaged as cantor in Muncacz, and within a few years he moved to Pressburg, where he also began his prolific career as composer and arranger of cantorial music. In 1907 Rosenblatt moved to Hamburg, assuming the position of chief cantor. His fame spread through his first recordings, made in 1905, and was enhanced by performances at large public gatherings, including the 1909 Zionist Congress, which was convened in Hamburg. Finally, Rosenblatt came to the United States in 1912 to serve as the cantor of the First Hungarian Congregation Ohab Zedek, located in Harlem. The United States would be not only where he spent most of the rest of his life but where his career as celebrity cantor reached its height.

In part, Rosenblatt's fame would be measured, by both his public and his family, in monetary terms. His 1954 biography, written by his son Samuel, recounts the cantor's salaries and fees for individual performances, in both sacred and secular settings. For instance, in 1927 Rosenblatt's gross income was more than $70,000, including a payment of $15,000 for conducting Rosh Hashanah and Yom Kippur services in Chicago. Soon thereafter, when the cantor left the congregation in Harlem for another synagogue, Anshei Sfard in Boro Park, Brooklyn, the biography notes that his new employer offered him "a ten-year contract at an annual salary of $12,000," which is vaunted as marking a "new high in cantorial remuneration." Rosenblatt's son also notes when his father's earnings became a matter of public attention, sometimes even regarding a loss of income. Thus, shortly after taking his position in Brooklyn, the cantor came down with pneumonia (having spent the holiday of Succos outdoors in inclement weather). The news of Rosenblatt's illness soon became public knowledge. "The press carried daily bulletins on the progress of his convalescence . . . from a malady that was estimated to have meant a loss to him of $10,000 worth of engagements."[3]

Cantors had already come to play a significant new role in immigrant Jewish culture by the time that Rosenblatt first came to America, after a generation of steady mass immigration of Jews from eastern Europe had been under way. The cantor's new stature in the immigrant community was articulated in terms of publicity, income, and, later on, use of new media. During what came to be known as the "cantorial craze" of the 1880s, immigrant congregations in New York City vied for who could employ the most renowned cantor for the largest sum. As the term "craze" implies, this was a phenomenon that began suddenly and did not last long—moreover, there was something less than rational about it, at least in retrospect. Brief though it was, the cantorial craze of the 1880s is a telling phenomenon of Jewish religious life in America, especially New York City, during the first decade of large-scale immigration from eastern Europe, and this phenomenon anticipates the culture of American celebrity cantors of the early twentieth century, epitomized by Rosenblatt.

Amid encounters with manifold disparities between the life that immigrants had led in Europe and their new life in America, cantors epitomized the religious experience that these Jews had left behind. The emotional power of the cantors' performances not only conveyed the congregation's prayers to heaven, according to traditional teaching, but also bore the affective charge of immigrant longings and uncertainties. These immigrants may have prized the sound of *khazones*, the music of the cantor, that much more due to its relative scarcity. During the 1880s few Jewish men who had come to the United States from eastern Europe were trained as cantors. More established Jewish communities in New York and other major American cities had their cantors, of course, but theirs was usually not an east European sound or idiom of performance. The concentration of new Jewish arrivals, most of whom came from small towns across a great expanse of eastern Europe to immigrant neighborhoods in major American cities, intensified the sense of scarcity of talented cantors who sounded "authentic" to their ears. For the immigrant cantor from eastern Europe, this was, in effect, a sellers' market.

The cantorial craze of the 1880s coincided with the emergence of a new figure in the Jewish landscape, both in Europe and America: the celebrity cantor. Thanks to mass immigration, increased urbanization and mobility, and the expansion of the Jewish press, highly admired cantors achieved unprecedented renown. Cantors attracted greater numbers of listeners in the large synagogues being built in European cities in the late nineteenth century, and they performed with greater frequency in recital and concert halls. Word of their artistry traveled not only by word of mouth but also in print.

In America, celebrity cantors came to play an emblematic role in immigrant life. Historian Jonathan Sarna argues that, for these immigrants, the celebrity cantor represented "the ultimate synthesis of the Old World and New . . . : observant yet rich, traditional yet modern. . . . He personified the great heritage of a European world-gone-by, yet succeeded equally well in Columbus's land of the future. In short, a cantorial performance simultaneously served both as an exercise in nostalgia and as living proof that in America the talented could succeed handsomely." Significantly, Sarna notes, this was "a synthesis most immigrants sought to achieve but few succeeded" in realizing.[4]

A case in point is the career of one of New York's first celebrity cantors from eastern Europe, Pinkhas Minkowski. Born in 1859 (and, by coincidence, in the same town as Rosenblatt), Minkowski was the son of a cantor and, as a boy, sang in his father's choir. The younger Minkowski had a traditional Jewish religious upbringing as well as some modern education, learning both Russian and German as a young adult. His musical education also expanded beyond traditional training in khazones, culminating in travel to Vienna. There he studied voice under the director of the Conservatorium, from which Minkowsky obtained a diploma. His cantorial career included positions in major cities in the Russian Empire: Kishinev, Kherson, Lemberg, and eventually Odessa.

In 1887 the newly built synagogue of congregation Kahal Adath Jeshurun, located on Eldridge Street in the Lower East Side—then the largest and most lavish of synagogues established by the east European Jewish immigrant community in New York City—lured Minkowski from his position in Odessa by making him a most handsome offer: a five-year contract with an annual salary of $2,500 (this at a time when the average New York City worker earned less than $450 a year), plus 1,000 rubles to release him from his contract in Russia, first-class passage to New York for him and his family, $300 to help him set up a home in New York, and six weeks' vacation every year. (At the time, the Eldridge Street synagogue was not paying its other employees so lavishly. The synagogue's secretary and bal-koyre—the man who chanted the weekly Torah reading—was paid only $300 a year.)[5] As one of the most well-paid cantors in America, Minkowski's artistry was the musical equivalent of the congregation's new synagogue, built in a hybrid of historical styles, including Romanesque, Gothic, and Moorish: both were grand, showy, costly, rooted in European tradition and enhanced by a modern aesthetic sensibility, whether state-of-the-art notions of sacred architecture or au courant musicology.

However, this match of synagogue and cantor did not prove to be long-lived. At first, the congregation was so taken with Minkowski that they offered him an annual bonus of $500. But by 1891 the synagogue's leadership was financially unable to offer the cantor this bonus. The following year, as the congregation was in the midst of reviewing the possibility of renewing Minkowski's contract, they received a letter from him stating that he had decided to return to Odessa.[6] Beyond the financial disappointment, it appears that Minkowski felt personally slighted by the congregation. Moreover, by going back to Russia, he returned to a much more established religious culture—indeed, once back in Odessa, he remained at the city's Brody Synagogue for three decades. In addition to leading his congregation in worship during those years, Minkowski composed and published sacred music and wrote musicological studies of Jewish liturgy.

Following Minkowski's departure, the leaders of the Eldridge Street synagogue did not pursue another celebrity cantor. The cantorial craze of the 1880s had waned, reflecting the dynamics of religious life in this rapidly expanding immigrant community. In the 1880s skilled cantors fluent in an east European style of khazones were in short supply and great demand. A decade later, as greater numbers of Jewish immigrants arrived in New York, men with the requisite musicianship were more readily available. The expense of star cantors also proved something immigrant congregations found hard to sustain. What had been a sellers' market quickly became a buyers' market. Rather than seeking out major cantorial talents in Europe, immigrant congregations could take their pick of newly arrived local talent. Thus, after Minkowski's departure in the summer of 1892, the Eldridge Street synagogue held auditions and eventually hired Yehezkel Borenstain. This cantor was engaged only for the High Holidays and paid five hundred dollars for his services, which including hiring a choir at his own expense, a financial burden Minkowski had been spared. Borenstain did not merit being offered a year's contract, and for several years the Eldridge Street synagogue hired cantors on a short-term basis, paying them thirty dollars per month.[7]

Minkowski might have remained in Odessa permanently, were it not for the Bolshevik Revolution. As Russia's new communist government made it increasingly difficult for religious institutions to continue to function, Minkowski decided to return to the United States in 1922. Although he was named the honorary president of the Jewish Ministers Cantor Association of America and Canada, he found it difficult to find a permanent post as cantor in the United States, and instead he performed special services in various American cities. This phase of Minkowski's career did not last long; in January 1924 he died at the age of sixty-five.[8]

Minkowski died a celebrity, honored by memorial services held in several cities. On the Lower East Side, more than one thousand people attended his funeral service, which included a performance by "two hundred cantors and one hundred choir singers." This ensemble performed under the leadership of Joseph Rosenblatt, who exemplified a new generation of celebrity cantors that flourished in the United States in the early decades of the twentieth century.

Although Rosenblatt's role at Minkowski's funeral suggests that the younger cantor succeeded the older one as a celebrity, Rosenblatt's fame was configured quite differently. Not only was the immigrant Jewish community of the United States in the early twentieth century different from the one Minkowski had encountered a generation earlier, but there was now an array of new vehicles for cantorial stardom, including an expanded press coverage, the publishing of sheet music, elaborately promoted concert tours, and the new media of sound recordings and, later, talking motion pictures. Over the course of Rosenblatt's remarkable career, all of these developments would prove strategic to his celebrity status.

Perhaps more than any of these innovations, Rosenblatt owed his celebrity to the advent of sound recording. He was one of the most widely recorded cantors of his generation, issuing dozens of 78 rpm disks during his American career, most of them on major labels such as Victor and Columbia.[9] He recorded several of the most popular works in the cantorial repertoire, such as "Kol Nidre," more than once. In addition, Rosenblatt also made recordings of Jewish art music, Zionist anthems, Yiddish folk songs, and even Tin Pan Alley Judaica ("My Yiddishe Momme"), as well as vocal recital standards in English ("The Last Rose of Summer") and Russian ("Song of the Volga Boatmen"). Several of Rosenblatt's recordings were issued to mark current events, such

Figure 11.1. Advertisement run in the *Jewish Daily Forward* by Columbia Records promoting a concert by Rosenblatt at Carnegie Hall, May 19, 1918.

as a version of the memorial prayer "El Male Rachamim" for victims of the *Titanic*, released in 1913, and Massenet's "Elegie," issued in 1917 for victims of World War I. Typically, his recordings listed Rosenblatt as both performer and arranger of the selections, thereby linking his virtuosity as a singer with his knowledge of the music as authoritative, his name serving, in effect, as a brand.

Rosenblatt extended the reach of his branding by publishing his arrangements of khazones and other works of Jewish vocal music in sheet music form. In addition to performing regularly at recitals and benefit concerts, as did other cantors, Rosenblatt was one of the few members of this profession to appear in vaudeville and films. Also unlike other cantors, his portrait became iconic, widely reproduced in news reports, advertisements, and cartoons in the Yiddish, Anglo-Jewish, and mainstream American press. Thus, through an extensive array of live, annotated, and recorded performances, compounded by exceptional appearances in the press, film, and popular theater, Rosenblatt

Figure 11.2. Sheet music cover for Jules Massenet's "Elegie," with Hebrew text by M. M. Dolitzky, promoting Rosenblatt's performance as recorded on Columbia Records. Published by S. Schenker, New York, 1921.

established his renditions of khazones as a (if not *the*) standard against which other cantors would be measured. Moreover, his persona and biography emerged as the epitome of the cantor as a public figure widely recognized beyond the synagogue.

By contrast, Minkowski never made recordings. This was not due to a lack of opportunity, but rather was a matter of conviction. At the beginning of the twentieth century, when the first commercial recordings of cantorial music were made, Minkowski denounced the Victrola as a "disgraceful screaming instrument." The cantor famously expressed outrage that in Odessa, cantorial recordings could be heard through the windows of prostitutes' rooms in the city's red light district.[10] Minkowski was not simply being a Luddite in voicing this outrage; he demonstrated an awareness that recordings of a performance of sacred music didn't simply document or preserve it, but transformed it. For example, in the early days of recording, the technology of the medium, whether wax cylinder or 78 rpm disk, limited the performance to a maximum length of three to four minutes.[11] Early recordings of khazones thus isolated from the full length of Jewish worship services, which can extend for hours in actual performance, discrete musical "numbers."

Most significantly, sound recordings are what the musician R. Murray Schafer calls *schizophonic* phenomena—that is, they separate sound from its original source.[12] In the case of khazones, recordings remove cantorial singing from the synagogue and the specific occasion of worship. Besides its removal from sacred place and time, the performance is separated from its original sacred intent—addressing God within the rubric of communal worship—thereby situating cantorial music in some other listening context. Cantors, record producers, marketers, and audiences have all demonstrated their awareness of this transformation. For example, many recordings of khazones feature instrumental accompaniment that would not be heard when this music is performed in those synagogues where playing instruments is forbidden on the Sabbath and holidays. The shift away from the context of worship is also signaled on many (though not all) recordings, in which cantors substitute the words Adoshem and Elokeinu for names of God traditionally uttered only when actually praying. Khazones was recorded not only by cantors but also by other singers, including several women, known as *khazntes* or "lady cantors." These women performed khazones in recitals, on recordings, and, later, on radio, but not in the synagogue. As is still the case today, Orthodox Judaism prohibits women from singing cantorial music in the synagogue; the practice of non-Orthodox Jewish movements training women to be cantors did not begin until after World War II. Thus, within the protocols of khazones itself, performers marked recordings of this music as being something other than worship.

The tension inherent in cantorial recordings between the traditional music that they reproduced and the new cultural economies, listening contexts, and social practices in which the medium positioned khazones exemplifies the challenge that Rosenblatt faced as a celebrity cantor. He addressed this challenge not only in his musicianship but also in the crafting of his public persona, which offered an image of a man who could reconcile the demands of Orthodoxy with the opportunities of modern popular culture, synthesized through his artistry.

Beyond promoting his musical talents through various media and marketing strategies, Rosenblatt cultivated public attention to his life outside the synagogue and other performance venues. Essential to his being recognized as the embodiment of Jewish religiosity in the early twentieth-century American cultural marketplace is this attention to what film scholar Richard Dyer would call Rosenblatt's "star text"—that is, an accumulating narrative of his performances, together with discussions of the cantor, both while performing and while not, which are publicly circulated and remediated.[13]

Thus, among the most well-known episodes in Rosenblatt's public biography concerns a performance he chose *not* to give: in 1918 Cleofonte Campanini, general director of the Chicago Opera, invited Rosenblatt to sing the lead role of Eléazar, a beleaguered Jewish goldsmith, in Jacques Fromenthal Halévy's *La Juive* for a fee of a thousand dollars per performance. Rosenblatt's refusal—despite assurances that he would not have to perform on the Sabbath or cut his beard—became the subject of national attention in both the mainstream and the Jewish press. The *New York Times*, for example, reprinted the Chicago Opera's letter to the president of Ohab Zedek, Rosenblatt's employer, in which the Opera stated that Rosenblatt had agreed to sing in *La Juive* only if the congregation would permit it.[14]

Rosenblatt took a proactive role in this public discussion, especially in the Jewish press, explaining the incident as both a confirmation of his piety and a validation of his musical talents by the non-Jewish world. The Jewish press, in turn, offered its own commentary on Rosenblatt's career. For example, Rosenblatt's struggle with the temptation to perform in the opera was limned provocatively in a cartoon that ran in the Yiddish satirical weekly *Der groyser kundes* (The big prankster) in May 1918. The cantor is shown, dressed in top hat and tails and gripping a prayer book, fleeing a scantily clad woman, labeled "Grand Opera," who beckons with outstretched arms: "Come, Yossele, a thousand dollars a night!" to which the cantor replies by praying: "Shma Yisroel [Hear, O Israel]!!!"[15]

Despite rejecting opera, Rosenblatt gave recitals in concert halls and, more provocatively, performed in vaudeville in the 1920s. He gave these performances to wipe out debts from bad investments he had made in a Yiddish newspaper and a *mikve* (ritual bath), both projects intended to enhance Orthodox Jewish life in New York. In Samuel Rosenblatt's biography of his father, the cantor's vaudeville appearances and concert tours are characterized not as compromising his commitment to khazones, but rather as extending his values as a pious Jew and a Jewish artist.[16] Indeed, the cantor's son championed his father's touring the vaudeville circuit as an opportunity to promote religious ideals:

His very conduct on the variety stage and the demands he made from the managers to satisfy his religious scruples were an ideal medium for teaching the non-Jewish masses of America something of the tenets of the Jewish faith while acquainting them with Jewish music. The announcements on the billboards that Josef Rosenblatt would not be heard on Friday evening

Figure 11.3. "Yosele khapt dem makhzer un loyft in shul arayn!" [Yossele grabs his prayer book and runs into the synagogue!]. Cartoon by Lola, published in the Yiddish humor weekly *Der groyser kundes* on May 3, 1918, after Rosenblatt refused to sing in the Chicago Opera.

or Saturday matinee, because he was observing his Sabbath, constituted a real *Kiddush Hashem*, a glorification of the Jewish religion. They evoked the profoundest respect and reverence in everybody.[17]

Samuel Rosenblatt claimed that press coverage of his father's vaudeville performances offered more opportunities to explain to the American public such Jewish religious practices as not pronouncing divine names in profane settings, keeping kosher, and not traveling on the Sabbath. These newspaper and magazine reports also provided the cantor with a public forum in which he could bracket his onstage performances of such selections as "The Last Rose of Summer" and the Yiddish theater song "Eyli, Eyli" within a public enactment of Jewish piety, reverence, and modesty. Rosenblatt similarly used the forum of popular culture to promote Jewish observance by turning a product endorsement into a valorization of piety. The publication of his arrangement of "Eyli, Eyli" in sheet music form was underwritten by the Loose-Wiles Biscuit Company, bakers of Sunshine Biscuits, and the back page of the sheet music featured the cantor's endorsement of their kosher products. "When I am traveling, they literally save my life," Rosenblatt explained, in Yiddish. "In all the Jewish homes that I visit throughout this country they serve Sunshine Kosher Cookies."[18]

This new use of popular culture for the promotion of a cantor's career—and, implicitly, the piety he embodies on behalf of his fellow Jews—was not without its critique, voiced not only by elites dismissive of popular culture themselves but also in works of popular culture, especially in the form of humor. Cartoons in the Yiddish and Anglo-Jewish press sometimes poked fun at Rosenblatt's celebrity status, variously likening him to a champion boxer or a stage idol.[19] At the same time, comic songs about cantors became a staple of American Jewish popular music, performed on the Yiddish stage, published in sheet music, and issued on recordings. Some of these songs address the phenomenon of the celebrity cantor directly, as in the case of "Hayntike khazonim" (The Cantors of Today), by Lipa Feingold, published in 1927. The song's lyrics play on a Yiddish proverb, *khazonim zaynen naronim*—cantors are fools:

> Men zogt bay undz yidn a vertl,
> Es gloybt zikh mir koym oyb s'iz vor.
> Men zogt, oyb du zest nor a khazn
> Dan iz er gevis shoyn a nar.
> Ikh ober gloyb s'iz nit emes,
> Vayl ikh hob a zakh vos bamerkt,
> Un ot vel ikh dos ibertsaygn
> Az di zakh iz gor poshet farkert.

> Vayl oyb es zol virklekh zayn emes,
> Dos yederer khazn iz a nar
> To zogt mir vi ken men zikh koyfn
> A hayzke dertsu nokh a kar?
> Un hobn in bank nokh mezumen
> Azoy az es khapt azsh a shrek
> Un oykh ken a yederer khazn
> Shraybn a fetinken tshek,
> Un arbetn arbet er oykh nit,
> Er zingt nor a mol dort derfar
> To gloybt mir dos er iz a khokhem
> Un er iz shoyn gor nit keyn nar.

> Zey hobn zikh ale fareynikt,
> Zey zaynen eyn gvaldike makht.
> Un der vos es zogt es iz narish
> Hot poshet a bilbl gemakht.
> Bay zey iz dos poshet a biznes
> Un yederer khazn iz star

Neyn fraynde, di zakh is nit emes,
Es gibt nit keyn khazn keyn nar

[Jews have a saying,
I'm not really sure that it's true.
They say that if you see a cantor,
It's certain that he is a fool.
But I don't believe that it's true,
Because I've noticed something,
And I will convince you
That the matter is quite the reverse.

Because if it were really true
That every cantor is a fool,
Then tell me, how he can buy
A house as well as a car?
And have money in the bank,
So much that it's frightening.
Every cantor can also
Write a nice, fat check.
As for work, he doesn't do that either,
He just sings sometimes.
So believe me, he's a smart fellow
And not a fool at all.

They've all united
And are a powerful force.
So whoever says it's foolish
Has simply said something libelous.
For them it's just a business;
Every cantor's a star.
So, my friend, it's not true—
No cantor is a fool.][20]

At least one cantor was in on the joke (or, perhaps, the joke was on him). The cover of the sheet music announces that "Hayntike khazonim" was "sung with great success by Cantor Mordechai Hershmann" and features a portrait of him in top hat and formal dress.

Cognizant of the challenges of performing as a cantor in popular culture venues, Rosenblatt strove to offer an image of the celebrity cantor as a dignified, rather than comic or venal, figure. His negotiation of this challenge is exemplified by what is doubtless the most famous of his performances in popular culture: a cameo appearance as himself in the 1927 feature *The Jazz Singer*.[21] At a strategic moment in the film, vaudevillian Jack Robin (played by Al Jolson, on whose life the film's plot is based) attends a recital by Rosenblatt, which stirs memories of Jack's father, Cantor Rabinowitz. This encounter foreshadows later scenes in the film, in which Jack's devotion to the theater reveals both its tension with and its indebtedness to khazones.

Rosenblatt's biography describes his participation in *The Jazz Singer* differently from what appears to have been the case, claiming that the cantor did not agree to appear in the film but only to record several "non-liturgical Jewish melodies" for its soundtrack. (In the film, he performs only one song, "Yohrzeit," and is seen singing it on a recital stage.) Moreover, the biography claims that Warner Bros. originally asked Rosenblatt to appear in the film as Cantor Rabinowitz (the role was eventually played by Warner Oland). Agents of the studio reportedly offered to pay Rosenblatt "$100,000 and appealed to him: 'Think of what it would mean for raising the prestige of the Jew and his faith if a man like you were to be held up as its representative to the non-Jewish public.'" Rosenblatt is said to have rejected the offer as well as a request to record sacred music for the sound track, including "Kol Nidre," which figures as a musical and dramatic motif in *The Jazz Singer*. "Under no circumstances," he is reported to have said, "would I permit that to pass my mouth anywhere except in a house of God."[22] (He did, of course, record Kol Nidre for both Victor and Columbia.) In this story of rejecting the proposals made by Warner Bros., Rosenblatt once more affirmed his commitment to khazones by discussing a role he chose *not* to perform—while, at the same time, identifying himself as that role's ideal performer.

Complicating the biography's claims of what Rosenblatt did or did not do in relation to *The Jazz Singer* is an article in *Moving Picture World*, which announced in late May 1927 that the cantor had agreed to appear in *The Jazz Singer*. Hailed as "the greatest Cantor in America, if not the world," Rosenblatt is reported to be participating in the film "as a singer, not as an actor. . . . Cantor Rosenblatt will appear as a singer and teacher of Cantors. He will take no part in the dramatic action of the production."[23]

This confusion about Rosenblatt's participation in *The Jazz Singer* may reflect not only the dynamics of negotiations with the cantor as the film was being produced but also some of the cantor's discomfort with his appearance in the film—especially in light of the cantor's own narrative, in which rejection of the opportunity to act in the film parallels his earlier rejection of a role in the opera. In fact, Rosenblatt's star text offers a distinct narrative in relation to *The Jazz Singer*, in which this commercial film venture validates his commitment to religiosity. In this narrative, Rosenblatt both refuses the role of the European cantor—who fails to find his way in the United States and, at the end of the film, dies as an honored but defeated figure—and enacts the role of the successful American cantor, who is able to stir the conscience of the wayward Jack Robin. Moreover, Rosenblatt does so from the stage, the same locus that tempts Jack to stray from his responsibility to the Jewish community. Thus, embedded within *The Jazz Singer* narrative in a counternarrative, in which the autobiographical exemplar is not Jolson, but Rosenblatt.

Rosenblatt subsequently performed khazones in two short films for Vitaphone and appeared as one of nine soloists in *The Voice of Israel*, a 1931 compilation of cantorial performances. In what would prove to be the final journey of his life, Rosenblatt traveled to Palestine in 1933 to appear in yet another film, *The Dream of My People*. This hour-long Zionist travelogue presents "the romance of the modern Jewish Renaissance" together with performances by the cantor, who is hailed in the opening credits as "The Greatest Omed [pulpit] Singer in His Last Song."[24]

Rosenblatt appears in *The Dream of My People* at selected moments to perform six solos. The first comes at the opening; the cantor, dressed in top hat and a morning coat, stands on Mount Zion, overlooking Jerusalem. As the camera pans the landscape, Rosenblatt is heard singing a selection of khazones, prerecorded with organ accompaniment. He then reappears at different sacred sites, including Jerusalem's Wailing Wall and Rachel's Tomb, singing a different selection from his repertoire at each location.

Figure 11.4. Rosenblatt sings at the Wailing Wall in Jerusalem, a scene from the 1933 film *Dream of My People*. Courtesy of the Library at the Herbert D. Katz Center for Advanced Judaic Studies, University of Pennsylvania.

During filming, Rosenblatt died suddenly of a heart attack while at the Dead Sea. News of his death is incorporated into the film's penultimate sequence. After Rosenblatt sings the Yiddish Zionist song "Aheym, aheym," the narrator abruptly intones, "Saw the land and died," as a collage of notices of Rosenblatt's death appears on screen, followed by footage of the crowds attending his funeral in Jerusalem. The film then concludes with a sequence on Tel Aviv, the "city of youth and gaiety."

As in *The Jazz Singer*, Rosenblatt is positioned in *The Dream of My People* at the juncture of two contrasting narratives, juxtaposing the cantor's star text against another Jewish trajectory. In the film's tourist narrative of Palestine, the cantor seems the embodiment of the diaspora Jew, who has come to venerate the old and admire the new, but who is ultimately unable to disencumber himself from a traditional, exilic sensibility and engage with modern political Zionism. Thus, after his interment, the tour proceeds to Tel Aviv, the Jewish "city of the future." At the same time, *The Dream of My People* offers a narrative that centers on the sacred, more so than on the secular, and on Rosenblatt, rather than on Palestine, in which the cantor figures as a modern-day Moses, a venerated Jewish leader who comes to see the "promised land" and then to die. Read this way, the film—another problematic commercial venture of Rosenblatt's, which, like his sound recordings and stage appearances, tested the traditional protocols of khazones—becomes a vehicle that successfully relates the final chapter of the cantor's life as the culmination of a sacred journey. Samuel Rosenblatt's biography of his father confirms this second narrative, explaining that the cantor had long wished that "his last pulpit might be in the Land of Israel."[25]

Notwithstanding its complex ambiguities, Rosenblatt's star text has been invoked to promote other cantors—and other commodities—in the Jewish marketplace, both during his lifetime and after his death. Cantor Charles Bloch's 1923 recording *Gems of the Synagogue* includes a "biographical sketch of the artist," which explains that the early musical talents of this New York City native brought him to Rosenblatt's attention. "After hearing [Bloch], Cantor Rosenblatt exclaimed, 'Er vet shoin zain a chazen' [he will surely be a cantor]." The sketch also notes that Bloch studied violin "at a conservatory and even played in concerts, but singing began to take up so much of his time that he was soon compelled to relegate the violin to a closet shelf." Bloch, we also learn, graduated from college and "studied and trained for the Opera"—yet despite these other possibilities, the reader is assured, "his first love has always been the heart-stirring music of the Synagogue."[26] In Bloch's star text, he not only is foreordained by Rosenblatt to be a cantor but also follows Rosenblatt's narrative by demonstrably resisting the lure of secular music making, while also evincing his command of it.

Rosenblatt's career entails a provocative conjoining of piety and entrepreneurship. His efforts to use new media and new cultural practices of public relations to promote his artistry and, moreover, his life story as devotional exemplars were not always successful. These efforts engendered considerable critique and parody and were sometimes exploited in the Jewish marketplace, especially after his death, for other purposes. Thus, in 1947 the *Jewish Daily Forward* ran an advertisement featuring a portrait and capsule biography of Rosenblatt; the ad's copy begins, "When Yossele Rosenblatt used to pray, Jews would happily pay the price. When it comes to enjoying the good things in life, people will always gladly pay the price for the best. This explains why so many housewives are ready to pay a few more cents for the rich quality and flavor of Yuban coffee."[27] As a case study in the interrelation of Orthodox Judaism and American capitalism, Rosenblatt's life and work suggest that, even as many Jews spoke of venal America as inimical to traditional religiosity, the possibilities for allying piety with the marketplace were being tested. In the course of these explorations, American Jews forged a new religious culture, characterized by an embrace of new media, celebrity culture, and entrepreneurial innovation.

NOTES

1. For a more extended discussion of the role of recordings and other media in the American cantorate, extending through the turn of the twenty-first century, see Jeffrey Shandler, *Jews, God, and Videotape: Religion and Media in America* (New York: New York University Press, 2009), ch. 1.

2. Details of Rosenblatt's childhood appear in Samuel Rosenblatt, *Yossele Rosenblatt: The Story of His Life as Told by His Son* (New York: Farrar, Straus, and Young, 1954), 3–57.

3. Ibid., 284, 293, 295.

4. Jonathan Sarna, trans. and ed., *People Walk on Their Heads: Moses Weinberger's Jews and Judaism in New York* (New York: Holmes and Meier, 1982), 13.

5. Annie Polland, *Landmark of the Spirit: The Eldridge Street Synagogue* (New Haven, CT: Yale University Press, 2009), 52–53.

6. Ibid., 55–56.

7. Ibid., 57.

8. Ibid., 62.

9. Discographies of Rosenblatt's recordings appear in Rosenblatt, *Yossele Rosenblatt*, 369–372, and Richard K. Spottswood, *Eastern Europe*, vol. 3 of *Ethnic Music on Records: A Discography of Ethnic Records Produced in the United States, 1893 to 1942*, (Urbana: University of Illinois Press, 1990), 1472–1480.

10. Pinkhas Minkovski, *Moderne liturgye in undzere sinagogen in Rusland* [Modern liturgy in our synagogues in Russia] (Odessa: Druk fun Kh. N. Byalik un Sh. Burishkin, 1910), 1ff., my translation; see also Mark Slobin, *Chosen Voices: The Story of the American Cantorate* (Urbana: University of Illinois Press, 2002), 60.

11. On the nature of early recordings, see, for example, Timothy Day, *A Century of Recorded Music: Listening to Musical History* (New Haven, CT: Yale University Press, 2000); David J. Steffen, *From Edison to Marconi: The First Thirty Years of Recorded Music* (Jefferson, NC: McFarland, 2005).

12. R. Murray Schafer, *The Soundscape: Our Sonic Environment and the Tuning of the World* (1977; rpt. Rochester, VT: Destiny Books, 1994), 91.

13. See Richard Dyer, *Stars* (London: British Film Institute, 1979).

14. "Rabbi [*sic*] Rejects $1,000 Fee to Sing in Opera," *New York Times*, April 15, 1918, 13.

15. Lola [Leon Israel], "Yosele khapt dem makhzer un loyft in shul arayn!" [Yossele grabs his prayerbook and runs into the synagogue!], cartoon, *Der groyser kundes*, May 3, 1918, 7.

16. See also Morris Clark, "'Inner Voice' Told Cantor Rosenblatt to Shun Opera Stage," *Musical America* 28, no. 8 (June 22, 1918): 33–34, a source Samuel Rosenblatt cites in his biography of his father.

17. Rosenblatt, *Yossele Rosenblatt*, 261–262.

18. "Eli, Eli, as Arranged and Sung by Cantor Josef Rosenblatt," sheet music (n.p.: Loose-Wiles Biscuit Company, n.d.).

19. See Rosenblatt, *Yossele Rosenblatt*, plates between 182 and 183.

20. Lipa Feingold, words and music, "Hayntike khazonim: humoresk / The Cantors of Today," sheet music (Brooklyn: Feingold, 1927); my translation.

21. *The Jazz Singer*, directed by Alan Crosland (Los Angeles: Warner Brothers, 1927).

22. Rosenblatt, *Yossele Rosenblatt*, 289–290.

23. "Cantor Rosenblatt's Voice for 'The Jazz Singer,' via Vitaphone," *Moving Picture World* 86, no. 4 (May 28, 1927), 273.

24. The two short films for Vitaphone are *Omar Rabbi Elosar* and *Hallelujah. The Voice of Israel*, produced by Joseph Seider (New York: Judea Films, 1931); *The Dream of My People*, directed by A. J. Bloome (New York: Palestine-American Film, 1934).

25. Rosenblatt, *Yossele Rosenblatt*, 337.

26. Cantor Charles B. Bloch, *Gems from the Synagogue*, sound recording (New York: Standard Phono, 1945), inside album cover.

27. "When Yossele Rosenblatt used to pray . . ." advertisement, *Jewish Daily Forward*, September 8, 1947, 3.

CHAPTER 12

How Matzah Became Square

MANISCHEWITZ AND THE DEVᵀLOPMENT OF MACHINE-MADE MATZAH IN THE UNITED STATES

Jonathan D. Sarna

The History of Matzah calls to mind the monumental composition by artist Larry Rivers, recounting thousands of years of Jewish history laid out against the background of the Passover matzah. To Rivers, the unleavened bread eaten on Passover seemed like the perfect canvas for his *Story of the Jews*. Matzah to him was not an object of Jewish history but rather a metaphor for it.[1]

Rivers might have been surprised to learn that matzah itself possesses a fascinating history, particularly in the modern era when, like the Jewish people, it underwent monumental changes brought about by new inventions, new visions, and migration to new lands. These changes transformed the character and manufacturing of matzah, as well as its shape, texture, and taste. They also set off a fierce and revealing debate among Europe's greatest rabbis that, in some respects, remains unresolved to this day.

This essay focuses on a little-known American chapter in the long history of matzah. It recounts the role of the B. Manischewitz Company in transforming both the process of matzah making and the character of matzah, and it points to the role played by rabbis and advertisers in legitimating this transformation. At a deeper level, it suggests that even "timeless rituals" are shaped by history's currents. The transformation of matzah, we shall see, reveals much about transformations within Judaism itself.

THE MANISCHEWITZES COME TO AMERICA

Sometime about 1886 Behr Manischewitz (he sometimes spelled it Ber and was often known as Dov Behr) emigrated to Cincinnati, Ohio, from the city of

Memel, then under Prussian rule.[2] Memel was a relatively new Jewish community—Jews had only received permission to settle there in the early nineteenth
century—and most Memel Jews, including the Manischewitzes, were immigrants from Russia and Poland; Behr himself was born in Salant.[3] During Behr
Manischewitz's youth, Memel served as the home of Rabbi Israel Salanter (who
lived there from 1860 to 1879), and according to family tradition, Behr was one
of his "best-loved pupils . . . and was so highly regarded for his learning and
devotion that the Gaon of Salant had designated Rabbi Dov Ber as his personal
Shochet."[4] Various elements of Manischewitz's later life reflected the Mussar
movement's influence.

We do not know precisely why Behr, his wife, Nesha Rose (sometimes
known as "Natalie"), and their three very young children left Memel for the
United States. One source claims that Cincinnati Jews from Salant, Lithuania,
compatriots of Behr's father, Yechiel Michael Manischewitz, needed a *shohet*,
knew that Behr was a certified and respected kosher slaughterer, and paid to
bring him and his family over to serve them. Rabbi Elias Hillkowitz from Salant
was a rabbi in Cincinnati at that time, and was a relative of Manischewitz, so
this is plausible. Another possibility is that Behr Manischewitz emigrated to
the United States in response to the 1886 Prussian expulsion of "Russians" (i.e.,
Jews) from Memel, which, in turn, came in reprisal for Russia's expulsion of
Prussians from Kovno.[5]

THE CHANGING WORLD OF MATZAH

Whatever the case, in 1888, after several years as a *shohet ubodek* and part-time
peddler, Manischewitz opened a matzah factory in Cincinnati. This was a common profession for Jewish immigrants, especially those trained in *shehitah*, for
matzah, too, was a Jewish food strictly regulated by Jewish law and requiring
supervision. Moreover, demand for matzah was rising steadily in the United
States, keeping pace with the growth of America's Jewish population, and the
industry as a whole was in the midst of a great transformation. Through the
mid-nineteenth century, most matzah had been baked by synagogues, which
either maintained special ovens of their own for this purpose or (as happened
in New York) contracted with commercial bakers whom they supervised. With
the collapse of the synagogue community and the subsequent proliferation of
synagogues in all major American Jewish communities, the now functionally
delimited synagogues spun off many of their old communal functions (including responsibility for communal welfare, the *mikvah*, and kosher meat), and it
was at this time, at midcentury, that independent matzah bakers developed.[6]

The *kashrut* of the matzah made by these new independent bakers became
a matter of considerable Jewish debate. In Cincinnati, in 1862, for example,
Orthodox Jews published a public notice warning that a matzah baker named

Mr. Simon "in no wise conducts himself in accordance with the requirements of Jewish law," The notice declared his matzah "chometz . . . no better than any other bread bought of any baker." New York's *Jewish Messenger* likewise expressed concern in 1863 over the lack of rabbinic supervision over private matzah bakers. Jews who came from stringent European backgrounds and were used to matzah made from wheat that had been continually "watched" since harvesting to prevent contact with water found the state of American-made matzah particularly disturbing. New York's Rabbi Moses Weinberger, a native of Hungary, deplored the fact that as late as the 1880s "most New York Jews used matsos made from ordinary market-quality flour," rather than "watched flour."[7] Given this background, it is easy to understand why an Orthodox Jew like Behr Manischewitz thought to enter the matzah business himself (so eventually did Rabbi Weinberger). Since demand was growing and local Lithuanian Jews trusted him to maintain the highest standards of kashrut, the business seemed to have substantial upside potential.

At the time that Manischewitz entered the matzah business, the industry was in a state of considerable flux. Much of the world's matzah was still made totally by hand. The process, which according to the later authorities must be completed within eighteen minutes, had been refined over many centuries and was characterized by a careful division of labor that is still found in handmade *shmurah matzah* bakeries today.[8] One person, usually an apprentice, measured out the flour. Another worker poured cold water into the batter. Then the mixture underwent a multistage process of kneading and rolling, usually performed by women. Next, the dough was scored or perforated, placed on a rolling pin or a long pole, baked (usually by a man) in a very hot oven, and sent off to be packed. Any dough not mixed, baked, and out of the oven within eighteen minutes was, of course, discarded. All the rolling pins and poles were then carefully sanded and wiped. The paper on the tables was changed. The workers washed their hands to get rid of any remaining dough. And the process started all over again. This is roughly how traditional matzah baking worked and still works. By Manischewitz's day it had become a highly gendered process—men and women had different roles—and it was divided into a series of well-defined sequential steps.[9]

In the nineteenth century, with the rise of industrialization, processes like this began to be mechanized, and in 1838 an Alsatian Jew named Isaac Singer produced the first-known machine for rolling matzah dough. Although this is often called a matzah-making machine, the machine actually covered only one part of the process—rolling—not the equally critical and very labor-intensive process of kneading the dough. Singer's machine, and variants of it, won approval from various rabbis and quickly spread into France, Germany, England, Hungary, and the United States (where it was discussed in Jewish newspapers as early as 1850).[10] The machine changed and shortened the process

of matzah baking, and also deprived many poor women of their meager livelihoods. At the same time, as machines are wont to do, it increased the supply of
matzah, which was critical given the rapid growth of the world Jewish population in the nineteenth century, and it also led to a reduction in the price of
matzah, since fewer hands were now needed to produce it.[11]

The Controversy over Machine-Made Matzah in Europe

Subsequently, the matzah machine became embroiled in a sharp and very
significant halachic controversy. The dispute was initiated in 1859 with the
publication of *Moda'ah le-Beit Yisrael* (Announcement to the House of Israel)
by Rabbi Solomon Kluger of Brody, and within the next few decades some eighteen other leading rabbis, particularly rabbis from Galicia as well as Hasidic
rabbis, came out in opposition to the machine; some of them went so far as to
declare machine-made matzah to be no better than *hametz*. Some two dozen
other rabbis, many of them from Lithuania, central and western Europe, and
Jerusalem strongly disagreed. Led by the influential *posek* Joseph Saul Nathanson, who published a work titled *Bittul Moda'ah*, annulling the announcement,
they vigorously defended the matzah machine; some insisted that machine-
made matzah was actually more kosher than the handmade kind, because there
was less possibility of human error.[12]

The arguments on both sides of the question were complex, and this is not
the place to rehearse them. But it is worth noting that in addition to strictly
halachic arguments around issues such as whether the machine fulfills the
requirement of *kavannah* (intentionality) in baking matzah, there were also
other issues involved in the debate. For example, there were technological arguments: is the machine fully reliable in preventing hametz from entering the
process? There were also social justice arguments—is it better to sustain traditional, expensive handmade matzah that provides work for poor people, or is it
better to encourage cheaper machine-made matzah that even poor people can
afford? Finally, and one suspects most important, the machine kindled arguments concerning modernity. Supporters of machine-made matzah promoted
the idea that modern technology could strengthen traditional Judaism; indeed,
some rabbis optimistically argued that technology could produce better and
more kosher matzahs than Jews had ever enjoyed before, at least since the
days of the Second Temple. Meanwhile, opponents of the machine feared that
machine-made matzah, like so many other innovations in matters of religious
tradition, would become a dangerous instrument of modernity, leading inevitably to assimilation, Reform, and apostasy. The Gerrer Rebbe, for example,
argued that supporters of the matzah machine sought as their long-term aim to
uproot the entire Torah. A later opponent insisted that the invention, from the
beginning, was intended to introduce reforms into the religion of Israel.[13] These

vituperative arguments were by no means settled by the time Manischewitz became involved in the matzah business. To the contrary, the Jewish world of his day was divided between those who accepted matzah made with the assistance of a machine and those who did not.

WHAT MANISCHEWITZ DID

Before Manischewitz himself publicly took a stand on this divisive issue, he faced a more prosaic problem: competition in his own back yard. In the early 1890s a dispute developed between his friend and relative, Rabbi Hillkowitz, and a new rabbi in town—almost certainly Rabbi Simon ("Rashi") Finkelstein, the father of Rabbi Louis Finkelstein, longtime chancellor of the Jewish Theological Seminary. As a result of this dispute, which seems to have had more to do with local power than with *halachah*, Finkelstein himself entered the matzah business against Manischewitz. Behr Manischewitz wrote back to his father in Salant, seeking help from that community's rabbi in the dispute. He feared that Finkelstein's competition would deprive him of his livelihood and believed that his competitor was impermissibly intruding into his domain (*masig g'vul*). But in the end all he received in return was a fatherly *mussar shmooze*. "Make peace," Yechiel Michael wrote his son, and he warned, in the best tradition of the then recently deceased Rabbi Israel Salanter, against any concern over honor and any involvement in quarrels and controversies "even if it will seem to you that the quarrel is for the sake of Heaven."[14] The advice was good, for Cincinnati was not like Memel or Salant, and competitors could not have been shut down even if the rabbis had wanted to do so. The advice also proved propitious, since in the course of time the Manischewitzes and the Finkelsteins became related by marriage. The only real way for Manischewitz to achieve success in America's capitalist economy, Behr came to understand, was by gaining a competitive edge—that is (1) by cutting the production costs of his matzah so that his profit margin would be higher, or (2) by making a better matzah, one that was superior in quality and therefore more desirable, or (3) by improving the image of his matzah so that people considered it superior to the competition and purchased it. Manischewitz managed to follow all three of these roads to success, and the rabbis of the Holy Land played a part in his strategy.

Most important, Manischewitz introduced a series of improvements and inventions that revolutionized the process of matzah baking the world over. Continuing a trend that Singer's matzah machine had begun and that would become very familiar in the twentieth century, he yoked modern technology to the service of religion. In 1899 he purchased the matzah bakery of Moses Bing in Cincinnati and announced "improvements on machinery...of such a nature as positively to surpass anything of its kind in this country."[15] By 1903 he was using at least three different machines as part of the matzah-making process:

one that partially kneaded the dough, one that rolled it, and one that stretched the dough, perforated it, and cut it. A separate electric fan kept the premises cool.[16] Later he introduced a gas-fired matzah baking oven (which allowed for better and more even distribution and control of heat) and an enormously important (and patented) "traveling-carrier bake-oven," a conveyor belt system that made it possible to automate the whole process of matzah baking: the dough was placed on one end and it slowly moved through the oven chambers emerging as evenly baked, identically shaped matzah on the other end. Jacob Uriah Manischewitz, who succeeded his father as president of the Manischewitz Company upon the former's untimely passing in 1914, is credited with more than fifty patents, including an electric eye that automatically counted the number of matzos in a box at a rate of six hundred a minute, as well as innovations in packaging and a special "matsos machine," introduced in 1920, which could produce 1.25 million matzahs every day and which he described, in 1938, as "the largest and most expensive single piece of machinery in any bakery in the world."[17] Thanks to all of these innovations, Manischewitz could produce more matzah, more cheaply, with less breakage, and with a much more regular and pleasing appearance than had ever before been possible.

The result was nothing less than a revolution in the matzah business, characterized by three major transformations: First, where before most matzah had been round, irregular, or oval-shaped, now, largely because of the demands of technology and packaging, it became square—in 1912, indeed, the matzot were specifically advertised as "Manischewitz's Square Matzoths." The issue of square matzah had been debated in the nineteenth century by Kluger and Nathanson, but most matzah, even that produced with the help of a rolling machine, remained round.[18] Matzah produced by Manischewitz and its mechanized competitors, by contrast, was invariably square (though in 1942, "special V-shaped matzoth were baked as part of the 'V for Victory' movement," during World War II).[19] Second, where before each matzah was unique and distinctive in terms of shape, texture, and overall appearance—no two were identical as is true of *shmurah matzah* to this day—now, every matzah in the box came out looking, feeling, and tasting the same. Matzah thus underwent the same processes of rationalization, standardization, and mechanization that we associate with the American management revolution wrought by Frederick Winslow Taylor.[20] Manischewitz matzah, in short, became a distinctive brand of matzah, with all that that implied. Finally, where before matzah was a quintessentially local product, produced on an as-needed basis in every Jewish community and not shipped vast distances for fear of breakage, now it became a national and then an international product—just like soap and cereal. In time, along with smaller matzah brands such as Horowitz-Margareten, Goodman, and Streits, Manischewitz would extend its market share to take maximum advantage of its ability to mass-produce matzah, and local matzah bakers who could not compete would go out of business. On a much larger scale, Cincinnati's Proctor & Gamble was doing the same thing at roughly the same time to the production of soap and detergent.

MARKETING CHALLENGES AND SOLUTIONS

But there is also a critical difference, extremely important for the student of religion, since in the case of matzah two very significant challenges had to be met before Manischewitz could take full advantage of these technological and business innovations and translate them into commercial success. First, the company needed to confront popular resistance to changing a long-familiar Passover ritual product. Matzah, after all, reflects and evokes a sense of tradition; it is, according to the Haggadah, "the bread of affliction that our fathers ate in the land of Egypt." This was hard to reconcile with Manischewitz's new-fangled machine-made square matzah, and the company had therefore to find some way to make its new matzah seem not only superior but also traditional and religiously authentic. Second, the company needed to confront what we have seen to be significant rabbinic resistance to machine-made matzah. Given the volatility of the issue, and the emotional energy invested in it by both sides of the controversy, Manischewitz had every reason to be nervous about the reception that the matzot made by its new machine would receive. It must have known that it would need powerful rabbinic endorsement for its matzot to succeed in the marketplace.[21]

Manischewitz confronted the first issue—how to make its matzot seem superior and authentic—through advertising. In Anglo-Jewish newspapers, the company described its matzot as being in all ways superior to the competition: they were produced in what the company called "a temple of kashruth, a palace of cleanliness, a gigantic structure of steel and glass, overflowing with light, air and sunshine."[22] In other words, they met the highest American food and health standards; they were, in their own way, therapeutic. Indeed, Manischewitz advertised at one point that "No human hand touches these matsas in their manufacture" as if this fact, rather than the production of matzot by hand, reflected Judaism's highest precept![23] By appealing to modern American consumer values to sell traditional food products, the company implied that purchasers of Manischewitz matzah could subscribe to the highest values of both Judaism and America.

When it advertised in Hebrew and Yiddish to more Orthodox customers, Manischewitz switched gears and emphasized its high standard of kashrut ("the most kosher matzot in the world"). In 1920 it published an "open letter" to the Jewish public in the *Yidishe Tageblat*, in which it touted its incomparable reputation for kashrut and announced technical innovations designed to make the world's best matzah even better. It also published regular ads and placed articles in the rabbinic journal *HaPardes* touting the company's "scrupulousness" in all aspects of the matzah-making process, as well as its utter reliability, attested to by the Agudath Harabbanim and Rabbi Pardes himself.[24]

In the early years, Manischewitz marketed its matzah as an elite product. It called them "fine matzos" and sold them in a cigar-type box that protected the contents and projected an aura of affluence. This, of course, was a clever attempt to give Manischewitz's square matzahs extra cachet. The company understood that if its matzah became the preferred matzah of rich and powerful Jews, other Jews would soon follow suit. Apparently the strategy worked, for at one point in the 1920s the company claimed that it delivered matzah "to 80 per cent of the Jewish population of America and Canada."[25]

Rabbinic Endorsements

As important as its advertising was, Manischewitz also understood that it needed powerful rabbinic endorsements. Without them it could not hope to legitimate its machine-made square matzah, much less win over customers used to eating handmade, round matzah on Passover. Vituperative controversies over machine-made matzah such as those that rocked Europe in the nineteenth century and divided Jerusalem in 1908–1909 were to be avoided at all costs.[26]

The company began with two great advantages peculiar to America. First, the majority of east European immigrants came to the United States from areas (such as Lithuania) where machine-made matzah had already won rabbinic sanction, and the immigrants tended in any case to favor accommodations to modernity; if not they would never have ventured to the United States in the first place. Hasidim comprised the strongest elements opposed to machine-made matzah, both in Europe and in Palestine, but in America their numbers prior to World War II were comparatively small and their leadership pitifully weak. American soil was described by one writer in 1918 as being "rather unfavorable for the seed of the Hasidic cult," and America's four Hasidic rebbes at that time had almost no Hasidic followers. Even had Hasidim decided to wage war against machine-made matzah in America, they would not have posed much of a threat.[27]

Second, even several rabbis opposed to machine-made matzah in Europe wrote early in the twentieth century to support its production in the United States. They understood that in the absence of machine-made matzah, the fast-growing American Jewish community might not have had sufficient matzah for its requirements, and they argued that in America, unlike in eastern Europe, there was no tradition of handmade matzah that needed to be upheld. Thus, even in matters of Jewish law there was a sense at that time that "America is different."[28]

Nevertheless, Manischewitz spared no effort to ensure that rabbis endorsed its matzah as appropriate even for the most religiously punctilious. As early as 1903 it announced that its bakery was open to all rabbis "seeking truth and righteousness," and through the years many apparently took the firm up on the offer.[29] For its fiftieth anniversary, in 1938 the company published a list of 124 "leading figures of the generation," most of them renowned rabbis (some by then deceased), who, it stated, had visited the bakery and attested to its high level of kashrut. The list was headed by Rabbi Abraham I. Kook, chief rabbi of Eretz Israel, and it included Rabbi Meir Shapiro of Lublin, Rabbi Meier Hildesheimer of Berlin, and thirty-two other European rabbis, largely from Poland and Lithuania, along with nine rabbis from the land of Israel, the chief rabbi of Cairo, the leaders of the Agudath Harabbanim in the United States, and dozens of other American rabbis from cities across the land.[30] A pamphlet entitled *Kashrut at Manischewitz* (1955) offered testimonials from some of these luminaries. According to its information, Rabbi Shapiro, the founder of Yeshivath Hachmei Lublin and of the Daf Yomi "ate only Manischewitz Matzos throughout the year," since he "was never sure of the strict kashruth of bread."[31] Most rabbis did not go that far, but especially in the United States the leading rabbis did agree to link their names to Manischewitz, thereby endowing its matzah with special prestige. At an annual ceremony in the weeks prior to Passover, rabbis gathered to tour the Manischewitz plant, to witness the baking of machine-made *shmurah matzah* prepared especially for the most fervent of Jews, and to enjoy a scrumptious banquet, complete with learned lectures from leaders of the Agudath Harabbanim. The setting, along with the prestigious rabbinical names associated with it, generated substantial publicity in Orthodox circles, buttressing Manischewitz's claim to be the most kosher matzah of them all.[32]

TIES TO ZION

In its fiftieth anniversary publication, published in *HaPardes*, Manischewitz paid special attention to the ties that it had forged with the Land of Israel. Letters in Hebrew from Jerusalem's Chief Rabbi, Zvi Pesach Frank, and the head of Yeshivat Merkaz HaRav, Jacob M. Charlap, appeared on facing pages near the front of the booklet, second in prominence only to the letter from the American Agudath Harabbanim. The Jerusalem rabbis, known supporters of machine-made matzah, extolled the kashrut and quality of Manischewitz's matzah, as well as the great love of Zion and openhanded generosity of Hirsch Manischewitz, Behr Manischewitz's son and the firm's vice president. Learned articles in the publication were likewise composed in Eretz Israel, by rabbis who had ties with Manischewitz. Indeed, the whole publication bespoke the firm's well-known love of Zion, and the respect that the leading religious figures in Zion had for Manischewitz.[33]

This relationship dated all the way back to the company's founder, who established close ties to Jerusalem early in the twentieth century. Behr Manischewitz even sent his sons, Max and Hirsch, to study there: Hirsch began his studies in 1901, when he was only ten years old, and remained in Eretz Israel for thirteen years studying successively at Yeshivat Etz Chaim (1901–1907), Torath Chaim (1908–1910), and Meah Shearim (1910–1914). Max, who was two years older, attended public school in Cincinnati and only subsequently sailed off to study in Palestine; he too studied for the rabbinate at Yeshivat Etz Chaim. Both brothers married daughters of what were later described as "well-known families in Jerusalem." Max married Edith Cohen in 1907 and Hirsch married Sarah Wolfe in 1910. Subsequently, the Manischewitzes took great pride in being "interrelated with the nicest families in the Holy City." Hirsch Manischewitz also took great pride in the prestigious rabbis with whom he had studied in Jerusalem. Twenty-five years later, his official biography in *Who's Who in American Jewry* still recorded the names of those rabbis, several of whom, notably Isaac Blazer, were well-known figures in the Mussar movement.[34]

Beyond these educational and familial ties, the Manischewitz family also made significant charitable donations to Eretz Israel. Hirsch Manischewitz, while studying in Jerusalem, organized a free loan society, a sick benefit foundation, and a relief fund for the poor; he also served on the board of the Kollel Amerika.[35] Upon the death of the family patriarch, Behr Manischewitz, in 1914, his sons established a small Jerusalem yeshiva in their father's name, known as the Rabbi Behr Manischewitz Yeshiva. Through the years, Hirsch Manischewitz took a special interest in this yeshiva and the Manischewitz Company made modest annual donations to it, ranging from $1,250 to $3,300. The yeshiva featured very prominently in the firm's fiftieth anniversary publication booklet.[36]

The fact that the Jerusalem yeshiva actually carried the Manischewitz name is somewhat curious. None of the best-known yeshivot in Eretz Israel at that time, including those where Hirsch Manischewitz himself had studied, carried the last name of a donor family, and one wonders why Manischewitz Yeshiva was different. Could not the yeshiva simply have been called Yeshivas Rabbi Dov Behr? In 1948, as part of a court case to which we shall return, a revealing reason was supplied. "Yeshiva graduates," the Manischewitz Company told the court, "teach as rabbis in Palestine, Europe and South America. They have the name Manischewitz associated with them and are helping to overcome the impression of Orthodox European Jews that American machine-made matzos are not kosher."[37]

The Manischewitz Yeshiva, in other words, formed part of a larger strategy aimed at utilizing the prestige of rabbis from Eretz Israel to legitimate the machine-made square matzot that Manischewitz produced and to help promote

them around the world. The rabbis who taught at Manischewitz Yeshiva sanc
tioned the use of machine-made matzah on Passover, and Manischewitz also
supplied the matzah that was actually served at the yeshiva on Passover. Indeed,
at least in the eyes of the company, the graduates of the yeshiva formed the vanguard of a worldwide matzah empire that, it hoped, would spread machine-made
Manischewitz matzah beyond the borders of North America to Jews throughout
the diaspora and in Palestine. As opposed to some of its other charity, which
was handled privately, Manischewitz in this case gave substantial publicity to
its association with Manischewitz Yeshiva. It viewed the yeshiva students it supported as future missionaries for its cause, as well as living symbols of those
Jewish values—piety, charity, and commitment to learning that would make its
matzah trusted and welcome in Jewish homes everywhere.[38]

Just after World War I, the Manischewitzes established one further link
between themselves and the rabbis of Eretz Israel. They brought over from Jerusalem Rabbi Mendel M. Hochstein, the son of one of Hirsch Manischewitz's old
teachers, and they made him the kashrut supervisor (head *mashgiah*) at their
bakery in Cincinnati; he also served as the rabbi of Congregation Anshe Sholom. Later, when the company moved to New Jersey, Rabbi Hochstein moved
with them, serving in addition as the rabbi of Brooklyn's aptly named Kehilath
Bnai Eretz Yisrael. In its advertising, Manischewitz regularly mentioned that
Rabbi Hochstein had trained and lived in Jerusalem. It knew that scrupulous
Jews in Europe would trust a Jerusalem mashgiah over an American one.
Indeed, when Rabbi Meir Dan Plotzki of Ostrova, on a visit to America, pronounced Manischewitz matzah to be thoroughly reliable ("there is none more
faithful to be found"), he revealingly singled out for praise "the constant super-
vision of one of the sages of Jerusalem"—Rabbi Hochstein.[39]

In short, a complex, reciprocal, and mutually beneficial relationship developed between Manischewitz and the rabbis of the Holy Land: each provided
the other with what they needed. Manischewitz provided material support
to Jerusalem charities and the Manischewitz Yeshiva, provided a position for
Rabbi Hochstein and treated Jerusalem's rabbis with special respect and status,
implying without ever saying so that they were the central rabbinic figures in
the Jewish world. In return, the rabbis provided them with public recognition,
the kinds of recommendations that they needed to expand abroad, and rabbinic approbation for their machine-made matzah. For years, the firm advertised that Rav Kook and later "the Chief Rabbinate of Israel" recognized that it
offered "the greatest possible assurance of kashruth." It also became the only
matzah in the world to receive certification from the Agudath Harabbanim
during the interwar years. Its "association with the Yeshiva in Palestine," it
admitted, "was of some aid in obtaining th[is] annual 'hechsher.'" As a result
of all of this, Manischewitz did for some time gain a reputation in Europe
as being the most kosher matzah of all. My own maternal grandmother in

London, scion of a distinguished Hasidic line, preferred Manischewitz matzah for this very reason and selected it over local English brands. This is particularly remarkable when one remembers America's traditional reputation among Orthodox Jews as being lax in matters of religion, a *treifene medinah*.[40]

The benefits that accrued to the Manischewitz Company from its contributions to Eretz Israel do not detract from the evident altruistic, philanthropic, and Zionist impulses of the Manischewitz family. Their interest in *tzedaka*, their love of Israel, and their support for religious Zionism—all are beyond question. Hirsch Manischewitz devoted the better part of his public activities to charitable Orthodox causes, mostly but not exclusively related to Eretz Israel. His brother, Max Manischewitz, sought to promote the industrial development of the *yishuv*; and in the 1920s proposed ambitious plans to open matzah, noodle, and macaroni factories in Jerusalem, as well as a kosher hotel. Indeed, the official Manischewitz logo, a heartfelt one, proclaimed in Hebrew "Next Year in Jerusalem."[41] Manischewitz's philanthropic and religious activities, however, were never wholly separate from its business considerations, particularly since the firm's religious reliability played a significant part in its marketing. Indeed, the interrelationship of business, technology, philanthropy, and faith helped to determine the success of the Manischewitz Company. Its reputation and religious ties, coupled with its technological prowess, business acumen, and clever advertising, go far to explain how its square, machine-made matzah won rabbinic sanction and how over the course of the first half of the twentieth century, this kind of matzah became normative and ubiquitous.

MANISCHEWITZ VERSUS THE COMMISSIONER OF INTERNAL REVENUE

Much of what I have described here would not be known but for a 1948 case in the United States Tax Court. The case arose when the Internal Revenue Service challenged the right of the Manischewitz Company to deduct a payment made to Manischewitz Yeshiva as "an ordinary and necessary business expense." It could not otherwise have deducted these payments, since the Jerusalem yeshiva did not qualify as a charitable organization ("to which contributions by corporations are deductible") under the tax code in effect at that time. Manischewitz fought the tax collection agency's challenge, and in so doing made the case that its donations to the yeshiva bore a direct relationship to its business, having been made (as per the law) "with a reasonable expectation of a financial return commensurate with the amount of the donation." In the course of the company's deposition it frankly set forth some of the benefits that its philanthropy produced, including, as mentioned, that it helped "to overcome the impression . . . that American machine-made matzos are not kosher" and that it was "beneficial in publicizing" the company's product. "Payments for support of the Yeshiva," the company candidly concluded "have been made from combined religious, charitable, personal, and business motives." The court solemnly agreed. Although there can be little doubt that the contributions to the seminary were prompted by a complex of motives," the precedent-setting decision declared, the deduction was legal, given that there were "reasonably evident business ends to be served, and the intention to serve them appears adequately from the record."[42]

CONCLUSION

The episode that we have recounted here is interesting in its own right as an unusual case study in the interrelationship of business, technology, charity, and faith and also for what it reveals about how religious innovations like square-shaped, machine-made matzah transformed the industry, won rabbinic approbation, and as a result achieved widespread public acceptance. What is especially noteworthy here is the fact that Manischewitz used rabbinic figures in Jerusalem to achieve this goal; the company did not exert parallel efforts to win support from the rabbis of Behr Manischewitz's native Lithuania. Traditional religious and Zionist motivations, as well as familiar east European prejudices concerning American Judaism, may well be sufficient to explain this anomaly, but a larger theme may be reflected here as well. For Manischewitz's turn toward Zion reflected a much broader challenge to east European rabbinic hegemony posed in the late nineteenth century by the rise of the two new centers of Jewish life: the United States and Eretz Israel. The reciprocal relationship that worked to the mutual advantage of Manischewitz and the Jerusalem rabbis formed part of a larger pattern of relationships that, at once, proclaimed American Jewry's independence from the rabbinic "establishment" in Europe and its desire to play a significant role of its own in Jewish life. The establishment of the Kollel Amerika Tifereth Yerushalayim in 1896 reflects some of this same dynamic, and it may be more than coincidence that, as we have seen, Hirsch Manischewitz served for a time on its executive committee. For similar reasons, one suspects, American Orthodox rabbis preferred to publish their Hebrew books in Palestine, rather than in eastern Europe. Later, the Orthodox Jewish lay leader Harry Fischel carried this tradition forward, doing much to strengthen ties between Orthodox lay leaders in the United States and the rabbis of Eretz Israel.[43] The rabbis of the *yishuv*, of course, had their own reasons for wanting to shift the center of Jewish life away from eastern Europe, and they had every incentive to cooperate with American Jewry to this end, particularly when the latter proved so wonderfully generous and philanthropic. Cooperation to advance the sale of Manischewitz matzah, in other words, is just one episode in a much larger and yet-to-be-written history tracing the emergence of rabbinic authority in the new centers of Jewish life, in the United States and Israel, and the ties that bound these new centers together.

For now, though, we have seen that the lowly matzah turns out to have a history that sheds light on subjects of far-reaching importance. The B. Manischewitz Company no longer exists today as an independent entity—it is now part of a great conglomerate—but its achievement should not be forgotten. For in the final analysis, what has been recounted here is not just the story of how matzah became square and machine-made matzah became normative. It is also the story of how traditional Judaism *itself* became normative in America—a story that involves, as we have seen, technology, business, politics, philanthropy, ties to Israel, and, above all, an ongoing commitment to Jewish law and Jewish life.

NOTES

I am indebted to Adina Gluckman for her able research assistance; to Shulamith Berger and Laura Alpern for making available materials that I would not otherwise have seen; to Gary Zola, Fred Krome, Kevin Proffitt, and the staff of the American Jewish Archives for making research materials available to me; to Meir Hildesheimer and Yehoshua Liebermann for permitting me to read their article on the controversy surrounding machine-made matzot prior to its publication; to Alan Feld, Menachem Friedman, Yaakov Horowitz, Jenna W. Joselit, and Shaul Stampfer for helpful suggestions; and above all to Moshe Sherman for inviting me to deliver the Selmanowitz Lecture at Touro College, for patiently awaiting the final version, and for permitting its reprint here. A preliminary version of this paper appeared in Hebrew in *Gesher* 45 (Winter 2000): 41–49.

1. Norman L. Kleeblatt, *Larry Rivers' History of Matzah: The Story of the Jews*, with Anita Friedman (New York: Jewish Museum, 1984).

2. "Manischewitz, Jacob Uriah," *Who's Who in American Jewry* 3 (1938): liii, provides the date of 1885 as the year of emigration, but other sources refer to the "mid-eighties." On the Manishewitz family, see Laura Manishewitz Alpern, *Manishewitz: The Matzo Family* (New York: Ktav, 2008) and my introduction thereto.

3. Yosef Shulman, "Memel," *Yahadut Lita* (Tel Aviv, 1967), 3:281–283; see also 195.

4. Immanuel Etkes, *Rabbi Israel Salanter and the Mussar Movement: Seeking the Torah of Truth* (Philadelphia: Jewish Publication Society, 1993), 242–255; *Kashrut at Manischewitz* (New York: Manischewitz, 1955), 1; "Rabbi Dov Behr Manischewitz," http://www.manischewitz.com/108years.htm; the brief biography in *Yahadut Lita*, 195, mentions only that he "served" Rabbi Salanter and received from him ordination as a "*shohet u-bodek*." Alpern (*Manishewitz*, 35) claims that the family only adopted the name Manishewitz in America.

5. Gerald Taft, "Background of Letters of Dov Behr Manischewitz and Family (December 14, 1987)," Manischewitz Letters to His Family in Russia, Correspondence Files, American Jewish Archives, Cincinnati, OH; Masha Greenbaum, *The Jews of Lithuania* (Jerusalem: Gefen, 1995), 285; Shulman, "Memel," 3:332; see also Joan Nathan, "The Bread of Our Affection," *Moment* 20 (April 1995), 31; Nathan, *Jewish Cooking in America* (New York: Knopf, 1994), 107. Note that the "Rabbi Eliayu Heshel" mentioned repeatedly in Dov Behr's letters is almost certainly Hillkowitz. See Dov Behr Manischewitz to Yechiel Michael Manischewitz, April 27, 1887, Manischewitz Letters, American Jewish Archives, and compare Jonathan D. Sarna and Nancy H. Klein, *The Jews of Cincinnati* (Cincinnati: Center for the Study of the American Jewish Experience, 1989), 67, 79.

6. Moshe D. Sherman, "Bernard Illowy and Nineteenth Century American Orthodoxy," (PhD diss., Yeshiva University, 1991), 30–31; Hyman B. Grinstein, *The Rise of the Jewish Community of New York 1654–1860* (Philadelphia: Jewish Publication Society, 1945), 306–310.

7. Barnett R. Brickner, "The Jewish Community of Cincinnati Historical and Descriptive 1817–1933" (PhD diss., University of Cincinnati, 1933), 122; Sherman, "Bernard Illowy,"

31n9; Jonathan D. Sarna, ed. and trans., *People Walk on Their Heads: Moses Weinberger's Jews and Judaism in New York* (New York: Holmes and M. iei, 1981), 73. Daniel Sperber, *Minhage Yisrael* (Jerusalem: Mossad Harav Kook, 1991), 2:141–142 chronicles the development of the stringency known as *shmurah matzah*, where the wheat is continually "watched" following its harvesting.

8. See *Shulhan Aruch*, OH 459:2 and also the discussion in the *Aruch HaShulhan*; for earlier authorities, see *Encyclopedia Talmudit* 16 (1980): 84–86.

9. For various accounts in Europe and America, see *Jewish Tribune*, April 4, 1925; Beatrice S. Weinreich, "The Americanization of Passover," in *Studies in Biblical and Jewish Folklore*, ed. Raphael Patai (Bloomington: Indiana University Press, 1960), 333–335; *New York Times*, April 9, 1995; Eve Jochnowitz, "Holy Rolling: Making Sense of Baking Matzo," in *Jews of Brooklyn*, ed. Ilana Abramovitch and Sean Galvin (Hanover, NH: Brandeis University Press, 2002), 72–77; compare T. B., *Pesahim*, 48b, and Steven Fine, "The Halakhic Motif in Jewish Iconography: The Matzah-Baking Cycles of the *Yahuda* and *Second Nurnberg Haggadahs*," in *A Crown for a King: Studies in Jewish Art, History and Archaeology in Memory of Stephen S. Kayser*, ed. Shalom Sabar, Steven Fine, and William M. Kramer (Berkeley, CA: Magnes Museum, 2000), 105–122.

10. Grinstein, *Jewish Community*, 308–309, 446; Sherman, "Bernard Illowy," 30–31.

11. Joseph Saul Nathanson, *Kuntres Bitul Moda'ah* (1859; rpt. Jerusalem, 1972) is the standard source for this history. I have also been fortunate to read an advance copy of an important study by Meir Hildesheimer and Yehoshua Lieberman titled "The Controversy Surrounding Machine-Made Matzot: Halakhic, Social and Economic Repercussions," *Hebrew Union College Annual* 75 (2004): 193–262.

12. *Moda'ah le-Beit Yisrael* (Breslau, 1859), http://www.hebrewbooks.org/13941; *Bittul Moda'ah* (Luou, 1859), http://www.hebrewbooks.org/13942.

13. The volumes by Kluger and Nathanson have been reprinted together in Jerusalem (1972). Abstracts of most of the major responsa may be found in *HeHashmal BeHalachah* (Jerusalem: Institute for Science and Halacha, 1978), 1:84–135. The best and most complete discussion in English is Hildesheimer and Lieberman, "Machine-Made Matzot," see especially notes 132 and 260 for those who considered machine-made matzah a tool in the hands of assimilationists and reformers. See also David Ellenson, "Jewish Legal Interpretation: Literary, Scriptural, Social and Ethical Perspectives," *Semeia* 34 (1985): 93–114; and Daniel Landes, "Response to David Ellenson," *Semeia* 34 (1985): 123–120; as well as Haim Gertner, "Gevulot Hahashpa'ah Shel Rabanut Galitsya . . . R. Shlomo Kluger Kemikreh Mivhan" (master's thesis, Hebrew University, 1996), 490–452 and works cited in note 20.

14. Yechiel Michael Manischewitz to Moshe Mendel Manischewitz, February 1892, Manischewitz Letters, Correspondence Files, American Jewish Archives.

15. Advertisement, *American Israelite*, March 30, 1899; April 12, 1900.

16. Rabbi Abraham Jacob Gerson Lesser of Cincinnati supervised the kashrut of Manischewitz at this time and describes this machinery and the whole process of matzah making at the plant in an "Open Letter" published in *Bet Va'ad La'hakhamim* 1 (Shvat 1903): 1. The description resembles the machine described by Rabbi Zechariah Joseph Rosenfeld in *Sefer Yosef Tikvah* (St. Louis, 1903), 6–11. Rosenfeld insisted that the fan did not really slow the fermentation process and therefore its presence had no halakhic implications (see 52–56, 102–105).

17. See patents 930, 673 (filed October 21, 1907), and especially 1,169,555 (filed October 28, 1911), U.S. Patent Office, Washington, DC; "Jacob Uriah Manischewitz," *Who's Who in American Jewry* 3 (1938–1939), liii; *Yidishe Tageblat*, January 9, 1920, 2; April 7, 1924, 6; Getzel Selikowitz, "The Matzo City," *Hebrew Standard*, February 13, 1920, 17; and *Kashrut at Manischewitz*, 1–2.

18. Some attached theological significance to the round shape. For different views, see Judah D. Eisenstein, *Otsar Dinim u-Minhagim* (New York: Hebrew Publishing, 1917), 248;

and Weinreich, "Americanization of Passover," 347; for the matzot advertisement, see *American Hebrew*, March 12, 1912; for the Kluger and Nathanson debate, see, for example, Nathanson, *Kuntres Bitul Moda'ah*, 2b, 14a.

19. *Universal Jewish Encyclopedia* 7 (1942): 414.

20. Samuel Haber, *Efficiency and Uplift: Scientific Management in the Progressive Era, 1890–1920* (Chicago: University of Chicago Press, 1964).

21. Solomon B. Freehof, *The Responsa Literature* (Philadelphia: Jewish Publication Society, 1955), 181–189, summarizes the controversy over machine-made matzah; see also Philip Goodman, *The Passover Anthology* (Philadelphia: Jewish Publication Society, 1961), 90–92; Eisenstein, *Otsar Dinim u-Minhagim*, 248; and "Matzah," *Ozar Yisrael Encyclopedia* (New York, 1907–1913), 6:277–278. Rabbi Zechariah Joseph Rosenfeld's *Sefer Yosef Tikvah* represented a pioneering attempt by an American Orthodox rabbi to determine the halakhic conditions under which machine-matzot—which, he admitted, were widely used in America—might be found acceptable. The book's *haskamot* indicate that the issue remained controversial. For more recent sources and a "Da'as Torah" opposing machine-made matzah, see Sholom Y. Gross, *Mitzvah Encyclopedia* (New York: Mosad Brochas Tova, 1981), 1:65–68.

22. *Hebrew Standard*, March 26, 1920, 9. The *Shulhan Aruch* OH 459:1 prohibits kneading in the sunlight for fear of fermentation, and most matzah bakeries were consequently in dark cellars. The speed and temperature in Manischewitz's factory apparently made this issue moot; see also the discussion in *Aruch HaShulhan* 459:3–4. In the Yiddish newspaper *Yidishe Tageblat*, April 3, 1922, 9, the Manischewitz Company specifically boasted that its founder "liberated" matzah "from the dark cellars and raised matzah baking to the level of an industry" (translation mine).

23. *Jewish Advocate*, March 6, 1919, 6. See T. Jackson Lears, "From Salvation to Self-Realization: Advertising and the Therapeutic Roots of the Consumer Culture, 1880–1930," in *The Culture of Consumption*, ed. Richard Wightman Fox and T. Jackson Lears (New York: Pantheon, 1983), 1–38.

24. *Yidishe Tageblat*, January 9, 1920, 2; *HaPardes* 4 (March 1931): 28; 6 (March 1933): 6, 34; and particularly the special section of *HaPardes* dedicated to the fiftieth anniversary of Manischewitz, 11 (March 1938): 27–53 (all translations mine).

25. Susan L. Braunstein and Jenna Weissman Joselit, eds., *Getting Comfortable in New York: The American Jewish Home, 1880–1950* (New York: Jewish Museum, 1990), 42, portrays the "fine matzos" sample box; the 80 percent claim is in Selikowitz, "Matzo City," 17.

26. Daniel Schwartz, "Pulmus matsot ha-mechonah be yerushalayim," *Sinai* 122 (1998), 113–128.

27. *Jewish Communal Register of New York City 1917–1918* (New York, 1918), 341–346, quote on 346; cf. Ira Robinson, "The First Hasidic Rabbis in North America," *American Jewish Archives* 44 (1992): 501–506.

28. See the letters and recommendations in Rosenfeld, *Sefer Yosef Tikvah*, esp. v; and sources cited in Schwartz, "Pulmus matsot ha-Mechonah," 114n8.

29. "Mikhtav Galui," *Bet Va'ad La'hakhamim* 1 (Shvat 1903), n.p.

30. *HaPardes* 11 (March 1938), supplement, http://www.hebrewbooks.org/12089.

31. *Kashrut at Manischewitz*, 3.

32. *HaPardes* 14 (April 1940): 19; cf. Weinreich, "Americanization of Passover," 347.

33. *HaPardes* 11 (March 1938), supplement, esp. 26–27.

34. *Who's Who in American Jewry* 3 (1938–1939): 702. The rabbis mentioned were "Rabbis Hochstern [Hochstein], Isaac Blasar, Zorach Braverman, Tuvia Rose, and Rabbi Hirsch of Slobodka."

35. Ibid., 702; *New York Times*, October 10, 1943, 49, col. 2.

36. The case of The B. Manischewitz Company, Petitioner v. Commissioner of Internal Revenue, Respondent, 10 T.C. 1139, at 1140, lists the firm's donations to the yeshiva from

1920 to 1947. The *Encyclopaedia Judaica*'s claim that the yeshiva closed in 1943 would thus seem to be in error (Jerusalem: Keter, 1971), vol. 11, col. 070.

37. Manischewitz v. Commissioner, at 1141.

38. Manischewitz v. Commissioner, at 1141–1142. For Hirsch Manischewitz's interest in shipping matzah to "Argentine and other Latin republics of South America, as well as to South Africa and many European countries, besides . . . the Holy Land," see Selikowitz, "Matzo City," 17.

39. *Kashrut at Manischewitz* , 3–4; Sarna and Klein, *Jews of Cincinnati*, 123; *Kashrut at Manischewitz*, 3.

40. Manischewitz v. Commissioner, at 1141–1142.

41. *Who's Who in American Jewry* 3 (1938–39): 702; *New York Times*, October 10, 1943, 49, col. 2; Nathan M. Kaganoff, ed., *Economic Relations and Philanthropy*, vol. 3 of *Guide to America: Holy Land Studies 1620–1948* (New York: Praeger, 19), 38, cf. 46.

42. Manischewitz v. Commissioner, at 1141–1144.

43. Simcha Fishbane, "The Founding of Kollel America Tifereth Yerushalayim," *American Jewish Historical Quarterly* 64 (December 1974): 120–136; Nathan M. Kaganoff, "American Rabbinic Books Published in Palestine," in *A Bicentennial Festschrift for Jacob Rader Marcus*, ed. Bertram W. Korn (New York: Ktav, 1976), 235–261; Herbert S. Goldstein, *Forty Years of Struggle for a Principle: The Biography of Harry Fischel* (New York: Bloch, 1928).

Contributors

MARNI DAVIS, an assistant professor at Georgia State University, studies and teaches American history and modern Jewish history. Her book on Jews and the alcohol industry is entitled *Jews and Booze* (2012). She has been the recipient of scholarly awards from the National Foundation for Jewish Culture, the American Jewish Archives, and the Feinstein Center for American Jewish History.

PHYLLIS DILLON, MA, is an independent scholar in the history of ready-made apparel and a consulting museum curator. She has worked for more than thirty-five years in museums as a textile conservator, curator, and arts administrator. She was the associate curator of the exhibition *A Perfect Fit: The Garment Industry and American Jewry 1860–1960* in 2005 at Yeshiva University Museum. She most recently helped produce the documentary *Dressing America: Tales from the Garment Center* (2009).

ANDREW S. DOLKART is the director of Columbia University's Historic Preservation Program and the James Marston Fitch Associate Professor of Historic Preservation in the School of Architecture, Planning, and Preservation. He has written extensively about the architecture and development of New York City, including three award-winning books: *Morningside Heights: A History of Its Architecture and Development* (1998), *Biography of a Tenement House in New York City: An Architectural History of 97 Orchard Street* (2006), and *The Row House Reborn: Architecture and Neighborhoods in New York City, 1908–1929* (2009). He is currently writing on the physical development of New York's Garment District.

ANDREW GODLEY is a professor of management at the Henley Business School, University of Reading. He has published widely in the area of retailing and marketing history, including *Jewish Immigrant Entrepreneurship in New York and London, 1880–1914: Enterprise and Culture* (2001), which provides a transnational comparison of Jews' involvement in the garment industry.

JONATHAN KARP is the executive director of the American Jewish Historical Society and an associate professor in the Judaic Studies and History Departments at Binghamton University, State University of New York. He is the author of *The Politics of Jewish Commerce* (2008), as well as coeditor (with Barbara Kirshenblatt-Gimblett) of *The Art of Being Jewish in Modern Times* (2007). His most recent book projects are *Philosemitism in History* (coedited with Adam Sutcliffe, 2008) and *The Rise and Demise of the Black-Jewish Alliance: A Class-Cultural Analysis* (forthcoming). He is completing a book titled *Chosen Surrogates: Blacks and Jews in American Culture* (forthcoming).

DANIEL KATZ teaches at the Empire State College, State University of New York. After receiving his PhD from Stanford University, Katz devoted his research to issues of labor and unions in American history. He has written extensively on issues on these topics and has been actively involved in labor organizing in New York City as well.

IRA KATZNELSON, Ruggles Professor of Political Science, Columbia University is an Americanist whose work has straddled comparative politics and political theory, as well as political and social history. His most recent books are *Liberal Beginnings: Making a Republic for the Moderns* (with Andreas Kalyvas, 2008) and *When Affirmative Action Was White: An Untold History of Racial Inequality in Twentieth-Century America* (2005). Other books include *Black Men, White Cities: Race, Politics, and Migration in the United States, 1900–1930* and *Britain, 1948–1968* (1973), *City Trenches: Urban Politics and the Patterning of Class in the United States* (1981), *Schooling for All: Class, Race, and the Decline of the Democratic Ideal* (with Margaret Weir, 1985), *Marxism and the City* (1992), *Liberalism's Crooked Circle: Letters to Adam Michnik* (1996), and *Desolation and Enlightenment: Political Knowledge after Total War, Totalitarianism, and the Holocaust* (2003). He is currently completing *Fear Itself*, a book dealing with American democracy from the New Deal to the cold war, and *Liberal Reason*, a collection of his essays on the character of modern social knowledge.

REBECCA KOBRIN is the Russell and Bettina Knapp Assistant Professor of American Jewish History at Columbia University. She has published widely on issues concerning American Jewish history and East European Jewish migration and is the author of *Jewish Bialystok and Its Diaspora*, a finalist for the National Jewish Book Award.

DAVID S. KOFFMAN is a Social Sciences and Humanities Research Council of Canada postdoctoral fellow at the University of Toronto's Department of History, where he is preparing his dissertation, "The Jews' Indian: Native Americans in the Jewish Imagination and Experience, 1850–1950" (2011), for publication.

ELI LEDERHENDLER is head of the School of History in the Faculty of Humanities at the Hebrew University of Jerusalem. He is the incumbent of the Stephen S. Wise Chair in American Jewish History and Institutions at the Avraham Harman Institute of Contemporary Jewry and is a coeditor of the institute's annual journal, *Studies in Contemporary Jewry*. His publications include *Jewish Immigrants and American Capitalism* (2009); *New York Jews and the Decline of Urban Ethnicity, 1950–1970* (2001), which won both the Koret Jewish Book Award in history and the Tuttleman Foundation Book Award; *Jewish Responses to Modernity* (1994); and *The Road to Modern Jewish Politics* (1989), which was awarded the National Jewish Book Award in 1990.

JONATHAN Z. S. POLLACK received his PhD from University of Wisconsin–Madison, where he is currently a fellow at its Institute for Research in the Humanities, completing his research on Jews in the scrap-metal business. He teaches American history at the Madison Area Technical College.

JONATHAN D. SARNA is the Joseph H. and Belle R. Braun Professor of American Jewish History in the Department of Near Eastern and Judaic Studies at Brandeis University, chair of the Hornstein Program in Jewish Professional Leadership, and chief historian of the National Museum of American Jewish History. Among his numerous publications is *American Judaism: A History* (2004), which was awarded the Everett Family Foundation Jewish Book of the Year Award, the American Jewish Historical Society's Saul Viener Prize for the Outstanding Book in American Jewish History, and the Weinberg Judaic Studies Institute 2005 Prize for Best Book in American Jewish Studies. He has also edited and coedited such volumes as *Jews and the Civil War* (2011), *America and Zion: Essays and Papers in Memory of Moshe Davis* (2002), and *Women and American Judaism: Historical Perspectives* (2001). His monographs include *Jacksonian Jew: The Two Worlds of Mordecai Noah* (1980), *JPS: The Americanization of Jewish Culture* (1989), *People Walk on Their Heads: Moses Weinberger's Jews and Judaism in New York* (1982), and *When General Grant Expelled the Jews* (2012).

JEFFREY SHANDLER is a professor of Jewish Studies at Rutgers University. He is the author of *Jews, God, and Videotape: Religion and Media in America* (2009), *Adventures in Yiddishland: Postvernacular Language and Culture* (2006), and *While America Watches: Televising the Holocaust* (1999). He is also the editor of *Awakening Lives: Autobiographies of Jewish Youth in Poland before the Holocaust* (2002) and the coauthor of *Entertaining America: Jews, Movies, and Broadcasting* (2003).

DANIEL SOYER is a professor of history at Fordham University, where he specializes in American immigration and urban history. His publications include *Jewish Immigrant Associations and American Identity in New York, 1880–1939* (1997), which won the Viener Prize of the American Jewish Historical Society; *My Future Is in America: Autobiographies of Eastern European Jewish Immigrants* (2006, coeditor with Jocelyn Cohen); and *A Coat of Many Colors: Immigration, Globalization, and Reform in New York City's Garment Industry* (2005, editor).

INDEX

Page numbers in italics refer to illustrations; those followed by T refer to tables and charts.